RĀJA YUDHIṢṬHIRA

A VOLUME IN THE SERIES

MYTH AND POETICS II

GREGORY NAGY, EDITOR

LEONARD MUELLNER, ASSOCIATE EDITOR

For a full list of titles in this series,
visit our website at www.cornellpress.cornell.edu.

A complete list of titles published in the original
Myth and Poetics series is available at the back of this book.

RĀJA YUDHIṢṬHIRA

Kingship in Epic Mahābhārata

KEVIN McGRATH

Cornell University Press
Ithaca and London

First published 2017 by Cornell University Press

Printed in the United States of America

Library of Congress Cataloging-in-Publication Data

Names: McGrath, Kevin, 1951– author.
Title: Rāja Yudhiṣṭhira : kingship in epic Mahābhārata / Kevin McGrath.
Description: Ithaca : Cornell University Press, 2017. | Series: Myth and poetics II | Includes bibliographical references and index.
Identifiers: LCCN 2016035979 (print) | LCCN 2016037419 (ebook) | ISBN 9781501704987 (cloth : alk. paper) | ISBN 9781501708213 (epub/mobi) | ISBN 9781501708220 (pdf)
Subjects: LCSH: Mahābhārata--Criticism, interpretation, etc. | Yudhiṣṭhira (Hindu mythology) | Kings and rulers in literature.
Classification: LCC BL1138.4.Y83 M34 2017 (print) | LCC BL1138.4.Y83 (ebook) | DDC 294.5/923046--dc23
LC record available at https://lccn.loc.gov/2016035979

Cornell University Press strives to use environmentally responsible suppliers and materials to the fullest extent possible in the publishing of its books. Such materials include vegetable-based, low-VOC inks and acid-free papers that are recycled, totally chlorine-free, or partly composed of nonwood fibers. For further information, visit our website at www.cornellpress.cornell.edu.

To Olga Davidson

ya eṣa rājā-rājeti śabdaś carati bhārata
katham eṣa samutpannas ...

XII.59.5

Contents

Series Foreword

Gregory Nagy

As editor of the renewed and expanded series Myth and Poetics II, my goal is to promote the publication of books that build on connections to be found between different ways of thinking and different forms of verbal art in pre-literate as well as literate societies. As in the original Myth and Poetics series, which started in 1989 with the publication of Richard Martin's *The Language of Heroes: Speech and Performance in the "Iliad"*, the word "myth" in the title of the new series corresponds to what I have just described as a way of thinking, while "poetics" covers any and all forms of preliterature and literature.

Although "myth" as understood, say, in the Homeric *Iliad* could convey the idea of a traditional way of thinking that led to a traditional way of expressing a thought, such an idea was not to last—not even in ancient Greek society, as we see, for example, when we consider the fact that the meaning of the word was already destabilized by the time of Plato. And such destabilization is exactly why I prefer to use the word "myth" in referring to various ways of shaping different modes of thought: it is to be expected that any tradition that conveys any thought will vary in different times and different places. And such variability of tradition is a point of prime interest for me in my quest as editor to seek out the widest variety of books about the widest possible variety of traditions.

Similarly in the case of "poetics," I think of this word in its widest sense, so as to include not only poetry but also songmaking on one side and prose on the other. As a series, Myth and Poetics II avoids presuppositions about traditional forms such as genres, and there is no insistence on any universalized understanding of verbal art in all its countless forms.

Acknowledgments

In this book, I am building upon models, concepts, and themes developed in my earlier works: *The Sanskrit Hero*, *Strī*, *Jaya*, *Heroic Kṛṣṇa*, and *Arjuna Pāṇḍava*. My method remains the same, that of closely reading the text, or *explication de texte*.

I remain thoroughly indebted to my colleagues in the Harvard Mahābhārata Seminar, chaired by Thomas Burke. He is someone whose excellence in the realm of intellectual generosity and practical humanism is—for me—both remarkable and unique, and his knowledge of archaic and classical India is, in my experience, matchless.

I am also profoundly and especially grateful to the following friends and colleagues for their liberal kindness: Peter Banos, Homi Bhabha, Amarananda Bhairavan, Pradip Bhattacharya, Sugata Bose, Edwin Bryant, Gurcharan Das, Olga Davidson, Maya De, Richard Delacy, Wendy Doniger, Diana Eck, David Elmer, Douglas Frame, Robert Goldman, Charles Hallisey, Lilian Handlin, Alf Hiltebeitel, Krutarthsinh Jadeja, Stephanie Jamison, Jayasinhji Jhala, Leonard van der Kuijp, T. P. Mahadevan, Leanna McGrath, Anne Monius, Susan Moore, Leonard Muellner, Gregory Nagy, Parimal Patil, Adheesh Sathaye, Amartya Sen, L. D. Shah, Oktor Skjærvø, Caley Smith, Guy Smoot, Romila Thapar, Pulin Vasa, Alex Watson, and Michael Witzel.

Finally, I am truly grateful to His Highness, Pragmulji III, whose assistance, hospitality, and friendship have been invaluable during my extensive fieldwork among the *kṣatriya* community in the Kacch of Western Gujarat.

1

The Beginnings

King Yudhiṣṭhira, during the narrative of the epic *Mahābhārata*, moves from a position of being a sometimes ingenuous and enduring *dharmarāja* to becoming the paramount ruler or *kururāja*. This book examines and analyses that trajectory and essentially follows the course of Yudhiṣṭhira's office from the point when he celebrates the *rājasūya* rite in the second *parvan* or 'book' to the moment where the ritual of the *aśvamedha* is conducted in the fourteenth *parvan*. As we shall see, the epic king—in the spiritual office of a sacrificer—is a figure who creates order through speech and sometimes via ritual death and the division of a victim; he is the primary point for this study.[1] Yudhiṣṭhira is the particular model from which we can move towards a more general picture of ancient kingship as it is represented by the epic. Yet indications of kingship in the *Mahābhārata* cannot be said to be synoptic, especially after the chaos that immediately follows the first *rājasūya* when disorder is generated—for at this point in the poem there are suddenly many competing notions of kingship. At the end of the poem, surprisingly, it is the Yādavas who triumph most when the many years of Yādava-Pāṇḍava alliance manages to secure ultimate power for the clan of Kṛṣṇa at Hāstinapura; as we shall see, Yudhiṣṭhira is the primary medium for this Yādava *jaya* 'victory'. Simply in terms of sanguinity Yudhiṣṭhira himself has more Yādava than Kuru blood, via his mother Kuntī, and in fact, in terms of mortality, he is genetically fully Yādava. In that sense one can rightly aver that the battle at Kurukṣetra is an engagement to the death between the Yādava allies and the Kurus: that is the essential subtext of the narrative.[2]

[1] In the *Iliad*, Agamemnon, as the paramount chief is also a *sacrificer* insofar as he is the only one to bear a *máxaira*, a 'knife', for the purpose of ritual (III.271).

[2] Janamejaya has more Yādava blood from his ancestral matriline—from Subhadrā and Kuntī—than any other single genetic lineal inheritance. In terms of the epic narrative, his principal great-great-grandfathers were Indra and Vasudeva. The epic can thus be conceived of as a contest between a matriline and a patriline in which the former is ultimately victorious. See Trautmann (1981) on the nature of matrilinearity as the typical Dravidian form of kinship. A logical extension of this model where the

There exists no single model of a *rāja* in the poem, but many types occur simultaneously, just as many kinds of religious culture coexist in the text as we know it today. It is this polyvalence or multitextuality of epic kingship that makes the poem both complex and unusually beautiful: the poem is a work of art and it is not 'history' nor does it represent any temporal record.[3] Kingship in epic *Mahābhārata* is a sign that is constantly moving among the poetry and the characters within that song; it is never consistent and is always changing in its signification and its properties, being persistently labile and fungible and yet remaining absolutely central. The problem of kingship in the epic is varied and diverse because the poetry of the great Bhārata Song assimilates and amalgamates numberless traditions and the reminiscence of many chronological periods as well as emulating others within one integral *Kunstsprache*; hence the epic retrojects an artificial and unreal world. The idea of kingship itself is a performative one, as we shall see, for kingship is not simply an office but an activity that requires relentless demonstration.

In this book I intend to argue three major principles concerning the nature of Yudhiṣṭhira's kingship. The first is that this is no singular and solo king. He is no autocrat but someone who consistently and always shares his authority with his brothers—half-brothers really—persistently allowing himself to be guided by them and by their joint chief, his wife, Draupadī. This is what can be called a 'fraternal kingship,' one where even the old king Dhṛtarāṣṭra has a voice in the family rule.[4] Secondly, there is also an active duality to Yudhiṣṭhira's sovereignty, at least until he receives his second coronation at Hāstinapura, for he shares decisive power with Kṛṣṇa. I have argued this and illustrated the point elsewhere in a previous work; as we shall soon see, this nature of *dualism* is profoundly intrinsic to the political culture of epic *Mahābhārata*. It is this effective double kingship that ultimately causes the Yādavas to secure the kingdom.[5] Thirdly, this dyarchy,

---

matrilineal group—the Pāṇḍavas—triumph over the patrilineal group—the Dhārtarāṣṭras—would be to argue that that the winning indigenous group is posed against the defeated intrusive group: such a line of reasoning construes the Dhārtarāṣṭras as the defeated Indo-Āryans and the Pāṇḍavas as the victorious Dravidians. If we could demonstrate that the Bhārgava clan was originally an indigenous group who had 'brahminised,' this would allow us to make further inferences about the nature of the epic poem as it came to be when first transformed by writing during the Gupta years.

3 Preliterate poetry is by nature multiform and polysemic and not 'rational'; as a system it is inclusive rather than exclusive.

4 The English word *kingdom* or *king* is from the OE noun *cyn* (race, family, kin), and hence *cyingdom* is that 'situation or location of kinship'. Moreover, kingship in this old English language usage concerns kinship, and not simply a singular rule. One can apply this idea to the late Indo-Āryan picture that is expressed in epic *Mahābhārata*.

5 McGrath 2013, chap. III.

which is so pendent upon the brothers and elders of the clan, also depends upon another element of political influence: that is, the *prajā* 'the people'. This of course is not composed of *hoi polloi* 'the many', but refers to what was in fact an oligarchy—often said by the poets to be made up of *brāhmaṇas*—that coheres about the central suzerainty at Hāstinapura. As we shall see, this active presence and voice is crucial in the practical functioning of kingly rule and constitutes what can be considered a *saṅgha* (an association or community).

All this changes once the poem moves towards its terminus, when Bhīṣma commences a discourse expounding his especial overview of kingship. Once the Śānti *parvan* begins, the nature of kingship—as explicated by the poem—becomes different from what went before, except for the brief coronation scene in the Āśvamedhika *parvan*, which portrays the victorious entry of Yudhiṣṭhira into Hāstinapura. We shall amplify and develop this point towards the end of the book: how it is that the 'early' Yudhiṣṭhira is arguably a pre-Hindu king, whereas what Bhīṣma demonstrates in his language is a more classical pattern of kingship that represents the early years of Hinduism.

***

This book also examines the nature of preliteracy as manifest by epic *Mahābhārata*. On the one hand there is the external drama of the poets standing before an audience, and on the other hand there is the internal success within the poem of Yudhiṣṭhira's immediate kinship group: these are the two tracks of the present study. One is based on verbal technique or *enactment*; the other concerns narrative or *myth*—and I would propose that the narrative development of this kind of preliterate poetry is essentially founded upon the dynamics of kinship relations.[6] If we are to comprehend the message of this late Bronze Age literature, we must necessarily understand the medium itself by which that information was once conveyed; knowledge of the former is impossible without comprehension of the latter.

These are simply two aspects of one movement: on the one hand there are the truths of performance or *how* the poets communicate, and then there are the truths of the poetry itself or *what* the poets communicate concerning kinship. In other words, how do the poets interpret the emotional quality of the words that they perform, and what is the information they convey during the performance? These are two different trajectories this book will elucidate, giving emphasis to the latter simply because it is more substantial or material. The narrative of

6 For those readers not familiar with the theoretical approaches to poetry as a preliterate phenomenon I have included a brief "Appendix On Epic Preliteracy" at the end of this book.

the poem is what reaches us today as a literary reality or myth, which we first interpret and then attempt to comprehend for its performative or enacted truth.

It was by their reconstruction of an ideal past—one that bears no relation to any historical reality—that the poets touched the audience, an effect that was magnified by the medium of theatre or poetic drama.[7] For us today, this understanding can only be tenuous and lightly captured, yet we cannot disregard that dimension; for what did such an illusion of the past and its kinship structure bring to a classical North Indian audience? This is the *mūthos* of the poem, where, firstly, the poem represents a 'repository of historical consciousness' that does not concern any historiographic tradition that we can know today. Secondly, that historical experience has been codified by methods other than by narrative—and to adumbrate this latter quality is the core project of this book.[8]

Equally, how did the actual presentation of that 'antiquarian' scene generate culture for an audience? I refer to the force of enactment or how the poets interpreted the story as they sang the song and charged their words with emotion during performance. Thus the questions remain: Are we able to retrieve how such an hypothetical audience interpreted the poem? Was the message different if the poets performing the Bhārata Song behaved or acted differently at different times? Are we as readers able to discern those shifting and varying qualities of performance? These are our joint tasks, particularly as we consider the poem's demonstrations of kingship: to distinguish or identify the metaphor of enactment in performance, where possible, and to understand the complex myth of narrative form.

***

Epic *Mahābhārata* coheres and integrates into narrative order various diverse and historically separate elements that are political, ritual, and also poetic. In this process we shall examine how kingship—*āryās* ... *rājānaḥ* (the Āryan kings)—in the myth and poetry of the great Bhārata Song provide this picture of stately office with its background substance and shadowy paradigms of kinship.[9] We shall examine these traces and aspects of politics that encompass and illuminate

[7] The Homeric *Iliad* similarly represents an idealised past in which several traditions were woven together and other more recent and nascent traditions, like the Athenian world for instance, were ignored.

[8] Romila Thapar, in at a talk given at Harvard on May 5, 2014, employed the phrase "repositories of historical consciousness," in referring to what she depicted as a politically clan-based and poetically bardic past; or, what I would describe as preliterate, premonetary, and pre-secondary urbanisation. I have summarised the temporal aspects of this myth of the poem towards the end of this book.

[9] *Āryās tu ye vai rājānaḥ* II.49.1.

the kingly presence of Yudhiṣṭhira in the poem. For instance, early on during their exile in the forest Bhīma says to his elder brother:

> rājyam eva paraṃ dharmaṃ kṣatriyasya vidur budhāḥ
>
> III.49.13
>
> The wise know that kingship is the highest dharma of a kṣatriya.

This *rājya* is the focus of the present study, a *kṣatriya* ideal of kingship that is ostensibly a Bronze Age type, but which is in fact a poetic model of the late first millennium BCE.[10] Mārkaṇḍeya, when he visits the Pāṇḍavas during their forest exile, remarks that *rājā vai prathamo dharmaḥ* (the king is the primary *dharma*), and he describes kingship as *purāyonir* ('the primal source' or 'womb') from which order appears in the kingdom just like light from the sun:

> āditiyo divi deveṣu tamo nudati tejasā
>
> III.183.26
>
> The sun among the deities overwhelms darkness in the sky with energy.

Towards the end of the poem, the old king, expressing a wish to cede the throne to Yudhiṣṭhira, tells the young king that *rājā guruḥ prāṇabhṛtāṃ* (a king is the *guru* of anything that breathes) (XV.2.19). In a sense, the poem itself, the epic *Mahābhārata* as heroic literature and the poetry of *kṣatriyas*, itself serves as an impersonal *guru* of a king's immediate community, of those who visit and attend the *sabhā*, the 'assembly', where the epic song must have once been performed. Just as a *guru* teaches and transmits knowledge so too does the king convey and manage the values of a community, sometimes by using 'force' and employing the *daṇḍa*. Similarly, epic *Mahābhārata* as the great Bhārata Song communicates these myths, archetypes, and values of human and kingly truth for North Indian society in early classical times. It also conveys to twenty-first century Indian modernity those ancient Indic archetypes of thought in a thoroughly living embodiment, and these have successfully entered the media of film and popular novels and the great spectrum of visual iconography.[11]

***

To repeat, my purpose in writing this book is not merely to comprehend the poetic systems at work within the poem nor to arrive at an understanding of

[10] My understanding of the term *kṣatriya* has been shaped by Hopkins 1888 in a most remarkable essay. I think of the *Mahābhārata* epic poem as representing a formulated Bronze Age society drawn from an unrecorded past that is both premonetary and preliterate in culture.

[11] See Tharoor 1989; Mankekar 1999; Sax 2002; Das 2009.

the historicity of the text—either in its transmission or in its temporal significance—but to understand the nature of the political culture that emerges from the poetry and its myth that is then dramatised by the poets' enactment. Let us commence by looking briefly at seven basic aspects or dimensions as to how the epic presents kingship as a myth of narration for its audience; then, in the next chapter let us examine how it is that Yudhiṣṭhira demonstrates the kingly office of 'sacrificer,' for he is *yajñaśīla* (one adept at sacrifice), says his half-brother Arjuna (IV.65.8).

i. Early Kingship

Firstly, allow me to recapitulate quickly how the poets introduce the idea of kingship. The poem begins in the usual epic fashion of retrojecting a narrative from an end-point that describes the death of a king or hero, in this case the king Parikṣit, the great-nephew of Yudhiṣṭhira; then the poem rehearses *how* such an incident occurred (I.44.4–5). The king's successor is then legitimised, in this case by two forms of constitution: firstly, the son Janamejaya is established as *nṛpa* 'king' (literally 'protector of men') by virtue of his lineage; and secondly, by election.[12]

sametya sarve puravāsino janāḥ
nṛpaṃ yam āhus tam amitraghātinaṃ
kurupravīraṃ janamejayaṃ ...

I.40.6

All the urban folk having assembled,
They called that killer of enemies king:
Janamejaya, who [was] champion of the Kurus.

When the timeless *ṛṣi* or 'sage' Vyāsa arrives at the sacrificial ground of Janamejaya the king asks him, his great-great-great-grandfather, that he tell of the origins of the clan war.[13] He says: *kathaṃ samabhavad bhedas teṣām* (how did their schism

[12] There is no indication in the epic as to what ultimately happened to the lineage of Janamejaya and the realm of *bhāratavarṣa* for the poem is a closed circle. Janamejaya is mentioned towards the end of the Harivaṃśa as wishing to conduct a horse sacrifice; there he is advised by Vyāsa and his sons and grandsons receive cursory reference (115.5ff.).

[13] Vyāsa is specifically a *brahmarṣiḥ kaviḥ* (a brāhmanical sage, Vedic poet) (I.54.5). 'Wizard' is a better translation of the word *ṛṣi*, but wizard has modern connotations that do not really tally with Bronze Age North Indian aesthetics. 'Shaman' would also be a possible translation, but such a word lacks the literary or verbally poetic qualities that *ṛṣi* bears.

rise?) (I.54.19). This is the actual question or moment that hypothetically generates the first singing of the epic poem.[14]

Vaiśaṃpāyana then declares that he will perform the epic, indicating a rubric of three elements: the gambling match, the time in the forest, and the *yuddha* 'battle' itself (I.55.4–5).[15] Having introduced himself and praised Vyāsa, his teacher, Vaiśaṃpāyana begins his story with the words:

> rājoparicaro nāma dharmanityo mahīpatiḥ
>
> I.57.1
>
> A king, named Uparicara, lord of the earth and always dharmic ...[16]

Hence kingship is the opening signifier of Vaiśaṃpāyana's poem. The narrative of the Kaurava clan, however, really begins with Śaṃtanu, the father of Bhīṣma, when he is said to be: *taṃ ... rājarājye'bhyaṣecayan* (they anointed him to kingship over kings) (I.94.6). There are seven generations, inclusive, between him and Janamejaya, and it is the latter's presence that persistently inhabits and activates the poem by virtue of his questions to the poet.[17] The poet gives Śaṃtanu the title of *rājarājeśvara* (lord of the kings of kings), a status that no one else in the epic enjoys, and it is as if he is signifying at this point in the Ādi *parvan* (the overlord, as it were) of the song (I.94.17). Śaṃtanu is also referred to as *adhirāja* 'superior king', again a title that no other sovereign receives in the epic

[14] I use the term "singing" to indicate the nature of epic performance, which is a convention I have employed in my previous *Mahābhārata* studies. Whenever I have heard epic poetry performed in present-day Gujarat it is always sonorous and accompanied by a musical instrument, usually the harmonium. The performance of epic is—for me—a process of great and often virtuoso drama on the part of a poet. For instance, in the Ambopākhyāna, which is the final section of the Udyoga *parvan*, the story is ostensibly related by Bhīṣma; that is, the poet imitates Bhīṣma, who in turn—during his performance of the narrative—imitates Satyavatī, Ambā, king Śalva of the Kāśis, the brahmin Śaikhāvatya, king Hotravāhana her maternal grandfather, Rāma, and others. Hence, the poet must run through a gamut of voices and emotions, both male and feminine, during this single small sub-narrative of the poem, imitating the tone and mood and affective force of each of these many epic characters; this is the drama of such performance as well as the great histrionic skills of an epic poet.

[15] This is soon reiterated as: *bhedo rājyavināśaś ca jayaś ca* (partition, and destruction of kingdom, and victory) (I.55.43). Vaiśaṃpāyana is the *śiṣya* 'student' of Vyāsa, and in fact it is his voice that performs most of the poem except for the four Kurukṣetra Books and small speeches here and there.

[16] This king came to rule the Cedi people, an extended clan who by then inhabited the southeastern regions that were later to be known as Kaḷinga, the people whom Aśoka was to defeat so savagely. This king "also annexed the adjoining countries as far as Magadha" (Pargiter 1922, 118).

[17] Of his rule, it was said by the poets: *vadhaḥ paśuvarāhāṇāṃ tathaiva mṛgapakṣiṇām / śaṃtanau pṛthivīpāle nāvartata vṛthā nṛpa* (O king, when Śaṃtanu ruled the earth the death of game, deer, and also of boar and cattle was not in vain) (I.94.13). Whether one can infer from this a Buddhist or Jain policy of *ahiṃsā* or 'non-violence' is questionable.

(III.159.24).[18] All the ancestors before his life exist in an almost atemporal past that is not directly connected to present time—as represented by the epic that is—and which has a strong influence upon—current time.

ii. The Associates

In the *Mahābhārata* kings exist in the company of heroes, and I think of the epic as an heroic or *kṣatriya* literature, a song tradition that derived from Indo-Āryan sources.[19] Heroes are *not* simply warriors and charioteers, but are also characters of great verbal ability, and I would certainly include women heroes here. The figures of Nakula and Sahadeva are thus not exceedingly heroic, not because their fighting is so unremarkable but because they *speak* so little.

Heroes were typically viewed as those who possessed energy, power, and physical potence along with an expedient violence, while kings were those who maintained authority, dictated the language of rule, and who both seized and gave away wealth at festivals and in gambling matches, causing wealth to circulate; such a view of kingship can be considered archaic.[20] In the *Mahābhārata* this distinction of king and hero sometimes fuses and blurs and is imperfect but the concepts have utility insofar as they facilitate analysis.[21] There is no formal

[18] The term is occasionally employed to qualify a non-mortal figure or is used in the abstract. The only other kingly usage that I was able to find concerned a minor and unknown ruler, Dantavakra, who is mentioned at II.28.3. Kubera is described by the poets with the unusual title of *rājarājo* (king over kings) at III.259.

[19] I have discussed this idea of heroic literature and epic poetry in McGrath 2013, chap. 1. The older term for this *varṇa* is *rājanya*, defined by MacDonell and Keith in their 1912 Vedic Index as: "the regular term in Vedic literature for a man of the royal family, probably including those who were not actually members of that family, but were nobles." As West (2007, 411) comments: "Not a single name of an Indo-European hero has come down to us, only Greek heroes, Germanic heroes, Celtic heroes, and so on, and those only because the medium of writing came in time to preserve them before the oral traditions died." (One could substitute the word "kings" here for "heroes.")

[20] By *archaic* I do not denote an archaeological era, as say, one indicated by a predominance of Painted Grey Ware, but rather to signify an unfixed and specifically unlocated culture that was both premonetary and preliterate and that prevailed in Northern and Northwestern India before secondary urbanisation became established in the middle of the first millennium BCE. The high *classical* is usually taken to refer to the Gupta era of the early first millennium CE. The Gupta Dynasty later sought to emulate those principles of social and aesthetic proportion that were considered to have *once* existed in earlier times. The Mauryan and Gupta periods were the only periods in antiquity when most of India was integrated into a uniform and single political unit. Epic *Mahābhārata* makes a pretence of such geopolitical unity.

[21] To apply this simple notion of epic category, one can observe that the chariot-song of Kṛṣṇa, the Gītā, is addressed, and even phrased, in heroic terms and does not mention any aspect of kingship or kingship's moral efficacy. See McGrath 2013, chap. V; and McGrath 2014.

expression of the king being a paramount landowner in the *Mahābhārata*; that form of terrestrial allegiance or loyalty is not present in the epic and to apply the idea of a feudal' system for Northern India at this time is thus not tenable. For instance, there is no mention of land during the gambling match in the Sabhā *parvan*; land is not considered a royal property that is available as a stake for betting (II.53.22ff.).[22]

As we shall see, there are strong indications of a less unified system of monarchic polity in the first half of the epic, where—either geographically or historically—the *saṅgha* supplies the political order rather than the *rājya*. *Saṅgha* is a term that literally means 'thrown together' and it is usually translated by the word 'community', whereas *rājya* specifically denotes 'kingdom' or 'realm'.[23] What is being indicated by this earlier form is a clan system where the elder males nominate a 'leader' or *dux* to guide them; this figure is less of a king in our classical sense than an oligarchic chief. Such a form of governance either precedes kingship or is a less institutional kind of rule.[24]

For instance, in the *Mahābhārata*, Vasudeva—the father of Kṛṣṇa—is sometimes cast more in the position of a chief than a *rāja*; he is overlord of an archaic polity or *janapada* where the *kṣatriyas* are organised in a *saṅgha* in which the *kula* or 'clan' was the significant unit.[25] Nārada refers to this at XII.82.25, when he

[22] When Yudhiṣṭhira makes the wager of *puraṃ janapado bhūmir* (town, country, terrain) these are all abstractions of wealth and there is no specified land *qua* property (II.58.7).

[23] In the Śānti *parvan*, both Yudhiṣṭhira and Bhīṣma refer to sociopolitical units called *gaṇas* 'companies'. These are less institutional than the *saṅghas* and perhaps less land-oriented and less fixed in domicile; in fact Bhīṣma describes them as: *jātyā ca sadṛśāḥ sarve kulena sadṛśās tathā* (all are like in castes and also like in clan) (XII.108.30). He says of these bodies that *dānena bhidyante gaṇāḥ* (the *gaṇas* are split by wealth)—meaning bribes (XII.108.13). In order for such societies to survive, Bhīṣma comments: *tasmāt saṃghātayogeṣu prayateran gaṇāḥ sadā* (therefore *gaṇas* should always aim for unions of companies). All of this *adhyāya* is devoted to the subject of the *gaṇa*. Nīlakaṇṭha comments: *itaretaraṃ gaṇā rājānaś ca prakarṣanti* (kings and *gaṇas* trouble each other) (XII.107.12). V. Agrawala (1952, 428) holds that the *saṅgha* and the *gaṇa* are "synonyms"; for me, however, to speak of any synonymity in the epic is to be necessarily reductive. J. P. Sharma (1968, 9–14) considers the various usages of *gaṇa* and *saṅgha*, noting that Fleet translated the word *gaṇa* as 'tribe'. A. Agrawal (1989, 51) remarks that when the Yaudheyas vanquished the Kuṣāṇas—and this must be in the last years of the first millennium—they struck coins with the impress *yaudheyagaṇasya jaya*, which he translates as 'victory of the Yaudheya republic'.

[24] By "earlier" here, I mean in the sense of nature rather than of duration. See McGrath (2004, chap. 2–3) on the etymon of *rāja*; also, Anthony 2007, 161: "[The] root (**reg-*) referred to ... a kind of powerful officer. This second root was later used to *king* in Italic (*rēx*), Celtic (*rīx*), and Old Indic (*rej-*), but it might originally have referred to an official more like a priest, literally a '*reg*ulator' (from the same root) or 'one who makes things *right*' (again the same root, possibly connected with drawing '*correct*' (same root) boundaries."

[25] In Dvārakā, when Arjuna abducts his future co-wife, there occurs a small scene where a *sabhāpāla* (officer of the assembly hall) oversees a meeting of the girl's distressed male kin. He is the one to sound the alarm when the abduction is announced and it is he who informs the assembled menfolk of

says to Kṛṣṇa: *saṅghamukhyo'si* (you are leader of an association). As we shall see, the families of Kṛṣṇa and of Yudhiṣṭhira tend towards this form of a dominant type of polity. Presently it is difficult to determine the geographical location or historical duration of the *saṅghas* as we have neither strong literal nor firm archaeological record. Writes Agrawala, "The *Janapadas* which were originally named after the peoples settled in them, dropped their tribal significance and figured as territorial units or regions."[26] "It seemed that the Bharatas lived round about Kurukshetra as a *Saṅgha* in Pāṇini's time."[27]

I would agree with such a view and would propose that these Bhāratas were organised in a lateral manner, one that privileged a matriline rather than a patriline, although we have no explicit evidence of this except in the poem.[28] The autocratic patriarchies that came later demonstrated a more monetary rather than a solely land and service based tenure of power, and by this account monarchy would have been more urban while the *saṅgha* system would be more topographical; hence I view the *saṅgha* arrangement as part an economic system that was premonetary. I shall return to this argument later in the penultimate chapter.[29]

Epic *Mahābhārata* retains a trace-memory of such older polities insofar as the epic poets were superimposing an heroic world onto a partially memorable, partially simulated, past.[30] In this model there are two kinds of time: the actual or 'real' premonetary and preliterate recalled-time of *janapadas*, and the literary time of a synthetic poetry of imitation where the culture is a matter of artifice rather than of any immediate representation. The latter medium supplants the

---

the outrage (I.212.10–15). There is no mention of the 'king' or of Vasudeva in all this; Kṛṣṇa and his brother Rāma are present however. Another word that also translates as 'clan' is *cakra*, which literally means 'wheel' or 'circle', but can denote a province or multitude, as in: *vṛṣṇicakra* (the Vṛṣṇi domain) (XV.44.34). This is a usage dating back to the form of encampment in ancient Indo-Āryan times.

26 See Agrawala 1952, 424. "For example, Pāñchāla was the name of a Kshatriya descendent of the Pāñchāla tribe and also of the king of the *Janapada*. Similarly, *Pāñchālāḥ* in the plural was the name of the country as well as the name of the Kshatriya clan" (Agrawala 1952, 425).

27 Agrawala 1952, 451. He describes the Bhāratas as *āyudhajīvin* (those who lived by the profession of arms). Pāṇini may have flourished in or around the fifth century in the region of Gāndhāra, presently in Pakistan. J. P. Sharma (1968, 9) comments: "The terms *gaṇa* and *saṅgha*, with reference to the republican form of government, do not occur until after the 6th century b.c."

28 By "lateral" I mean 'by election'—as opposed to a more *vertical* form of nomination that is generated by lineage.

29 My original ideas concerning premonetary society were inspired by Simmel 1900; Seaford 2004 offers a substantial and modern bibliography on this field, as does the work of T. K. Earle and of le Goff. See Rapson 1897.

30 I would tentatively aver that these older kinds of kingly polity long preceded the formulations of *dharmaśāstra*.

former and *re*-presents it in a compounding of many disparate events in what is in fact a montage. The representation itself takes place in a third form of time, that is, the time of actual performance. Hence there occurs a compounding of the historical, the mythical, and the performative, which coalesce into a single instance or event that has been simply transmitted and then recorded in our present text of the poem.[31]

It is thus telling that the epic commences with *śaunakasya kulapater* (a sacrifice of the clan-lord Śaunaka).[32] The fact that he is not a *rāja* suggests something of that old and archaic world is being signalled or installed at the immediate outset of the poem (I.1.1).[33] The poet then tells his audience that the epic concerns *ayaṃ kuruvaṅṣaś ca yadūnāṃ bharatasya ca* (and this Kuru lineage of the Yadus and of Bharata), a song about the joining of these two great clans (I.1.44).[34] At the end of the poem a Yādava rules at Indraprastha and a nominal Bhārata at Hāstinapura.

Throughout the initial two-thirds of the poem this memory of the *saṅgha* appears to linger, if not obviously as an explicit institution then at least in terms of its operation and practice, something the poets presume. This preliminary *parvan* of the poem is multifarious and profoundly diverse in its narrative

[31] Those initial editors who originally assembled the *Mahābhārata* were working as anthologists, drawing together into one series many accounts and versions of poetic tradition. In this process they eliminated much that was peculiarly local or socially specific in order to render a uniform and 'Pan-Indic' text. I have included an "Appendix On Epic Time" at the end of this book, summarising my views on this subject.

[32] While in the forest, Yudhiṣṭhira meets with a Śaunaka at III.2.60; this might not be the Śaunaka who instigates the opening ritual of the poem. If it is, he must be extremely aged at that point, being by then three generations in time removed from the forest encounter with Yudhiṣṭhira. Again, preliteracy is not overly concerned with rational time or sequence but more with synchronic structures.

[33] The title is repeated at I.4.1, in the hiatus between the Pauṣya and Puloman episodes. Obversely, the term *rāja* is employed to simply denote seniority or leadership, as in the expression *dāśarājo* 'fisher-king', where the father of Satyavatī is indicated: he is a chief of ferrymen or fishermen (I.94.47). *Rāja* here simply indicates the most senior rank in a particular social hierarchy. At XII.146.1ff., there is another Śaunaka or 'descendent of Śunaka', who is explicitly said to be a *brāhmaṇa* called Indrota. In this passage Śaunaka is described as speaking with Janamejaya. The question then is, if these two are identical could a *brāhmaṇa* become a *kulapati*? This is a fine question. *Kulapati* is a term that later came to be sometimes used for the head of a large educational institution.

[34] Parpola (2015, 93–94) comments: "The Rigveda mentions by name some thirty Aryan tribes and clans. A term meaning 'five peoples' is used throughout the Rigveda to refer to the major tribes, of which four are regularly paired: Yadu with Turvaśa, Anu with Druhyu. These four tribes seem to have been among the first wave of Indo-Aryan speaking immigrants to the northwest of the subcontinent from Afghanistan. A fifth tribe, Pūru, together with its ally or subtribe Bharata, appears to have arrived later, again from Afghanistan ... The first Kuru king mentioned in the Rigveda is Kuruśravaṇa, a descendent of Trasadasyu [a Pūru], suggesting that the Pūrus moved to the area later called Kurukṣetra ... Alexander the Great defeated King Pōros, whose Middle Indo-Aryan name Pora comes from the Sanskrit *Paurava*, a 'descendent of Pūru'; his realm lay between the Jhelum and Ravi rivers."

formations and the epic appears to commence twice, insofar as the poet who opens the performance of this text is introduced twice, and almost identically (at I.1.1 and then at I.4.1).[35] From the initial opening, with a short series of comments on the relations between the poets of the epic, there occur two brief summaries of the epic or modes of the work.[36] One begins with Pāṇḍu and the other opens with Dhṛtarāṣṭra, two brothers and kings whose tenure begins the drama *proper* of the Bhārata Song.[37] The first synopsis describes the doings of the young Pāṇḍava boys and ends with the war at Kurukṣetra, while the second version begins with Draupadī's *svayaṃvara* or 'marriage contest' and concludes with the events closely following the great battle.

Immediately before this first account is mentioned, Yudhiṣṭhira makes his initial entry to the poem and is described as: *yudhiṣṭhiro dharmamayo mahādrumaḥ* (Yudhiṣṭhira, made of *dharma*, [is] a great tree) (I.1.66). A few lines later the poets say that, as he entered Hāstinapura as a youth:

> yudhiṣṭhirasya śaucena prītāḥ prakṛtayo'bhavan
>
> I.1.80
>
> The members-of-the-polity were happy with the purity of Yudhiṣṭhira.

The poets are thus indicating the presence of popular approbation in the formation of a prince; this is not an autocratic nor a unitary kingship but a political community. Indeed, when Duḥṣanta initially rejects the mother of his son who has just presented him with their offspring it is because *bhavedd hi śaṅkā lokasya* (for there might be suspicion among the world) (I.69.36). In other words, the king cannot simply expect that lineage counts in the succession; the affirmation of the populace is also required. This boy is, of course, Bharata, from whom the poem and also the modern country of Bhārata, India, receive their name.[38] Likewise, Bhīṣma in the Udyoga *parvan*—in a speech recapitulated by Kṛṣṇa—tells of how, when his own father passed away the subjects approached him requesting that he become their next ruler, crying: *rājā bhava ... naḥ* (be our king!) (V.145.25). Yet when the epic describes Pūru, who precedes Duḥṣanta in time, it states that his father, the great Yayāti, *pūruṃ rājye'bhiṣicya* (anointed

35 See Bhattacharya 2012.

36 I have examined the complex and internal relations between *Mahābhārata* poets in McGrath 2011.

37 The first summary runs from I.1.67 to 1.94; the second goes from I.1.102 until 1.159. These two summaries are then magnified in the *anukramaṇī* (list of chapters) (I.2.34–69), and the *parvasaṃgraha* (digest of books) (I.2.72–234).

38 The poets say that Vyāsa spent three years composing the great Bhārata Song (I.56.32); and, likewise, Śakuntalā carried the foetal Bharata for three years before giving birth to the child (I.68.2). Both are periods of thirty-nine complete lunations.

Pūru into kingship), and this admission was without any popular recognition (I.69.46).[39] Thus kingship in certain geographical places—or in certain parts of the poem—projects a prerogative of bestowal by a kingly father towards the senior princely son, yet in other regions, either in terms of place or of poetry, the consent of the people who are subject to such rule is required. This latter model is, I would submit, an aspect or extension of the *saṅgha* kind of polity.

When Kṛṣṇa—on his ambassadorial mission to the court at Hāstinapura with the intention of securing peace between the two moieties of the community—pleads with king Dhṛtarāṣṭra to restrain the waywardness of his sons, he says:

> bruvantu vā mahīpālāḥ sabhāyāṃ ye samāsate
>
> V.93.51
>
> Let the great kings who have assembled in the sabhā speak!

It is their voice and admonishment he is asking Dhṛtarāṣṭra to hear and so to modify his policy, or lack of policy; he is asking the *rāja* to attend to the concerns and expressions of the senior members and elders of the clan, to be responsive to his *saṅgha* in a literal sense of 'combined together'. This is not a picture of king as an individual suzerain.

Later, Kṛṣṇa advises Duryodhana, who at this point in the epic is challenging *all* authority in his attempt to take control of power in the kingdom:

> tvām eva sthāpayiṣyanti yauvarājye mahārathāḥ
> mahārājye ca pitaraṃ dhṛtarāṣṭraṃ janeśvaram
>
> V.122.59
>
> The great warriors will install you as heir-apparent,
> And father Dhṛtarāṣṭra, lord of the people, as Mahārāja.

Manifest here is the understanding that the great warriors of the kingdom will be the ones to establish both kingship and its succession. Concerning the installation of Dhṛtarāṣṭra, the poets comment that:

> tataḥ sarvāḥ prajās tāta dhṛtarāṣṭraṃ janeśvaram
> anvapadyanta vidhivad yathā pāṇḍuṃ narādhipam
>
> V.146.7

[39] Bhīṣma is said to unceremoniously anoint his stepbrothers into kingship at I.95.5 and 12. Similarly, *abhiṣicya tu taṃ rājye dilīpo vanam āśritaḥ* ([king] Dilīpa, having anointed him [his son] into kingship departed toward the forest) (III.106.40); and likewise, King Parikṣit anoints his eldest son *rājye* 'into kingship' (III.190.43). Dyumatsena, the father-in-law of Sāvitrī, receives his anointment from the *purohita* 'domestic priest', who also anoints his son *yauvarājye* 'as crown prince' (III.283.11).

> Then, sir, all the populace accepted king Dhṛtarāṣṭra
> According to injunction, as they had accepted Pāṇḍu as king.

One must recall that many of the heroes of the epic are not quite human. They are born with one divine parent, as with the Pāṇḍava half-brothers, or born without a human parent, as with Droṇa or Kṛpa, or even sometimes, as with Draupadī, born without any human or humanlike generation.[40] The poem in its core narrative deals with these strangely heroic creatures who are *like* mortals: this is a simile which is often vague and forgotten. These strange beings, the heroes, dramatise and represent the contentions and organisations that inform the Bhārata narrative as it describes and portrays how both kinship and kingship occur in this uncommon half-world of the epic.

Heroes and kings in the epic are both superhuman and at times supernatural, yet their political selection and maintenance is necessarily quite human. What we have seen here is a situation where the *ordinary* folk—in the world of epic performance and poetry—participate in the creation and in the practice of kingship by strange *mythical* figures who are not always human beings. The poem blurs this relation just as it blurs the difference between old-time *saṅghas* and the later *rājya*. One wonders what actual weight a popular voice held in the polities of the Mauryas or of the Gupta dynasties, in the world of the poem's early historical state?

As we shall see, the problem is that several *kinds* of kingship are joined together in the poem in a fashion that is not always seamless. It is this vast inclusiveness of poetic materials—which the editors and poets assembled and which lies at the basis of our present Pune text—that makes for such a great and canonical work of art, one that inhabits the very core of what it means today to be part of the diverse and cosmopolitan state of India.

iii. Duality

Concerning the *natural* aspects of kingship in ancient times—as it is represented in the poetry of the *Mahābhārata*—there appears to be what Lévi-Strauss has referred to elsewhere as an "idéologie bipartite," which also adheres about this social activity.[41] There certainly exists a dual quality of kingship as it concerns

[40] See McGrath 2012, concerning what makes for the *semi*-divine and the half-human in epic *Mahābhārata*, particularly as this applies to Arjuna.

[41] Lévi-Strauss (1991, 19:313): "le dualisme diamétral ne constituait pas à lui seul un modèle adequate pour comprendre le fonctionnement des organisations dualists dont le dynamisme requiert qu'on fasse

Yudhiṣṭhira and Kṛṣṇa or Dhṛtarāṣṭra and Vidura; there is also the pattern of two brothers who either compete for, or divide, a throne or kingdom, and this is further magnified by the contention between two moieties of the Kuru clan.[42] It is as if a certain dualism is intrinsic to the functioning of kingship in this literature, one that is profoundly inherent to the very culture or social philosophy of *kṣatriya* life. Similarly, in terms of the hero as a category, such a pattern is demonstrated by the signal duality that exists between a charioteer and his hero and also between select heroes themselves with their fixed *bhāgas* or 'formal opponents' in combat—what nowadays might be referred to as an 'opposite number.'[43]

This mysteriously inherent duality that lies at the heart of the poem is simply a poetic technique or mnemonic dexterity that the early preliterate poets applied as a particular instrument of creativity.[44] This was less a condition of their performative skills than of their cognitive manner, and this kind of poetic perception and its dynamic is fundamental to *Mahābhārata* rhetorical form.[45]

Stylistically speaking, the poets always have an interlocutor—either Janamejaya or Dhṛtarāṣṭra—and there is virtually never any form of speech that exceeds the pattern of a dialogue: that would be *too* dramatic for a single poet

appel à d'autres principes." In this book and in La Pensée Sauvage, Lévi-Strauss is primarily concerned with formulating synchronic structures; whereas what I am proposing here, in terms of how the preliterate *Mahābhārata* poets worked, concerns a performative and diachronic system of effort, imagination, and composition.

42 In the extreme case there are the two brothers who were *dvidhaivaikaṃ yathā kṛtau* (two made as one); these are Sunda and Upasunda who lived at Kurukṣetra and killed each other (I.201–204).

43 In McGrath 2013, chap. III, I examined at length the phenomena of dyarchy as it occurs between Yudhiṣṭhira and Kṛṣṇa. Puett (2002, 226–236), in his discussion "Kingship and Sacrifice: From Granet to Dumézil and Back Again Through Sahlins," describes the "classic study of kingship, *Mitra-Varuna*" of Dumézil and the "basic dualism in concepts of sovereignty: a passive, sacerdotal form of kingship, and an active, militaristic form. It is in these terms that he [Dumézil] analyzed the first legendary rulers of Rome: Romulus, the exemplar of violent aggressiveness (*celeritas*), and Numa, the model of sacerdotal powers (*gravitas*)." (Puett 2002, 226–227.) Puett (229) similarly quotes from Sahlins (1985, 91): "Numa, Romulus's successor, weans Rome from war and founds the priesthood and cult, means of civic order ... Thereafter the Latin kingship will alternate between *celeritas* and *gravitas*, magical war kings and religious peace kings." In McGrath 2004, chap. III, the figure of the *bhāga* is discussed in terms of warrior symmetry. The "Appendix On Epic Time" towards the end of the present book develops this concept of dualism summarily.

44 Other instruments of this system of epic poetics would include composition in performance, the use of themes and formulae, and the ability to either contract or expand a poem's presentation at will, depending upon the needs and wishes of an audience. See Lord 1960.

45 See, for instance, Anthony (2007, 135), where he comments upon "the Indo-European fascination with binary doublings ... which reappeared again and again, even in the metric structure of Indo-European poetry; the theme of pairs who represented magical and legal power." This latter motif could certainly be said to apply to the Yudhiṣṭhira-Kṛṣṇa alliance. One thinks of Romulus and Remus in the founding of Rome in such a light where twinning is the essence or paradigm of the myth.

to manage alone. By *thinking* in such bipartite terms as they *sang* the epic the poets were thus able to find themselves and their characters—the heroes—more naturally, as it were, and such a dual kind of cognition enabled them to always perform with a structure in mind.[46] This profound patterning of dualism within the poetics of epic *Mahābhārata* concerns both its mnemonic system and also how it *works*; once writing, and therefore prose, becomes the creative process—rather than unlettered performance—such a practice of intellectual duality loses its compulsion and its conceptual imperative as the need for a mnemonic is replaced by written form.

Addressing kingship in particular, this dual formation is sustained for the poem in addressing two successive kings as patrons, one narrative framing another: the poet Vaiśaṃpāyana sings to king Janamejaya, and—within that poetic structure or stream—at the centre of the epic Saṃjaya the poet sings his part of the Bhārata Song to the old blind king Dhṛtarāṣṭra.[47] Then there are two significant kings—as characters—within the *Mahābhārata* narrative writ large who move in constant parallel, Dhṛtarāṣṭra and Yudhiṣṭhira, neither of whom are dynamic or strong kings: the old patriarch is overruled by his son Duryodhana, and, as we shall see, the elder Pāṇḍava is frequently directed by his heroic kinsman and victorious ally, the Yādava Kṛṣṇa.

In steady counterpoint to the constant focus the poem brings to Yudhiṣṭhira is the presence of his cousin, Duryodhana, who slowly manages to overtake the political order at Hāstinapura and to dominate the polity there, leading it into a totally destructive war.[48] The powerful character that Duryodhana brings to

46 Preliterate poetry is perhaps by nature informed by such dualistic cognitive process for that is how the poets *thought* as they arranged and composed their verses, almost in the manner of syllogism—in terms of narrative formation rather than as a means of proof. Once written prose comes into existence and use the thought process of the poets becomes different, it is not just the case that the system of record changes. There exists a medium, the message, and also the activity of cognition, which organises the message. See McGrath 2016 on the mnemonic process of these Late Bronze Age poets.

47 This model of performance is actually reversed on one occasion and it is as if the poets or editors have mistakenly introduced the names of Dhṛtarāṣṭra and his poet Saṃjaya in a reverse order: for in this one speech it is the old king who behaves like a poet, singing of the youthful deeds of Kṛṣṇa to his interlocutor, Saṃjaya (VII.10.1–42). This instant in the poem is an odd reordering of the usual verbal structure. It is ironic that Janamejaya, who—during most of the epic's events—was not even born, remains such a constant and steady presence in the poem—in terms of the dynamics of its engendering. As an aside, Śiśupāla also mentions certain of Kṛṣṇa's youthful deeds beginning at II.38.4ff.: it is rare in the epic for such reference to another tradition of poetry to occur like this.

48 When Saṃjaya actually begins to sing about the onset and events of battle at Kurukṣetra, his first line is: *bhrātṛbhiḥ sahito rājan putro duryodhanas tava* (O king, your son Duryodhana, with his brothers ...) (VI.42.2). Duryodhana brings a highly charged contrast to the presence and character of his cousin and rival for the throne, and one wonders if there was perhaps once a *duryodhanakathā*, 'a Duryodhana Epic' that has been drawn into this larger poem and renovated; in the same way that the hero Diomedes

the epic supplies the *Mahābhārata* with a peculiar dimension of kingship: what exactly did the poets or proto-editors intend the son of Dhṛtarāṣṭra to represent? Duryodhana is of course thoroughly mortal, although his birth and that of his hundred brothers was unnaturally facilitated by Vyāsa; whereas Yudhiṣṭhira is half divine, his father being the deity Dharma and his brothers are in fact only half-siblings. Duryodhana is the biological grandson of Vyāsa; Yudhiṣṭhira is not and is in fact mortally connected—via the matriline—with the Yādava people. There is thus an asymmetry between the two moieties of the clan, a distinction that continues to run in various forms throughout the poem.

Sustaining this dual system, Duryodhana and Yudhiṣṭhira move in effective counterpoint throughout the epic and it is the folly of *both* these regnant figures that conduces to the destruction of the Kuru kingdom in the war at Kurukṣetra.[49] Duryodhana certainly receives the ascription of 'king' from the poets, but this is complimentary or simply part of the drama of the poem and somewhat unfounded in reality. For instance, at one point he is said to be *rājānaṃ kauravyaṃ dhṛtarāṣṭrajam* (the Kaurava king, son of Dhṛtarāṣṭra) (IV.24.7). The merging of Duryodhana into the role or place of kingship is something that the poets accomplish with a degree of abbreviation, for nowhere is it indicated that he ever received the *abhiṣeka* 'the royal unction'; this is a curious blurring of title for at no time does Dhṛtarāṣṭra ever relinquish his own paramount status. Thus, for much of the epic narrative there are two kings contending in the kingdom, emotionally, violently, and morally, with the grey figure of Dhṛtarāṣṭra as a titular eminence from another generation and era in the background. It is this duality that charges the narrative with its impetus and force.

---

in the *Iliad*—especially in Scroll V—appears to have been drawn from another, and probably his own, epic tradition. Burgess (2001) has shown how the Song of Achilles drew extensively from an "earlier" tradition of Memnon.

49 Kurukṣetra (field of Kuru), so named because the ancestor, Kuru, long ago, had performed a great *tapas* 'spiritual exertion' there (I.89.43). It is a moot point as to why the family of Dhṛtarāṣṭra are referred to as 'the Kurus' while their cousins, the Pāṇḍavas, do not usually receive this title even though they are equally 'Kuru' by nominal descent or lineage: Kuru is the unmarked term and Pāṇḍava is the marked term. Is this possibly a remnant indicating that the Dhārtarāṣṭras are come of an older poetic tradition than the Pāṇḍavas or is it due to the fact that Pāṇḍu is not the generator of his sons whereas Dhṛtarāṣṭra does actually possess paternity over his sons: that is, the Pāṇḍavas have *no* genetic connection with Kuru. Concerning the question of Kaurava antiquity one might note that there are ten chiefs or kings of the Kaurava force: Śakuni, Śalya, Jayadratha, Vinda and Anuvinda, Sudakṣiṇa, Śrutāyudha, Jayatsena, Bṛhadbala, and Kṛtavarman, and there is a reference to the Battle of the Ten Kings in RV VII.18; see McGrath 2004, 56–57. Yet in the Ādi *parvan*, there is also a reference to a battle with ten armies, but this time it is the ten armies of the Pāñcālas who are attacking the Bhāratas (I.89.33). It is not possible to find historical contingency in the *Mahābhārata*, although one can always speculate; the poem represents no single temporal moment and is a compounding of many social conditions, times, and beliefs.

Vidura blames Dhṛtarāṣṭra in the Fifth *parvan* when he says that:

āhitaṃ bhārataiśvaryaṃ tvayā duryodhane mahat

V.38.43

Great lordship over the Bhāratas has been delivered by you to Duryodhana.

Later, during the Karṇa *parvan*, Kṛṣṇa himself—in drawing Arjuna's attention to Duryodhana—refers to the Kaurava as, *rājā sarvasya lokasya* (king of all the world), which is a precise description, except that there is also *another* king of all the world at that moment with whom Kṛṣṇa is profoundly connected, and that is, of course, Yudhiṣṭhira. (VIII.43.4).

There is thus an essential narrative form in the poem, in terms of how the poets are always *doubling* the figures and the actual process of the song's development; it is this manner of poetics that firmly underlies, and also constitutes, the phenomenon of kingship as demonstrated in epic *Mahābhārata*.[50] As stated above, I would argue that this is a profound condition of preliterate poetics at work, being the nature of *how* the poets thought as they composed their song during performance. It is as if their system of thought-in-action or composition was necessarily fugal or founded upon successive counterpoint.

iv. Magadha

Johannes Bronkhorst makes the interesting claim that, "the first written version of the *Mahābhārata* dates from the time when Brahmanism was trying to reach out toward the east into regions that had an altogether different culture until that time. Moreover, it was concerned with the imposition of Brahmanical culture on kings and kingdoms that had not adhered to it so far. We may assume that the *Mahābhārata* was an instrument in this Brahmanical effort to spread into the territories of Greater Magadha."[51] This is a fascinating assertion concerning what the poem at one point refers to as *rājadharmaḥ sanātanaḥ* (the perpetual dharma of a king) (V.20.3). Bronkhorst thus connects a moment of written composition or record with an historical and demographic movement, and this is a most useful hypothesis in terms of its potential historicity. In what follows we shall explore this proposition and its grounds of inference—for such a declaration

[50] A glance at the opening hundred lines or so of the Homeric *Iliad* reveals a similar pattern of duality, in terms of how the poets generate the movement of the poem.

[51] Bronkhorst 2007, 97.

makes presumptions as to the performance of the epic as well about the nature of such literary efficacy.

Given the multifarious and highly diverse structure of the *Mahābhārata* as we presently know it, where *kṣatriya* poetry is fused with edifying and didactic song, it is almost impossible for a reader today to reconstitute a performative praxis for the poem: we can guess and accept hints, but that is all. This praxis is the necessary subtext of Bronkhorst's hypothesis. How exactly was it that a poem accomplished such a feat, and what were the performative conditions and their potential efficacy? And if we cannot discern the latter, how can we propose the former? At some unidentifiable point long ago the poem was assembled in a fashion of *bricolage*, with many various components joined together into a unified whole that somehow, and quite mysteriously, now succeeds as a composite work of art.[52] How and why that structure emerges are the questions that must be answered before Bronkhorst's statement can be successfully applied to historical conditions. Also, how in fact did that conviction of epic performance and enactment succeed? Bronkhorst's assumption however is a crucial point if we are to understand how the Bhārata Song once thrived not simply as a work of art but as an ideological representation of kingship within an active polity; he has raised *the* crucial question.

The *brāhmaṇa* clan of the Bhārgavas may have been connected with this 'migration,' given the preponderance of references in the poem to this social or political group.[53] Cyavana, Rāma Jāmadagnya, and Mārkaṇḍeya, for instance, are of this order, and many of the *Mahābhārata upākhyānas* 'secondary tales' concern members of the clan and their doings.[54] Ugraśravas, the poet who recites the outermost ring of the song, says—almost at the outset of the performance—that, *imaṃ vaṃśam ahaṃ ... nigadāmi ... bhṛgoḥ* (I declare this lineage of Bhṛgu) (I.5.6–7).[55]

52 In McGrath 2013, chap. I, I examined this idea of *bricolage*, a term and concept I had drawn from the work of Claude Lévi-Strauss.

53 However, the Sabhā *parvan*, the Virāṭa *parvan*, the Śalya *parvan*, the Sauptika *parvan*, and the Strī *parvan*, all possess scant reference to the clan of Bhṛgu.

54 See Sukthankar 1944, 278ff. Sukthankar (1944, 316) states: "The Anuśāsana, for some reason that is not yet quite clear, is the richest in Bhārgava material." Sathaye (2010) offers a good summary and analysis of Sukthankar's work. Hiltebeitel (in 2011b, 150) states that "Fifty-seven of the sixty-seven *upākhyānas* ... occur in parvans 1.3.12 and 13 where stories cluster most densely." Hiltebeitel (2011b, 149) also makes the observation: "Calculating from the roughly 73,900 couplets in the Critical Edition, the full total for the 67 *upākhyānas* is 10,521 couplets or 13.87%." He adds that "A count has to be approximate because the *Mahābhārata* contains prose passages. One also has to count all couplets as '*ślokas*'."

55 This occurs, of course, at what is known as the 'second beginning' of the poem. The 'actual' poem, however, the *bhārata* itself, does not itself commence until I.55.

One wonders if the great destruction of *kṣatriyas*, which Rāma repeatedly conducted near Kurukṣetra, was not in fact an annihilation of Buddhist kingdoms that were situated to the east of the Gaṅgā-Yamunā *doab*, for it is often said by the poets that, *rāmaḥ ... asakṛt pārthivaṃ kṣatraṃ jaghāna* (Rāma repeatedly killed the princely *kṣatriya* order) (I.2.3). This is an interesting hypothesis which I have heard from friends in Gujarat but which cannot be proven, yet it does possibly support the inference which Bronkhorst drew from his reading of the poem.

The great Sukthankar notes that, "the name of Bhṛgu is chosen to exemplify the dangers incurred by those who oppress Brahmins ... the Bhārgava heroes occupy a surprisingly large portion of the canvas—which is said to depict the Bhārata War."[56] Allow me here to quote significantly from Verardi: "whereas the idea of state and society the Buddhists had in mind was compatible with the extremely varied peoples inhabiting the subcontinent, the Brahminical model implied their forced incorporation into the well-guarded perimeter of an agrarian society. It was not just a state society that, especially from the Gupta period onwards, started being established in vast portions of India but a *varṇa* state society ... the imposition of the rules of the *varṇa* state implied much violence."[57] It is the violence of the poem itself, with its immense range of lovely and natural similes that stand for such a social and political shift, that was married to a geographical movement of peoples.

It remains to be said, however, that Bronkhorst has raised a necessary question as to *how* the poem once functioned and also as to the importance of the poem's projection of a particular kind of expansive rule, that is, kingship. As we shall see, the epic proposes two different kinds of kingship, one that is founded on what we might call 'nature' and the other on what could be termed as 'culture.'

v. The *Dharmarāja*

The poem poses an unusual status for time, insofar as Yudhiṣṭhira is the *dharmarāja* during a period when *dharma* only obtains on earth to the extent of one quarter of its full potential, due to the fact that the *kali yuga* (the age of *kali*), or what Hesiod described as an Iron Generation, commences with the beginning

56 Sukthankar 1944, 329.

57 Verardi 2011, 11–12. The Śānti and Anuśāsana *parvans* describe at great length the necessity of such 'force' or 'violence'—what is called the *daṇḍa*.

of the battle at Kurukṣetra.[58] This is ironic, for the great probity and moral clarity of Yudhiṣṭhira is constantly distressed or thwarted by situations that demand actions that cannot be considered to possess full *dharma*; thus his kingship, or the potential of his kingship, is persistently deflected or constrained, for moral success is only possible in one quarter of all that is thought, spoken, or acted during this aeon. Most of the *Mahābhārata* addresses this asymptotic condition of *adharma*.[59] As a poem, then, epic *Mahābhārata* is a work about the preponderant condition of *adharma* in the world; it is not a poem about *dharma*.[60] By *dharma* I understand what can be considered as the 'animating principle of social consciousness'—and, if one comprehends *dharma*, one understands the practical and active nature of a society.[61]

In the *kṛta yuga*, the first of the 'ages', everything is stable and virtually imperishable; there is no exchange, *na krayavikrayāḥ* (no buying nor selling), and there is no economy for only a natural state of production exists, and there are even no separate or solely supernal deities at that original prelapsarian moment of time (III.148.12). During this ideal era there were no uniquely supernatural beings, and no rituals for all existence was then in complete harmony and equilibrium (XII.59.14). By the time that the *kali yuga* is about to commence, however, everything is friable and subject to decomposition and mutation, even *dharma*; thus the extraordinary virtue of a king-hero like Yudhiṣṭhira is also subject to impropriety and instability, for the random overpowers any fixed order or equilibrium in both the social—or human—and the natural worlds. As we shall see there are many competing surveys of *dharma* in the poem as we have it now because in a *kali yuga* the state of *dharma* is necessarily diverse, various,

58 The monkey-hero Hanūmān—who in some traditions has the same father as Bhīma—describes the four *yugas* to Bhīma at III.148.10–37. He says, *pādenaikena kaunteya dharmaḥ kaliyuge sthitaḥ* (O Kaunteya, in the *kali yuga dharma* is only stationed with one foot) (III.148.32). The sequence and qualities of the *yugas* are also iterated by Bhīṣma at XII.70.7–28.

59 Kṛṣṇa states that the *kali yuga* is about to commence at V.140.6.

60 It is ironic that from a work of 'fiction' an audience can receive edification as to the 'truth' of moral value; in this case it is the *adharma* made manifest in the epic by the poets that leads an audience towards a greater awareness of the nature of what is morally correct in human behaviour. As Sen (2009, vii) has remarked, it is from an awareness of *injustice* that Yudhiṣṭhira forms his views on what is *right*. A contemporary Delhi intellectual has described the poem thus: "The Mahabharata is a labyrinthine epic about deceit and betrayal." Varma 2004, 36.

61 In a talk given under the auspices of the Hindu Studies Colloquium at the Center for the Study of World Religions on September 20, 2012, James Fitzgerald wisely asserted that, in its original sense, *Dharma*, in a personified form, was associated with the Vedic divinity Yama insofar as both—as *psychopomp*—were the conductors of an individual soul towards a future existence. Fitzgerald has an excellent overview of "Dharma and its Translation in the *Mahābhārata*" (Olivelle 2009, 248–263).

and contentious.[62] Similarly, because the poem has been accumulated over the centuries and millennia into a singular whole—a unit epic—there are of course present in its verses many historically different qualities and identities of *dharma*, particularly as they relate to kingship.[63] Time in the poem thus takes on many different forms and realities, almost all of which—except for the specific names of months—are simply metaphorical.[64]

Kuntī, in her allegorical discourse with Kṛṣṇa, her nephew, when she speaks of what makes for a good *kṣatriya* and a strong king, says:[65]

daṇḍanītyāṃ yadā rājā samyak kārtsnyena vartate
tadā kṛtayugaṃ nāma kālaḥ śreṣṭhaḥ pravartate

V.130.14

When the king keeps entirely a policy of judicious force
Then the best time, namely the Kṛta Yuga, commences.

One should note that this is Kuntī's extremely *kṣatriya* view of time and not the traditional ordering of *yugas*. In her telling of the metaphor of time, she marks strong kingship as the sign of the golden age.[66] She also adds:

yugasya ca caturthasya rājā bhavati kāraṇam

V.130.16

The king is the cause of the fourth age.

62 Das (2009) brings a modern view to this problem. In 262n12 of this essay, he makes the comment about "... the epithet *dharmarāja* shared by Yudhiṣṭhira and Yama, the Lord of Death."

63 A king could be said to be the chief interpreter of *dharma* in a society and it is his verbal pronouncement of such decisions that go to constitute the activity and enforcement of *dharma* in a community. As the son of personified *Dharma*—who in the *Mahābhārata* is a divine figure although this is not traditionally the case—Yudhiṣṭhira meets with his father in the forest and answers the enigmatic and riddling questions that his senior poses (III.297ff.). Since, during the *kali yuga* there is no forthright and absolute understanding of *dharma* in human and natural society, and, as *dharma* is out of balance, an unusual moral intelligence is thus required before what is *right* can be correctly interpreted. Hence the speech of the divine figure, *Dharma*, is a message that possesses many possible interpretations; it is a message that is enigmatic and riddling. Vyāsa makes the claim that, towards the end of the poem when the spirit of Vidura enters Yudhiṣṭhira's body, this is a representation of the divine *Dharma* itself entering the body of the king (XV.35.16). Again, such divinisation and personification of *dharma* is a peculiarly epic conceit. At XV.38.6, Kuntī claims that she has been informed that she is the *dharmasya jananī* (the mother of Dharma), who in this case is actually Yudhiṣṭhira himself.

64 The "Appendix On Epic Time" is to be found at the end of this book.

65 The word she uses for 'allegory' here is *upamā*, a term that can also be taken to mean 'simile' (V.130.8).

66 In McGrath 2009, chap V:4, I examined these edifying speeches of Kuntī.

This is the era in whose beginning the Song of the Bhāratas is historically placed, the *kali yuga*. Kuntī closes this part of her exhortation by saying that a firm king during this later period should rule in the manner that exemplifies constraint:

> sāmnā dānena bhedena daṇḍenātha nayena ca
>
> V.130.30
>
> By conciliation, by material influence, by division, also by force and by design.

Later in her long peroration she says that *svargadvāropamaṃ rājyam atha* (kingship is like a door to heaven) (V.132.29). If epic *Mahābhārata* is a poem concerned with kingship, then in a sense the epic is arguably a medium or gateway and a human representation of that *heavenly doorway* in verse or song. If *svarga* is a place of harmony, then according to such a view the epic *Mahābhārata* is a place where kingship finds such ideal stability. As Vyāsa says to king Yudhiṣṭhira during the early course of the Śānti *parvan,* when all the immediate clan gather about the grieving king in order to revive his desperately mourning spirit—for so many of his kin and heirs have been killed—hoping to inspire his new kingship and its regime:

> rājā hi hanyād dadyāc ca prajā rakṣec ca dharmataḥ
>
> XII.32.8
>
> For a king should kill, and he should give, and he should protect people rightly.

It is by these three activities that good kingship secures its equilibrium, that is, as represented *by* the poem: the king punishes, he donates, and he protects.

Listening to the production, to the singing of epic poetry, was a medium for *kṣatriyas* to enter into that world of the ancient long-dead heroes and for an audience to experience some of the emotions those heroes endured, in that *supra*-mortal world of the poem, as they struggled to apprehend an always elusive *dharma*. The performance of the poem for a *kṣatriya* audience was a medium by which kings and warriors—in their minds and affect—could participate in that old-fashioned world and so could possibly *learn* about how to conduct both themselves and their charges in their contemporary moral life itself. This experience of an audience was one of emotional pleasure due to the similes and the compound beauties of the myths that were being sung. Even death, physical pain, and grief—that is, all the ordeals the pursuit of an evasive *dharma* entails in an unstable life and society—were made aesthetically pleasing via the performed similes of the epic.

vi. The Text

Let us consider the *nature* of the text as we have it today with the Critical Edition of Pune (PCE). Sukthankar makes the significant comment—concerning the narrative nature of the poem—when he says of the epic that "It is a rapid motion picture reel of many ages of Indian culture—not necessarily factitive history—arranged in a naïve fashion: something like the sculptured panels on the gateways and the railings of the Buddhist Stūpa at Sanchi or the mural frescoes of Ajanta, with tableaux telescoped all in one plane, without much regard to perspective or with its own peculiar technique of perspective."[67] Both works of art, at Sāñchī and Ajanta—and I would certainly include the sculpture of Bharhut here—were celebrating the awakening spiritual awareness of a young king and demonstrating his deeds. Such were the compressed patterns of montage, especially as it relates to bas-relief, in that period between Mauryan and Gupta hegemony when the great Bhārata Song as we know it today came to be assembled in a form akin to what we have received and now understand as the *Mahābhārata*. These were *patterns* of narration rather than narrative *sequences*, as we understand narrative in the West today.[68]

This was an imagined former era where *kṣatriyas* employed chariots as both war vehicles and as vehicles of prestige and status.[69] This was also a period when the old world of Indra and the Indo-Āryan deities gave way to, or was displaced by, a newer divine macrocosm that—in the medium of the *Mahābhārata*—came to be principally overseen by Viṣṇu and his *aspects*, particularly as expressed by the icon of *naranārāyaṇau* (Nara and Nārāyaṇa).[70] In that older world, *tejas*

67 Sukthankar 1944, 333. By "perspective" here we can perhaps understand 'conventions of narrative.'

68 The use of visual aids by contemporary and recent poets who sing or sang epic poetry also demonstrates such 'non-sequential' narrative form. These are the *pata/paṛ* used by poets today and in the last two centuries; see, for instance, J. D. Smith 1991, plates 5 and 10. The British Museum has a collection of such painted and glazed paper *patas* that have been used by itinerant singers of both the *Mahābhārata* and *Rāmāyaṇa*; these are all shown in the Museum online database.

69 The material elements of a *ratha* 'chariot' are given at VIII.24.66–106, and depict the *ratha* of Śiva; this is the best description that we presently have for the technically specific components of such a vehicle. These parts are here also supplied with symbolic dimensions so that the vehicle of the chariot represents both geography and religious culture: this is a physical chariot supplied with exact cosmic significance. Śalya at VIII.28.6–8 informs Karṇa of the necessary practical skills of a charioteer. Chariots are a key signifier in Bronze Age heroic literature, as Anthony (2007, 462) writes: "This heroic world of chariot-driving warriors was dimly remembered in the poetry of the *Iliad* and the *Rig Veda*. It was introduced to the civilizations of Central Asia and Iran about 2100 BCE, when exotic Sintashta or Petrovka strangers first appeared on the banks of the Zeravshan."

70 Belvalkar (1961, ccii), in his Introduction to the Śānti *parvan*, observes that " ... the real Śāntiparvan ends with adhyāya 320, which can imply that, at some stage in the growth of the Epic, the Nārāyaṇīya Section did not form an integral part of the Mokṣa-parva sub-section. By a consideration of the

or 'energy' was the substance of excellence and this was displaced by a world where *yoga* or 'psychic strength' supplied the ground for princely and heroic triumph. Similarly, the naturalistic and migrant world of the Ṛg Vedic peoples with its *soma* rituals of inspired intoxication and praise-singing was slowly being overtaken by the more settled world of *brāhmaṇa* ideology—itself possibly a liturgical response to Buddhism and Jainism—where the solemnity of a highly organised sacrifice came to be considered as central to and supportive of an efficient polity.[71]

Concerning the preliterate-literate nexus of the epic, how the Bhārata Song became the *Mahābhārata*, or how it was that the spoken poem became a *written* and material work of art and then that text itself developed, there is still much to be known and such textual research will weigh importantly in the future of *Mahābhārata* Studies. Let us briefly quote from three editors of the Pune Critical Edition, beginning with Franklin Edgerton, the editor of the Sabhā *parvan*.

In his comments on this work he wrote: "It is quite true, as Sukthankar properly emphasizes, that the reconstruction is not an 'ur-Mahābhārata' ... But I believe that it is to *all Mahābhārata* manuscripts now accessible to us approximately what the Alexandrian text of Homer is to the Homeric tradition since its time."[72] Similarly, looking backward towards an unidentifiable textual time, Sukthankar wrote that: "It must, however, be admitted that although in most cases the compilers of our Purāṇas appear to have drawn their material from the *Mahābhārata*, there may be—indeed there *must* be—a few cases in which both the *Mahābhārata* and the Purāṇas may have drawn independently upon a third common source. We can also say this with regard to episodes like the Sāvitrī episode, which likewise occurs in the Matsya Purāṇa, where it is narrated in an entirely different manner from that in the epic, and where all traces of mutual relationship are absent or obliterated, except for two or three common stanzas and stray pādas."[73] Thirdly, Dandekar wrote about the Anuśāsana *parvan*, commenting on its "extensive passages": "The scope and nature of the contents of this *parvan* were such that literally any topic under the sun could be broached

---

grammatical peculiarities of the Nārāyaṇīya sub-section by itself, as compared to those of the rest of the Epic, we have also found a further independent confirmation of such a view ... We have seen how, in the present version of the Bhagavad-gītā no less than of the Śāntiparvan, sage Bhṛgu makes his ubiquitous presence felt—or at least recorded—on all important occasions."

71 See Verardi 2011, I and II. By the term "ideology" I understand: "a system ... of ideas, strategies, tactics, and practical symbols for promoting, perpetuating, or changing a social and cultural order; in brief it is political ideas in action." Friedrich 1989, 301.

72 Edgerton, on p. xxxvi of his Introduction to the 1944 edition of the Sabhā *parvan*, Pune.

73 Sukthankar in his Introduction to the 1942 Pune Edition of the Āraṇyaka *parvan*, Part 1.

and discussed in it. Indeed, the redactors of the Epic, through the ages, seem to have seen in the Anuśāsana, almost the last opportunity for the free play of their propensities. And they must be said to have availed themselves of this opportunity to the fullest extent. This has resulted in poor Yudhiṣṭhira being represented as putting to his grandsire some of the most elementary questions—often without rhyme or reason. Not infrequently, these questions serve as mere excuses for introducing a legend or a doctrine fancied by the redactor."[74]

***

In sum, there existed an ancient preliterate state for the poem in its many parts and variations, and then there occurred a period after a point of textual integration and refinement when that written text also began to undergo change and fluidity. This represents the cultural relationship that exists between models and copies, where the former were ultimately hypothetical while the latter are always conventional. What the original canon must have been is lost to us now, like a Platonic ideal, but it nevertheless informs the sequence of poetry over the centuries, becoming simultaneously embellished and refined.[75] The poem does refer to its own hypothetical Bhārata *ur*-text, which has now been integrated into the larger and more complex *Mahābhārata*, but this we are no longer able to soundly reconstruct and might scarcely conceive of as a reality.

> catur viṃśati sāhasrīṃ cakre bhāratasaṃhitām
>
> I.1.61
>
> He [Vyāsa] made the collected Bhārata—twenty-four thousand [verses]. [76]

Certainly, the structural details of the poem—as I have partially demonstrated in my earlier works—are so precise and refined, particularly in the use of ring composition, that one can infer that at some point in the early history of the written text there occurred a formal organisation of the complete work as we know it today. For instance, the opening of subsequent *parvans* usually refers back to the closing events of the preceding *parvan*, thus bringing a continuity or metonymy—a *cinematic* effect—to the whole. Nevertheless, the stylistic differences among the various *parvans* and even among—in some cases—the

[74] Dandekar (1966, xlvii) in his Introduction to the Pune Anuśāsana *parvan*.

[75] I am grateful to Gregory Nagy for this hypothetical distinction between model and copy.

[76] If one adds up the number of verses given in the *parvasaṃgraha* 'digest' of the poem, from the installation of Bhīṣma as *senāpati* 'commander' to the Sauptika *parvan*, for the eighteen sub-*parvans*, the number of verses amounts to 23,795. I argued for this conception of the core *Jaya* epic in McGrath 2011. These figures are supplied at I.2.154–190.

sub-*parvans*, would indicate an aggregation of different traditions of poetry. To make an analogy: it is sometimes as if the poetry of Milton were to be joined with the poetry of Wordsworth for the stylistic disjunctions are so great despite the fact that the details of the narrative are often consistently sophisticated in their particular arrangements and are able to supply the poem with an internal binding of a carefully synthetic and aggregate form.

The complete absence of any reference to Buddhism or Jainism in the epic is uncanny, given the social and religious preponderance and the ferment of these two spiritual cultures in the second half of the first millennium BCE. Would this, I wonder, argue for the fact that the text of the poem as we know it now comes from a period long before Buddhism and Jainism flourished? Or conversely, there are mentions of the Yavanas in the poem, usually on the side of the Pāṇḍavas: would these 'Greeks' be indexing the colonist forces that Alexander left behind him in the Northwest when he retreated? This would certainly indicate a *terminus post quem* for some of the materials in the epic. The problem is compounded, however, by the fact that the language of the poem as we have it presently is classical while the material culture represented in much of the poem is archaic: there is no obvious symmetry there.

To view this situation or condition from another point of view: in the enormous geographical region—mostly in Northern and Northwestern India—portrayed or represented by epic *Mahābhārata*, and whenever one identifies its historical moment, there must have been tens of hundreds of minor cultural groups extant. These were societies that could be specified by their ecological or terrestrial culture, by their linguistic or dialectical culture, by their ritual or dietary culture, and by political or kinship-based cultures. Nevertheless, the epic compounds all these distinctions into a single literary and poetic text, one of uniform taste and common iconography that is essentially Pan-Indic and where there exists essentially only one single ethnological and cultural group, specifically, the Kuru society of *bhāratavarṣa* and its environs.[77] This is of course literary, mimetic of an idea rather than of any 'reality,' as well as being an object of wonderful and beautiful artistry; it is a gorgeous tapestry of a myriad of pictures. These poets were thus extraordinarily gifted in causing their audience to visualise the poem as they performed it.[78]

77 "In agreement with the Great Epic and the Purāṇas, the *Jambudīva-paṇṇatti* derives the name of Bhāratavarṣa from king Bharata whose sovereignty was established over it. It speaks of six divisions (*bhedā, khaṇḍā*) in Northern India, and of three divisions in Southern, Eastern, Western and Middle." Law 1941, 14.

78 Strauss Clay (2011) has finely studied the visual mnemonics of *Iliad* and how it is that the poets *visualise* their work for an audience.

The recent fine arguments of Mahadevan and Hiltebeitel that propose a possible textual aetiology for the epic—particularly that of Mahadevan—are salient innovations or steps in scholarship. Mahadevan proposes that "the first written *Mbh*, already the complete 18-*parvan* epic [begins] in the Kuru-Pāñcāla country, ca. 3rd–2nd BCE, in a Mauryan Brāhmi script." Hiltebeitel posits that, "the CE archetype in toto ... would have been redacted in writing ... during the Gupta period."[79] The articles on this theme by these scholars represent what will become a most fruitful source of enquiry in the field of *Mahābhārata* Studies for there remains so much that is unclear in how the epic was transformed from a series of centrifugal poetic songs into a uniform and centralising work of art. How was it that the various *parvans* came to receive their organisation and can we trace the process of these tangible units in any sound philological manner?

Speaking from the position of one engaged in the study of the performative art of preliterate poetry I would address such propositions by directing our attention to the skills of itinerant rhapsodic poets. These poets were possibly illiterate during a period where literacy did exist; they were poets who had internalised in their memory a complete Bhārata Song and were able to *recite* that song at will, either completely or in part. Such poets, in their wandering and royal commissions, would transmit their performative and unwritten texts about the subcontinent. Preliteracy and literacy are *not* mutually exclusive traditions of a medium of expression; they can co-exist and did co-exist—and this is even true today.[80] The point is that transmission of texts need not always be literal or even physical.[81]

What we have now as an epic *Mahābhārata* is an extensive palimpsest of magnificent humanity and creativity resulting from many centuries, if not millennia, of poetic experience, stretching back towards an indefinite time before secondary urbanisation and continuing through the Aśokan era towards the years of Samudragupta. In the Pune Critical Edition what we now have is a

[79] Mahadevan 2011, 50. Hiltebeitel 2011a, 87.

[80] I know this from my own fieldwork in contemporary Gujarat where illiterate songsters still perform the Song of Rāja Ramdev Pir.

[81] Hiltebeitel (2011c, 13:F) makes an excellent examination—based on textual similarities—that compares the Buddhacarita of Aśvaghoṣa with the Jarāsaṃdhavadha *parvan* in the *Mahābhārata*. I would always approach such a question from a position of verbal or preliterate transmission rather than focussing on the literal or material passage of physical texts themselves. On this occasion I would propose that Aśvaghoṣa and the *Mahābhārata* poets were simply drawing upon a similar oral and performative tradition of mnemonic practice. However, it is not the case that one interpretation is wrong and the other right: these are merely two different methods of analysis as part of an ongoing heuristic and humanistic discourse.

poem where the metonymy between sections allows a certain fusion of narrative: the joints have been smoothed and small alterations in the poetry equip the whole text with an air of coherence, even though—at times—the juxtapositions can be strangely abrupt.[82]

***

There is little in the poem of direct historical record or reference which would—in the manner of Bronkhorst—allow us to refer to a particular moment of historical kingship; yet concerning this question of the *actual* or temporal setting of the poem and its early *literal* presence, I personally would like to think of the epic as being transcribed into written form—in a fashion that is presently indeterminate—during the time of Samudragupta who flourished between 353 and 373 of the Common Era.

There exists little firm evidence, however, to support such an unfounded opinion, although in the Āśvamedhika *parvan* there does occur the statement that: *rājādhirājaḥ sarvāsāṃ viṣṇur brahmamayo mahān* (Viṣṇu, sovereign king of all, the great one made of Brahma) (XIV.43.12). This is the only time in the poem that the word *rājādhirāja* is employed, and curiously this is a term that was used by Samudragupta on coinage that celebrated his accomplishment of the *aśvamedha*.[83] Sharma comments on such a memorial coin: "On his Aśvamedha type of coins we have the legend on the obverse '*Rājādhirājaḥ Pṛithivīm avitvā divaṃ jayatyaprativāryavīryaḥ*'. The king of kings, having gained the earth, conquers heaven, with his irresistible heroism."[84] Chapter Fourteen of the *Mahābhārata* records and celebrates Yudhiṣṭhira's sponsorship of a performance of the horse sacrifice, and, as an interesting aside, in this *parvan* Yudhiṣṭhira is actually called a *rājarṣi* 'royal seer', someone of great mystical authority and power (XIV.14.1).

Verardi speaks of the period of Gupta régime as, "an age of strictly orthodox rule ... Buddhism was tested very hard," and, "Samudragupta was unsympathetic, if not overtly hostile, to Buddhism."[85] There are just a few tenuous references in the poem to *caityas* 'funeral monuments' and to *eḍūkas* 'ossuary structures',

82 As in the bas-relief narratives expressed by the carvings from Sāñchī, where the aesthetics of pattern are more dominant than the rules of sequence.

83 This word is unusual enough for Nīlakaṇṭha in the Bombay text to take note of it and gloss it as *īśvaratvaṃ aiśvaryaṃ narādīnāṃ* (sovereignty, lordship of humans etc.).

84 T. R. Sharma 1989, 92. A. Agrawal (1989, 126) remarks on the horse sacrifice that it was: "the revival of an old Vedic rite the performance of which had not been witnessed for a long time."

85 Verardi 2011, 128–130.

which could possibly indicate Jaina or Buddhist architecture.[86] There is also the mention in the Droṇa *parvan* of an *upaniṣad*, when Bhūriśravas is about to enter a state of *prāya* or 'meditative suicide'.[87]

> sūrye cakṣuḥ samādhāya prasannaṃ salile manaḥ
> dhyāyan mahopaniṣadaṃ yogayukto'bhavan muniḥ
>
> VII.118.18
>
> Having turned his attention to the sun and tranquil mind to acquiescence in motion,
> The renunciant, meditating on the great Upaniṣad, was engaged in yoga.[88]

Such a reference offers the analyst another possible dating, since Upaniṣadic literature can be said to find its origins in the middle of the first millennium BCE.[89]

***

To repeat, the epic as we presently know has been so profoundly synthesised from many poetic sources and historical periods to the extent that it simply retrojects an idealised composite view of an heroic *past*, one that is Bronze Age in material culture and both preliterate and premonetary.[90] All these elements have been drawn into a single synoptic form and the resultant multitextuality of the poem has been smoothed at its narrative seams. Sometimes disjunctions

86 III.188.64 and 66: *eḍūkān pūjayiṣyanti* (they will worship bone-houses). There is the curious mention of king Gaya, a *rājarṣi* 'royal seer' who celebrated *hiraṇmayībhir gobhiś ca kṛtābhir viśvakarmaṇā* (with gold cattle made by Viśvakarman); one wonders if these statues were worshipped? In the same passage, Gaya, who is said to be the ruler of a land where there were many *caityas* '*stūpas*' (III.121.11–12).

87 This is traditionally a Jain practice that is sometimes even performed today. Candragupta Maurya is said to have ended his life as an old man in this manner in the later years of the third century BCE. His grandson was Aśoka. Kṛṣṇa's father is said to determine to die in this fashion at XVI.6.21.

88 As an interesting aside concerning this episode in the poem, Sātyaki decapitates Bhūriśravas while the latter is in a state of *prāya*; in defending his action he says: *api cāyaṃ purā gītaḥ śloko vālmīkinā bhuvi / pīḍākaram amitrāṇāṃ yat syāt kartavyam eva tat* (then this verse was formerly sung on earth by Vālmīki: whatever is a tormenting of enemies—that should be a duty) (VII.118.48). This is a rare instance where the *Mahābhārata* poets quote from the Rāmāyaṇa tradition.

89 At I.1.191, the poem refers to itself as *upaniṣadaṃ puṇyāṃ* (an auspicious *upaniṣad*). Another instant of possibly empirical dating evidence occurs in the Karṇa *parvan* at 49.89, where the *asim* 'sword' of Arjuna is said to be *ākāśanibhaṃ* (like the sky); that is, the blade exhibits a *blueness*. This would indicate a quality of steel, actually *wootz* or Damascus steel, whose production was only developed in Northern India in the third century BCE. See Figiel 1991, 10–11.

90 Before battle occurs there occurs the kingly rite of *lohābhihāra* (the washing of weapons); the sign for such weaponry here is being given as *loha* (that which is red or coppery), which I take to indicate bronze. This ritual is mentioned by the *dūta* Ulūka at V.157.18 and 11, just prior to the opening of hostilities at Kurukṣetra.

do nevertheless occur—the *leaps* in the sequence of events and characters—and these occasionally supply the narrative with a powerful appearance of bricolage and serial abruptness bringing a certain post-modern air to the work. Such cracks in the surface of the song make one wonder if these moments actually reflected certain intentional changes in those original and early performative conditions—that is, if such instances indicate a ritual movement? For certainly, the poem itself proclaims that it was initially presented as a complete 'event' during a sacrificial ritual and that must have supplied a strong tempo and definition to the epic, explaining the many disjunctions or deviations from diachronic narrative form.

For us today, as literary analysts, what is interesting is that it is actually possible to track the different forms of kingship within the poem indicating this creative aggregation that once occurred due to the nature of the poetic tradition in those times. As we shall see, both archaic and classical paradigms of kingship co-exist within the poem. It is as if the epic is itself representing an historical view of kingship in its development over the ages and that the editors of the written text were summarising the temporal narrative of kingship over the centuries for the sake of their audience. The present version of the poem as we have it is a poetic record of how kingship developed in time up to what I would propose is the early Gupta period. This certainly indicates an awareness of and an attention towards what can be called the 'historical.'

vii. Terms

As a final point to close these introductory remarks, my effort in this book, as it has always been in my other works, is—through the thoroughly empirical *close reading* of words, of sentences, and especially of similes—to apprehend not only the possible truths available in the poetry and its narrative, but also in the culture that encapsulates and conveys that song.[91] To quote Bronkhorst once again: "One can thus maintain, as I do readily, that the study of implicit preconceptions or intuitions of Indian thinkers is an integral part of the effort required to understand Indian philosophy."[92] For "Indian thinkers" one could say *epic poets*,

[91] In close reading it is always the repetition of a word, simile, metaphor, or phrase that reveals the underlying truth at work *beyond* or *behind* the term; this is not simply a cognitive disposition but one that is indicative of cultural form.

[92] Bronkhorst 2011c, 136. Or, to phrase the question in another fashion, drawing upon the work of Hurford (2007, xi), how is it that "meaning precedes words"? Hence, what is the thought concerning leadership that must have preceded the production of this poem?

and, in that sense, this book represents an effort to comprehend some of their cultural "preconceptions or intuitions" that are never explicit and require to be vigilantly perceived in the *nature* or natural being of their poetry. This requires a particular act of reading on the part of the analyst, a form of inferential *reading* that is acutely sensitive to all possible expressions and especially to communication that is not directly overt—to expression or rapport that we presume to be mutual between poet and audience.

A king, in the sense of Dumont, is that person who occupies the apex of all social hierarchies and the exchange of services that exist within those levels and social stations.[93] His office concerned the entitlement of land, the utility of force, and the practice of judgement where situations were contested; he also sponsored and participated in certain forms of solemn ritual.[94]

The term *rāja* is just one common word indicating the general status of 'king', and there exist many epic synonyms that refer to this supreme rank. As we shall see, it is possible for there to be several persons who receive the title *rāja* at many concurrent points in the narrative: the word is neither exclusive nor singular in its usage, and it is a highly unmarked term. For instance, during the ritual coronation of Yudhiṣṭhira in the Śānti *parvan*, which is *the* paragon royal anointment, both Yudhiṣṭhira and Dhṛtarāṣṭra are referred to by the poets as *rāja* without any distinction (XII.39). As we shall also see, this term is highly labile and constantly—almost like a coin—being moved from person to person.[95] This holds true until Book Twelve of the epic opens, and there, in his teaching on *rājadharma* (the lore of kings) the ancient kingly preceptor Bhīṣma, the most senior of the princes in the poem, uses the term *rāja* in his discourse as *the* primary signifier for kingship, only sometimes employing other words like *pārthiva* or *narādhipa*. He uses many other terms when he addresses Yudhiṣṭhira in the vocative.[96] Kingship in this secondary and patently didactic part of the poem, however, as we will also explore, means something very different from what has been indicated in the previous eleven books of the epic.

93 Society as portrayed by the poem is premonetary; in premonetary societies, since there is no 'market' as we understand the term today, and the economy is founded upon an exchange of services and not simply upon an exchange of objects. Barter as a system of exchange or economic circulation presupposes a market. I am excluding long-distance trade from my model, which is well attested from the late Neolithic times, and was founded upon a medium of barter.

94 Dumont 1966.

95 I think of the epic term *rāja* as being non-specific, like the English title of "lord." It refers simply to an unmarked, elevated, and titular status, and does not only indicate supreme or paramount office.

96 When Bhīṣma quotes from the words of the divine Bṛhaspati who is addressing the king of Kosala as *mahārāja*, he supplies a list of synonyms for 'king' beginning with *bhūmipaḥ* (XII.68.32ff.), and concluding with *rājā bhojo virāṭ samrāṭ kṣatriyo bhūpatir nṛpaḥ* (XII.68.54).

Mahīpati 'lord of the earth', *nṛpa* 'protector of humans', *īśvara* 'lord of rulers', *bhūmipa* 'protector of the earth', *kṣitipa* 'protector of the land', *mahīpāla* 'protector of the earth', *narendra* 'Indra of men', and *nareśvara* 'lord of men' are some of the equivalent words or epithets denoting a ruler who possesses the highest office of kingship. However, when Yudhiṣṭhira is at last installed as paramount chief, the title the poets give him is not *rāja* but *patiṃ pṛthvyāḥ* (lord of the earth) (XII.40.15). It is my impression that this word *pati* or *nṛpati* constitutes the marked term that signifies the supreme officer in a kingdom. The term *cakravartin*—meaning either 'the one who turns the chariot wheel' or 'the one who turns the wheel of *dharma*',—is a rare word in the epic, and it is *never* applied to Yudhiṣṭhira.[97] It is a title that is more imperial than kingly and an epithet that became typically Buddhist or Jaina.[98] It is typical of the *Mahābhārata* poetics that the epic employs this term, which came into use in the later part of the first millennium BCE only to designate kings of an ancient and folkloric past. We shall consistently observe this kind of activity in the poem where virtually all indication or reference to Buddhist or Jaina experience and record is simply elided, sometimes leaving a vague shadow.

I have commented on the practice of *epic synonymy* elsewhere.[99] The vast extent of region and geography, as well as social and political culture, which the Critical Edition of the *Mahābhārata* incorporates and unifies, has conduced to this highly syncretic inclusiveness of a vast spectrum of linguistic phenomena. In epic *Mahābhārata*, there exists a great profusion of synonymity, due to the spatial, temporal, and cultural diversity of the poem's sources and words: these lose their historical or local specificity in such a lengthy process of assimilation.

In a previous study I showed how the epic narrative was blended and fused by the poets and also by later editors; there I drew upon an idea of Claude Lévi-Strauss—the concept of bricolage—demonstrating how the great variety and diversity of narrative movement might possibly have been made to cohere.[100]

97 Similarly the epic is unfamiliar with the term *avatāra*, a word drawn from classical Hinduism. See Hiltebeitel 2011c, 589ff.

98 Rosenfield (1967, 175) notes: "Although the idea of the *cakravartin* was one of the fundamental and widespread concepts of Buddhism, it was only in the so-called Āndhra country along the Kistna River in the Deccan that this icon flourished." At III.88.7, the eponymous Bharata is described as: *bharato rājā cakravartī mahāyaśāḥ* (King Bharata, a greatly glorious Turner of the Wheel); he was also a great sacrificer. At III.107.1, the *cakravartin* is Bhagiratha, a great archer and great charioteer, a king from the antique past; at XII.27.10, the king is Ugrāyudha; at XIII.14.133, Māndhātā is named; at XIII.75.26, Purūravas is so called; and at XIII.151.42, Duḥṣanta is likewise mentioned.

99 McGrath 2004, 24n90.

100 McGrath 2013, chap. 1.

I refer to how the Vedic and the proto-Hindu world, the archaic and the classical, the heroic and didactic, were all assembled and finely amalgamated into a single multifarious poem.[101] In this present study I shall show how the poets and editors employ terms in a manner that is without judgement and in a fashion that allows a multitude of meanings to be derived from or projected by a single word. The poets use the ideas of *king* and *kingship* with great semantic breadth, and this is a practice that brings to the epic a wonderful vivacity or complexity—a verbal activity that verges on the pleasurably irrational or inexplicable. There is no single kind of king in the epic, but many simultaneous offices that contrast or even mutually contend for supremacy. The word *king*, however it is rendered in the Sanskrit, is a term about which many elements of the narrative coalesce. Epic *Mahābhārata* does not project one uniform concept of kingship but collates many aspects of this paramount political model; Yudhiṣṭhira acts simply as a master signifier in this account, and he even shares his power—for duality, as we shall see, is an important architectonic method in these arrangements as is the ever-present *saṅgha*.

***

What this book is ultimately directed at is the cultural and social position of kingship as represented by Yudhiṣṭhira in the poem: the myths and narratives of kinship and the drama and metaphors of performance. I am not primarily concerned with the *śāstra* of kingship and its artistry, its techniques and realistic practice as generally spoken by the personage of Bhīṣma—sometimes via the theatre of other voices—which are to be found towards the end of the poem. Other scholars, like Bowles, Fitzgerald, and Hiltebeitel, have studied these aspects of kingship, and are far more competent than I am in their certain comprehension of that field.[102]

In this book I proceed in the intellectual tradition of the Parry-Lord-Nagy system of analysing oral poetics, thinking of the great Bhārata epic as a 'multitext' of persistent vitality, just as I have done in my previous works.[103] Similarly, I also follow closely in some of the conceptual forms developed by Benveniste,

[101] The Homeric poets, Shakespeare, Wagner, Lönnrot, even Joyce, all worked similarly; this is simply the nature of literary *making*. The past is *always* incorporated and modified, that is the nature of human culture, for nothing is unique or discrete and apart from an ongoing metonymy or continuity; nothing arises simply from itself *sui generis*.

[102] Bowles 2007; Fitzgerald 2001 and 2006; Hiltebeitel 2010 and 2011.

[103] Bird 2010; and Dué and Ebbott (2010, 153–165) describe such a "multitextual" form. Dué and Ebbott (19) also draw upon the Parry-Lord-Nagy system of analysing oral poetics when they write about "the natural multiformity of composition-in-performance." It is this centripetal quality of an epic tradition that I accept as the primary underlying poetic of *Mahābhārata*.

Watkins, West, and Frame.[104] Epic poetry as verbal *system* and *form*—this is where we begin.

> satyadharmaparo dātā viprapūjādibhir guṇaiḥ
> sadaiva tridivaṃ prāpto rājā kila yudhiṣṭhiraḥ
>
> VII.33.3

> Intent upon dharma and truth, liberal, with qualities venerating brāhmaṇas and OTHERS,
> Thus indeed good king Yudhiṣṭhira obtained threefold heaven.

This book draws attention towards who those "others" might possibly have been. For earthly kings, just like the supernal Indra or Prajāpati, or even Viṣṇu, were once objects of reverence. If this ritual admiration was correctly promoted, reciprocity was always engaged—in how the cosmos and its rulers distributed material life and its benefits. Epic song, as 'ritual admiration,' thus went to compose what could be viewed as this propitious *dharma* or good holdings on earth for a warrior and kingly audience.[105] The performance of epic song possessed a manner of dharmic *causality* itself, vis-à-vis its audience and their community.

***

The singing of epic poetry as a ceremonial rite was one means of implementing this model of universal exchange in which ideals of kingship underlay the practice of an heroic religion, one where heroes received worship, just as they still do in the subcontinent today, both locally and also nationally.[106] In a communal

[104] Parry 1932; Lord 1960; Nagy 2010, 2013. Benveniste 1969; Watkins 1995; Muellner 1996; West 2007; Frame 2009.

[105] I would perhaps omit the Mahādeva Śiva from this series because of his deeply antinomian position vis-à-vis the sacrifice; see IX.18.

[106] Concerning 'heroic religion' in antiquity and the role the great Bhārata Song played in such ritual attention, witness the many references to the great Bhārata Song as a 'Fifth Veda', that is, as a numinous text. We possess no firm evidence of the ritual events or occasions on which to found any inference about such religious praxis, but there are a myriad of references relating to the efficacy of such sacred performances that are frequently reiterated throughout the epic. The first and the last *adhyāyas* of the poem in the PCE contain constant indications as to the moral and spiritual force to be obtained from the declamation, or the 'causing to be heard,' of the poem. In other words, the epic possesses a *super-natural* efficiency that will affect the agent or patron of such performance; for instance, the poets say at the end of the epic: *nārado'śrāvayad devān* (Nārada caused the deities to hear [this poem]) (XVIII.5.42); *kārṣṇaṃ vedam imaṃ vidvāñ śrāvayitvārtham aśnute* (A wise one, having caused to be heard this Kṛṣṇic Veda obtains benefit) (I.1.205); and whoever recites or performs the epic *sa … gacchet paramaṃ … siddhim* (he would go towards extraordinary perfection) (XVIII.5.44). The initial and final chapters of the poem are replete with statements like this concerning the spiritual consequences of the epic's performance. Heroes, insofar as they are the elements of such ritual, are thus party to the religiosity of the event.

situation where there exists no habit or expectation of conceptual innovation, it is the emphasis that is placed upon a biased reproduction of the past—via performative metaphor—that supports and sustains the currency of social custom and practice. It is the aim of this book to show how epic *Mahābhārata* worked in such a light, revealing the meanings and techniques behind the words that so dramatised as well as aestheticised, the action and style of kingship as an art. It is the portrait of Yudhiṣṭhira that reveals such ancient activities for us.

Ultimately, in the succession that finally dominates at Hāstinapura, it is the Yādava clan—through the matriline of Kuntī—that finally succeeds most efficiently, with a son of Kṛṣṇa established as king at Indraprastha and his great-nephew settled on the throne at Hāstinapura.[107] This is the poem's fundamental and ultimate teaching about how kingship might or should succeed—that is, its deepest and quite shadowy myth. Despite all the dramas of morality and ethics, and despite the horrors and cruelties of internecine war, it is this subtlety of kinship that is seen to finally succeed and one that wins via the ways of the matriline. Yudhiṣṭhira allows his close ally Kṛṣṇa to advise him in almost all crucial decisions and policies, and it is Kṛṣṇa's particular and timely absences that cause the Pāṇḍava clan to go awry in their judgement and behaviour. In the end it is actually the organisation of marriages that leads to the real *jaya* 'victory' in the poem, a triumph that goes to the lineage of Yadu. The division that first occurred between Yadu and Pūru, descendents of Yayāti, becomes at last reunited.

In the next chapter, we shall examine some of the *mythemes* that express paradigms and manners of kingship, and then focus especially upon the image and ideal of a sovereign as *sacrificer*, as exhibited by three specific models (because there are two royal rites that frame the battle of Kurukṣetra, itself expressed by the poets also as a *rite*). Chapter 3 describes how the poets depict Yudhiṣṭhira as he is finally installed at Hāstinapura, and this allows us to glimpse certain fundamental qualities of Kuru sovereignty. The chapter also examines how the ideal practice of kingship is verbally regarded and expressed during the poem, culminating in what is taught by the recumbent and ancestral arch-hero who speaks to his king concerning the function and ways of suzerainty. Bhīṣma's

107 Yudhiṣṭhira is of course not biologically descended from Pāṇḍu; his only human genetic inheritance comes via Kuntī, Kṛṣṇa's paternal aunt. In terms of mortality, he is solely Yādava and has no genetic connection with Śaṃtanu, Vyāsa, or Bhīṣma. To quote from Parpola (2015, 148): "To consolidate their rule, the victorious Pāṇḍavas grafted themselves on to the Kuru genealogy as cousins of their former foes, the defeated Kauravas. In this regard, the latest version of the *Mahābhārata* was intended as a form of political propaganda." Let us recall that Bhīṣma is the only directly lineal descendent of Kuru in the poem.

verbal modelling of a monarchic system is very different, as we shall see, from the system of kingship woven by the poets in the previous eleven books of the epic. In the final chapter, we look at how it is that the last four *parvans* of the poem present multifarious aspects of death for the surviving heroes and what this tells us about the Bhārata king and kingdom.[108]

[108] There are so many *Mahābhārata's* today in the subcontinent: vernacular, dramatic, cinematic, sculptural, literary, ritual, and cult-oriented, and more than one Sanskrit version of the poem. The epic is perhaps the *charter myth* of modern India although the relationship between literature and history, or poetry and experience, is by no means a firm and fixed system. This present book has as its text the Critically Edited version of the poem—the *mahābhāratasaṃhitā*—which Viṣṇu Sukthankar and his colleagues assembled or constructed in the mid-twentieth century at Pune: the PCE. I have occasionally drawn upon the commentary of the *paṇḍita* Nīlakaṇṭha, which is usually appended to the Bombay text, the so-called *vulgate* edition of the epic. Sörensen's Index and Vettam Mani's *Purāṇic Encyclopaedia* have provided invaluable references for this research. The online text of the epic, meticulously prepared by J. D. Smith, has been of great utility in locating words and in tracking word change: http://bombay.indology.info/mahabharata/welcome.html.

2

KINGSHIP

In this chapter, let us first examine how the idea of kingship is raised in the initial stages of the poem and note how the poets develop this for an audience in the course of the narrative: how it is that kings secure their office, and what it is that kings should accomplish. Then, let us focus upon one predominant practice of kingship, that is, the king as a *sacrificer*, and see how this ancient and primary function of a prince or chief manifests itself in the verses.[1] We shall examine three royal rituals: the king's anointment, the rite of battle, and the horse sacrifice.

To begin, let us see how Yudhiṣṭhira enters the Bhārata Song. When Kuntī's first legitimate son was born, the initial son to be born of this generation and so the elder of Duryodhana, *vāg uvācāśarīriṇī* (a bodiless voice spoke), saying: *yudhiṣṭhira iti khyātaḥ* (he is known as Yudhiṣṭhira). Hence the heir receives the name of 'one who is steadfast in battle' (I.114.5–6).[2] The first words that Yudhiṣṭhira himself speaks in the poem are said to be *śanair dīnam* 'quiet, distressed':

> saganạ̄s tāta vatsyāmo dhṛtarāṣṭrasya śāsanāt
>
> I.131.14
>
> Sir, along with our gaṇa we shall dwell, according to the command of Dhṛtarāṣṭra.

There are two crucial and telling elements in this first statement: one is the reference to the *gaṇa*, 'the companions' or 'association', and the other is the explicit

[1] Manusmṛti has it that *yajeta rājā kratubhir vividhair* (the king should sacrifice with various rites) (VII.79).

[2] Then, in the subsequent *adhyāya*, the poets claim that, concerning the sons of Kuntī: *nāmāni cakrire teṣāṃ śataśṛṅganivāsinaḥ* (the ones who lived on the Hundred Peaked Mountain made their names). These are the mountain-dwelling *brāhmaṇas* (I.115.19). Preliterate poetry, as we understand it in epic *Mahābhārata*, does not really make great efforts to achieve rational or logical consistency; such is not a primary criterion in this kind of poetry.

concord that is expressed concerning the ruling of the old king, his elder nominal kin. We shall develop these two points below and show that these components of Yudhiṣṭhira's opening line encapsulate how he behaves throughout the course of the poem. The adjectives that qualify this primary speech—so full of acceptance and accord—describe how mild and pacific is the manner of this prince. Thus we have Yudhiṣṭhira in minute and yet precise detail.

As the unmarried and juvenile Pāṇḍava brothers set off towards the town of Varaṇāvata, as directed by the old king who is himself already being propelled by his jealous and resentful son Duryodhana, the audience again hears of Yudhiṣṭhira in a fashion that will soon become typical of his activity in the poem. The *paurān duḥkhān* (the unhappy people) are vocally complaining about the departure of their favourite and contemning Duryodhana and his father; Yudhiṣṭhira, his chariot already yoked, dismisses them and advises that they do not abandon Hāstinapura in order to follow the Pāṇḍavas. He says:

pitā mānyo guruḥ śreṣṭho yad āha pṛthivīpatiḥ
aśaṅkamānais tat kāryam asmābhir iti no vratam

I.133.14

Father is to be esteemed the best guru.
It is our vow to do unhesitatingly what the lord of the earth says.

Again, we observe crucial elements in the persona of Yudhiṣṭhira: that devotion of the populace to him, his concern for them, and his commitment to the rulings of his nominal or guardian uncle, whom he here—following tradition—refers to as his father. Also, Yudhiṣṭhira does not speak in the voice of a single prince, even though he is potentially heir-apparent, but in terms of himself *and* his brothers. This will always be the case with Yudhiṣṭhira: he is *not* a solitary and single figure of kingship, but whatever office or station comes to him becomes actively fraternal in practice.[3] Kingship that is unique or 'monarchic' is—as I shall argue in another chapter—an historically 'later' political model. This latter formation of polity involves another manner of kinship organisation where descent is only from eldest son to eldest son, rather than from a model of descent that coheres about the sons of sons.

Let us now briefly revisit our five diverse points from the previous chapter concerning the opening manifestations of kingship in the epic, before turning to more specific depiction, where a king serves as sacrificer.

3 This fraternal bond is also present on an intimate level where the brothers even share their *mahiṣī* 'chief wife', Draupadī. The motif of a royal woman with five partners is repeated by Damayantī, with her five suitors: Nala, Indra, Agni, Varuṇa, and Yama (III.52.4); and by Kuntī with her five husbands, Pāṇḍu, Sūrya, Dharma, Vayu, and Indra.

i. Early Kings

Firstly, let us look at how the idea of past and antecedent kings is initially amplified in the poem: What are those initial myths of kingship? When Saṃjaya, in his first major speech of the Ādi *parvan*, sings to the melancholic Dhṛtarāṣṭra a litany of twenty-four earlier kings he acknowledges their fame and achievements and the absolute necessity of death (I.1.163–182).[4] This sequence of kings is applauded and made up of the *mahotsāhān mahābalān* (the very powerful, very strong), and they are characterised as being:

> mahatsu rājavaṃśeṣu guṇaiḥ samuditeṣu ca
> jātān divyāstraviduṣaḥ śakrapratimatejasaḥ
>
> I.1.164
>
> Born in great royal dynasties and elevated with virtues,
> [They are] cognisant of divine weaponry, equal to Śakra in energy.

Having subdued the earth with *dharma*, having sacrificed most liberally, these kings then obtained *yaśaḥ* 'glory' (I.1.165). For the poet Saṃjaya, these lines encapsulate the pattern of ideal epic kingship.[5] None of these qualities, of course, can be attributed to the old Dhṛtarāṣṭra, except his famed lineage, and the first of the kings mentioned by Saṃjaya, Vainya, is described as a *mahārathaṃ vīraṃ* (a warrior possessing a great chariot); that is, Vainya is being described not in kingly terms but in heroic terms (I.1.166).[6] Once Bhīṣma opens his great narrative in the Śānti *parvan* this distinction of king and hero becomes rigid and exclusive, for the picture of a prince that Bhīṣma portrays becomes completely different, as we shall see, from the image of kingship in the poem prior to that moment.

Let us see how the word and the idea of *rāja* are used in various ways by the poets during the commencement of the epic, demonstrating how "a word's metrical, verbal, and syntactical contexts can function to support polysemy," focussing especially on the second of these dynamics and illustrating certain aspects of Bhārata kingship that we have not yet mentioned.[7] Janamejaya is the first *rāja* to be spoken of in the epic, at I.1.18, and it is the audience on the outer

[4] King-lists are given on several occasions during the course of the poem, as at I.89.5–90,95; and at XII.29.16–136. They bring an air of 'authenticity' or historical 'facticity' to the epic.

[5] In a similar fashion, Dhaumya, the domestic priest of the Pāṇḍavas, later, at IV.4.9–44, describes the conduct of a king's dutiful servant. *Mahābhārata* possesses a steady pedagogical quality on many levels.

[6] A *mahāratha* is also a standard of rank, higher than a *ratha* and less than an *atiratha*. Bhīṣma catalogues the Kaurava forces according to this standard, the *rathasaṃkhyā*, beginning at V.162.17ff.

[7] Muellner 2012.

rim of the poem, the *ṛṣayas* 'the sages', who make this mention. Next, the old ruler Dhṛtarāṣṭra is termed *rāja* at I.1.65, where he is also said to be the *mūlaṃ* 'the root' of the clan. The first explicitly significant mention of kingship as it pertains to the Kauravas, and a king's primary duty occurs in the thirty-seventh *adhyāya* 'chapter', where the grandson of Arjuna is being recalled. It is said that:

> parikṣit tu viśeṣeṇa yathāsya prapitāmahaḥ
> rakṣaty asmān yathā rājñā rakṣitavyāḥ prajās tathā
>
> I.37.25
>
> For as Parikṣit especially protects us like his great-grandfather [did],
> Thus a populace is to be protected by a king.

The ideal of kingship is more fully delineated when the poets speak of Yayāti who having received the benefit of youth a second time, is said to rule:

> devān atarpayad yajñair śrāddhais tadvat pitṝn api
> dīnān anugrahair iṣṭaiḥ kāmaiś ca dvijasattamān
> atithīn annapānaiś ca viśaś ca paripālanaiḥ
> ānṛśaṃsyena śūdrāṃś ca dasyūn saṃnigraheṇa ca
> dharmeṇa ca prajāḥ sarvā yathāvad anurañjayan
> yayātiḥ pālayāmāsa sākṣād indra ivāparaḥ
>
> I.80.3
>
> He satisfied the deities with sacrifices, likewise the ancestors with obsequies,
> The poor with favours, and the twice-born with desired rites,
> Guests with food and drink, the community with nurture,
> The śūdras with kindness and the servile with restraint;
> Gratifying all the populace with suitable dharma, Yayāti protected,
> Matchless, like Indra himself.

Note that here the first function of the king is that of a *sacrificer*, and the cosmic model of kingship is supplied by Indra, the *devarāja* (king of the deities), the warrior deity. Note also that one of the common epithets for, or titles of, Indra is *śatakratu* (the one who performed a hundred sacrifices).[8] He is also the divine figure who signifies rainfall and the thunderous monsoon and as an extension of this idea—by metonymy—Satyavatī says to Vyāsa when she is urging him to

8 *tvam eva rājā* (You are king!)—so Indra is addressed at III.218.19, and at II.41.3 there is even reference to *śakrābhiśeke* (in the royal anointing of Indra). If Indra supplies the *kṣatriya* icon of kingship on a supernal level, perhaps one can argue that Prajāpati later becomes the figure of divine overlordship for the *brāhmaṇa* class? Yudhiṣṭhira actually meets with Indra *in person* at III.162.9ff., something that can be said neither of Dhṛtarāṣṭra nor of Duryodhana. Indra then announces: *tvam imāṃ pṛthivīṃ rājan praśāsiṣyasi* (you, king, will rule this earth). No one else, of course, receives such prognostication.

procreate and sustain the lineage: *arājakeṣu rāṣṭreṣu nāsti vṛṣṭir* (there is no rain in kingless kingdoms) (I.99.40).[9] In other words, myths and metaphors of kingship, fertility, and Indra are intrinsically involved in this poetry, and one must presume that the singing of epic poetry itself possessed some kind of social, if not natural, efficacy.[10]

When Yayāti wishes to supercede the succession, putting aside his elder son in favour of the younger brother—that is, he wishes to anoint Pūru rather than the elder Yadu as *nṛpati* 'king'—then the *varṇā* 'castes', *brāhmaṇapramukhā* (headed by the *brahmins*), question his right (I.80.12). Once again we see a certain tension between two brothers concerning the idea of what makes for a king, as well as the need for social or communal consensus before a king can behave potently. We shall study this situation below, where an elder brother is surpassed in the succession by a younger brother for it is a particular feature of *Mahābhārata* kingship patterns. Here, the poets say that *paurajānapadais tuṣṭair ... abhyaṣiñcat tataḥ pūruṃ rājye* (then he anointed Pūru into kingship with the satisfaction of town and country-folk) (I,80,24). Yayāti then retreats from political and princely life, and *vanavāsāya ... purāt sa niryayau* (he departed from the town for the purpose of a forest life)—that is, he takes up the life of a renunciant.[11]

We see this practice again and again in the epic, where an old king withdraws from rule and court life and goes to live in the forest accompanied by his wife or wives and a few assistants while the appointed son assumes rule over the kingdom. This is what Dhṛtarāṣṭra does and also what Yudhiṣṭhira eventually does towards the close of the epic, and I would argue that this is an aspect of archaic patterns of kingship, so unlike the paradigms of classical kingship that

[9] This idea of the propriety of the king being influential upon the well-being of his people and the natural world—especially rainfall—recurs throughout the poem, as at I.163.14–23, and at II.30.1–7; for instance, this sentiment is repeated and amplified at length at I.102.1–11 when Bhīṣma is regent. Curiously, the kingdom is here said to possess *caityayūpaśatāṅkitaḥ* (hundreds of sacrificial posts and funeral monuments) (I.102.12). *Yūpas* are associated with the Vedic ritual, and *caityas* are thought to be the Buddhist or Jaina mounds where sacred bones were interred. *Caityas* are mentioned again at III.17.3.

[10] Ugraśravas, the poet, says: *ya idaṃ śrāvayed vidvān sadā parvaṇi parvaṇi / dhūtapāpmā jitasvargo brahmabhūyāya gacchati* (Whatever wise one would perform this [poem], *parvan* by *parvan*, error-cleansed, heaven-won, he goes towards Brahmā) (XVIII.5.35). In other words, the performance of the poem possesses moral—if not cosmic—efficacy.

[11] Pratīpa does the same, when he anoints his son Śaṃtanu—father of Bhīṣma—into kingship and then he leaves for the forest. The wording is formulaic and almost the same: *sve ca rājye'bhiṣicyainaṃ vanaṃ rājā viveśa ha* (the king anointed him in his own kingship and entered the forest) (I.92.23). One can say that the idea of the sentence is actually more formulaic and impulsive than the precise wording of the sentence. Formulae are not always strictly morphological but can be conceptual.

Bhīṣma outlines in his four discourses.[12] When Bhīṣma begins to speak in the early sections of the Śānti *parvan* the nature of kingship in the poem suddenly translates into a very different system of rule as that 'older' world of Yudhiṣṭhira's long period of struggle becomes conceptually superceded.

ii. The Associates

Returning to this idea of an associate presence of the populace in the organisation of kingship, when the theme of *bheda*—as dissension or rupture that separates two elements of society—enters the poem in the First *parvan* of the epic, the poets say that the *paurāḥ* 'townsfolk' are dissident concerning how it is that old Dhṛtarāṣṭra is ruling at Hāstinapura when he had previously been excluded from kingship on account of his blindness.[13] They say among themselves:

> abhiṣiñcāma sādhvadya satyaṃ karuṇavedinam
>
> I.129.7
>
> Now, let us anoint correctly the truthful knower of compassion.

This of course refers to Yudhiṣṭhira, and once again the poets make much display of the presence and influence of the populace in the princely succession. It is when Duryodhana comes to learn of these murmurings that his envy and ambition become further incensed. He says to his father:

> abhaviṣyaḥ sthiro rājye yadi hi tvaṃ purā nṛpa
> dhruvaṃ prāpsyāma ca vayaṃ rājyam apy avaśe jane
>
> I.129.18
>
> O king, if you had been firm in the kingdom, as before,
> Certainly we would obtain kingship—even contrary to the people.

After the gambling session in the Second *parvan* and the exile of the sons of Pāṇḍu, the poets tell us of how the *paurāḥ* once again become subversive, *garhayanto* 'reproaching' Duryodhana and his companions, complaining about the clan and how it endangered and threatened their households (III.1.11–12). They say:

[12] The four discourses concern *rājadharma*, *āpaddharma*, *mokṣadharma*, and that which is *anuśāsana*.

[13] Dhṛtarāṣṭra, the poets say, was excluded from kingship in favour of Pāṇḍu, even though Dhṛtarāṣṭra was the elder brother: *dhṛtarāṣṭras tv acakṣuṣṭvād rājyaṃ na pratyapadyata* (Dhṛtarāṣṭra did not attain the kingdom because of blindness) (I.102.23). The poets do not indicate, however, who actually made this decision, if it was indeed the *saṅgha*.

neyam asti mahī kṛtsnā yatra duryodhano nṛpaḥ

III.1.15

This earth is not entire where Duryodhana is lord.

The people then follow the Pāṇḍavas as they set off on their exile, preferring Yudhiṣṭhira's lordship that is not *adharmeṇa* 'lawless'.[14] They say that he oversees them in order that *kurājādhiṣṭhite rājye na vinaśyema* (we might not perish in a kingdom where a bad king is established) (III,1,20). Even when the Pāṇḍavas are already at Kāmyaka in the forest, the people of Indraprastha come to them plaintively; they cry and weep, *hā nātha hā dharma* (O ruler, O Dharma), not wanting the son of Dhṛtarāṣṭra to dominate them (III.24.8–12). Yet, later, the poets tell of how, after Duryodhana's accomplishment of the *vaiṣṇavo yajña* (the rite of Viṣṇu):

janāś cāpi maheṣvāsaṃ tuṣṭuvū rājasattamam

III.243.1

The people then praised the great archer, the excellent king.

(Such is the fickle mood of the populace or the irrational nature of the preliterate tradition of synthesis.) One can rightly infer, therefore, that kingship is in no way absolute in terms of its epic demonstration, and a certain degree of popular consensus is incumbent for firm rule; the *dharma* of kingship at this point is neither arbitrary nor autocratic. There is always the rider, however, that epic polity and society reflect no historical or social reality and are just a representation of an ideal community that is retrojected into a make-believe and poetic past: the poets do have a particular aim in mind. As we have noted, the kingship manifest in the poem does not reflect an actual reality but more of a supposed political situation; moreover, as we cannot reconstruct what epic performance was *like* we cannot truly claim to understand the message or judgment of the poem.

Thus, in the story of the Rāmāyaṇa, related by Mārkaṇḍeya to Yudhiṣṭhira, when the old king Daśaratha determines that he wants to establish his son in the succession, the poets say that:

sa raja ... mantrayāmāsa sacivair dharmajñaiś ca purohitaiḥ
abhiṣekāya rāmasya yauvarājyena bhārata ...

III.261.7

[14] These twelve years in the forest are not so arduous nor indigent for at the terminus of this period Yudhiṣṭhira sends away his family priest, Dhaumya, *sūdopaurovaiḥ* (with the kitchen-heads and cooks), and also, *nāryo draupadyāḥ ... paricārikāḥ* (the women servants of Draupadī), along with the drivers of chariots (IV.4.2–4).

The king consulted with wise companions and with priests
For the anointing of Rāma as heir-apparent, O Bhārata.

Rāma has come of age in a satisfactory manner, and his father prepares him ritually to enter the lineage, but this is accomplished only with the consensus of his community of advisors. This is all simply overturned by the schemes of a mistress of course, and then the judgement and desire of the old king is sufficient to achieve another new and remedial plan (III.261.25). Kingship in this sense, in terms of its renewal, is thus shown to possess a certain fungible quality that centres upon the king as the most senior determining agent, but one who exists among a company of associates. The *morality* of the epic is neither lucid nor explicit, yet the active political voice of a populace as it participates in kingly office is both prominent and subtle in the text. I would argue that such is the necessary component of *saṅgha* political dynamics.[15] This is more of a corporate system of rule than what we usually conceive of when we speak of kingship *qua* monarchy or autocracy.

iii. Duality

Let us return to this idea of intrinsic and necessary duality, the twofold quality that underlies the generation of a king, and see how such a pattern unfolds vis-à-vis kingship's arising in the early chapters of the poem. Śaṃtanu is actually the first king to rule from Hāstinapura, and the *Mahābhārata* is said to proclaim his story (I.93.46 and 94.10). During his rule, the poets announce that:

na cādharmeṇa keṣāṃcit prāṇinām abhavad vadhaḥ

I.94.15

There was no adharmic death of any living being whatsoever.

He speaks to his first-born son, addressing him as *bhārata* at I.94.62 and calls him a *śūra* 'hero'; this son is of course soon to be known as Bhīṣma, a prince who agrees to forsake the inheritance of kingship and to remain a virgin so that his father might find love with the ferry-girl Satyavatī, the daughter of a fisher-king.

[15] J. P. Sharma (1968, 15) comments on "the role that the people, or rather the heads of the families, played in 'electing' one of their fellow men to the kingship or chieftaincy of the tribe." He refers to the institution of the *saṅgha* or *gaṇa* variously as a non-monarchy, aristocratic government, republic, or oligarchy. He adds, "some of the tribes or 'political communities' had a king who was appointed, rather than elected, for life by the elders of the tribe or political community, while others were governed by a *sabhā* or an aristocratic oligarchy ... some tribes had both a *sabhā* or council, and a *samiti* or an assembly, while some appear to have had an assembly (*samiti*) and an unspecified number of kings (*rājānaḥ*)."

Bhīṣma consents to the male offspring of that union receiving the royal title: *sa no rājā bhaviṣyati* (he will become king of us) (I.94.79). Thus, Bhīṣma becomes the guardian of kingship at Hāstinapura and its constable, standing aside in favour of his half-brother.

Of the two subsequent sons born to Śaṃtanu—again, there occurs this phenomenon of two brothers—the elder, Citrāngada, dies, and the line proceeds from his younger sibling, Vicitravīrya, although not in terms of sanguinity, but by virtue of affinity. More specifically, descent comes through his wives only via the insemination accomplished by the step-brother of Bhīṣma, Vyāsa; Vicitravīrya is referred to at this point by the unusual term *rājā sa kauravaḥ* (that king Kaurava) (I.96.41).[16] Sexual reproduction in the epic is nearly always so complex and often proceeds laterally before it descends vertically: the woman enjoys intercourse and conceives not from her husband but from another male figure—human or divine.[17] These two stepbrothers, Bhīṣma and Vyāsa, although not kings themselves, actually engineer or supervise the process of kingship at Hāstinapura, and they can be viewed in a locative sense insofar as Bhīṣma comes from the Gaṅgā, his mother, and Vyāsa comes from the Yamunā, where his mother plied a ferry. The intermediate area, the 'doab', is known as the *kurujāṅgala* (the Kuru wilderness).[18]

We have already noted how the template of two brothers, who for one reason or another separate, is established early on in the epic with the two sons of Yayāti by two different women. Yadu and Pūru are the ancestral figures in the poem who establish the two lineages that—at the time of Kurukṣetra—focus the narrative of the song: these are the Yādavas and the Kauravas.[19] At the close of the epic the office of king in Hāstinapura belongs to a Kuru—although as we have noted, genetically he is more Yādava than Kuru—and at Indraprastha it stands in the Yādava line; and so the bipartition of lineage that descended from Yayāti is closed. It is often the case that an elder brother is typically displaced from the succession by a younger brother, and in terms of such a dual patterning

16 Vyāsa was born of a previous union that Satyavatī enjoyed before she met Śaṃtanu. Thus both Śaṃtanu and Bhīṣma are without enduring progeny and no male lineage exists; Satyavatī, with Parāśara, grandson of Vasiṣṭha, is whence the line descends for a while. Pūru's lineage thus becomes closed and only the lineage of Yadu is eventually successful, in terms of longevity, via Subhadrā.

17 I have covered this topic in an earlier work (McGrath 2009).

18 First mentioned at I.102.22.

19 Yadu and Pūru are born at I.78.9–10. Kuru is descended from Pūru. To repeat from above, as Bhīṣma and Śaṃtanu produce no progeny the line of Pūru is thus genetically, but not nominally, closed. Vaiśaṃpāyana recounts the long lineage from Pūru down to the two sons and one grandson—Aśvamedhatta—of Janamejaya beginning at I.90.5–96. Curiously, this list is given in form of rhythmic prose.

or fraternal fission we can observe the connection between Vyāsa and Bhīṣma, between Dhṛtarāṣṭra and Pāṇḍu, between Karṇa and Yudhiṣṭhira, to name a few of these *duos* who separate over the issues of sovereignty as it concerns kingship.[20] One could even argue, although the evidence is minimal, that Balarāma and Kṛṣṇa were in mild competition for princely authority at Dvārakā; for certainly, their relation is not an easy one or an openly explicit one.[21]

Pāṇḍu had been *mahīpati* 'king' at Hāstinapura, displacing his elder brother on account of the latter's blindness (I.102.23).[22] As a king he was not domestically content and the poets say of him that he was *jigīṣamāṇo vasudhāṃ* (desiring to conquer the earth) (I.102.7). Historically, it was only with the advent of the Mauryas that this impulse towards empire found fruition; then later, with the Guptas, an imperial hegemony was once more achieved. In the next lines it is said that the Dārva, king of Rājagṛha, the first Magadhan capital, was killed in this progress of Pāṇḍu.

Dhṛtarāṣṭra, even when Pāṇḍu is still ruling, declares of Yudhiṣṭhira that *rājaputro jyeṣṭho naḥ kulavardhanaḥ* (he is the elder royal son and the one to make our clan flourish)—thus according him the nomination of succession (I.107.26).[23] When Pāṇḍu determines to leave Hāstinapura and live the life of a forest-dweller, he removes his regalia and a messenger goes to inform his brother (I.110.36–40). Once Pāṇḍu is deceased, the poets merely refer to Dhṛtarāṣṭra as *rāja* (I.119.1). Soon, the eldest son of the new king is envious, and lusting

[20] Bhīṣma's father, Śaṃtanu, had an elder brother, Devāpi, who had similarly forsaken the palace and lineage and had gone to live in the forest leaving Śaṃtanu to rule. One could also cite the governing presence of Dhṛtarāṣṭra and his half-brother, Vidura, who dominate at Hāstinapura. When Kṛṣṇa and Karṇa converse in private together on a chariot in the Udyoga *parvan*, Kṛṣṇa reminds Karṇa that he could become king because: *pāṇḍoḥ putro'si dharmataḥ* (You are the rightful son of Pāṇḍu), even though born before his mother's marriage (V.138.8–9). In the story told by Mārkaṇḍeya at III.190, two brothers are described, the younger of whom succeeds: Śala is displaced by Dala.

[21] The original model perhaps is the IE pattern of male twins, one who is recessive and one who is dominant. This arguably, in terms of myth, underlies such a poetic structure, operating during metaphorical enactment. To paraphrase Nagy (2010, 62), the former concerns absence while the latter deals with what is present.

[22] He receives the unique epithet *nāgapurasiṃha* (lion of the city of the elephant), or Hāstinapura, at I.105.21.

[23] Not long after this moment in the poem the audience hears of how Kuntī conceived her son Yudhiṣṭhira and of how he and his two younger brothers were born (I.114.1–7). Then, one hears that Duryodhana was born (I.114.14). This is perhaps what we might cite as an example of the *multitextual* nature of the epic, its form cannot in any way said to be simply diachronic, for the poem constantly repeats events and retells moments of the narrative from a novel point of view and often presents its movement as a retrospection where the audience will hear of a conclusion before it learns of the development towards that point. This makes for a work of art that is both—for modern readers—complex and irrational; yet it is upon this sophisticated and multifaceted ordering that the beauty of the poem is founded.

after power plans to bind his rival cousins, Yudhiṣṭhira and Arjuna, and then, he claims *praśāsiṣye vasuṃdharām* (I shall govern the earth) (I.119.27). This is the first occasion in the poem where Duryodhana's envy and ambition is stated in direct speech as the duality of contention shifts from brothers to cousins. His father, the old blind Dhṛtarāṣṭra, remains *rāja* but becomes increasingly weak and overruled by his favourite child who is soon directing the kingdom. In the early chapters of the Āraṇyaka *parvan*, when the Pāṇḍavas have taken up their forest residence, Vidura is still advising his king to determine the succession in favour of Yudhiṣṭhira. This is the prerogative of Dhṛtarāṣṭra, says Vidura: *pāṇḍoḥ putraṃ prakuruṣvādhipatye* (make the son of Pāṇḍu sovereign) (III.5.12).[24]

When Drupada, the father-in-law of the Pāṇḍavas, first learns whom his daughter is going to marry, he is delighted that it was Arjuna who had won the hand of Draupadī. Then, hearing of Duryodhana's plots to kill the brothers, Drupada contemns him: *vigarhayāmāsa tadā dhṛtarāṣṭraṃ janeśvaram* (then he reviled Dhṛtarāṣṭra, the chief) (I.187.15). The term used here is *janeśvara*, literally 'lord of men', and it is a word that is not often used to denote high office in a kingdom. The division between brothers for a throne—a paradigm that is intrinsic to the poem—has become a contest between cousins: structurally and genetically the situation is the same although it has become fatally bitter and one generation removed. Bhīṣma, in the Ādi *parvan*, comments on how he views this situation:

> atha dharmeṇa rājyaṃ tvaṃ prāptavān bharatarṣabha[25]
> te'pi rājyaṃ anuprāptāḥ pūrvaṃ eveti me matiḥ
>
> I.195.7
>
> O bull of the Bharatas, as you obtained the kingdom by dharma,
> They too attained the kingdom first. Such is my opinion.

There is much ambiguity in the poem as to what constitutes sovereign right, and the Pāṇḍava claim is not always distinctly correct, not morally, as we shall see. Certainly, true kingship is only for those who have experienced the *abhiṣeka* 'royal unction'; without receiving that anointment of the head no one can legitimately claim to be a suzerain king. This does place Duryodhana—given his claims and his actions—in a peculiar light for he never experiences the

[24] On should recall that Dhṛtarāṣṭra and Vidura are paternal half-brothers, being sons of the same father.

[25] I can find no reason why the terms *bhārata* and *bharata* are used synonymously to stand for the 'offspring of Bharat', meaning '*bhārata*'. It is an unusually inexact usage.

rite.[26] Secondly, it is the sponsorship and accomplishment of the *aśvamedha* (the horse sacrifice) that truly qualifies an anointed king as one who is effectively and rightfully potent. Neither Dhṛtarāṣṭra nor his son can make a claim to such distinction and only Yudhiṣṭhira achieves this position.[27] Even Janamejaya, the patron of the poem *in toto* as we know it, ostensibly never accomplished this ritual; his only grand rite was that of the *sarpayajña* (the snake sacrifice), mentioned in the Ādi *parvan* and in the final lines of the epic (I.47.1ff.).[28]

The Pāṇḍava view and practice of kingship demonstrates a great deal of expedience rather than any consistent propriety. What is soon happening at this early moment in the poem is that Bhīṣma—as guardian of the kingdom—is proposing, for the first time ever in the narrative, that the kingdom be partitioned between the two sides of the clan: *teṣāṃ ardhaṃ pradīyatām* (let them be given half); and so this dualism between moieties becomes institutionalised (I.195.19). It is the Dhārtarāṣṭras however who have succeeded to the patriline in that they are the direct descendents of Vyāsa, the son of Satyavatī, wife of Śaṃtanu; for the Pāṇḍava sons were—as we have observed earlier—not in fact procreated by their father Pāṇḍu, but by divine agency.[29] Thus, in terms of patriline, it is Duryodhana who is in the direct succession, not Yudhiṣṭhira, and if that is to be the active principle of succession, then he may rightfully claim the throne. As is typical of epic *Mahābhārata*, *dharma* is never explicit nor overt due to the fact that the *kali yuga* is about to engage, and *dharma* is therefore to be always in abeyance by three-fourths of its full potential. Again, it is this super-complex artistry of the poem that makes for a work of impenetrable or irreducible beauty. Karṇa responds to Bhīṣma's proposal—and he is *the* hardline

26 Perhaps Duryodhana received the royal anointment as part of the *vaiṣṇavo yajña*, although this is not stated, and, as the ritual is unique, one cannot infer such. In the Karṇa *parvan*, the poets claim—in the voice of Arjuna speaking to Kṛṣṇa—that *rājā dhṛtarāṣṭraḥ ... duryodhanam ... rājye'bhyaṣecayat* (king Dhṛtarāṣṭra anointed Duryodhana into kingship) (VIII.52.9). That is all, however, and there is no other mention of this occurrence.

27 The poets say that *aśvamedhaśatair īje dhṛtarāṣṭro* (Dhṛtarāṣṭra sacrificed with an hundred *aśvamedhas*) (I.106.5). However, at I.114.5, Nīlakaṇṭha comments on how his condition of being *garbhāndha* 'congenitally blind' precluded him from acting in this manner of a true sacrificer. A hundred *aśvamedhas* is also poetic *hyperbole*, for such is not practically feasible within a single life span.

28 At I.3.1ff., Janamejaya is said to sponsor a *sattra* at the site of the battle of Kurukṣetra. In the Harivaṃśa, which is a poem come from a completely separate poetic tradition, it is said that Janamejaya does intend to sponsor an *aśvamedha* (115.6).

29 The Pāṇḍavas are joined lineally through the matriline to the Vṛṣṇi-Andaka, or Yādava clan, a kinship pattern that is sustained by Arjuna's marriage with Subhadrā; by marriage with Draupadī they are united with the Pāñcālas. Thus, the procreation Vyāsa accomplishes continues the matriline of Satyavatī, and *not* the patriline of Śaṃtanu. As we have seen, this reproductive paradigm is typical of epic *Mahābhārata*, where a woman procreates *not* with her husband but with another male.

proponent of war—with a story about a king of Magadha who was weak and whose minister took over sovereign management and rule; yet kingship nevertheless remained with Ambūbica, the king, despite his fecklessness and despite the overbearing minister (I.17–24).

Thus—presumably because of the onset of the *kali yuga*—the *dharma* of succession and right kingship is a state that always appears to stem from fraternal contention, creating ambiguity, and therefore rivalry, in a polity. Material and physical audacity, communal popularity, clan acceptance, and a strangely undefined genetic sensibility—all these four components are the sufficient strands that make for a right king. The opposite of good kingship is thus what the poets describe as *bheda* 'partition', and it is the struggle about this dualistic term that lies at the very core of epic *Mahābhārata*.

iv. Magadha

Going back one step to the steady, if not mysterious, refrain concerning Magadha, once the Pāṇḍava brothers had married into the Pāñcāla clan, they became potentially super-powerful. Because of this alliance, when they returned to Hāstinapura, the old king Dhṛtarāṣṭra—as we have seen—divided the territory and gave the brothers *ardhaṃ rājyasya* (half of the kingdom) (I.199.26).[30] In this division of the kingdom, it is not clear as to the nature of land tenure; that is, whether the king 'owns' the terrain or simply dominates it politically and receives fiscal due. The new town of Indraprastha, along with its amazing *sabhā*, is built upon the shore of the Yamunā, while the Dhārtarāṣṭras remain at Hāstinapura on the Gaṅgā, and the division of the *paitṛkaṃ dravyaṃ* 'patrimonial inheritance' is established; yet at this point in the narrative, discord has not yet become manifest nor violent, it remains civil.[31] It is said of Yudhiṣṭhira that *pālayāmāsa dharmeṇa pṛthivīṃ* (he maintained the earth with *dharma*) (I.200.6). This period of rule at Indraprastha appears to last for more than a decade, for Arjuna—in breach of the conjugal accord made between the brothers concerning Draupadī—is said to depart for a period of *dvādaśa varṣāṇi* 'twelve years' before

[30] The Pāṇḍava 'brothers' are, of course, in fact co-uterine half-brothers, born of four different progenitors and two mothers. The armed alliance with which Yudhiṣṭhira goes to Kurukṣetra is with the Pāñcālas, the Yādavas, and the Vairāṭas, each clan being joined with the Pāṇḍavas by marriage as well as agreement. The sexuality of Arjuna is a crucial element in the formation of these coalitions.

[31] Let us recall that Vyāsa comes from the Yamunā while Bhīṣma comes from the Gaṅgā: these two figures are the two living elders of the clan, and it is as if the kingdom becomes dyarchic once more, not just politically, but geopolitically.

returning, a period that matches their later forest retreat (I.205.30). The poets blur this passing of time, however.

However, even while Yudhiṣṭhira, along with his brothers, rule from Indraprastha, they *jaghnur anyān narādhipān śāsanād dhṛtarāṣṭrāsya rajñaḥ* (from the command of king Dhṛtarāṣṭra—they struck other kings) (I.214.1). At this point in the poem, Yudhiṣṭhira thus continues to offer fealty to his nominal paternal uncle and the arch-hero Bhīṣma who advises the aged king. Full kingship has not yet come to the elder Pāṇḍava even though the poets already refer to him as *rāja* (I.214.7). He is not yet a *pati*.

The first time that Yudhiṣṭhira is referred to as *ajātaśatru*, an epithet that points to the fact that his 'enemies are unborn', occurs in the Ādi *parvan* when his mother Kuntī is addressing him; this is not an uncommon title for Yudhiṣṭhira in the epic. Historically, Ajātaśatru was also the name of a son of king Bimbisara of Magadha who flourished during the years 491–461 BCE and who violently displaced his father in order to secure kingship. Ajātaśatru was also the title of Bindusara, the father of Aśoka who ruled between 298 and 272 BCE and was a *rāja* who favoured the Ājīvika sect. This first Ajātaśatru extended the kingdom of Magadha westward as far as the Indus, and he established the capital city of Pāṭaliputra, which remained a great city under the Maurya and Gupta dynasties.[32] The allegiance of the Magadha kingdom to the Pāṇḍavas at the great battle of Kurukṣetra is directed by a king named Jayatsena, the son of Jarāsaṃdha (V.19.8). As the armies are depicted in their assemblage prior to moving towards the battlefield, the chief of the Magadha force is said to be Sahadeva (V.154.10).

Yet it is also stated that the army of the king of Magadha is with Duryodhana, and in the early days of battle, there is a small scene where this army is urged on by him. This is an elephant force and not a gathering of chariots.

> duryodhanas tu saṃkruddho māgadhaṃ samacodayat
> anīkaṃ daśasāhasraṃ kuñjarāṇāṃ tarasvinām
>
> VI.58.31
>
> The wrathful Duryodhana urged the Māgadha force
> Of ten thousand bold elephants.

These elephants are soon completely destroyed by Bhīma who is repeatedly likened to the deity Rudra, being *raudrātmā*, and he is said to be:

[32] This is now the modern Patna in Bihar.

atiṣṭhat tumule bhīmaḥ śmaśāna iva śūlabhṛt

VI.58.61

Bhīma stood in the tumult like the Trident Bearer in a burning ground.[33]

There is a curious ambivalence on the part of the poets or editors as to which side the forces of Magadha fought with at the battle. It is as if the compilation and assimilation of poetic traditions drew upon so many different sources that rational collocation of theme and narrative was not always possible—or not even desired or even a criterion.

v. The *Dharmarāja*

Finally, let us now turn from these considerations of some of the dimensions of kingship in the poem, noting how those ideas developed throughout the early narrative, and let us look at what is the central component of Yudhiṣṭhira's epic identity: a quality that lies profoundly pivotal to his ostensible position of king, at least in a nominal sense. As *dharmarāja*, Yudhiṣṭhira only speaks the truth and never retracts a testimony; ideally his thoughts will never wander from what is right. He says, *anṛtaṃ notsahe vaktuṃ* (I am not able to speak untruly) (III.49.27).[34] In fact, the words of a king should always be a *speech act* and be efficacious in their causative nature.[35] In a preliterate society, where law cannot

[33] In terms of simple analysis here, Śiva is set in counterpoint to a force that is not Indo-Āryan in form, elephants being indigenous. The Indo-Āryans valued chariots, and chariot fighting was the highest-ranking manner of warfare. The Mahādeva is also—reputedly—not an Indo-Āryan deity.

[34] I would strongly assert that this verbal potence of a king is an aspect of kingship during times of preliterate culture. Scholars like Olivelle, however, would propose that such an ethical quality of epic kingship demonstrates more historical conditions. Olivelle (2009, 83), speaking of the *dharma* of a king, comments: "The use of *dharma* ... as the central concept in defining a new imperial ideology, the ethical ideology of the Maurya empire articulated by Aśoka in his edicts, could not be ignored even by the scholastic Brahmins working within the Vedic *śākhās*. In his brief edicts, Aśoka uses the term about 111 times."

[35] For speech act theory, see Austin 1962; Searle 1969. At I.133.18ff., Vidura speaks to Yudhiṣṭhira enigmatically in riddling form, which the latter comprehends; at III.297.26ff., a *yakṣa* similarly speaks to Yudhiṣṭhira with riddles; and at III.177.15ff., Yudhiṣṭhira satisfies a verbal test that a snake poses. On all three occasions, the prince is able to understand and to respond to the coded messages, such is his cognisance of language. In the Āraṇyaka *parvan*, Yudhiṣṭhira makes a truth act, a particular form of speech act, in which he causes a *yakṣa* to revive the dead Nakula: the expression *nakulo yakṣa jīvatu* (Yakṣa, let Nakula live!) is repeated three times, each imperative being conjoined with a statement of Yudhiṣṭhira's own personal and unimpeachable veracity (III.297.71–73). See Brown 1972 for a description of truth acts.

be physically recorded, it is the language of the ruler that generates not only judgement, but also justice. He says:

> na me vāg anṛtaṃ prāha nādharme dhīyate matiḥ
>
> I.187.29
>
> My speech utters no untruth, my mind does not reflect on adharma.[36]

It is for these reasons that he receives the *dharmarāja* title, an epithet no other prince attains in the poem. Kingship in the first millennium was performative; there existed no constitution by which that work was regulated and to which a king had to conform. Hence there were many possible *kinds* of kingship; and just like ritual, such a social dynamic could go terribly wrong. One of the practical aspects of maintaining *dharma* in a community found its place not only in the right *speech* of the king, but in his activity as a sacrificer.[37] If a ritual was to be effective and possess causality, the language used during the rite had to be faultless—both morally and linguistically—for as one who was patron of a sacrifice the king entered upon a domain of meaning that was both superhuman and durable.[38] Let us now examine this feature of Yudhiṣṭhira, commencing with how the priestly king is wakened to his royal office at the outset of a day.

When, during the Jayadrathavadha *parvan*, the poets describe how Yudhiṣṭhira is roused in the morning, they lavish great lyrical detail on the musicality and poetry of the occasion, and it is as if his kingly personage during the *levée* marks an instant of almost cosmic beauty, and the poetry itself is being aroused as its first patron returns to consciousness. This is the only such occasion or description of a princely awakening in the poem and one of the few accounts that is detailed and 'realistic' (or non-formulaic) in style, being concerned with small material features and mundane facets of kingly life. It is as if the poets are describing what they have actually witnessed rather than what they have merely

36 Repeated at I.188.13.

37 The epic begins—at least by the third *adhyāya*—with a sacrifice: *kurukṣetre dīrghasattram* (a long *sattra* in the field of the Kurus), which is being attended by Janamejaya, the great-grandson of Arjuna and great-great-nephew of Yudhiṣṭhira (I.3.1). Janamejaya was then king at Hāstinapura. In the Ādi *parvan*, there is also another important sacrifice, that of the snake, which commences at I.48.4. Anthony (2007, 408–409) writes: "Indo-Iranian identity was linguistic and ritual, not racial. If a person sacrificed to the right gods in the right way using the correct forms of the traditional hymns and poems, that person was an Aryan ... Rituals performed *in the right words* were the core of being an Aryan."

38 On a related note, Bhīma remarks that *na hi yācanti rājāna eṣa dharmaḥ sanātanaḥ* (kings do not request, this is the eternal *dharma*) (III.152.9). In other words, kings should only give or they should simply take. As we shall soon observe, the 'giving' occurs after the sacrifice, while the 'taking' occurs before the rite.

heard.[39] The situation is of the war-camp at Kurukṣetra, as the narrative rests between the death of Yudhiṣṭhira's nephew Abhimanyu and the death of the Sindhu king Jayadratha, one of the boy's slayers. Saṃjaya describes the scene to his interlocutor Dhṛtarāṣṭra:

paṭhanti pāṇisvanikā māgadhā madhuparkikāḥ
vaitālikāś ca sūtāś ca tuṣṭuvuḥ puruṣarṣabham
nartakāś cāpy anṛtyanta jagur gītāni gāyakāḥ
kuruvaṃśas tavārthāni madhuraṃ raktakaṇṭhinaḥ

VII.58.2

Bestowers of honey and milk, eulogists, those who clasp hands,
And panegyrists and poets, reciting, they praised the bull-man.
Then dancers danced and sweet-voiced singers sweetly sang songs—
The Kuru lineage, your affairs ...

Various kinds of drums are sounded, instruments are played, as the king is awakened and goes to perform his ablutions, and he is:

āplutaḥ sādhivāsena jalena ca sugandhinā

VII.58.10

Bathed with fragrant sweet-smelling water ...

After he is anointed with unguents and dressed: *sragvī cākliṣṭavasanaḥ prāṅmukhaḥ prāñjaliḥ sthitaḥ ... jajāpa japyaṃ* (well attired, wearing a garland, stood facing east, hands together, he murmured a prayer). Then the following occurs:

tato'gniśaraṇaṃ dīptaṃ praviveśa vinītavat

VII.58.12

Then modestly he entered the shining fire chamber.

Presumably this is where the *agnihotra* (the morning fire-worship) is performed. Yudhiṣṭhira then continues on to meet with learned *brāhmaṇas*, where he listens to them and offers gifts, as well as nominally conducting rites himself, ceremonially touching various insignia and food offerings. This is certainly an orthodox and orthoprax situation that is thoroughly founded in brahminical culture. Yudhiṣṭhira then moves to another room where he sits upon a costly and precious throne and puts on kingly garments and ornaments brought to him by servants.

39 I previously examined (in further detail) this distinction between what is *seen* and what is *heard* in epic poetry (McGrath 2011, chap. II).

The poets say—with nice hyperbole—that *rūpam āsīn ... dviṣatāṃ śokavardhanam* (his beautiful appearance was the cause of grief for his enemies) (VII.58.22–25). More poets and eulogists sing his praises until the scene abruptly terminates with *nisvano mahān* (a very great sound):

> nemighoṣaś ca rathināṃ khuraghoṣaś ca vājinām
>
> VII.58.28
>
> The roar of wheel-rims of chariots and roar of horses' hooves.

This announces the arrival of his ally Kṛṣṇa and almost co-sovereign.

It is as if the scene draws upon an observed ritual template, being particularly precise in its fashion of portraying a great king in his matutinal form, proceeding from his bed towards the throne and accomplishing certain almost sacerdotal customs on the way, and the audience sees here a king of quasi-priestly manner. The magnificence and detail and sheer wealth that is depicted is in powerful contrast to the surrounding war camp where the end of the known world is being brutally and horribly enacted; the narrative is in fine counterpoint to the previous scene of formal lamentation for a fallen juvenile hero, and the action prior to that, which described his gallantry, bravery, and death.[40] It is rare in the Bhārata Song to have such domestic or 'realistic' details; preliteracy as manifest in epic poetry does not often engage with individuality, and there is little delineation of such exacting specificity as it occurs in the above passage.

Depiction is usually formulaic, and there is little, for instance, that informs an audience about exactly what Yudhiṣṭhira—or any other hero—actually looked like; simile and epithet, which are cliché in origin, render such points generally. The audience hears that Yudhiṣṭhira possesses *pracaṇḍaghonaḥ* (a big nose), and that he is also *jāmbūnadaśuddhagauratanur* (possessing a body that is fair and pure as river-gold), at XV.32.5, but that is really all that is ever told about his individual personage.[41] Epic *Mahābhārata* as a preliterate medium hardly ever touches upon such temporally explicit qualities, of person, event, or landscape. The 'truth' of epic poetry lies in its use of simile, metaphor, and myth, and not in any engagement with the particular or historically precise, and its typologies are of greater worth than its detailed elements: hence the *timelessness* of the poetry, its pictures and its fully Indic panorama.

[40] Faust (2008, 14) writes of a more recent occasion and the similar importance of *how* a warrior dies: "News of a Good Death constituted the ultimate solace—the consoling promise of life everlasting."

[41] These words are a repetition of what Draupadī said to Jayadratha when he was attempting to abduct her, and in that sense they must be close to formulaic insofar as what is being repeated has been *heard* before and elsewhere (III.254.7).

***

To recapitulate what was said in the first chapter, enactment concerns what is being seen or heard, and this involves expression in both technique and voice: *how* the poets work or speak, their verbal *nuance*, and their physical gestures, and how it is that they impart particular emotion to the words that an audience receives. In other words, what is it that the *sound* of the poem itself communicates, apart from the signification of the words? Myth, however, concerns how the poets accomplish this in terms of narrative and the kinship represented therein; that is, *what* goes to constitute the nature of this truth. The former is dramatic, while the latter is poetic. It is the reciprocity between these two rhetorical forms—performance and composition—that makes for a text; the former is difficult for us moderns to grasp, however, because we are unable to perceive what the gestures of the poet must have been like, and, similarly, it is not always possible to discern the mood of a word or phrase's expression.[42] The myth of a king as a sacrificer must needs be enacted by the dramatic presentation of the poets who cause an audience to interpret the metaphors the poets vivify and activate during performance. It is up to the poets to display during their action and declamation—the details of drama and theatre in how they performed—how it is that this underlying ritual form brings energy to the nature of epic narrative. How would a classical audience understand this hieratic function of kingship and its extended passion, and how would they perceive this movement in the poem? What exactly would the poets emphasise in their enunciation?

Draupadī, early on during their time in the forest, in a virulent and truly contemptuous and eloquent diatribe against her principal husband, mentions that:

> aśvamedho rājasūyaḥ puṇḍarīko'tha gosavaḥ
> etair api mahāyajñair iṣṭaṃ te bhūridakṣiṇaiḥ ...
>
> III.31.16
>
> The horse sacrifice, the royal unction, the lotos rite, the one-day soma rite,
> So you offered with these sacrifices and copious offerings ...

Even though the horse sacrifice has not yet occurred in the story and two of the other rites are unknown to us at this point, Draupadī is here depicting the vital, and arguably central, aspect of ancient Indian kingship; this is what kings do, as

[42] It is as if we only have the musical score to supply us with an indication of the sound of an orchestral symphony, and we lack any experience of how all the instruments would sound or how they were conducted.

well as fighting and enforcing the law that sustains social hierarchy.[43] She does not question his propriety in this sacral role, but it is Yudhiṣṭhira's behaviour in the more potentially violent aspects of rule that she cynically criticises in her speech. He says to her, soon after this exchange, *yaje yaṣṭavyam* (I sacrifice that which is to be sacrificed); for him, that is the essential nature of his office of *dharmarāja* (III.32.2).[44] Let us now turn to the three crucial sacrifices of *rāja* Yudhiṣṭhira.

1. The *Rājasūya* Sequence

The *rājasūya* of Yudhiṣṭhira does not truly fulfill his title or role as a *sacrificer* because the sequel to the rite goes horribly wrong, and he who had momentarily been paramount soon becomes instantly abject, excluded, and exiled. In fact, due to the production of this ritual the stability of the kingdom, as well as the unity of the narrative itself, becomes disorderly. Even the sensibility the poets evince for the concept or practice of kingship in *bhāratavarṣa* loses its sense of accord and integrity, becoming thoroughly divergent. The consequences of the ritual lead directly into the central didactic parts of the poem, that is, the Āraṇyaka *parvan*, which is one of the most edifying books of the *Mahābhārata*, and, which, in terms of narrative series, is extremely eclectic. The *aśvamedha* rite as later sponsored by Yudhiṣṭhira is ostensibly successful and coherent; the *rājasūya*, however, appears to cause terrific disorder—in terms of Kuru kingship—and in fact facilitates if not generates irreversible schism in the kingdom. Let us now analyse both these aspects of the ritual, its occurrence and its dire efficacy.

With the performance of this rite, which the *ṛṣi* Nārada has convinced Yudhiṣṭhira to accomplish, the stakes of kingship and rule become suddenly much more serious, insofar as the Pāṇḍava is announcing his supreme status to the world and particularly towards his Kaurava kin. This is a conspicuous challenge to his old uncle Dhṛtarāṣṭra and to his cousins, and the rivalry between the two moieties of the clan quickly gathers pragmatic force. Says Nārada:

43 In my experience of the Kacch of Gujarat this remains the only function of kingship today in the early twenty-first century: that of the sponsoring of important rites and the symbolic participation therein.

44 Taking this idea back one step, it is Hanūmān who states that *dharmād vedāḥ samutthitāḥ / vedair yajñāḥ samutpannā yajñair devāḥ pratiṣṭhitāḥ* (from *dharma* the Vedas arise, the sacrifice is produced by the Vedas, the deities are established by sacrifices) (III.149.28). Hence one can understand the king's dependence upon the *brāhmaṇas* insofar as they are the scholars and knowers of Veda. *Dharma* is here said to find its origin in *ācāra*, 'custom' or 'ordinance'; curiously this is not said to be of divine origin.

rājasūyaṃ kratuśreṣṭham āharasveti bhārata

II.11.66

Bhārata, perform the highest rite, the rājasūya.

He adds to this injunction, however, the rider that:

yuddhaṃ ca pṛṣṭhagamanaṃ pṛthivīkṣayakārakam

II.11.69

War follows, the cause of the ruin of the earth.

In the Harivaṃśa, the poet likewise claims that:

hetuḥ kurūṇāṃ nāśasya rājasūyo mato mama

115.14

The cause of that destruction of the Kurus, to my mind, was the rājasūya.

One consequence of this ultimate ritual is that the sponsor can then claim the title of *samrāj* 'sovereign', the superlative kingly rank (II.12.11). As is typical with *rāja* Yudhiṣṭhira—until he finally becomes *kururāja* after his victory at Kurukṣetra—he always defers in major decisions to his ally and maternal cousin, Kṛṣṇa, and before instituting the rite, Yudhiṣṭhira asks for Kṛṣṇa's confirmation of this policy:

tatra me niścitatamaṃ tava kṛṣṇa girā bhavet

II.12.37

Here, my certitude would be with your word, Kṛṣṇa.

This is something that I have demonstrated in an earlier work, this almost double sovereignty, or dual kingship, that appears to exist between these two figures, an alliance of king and hero; this immediately ceases once Yudhiṣṭhira actually achieves complete power after his victory at Kurukṣetra.[45] It is as if the essential war alliance of Pāñcālas and Pāṇḍavas is managed according to a double authority or dyarchy in which Kṛṣṇa possesses the dominant voice, while it is Yudhiṣṭhira who really holds the access to power.[46]

[45] See McGrath 2013, chap. III. The trace of dual kingship is apparent in the *Iliad* where *atreída dè málista dúō kosmētore laōn* (the two sons of Atreus, chiefs of the people), as a verbal formula, is repeated (I.16).

[46] One should recall that Kṛṣṇa is personally an ally of the Pāṇḍavas, but the Yādavas or Vṛṣṇis are not party to this treaty. In ancient Sparta a dual kingship is obtained for a period towards the middle of the first millennium BCE; see Forrest 1969. Dumézil (1948 and 1977) also discuss this archaic political model where two equal consuls held supreme power in Rome. Kristiansen and Larsson (2005, 280) comment that "the institution of twin rulers as it unfolded ... was linked to the adaptation of

Similarly, it is as if there exists a dual authority at Hāstinapura, shared between Dhṛtarāṣṭra and his half-brother Vidura, for Droṇa makes the telling comment in the *sabhā* that Pāṇḍu, *rājā kurūṇāṃ* (king of the Kurus), had bestowed kingship:

jyeṣṭhāya rājyam adadād dhṛtarāṣṭrāya dhīmate
yavīyasas tathā kṣattuḥ kuruvaṃśavivardhanaḥ

V.146.4

The thriver of the Kuru lineage gave the kingdom to
The wise Dhṛtarāṣṭra, the elder, as to the younger charioteer [Vidura].[47]

For some reason, the possibility of a dual kingship shared between Yudhiṣṭhira and Duryodhana is not even considered by the poets; it is as if there exists an almost organic antipathy between these two *kṣatriyas*, or that their two poetic traditions were inherently separate in nature. There is little symmetry—in a narrative sense—between the two cousins, for Yudhiṣṭhira is overtly married and familial, whereas Duryodhana's kinship relations, except those with his mother and father and a few brothers, remain unmentioned. Duryodhana is cast more in the role of an intransigent hero—just like Karṇa—whereas Yudhiṣṭhira is certainly *not* an heroic figure but a quietly charismatic prince aspiring to kingdom. Yet, having achieved this ambition, his days are charged with remorse, grief, and guilt, while Duryodhana is of course dead.[48]

***

Some time before Yudhiṣṭhira performs this major rite, Kṛṣṇa informs him—at great historical length—about the kings who lived and ruled in Northern India, and he tells Yudhiṣṭhira about a particular ruler in Magadha called Jarāsaṃdha who had been harassing Kṛṣṇa's town of Mathurā.[49] That king, says Kṛṣṇa, had

---

the institution of warrior aristocracies." This was a "division of power between the priest king and the warrior king" (ibid., 281).

47 Similarly, *siṃhāsanastho nṛpatir dhṛtarāṣṭro mahābalaḥ / anvāsyamānaḥ satataṃ vidureṇa mahātmanā* (the powerful king Dhṛtarāṣṭra, seated on the lion-chair, always attended by the great-souled Vidura) (V.146.11). Lévi-Strauss (1991, chap. 19) discusses what he calls "bipartite ideology" as it concerns twins who are in a position of administering rule; he comments on Dumézil's views concerning dual sovereignty. Oosten, in Claessen and Oosten (1996, 221–238), considers this intrinsic dual nature of ancient kingship from both a mythical and historical point of view.

48 Let us again recall that of the two, only Duryodhana is in the direct patriline that descends from Vyāsa; his father, Parāśara, was a son of Vasiṣṭha, who was a son of Brahmā. Duryodhana is also a nominal Kuru; Yudhiṣṭhira is not.

49 Kṛṣṇa is arguably making use of the Pāṇḍavas here in order to dispose of a king who had been oppressing and displacing his own people, the Vṛṣṇis. When he, along with Arjuna and Bhīma, arrives at Magadha, the poets describe that king as *jarāsaṃdhaṃ samarcayan paryagni kurvaṃś ca nṛpaṃ*

captured and imprisoned almost a hundred other rulers, and, if Yudhiṣṭhira was to succeed in his *rājasūya*, he needed first to destroy Jarāsaṃdha (II.13.1–68).[50] This is accomplished with expedition, and then the four brothers, on behalf of the king, pursue a *digvijaya* (a conquest of the directions), overrunning by force dozens of kingdoms throughout nearly all of Northern India, such domination being a necessary condition for the success and efficacy of the *rājasūya* (II.23.13–19).[51]

The epic here demonstrates what appears to be historical verisimilitude in the listing of the kings who succumb to these assaults in an area that exceeds several thousand square miles; this is an extraordinary onomastic catalogue of persons and places, and the *reality* of such an extensive campaign would have required years of armies being in the field. This compression or confounding of myth and historicity supplies the poem with authentic force and substance. Yet it is as if the poem is suddenly—with the *digvijaya*—becoming fanciful, for the time and resources needed to accomplish such a venture would have been gigantic, and this aspect of the campaign is not touched upon by the poets except in formulaic fashion. Yet suddenly, the narrative of Yudhiṣṭhira assumes a very different tone, as the young prince instantly becomes an omnipotent *rāja* and the poem moves to a completely new thematic register.

It is Bhīma who is allotted the eastern provinces and he is the one to overrule the Māgadhans (II.27.14ff.). It is notable that Karṇa, who is the chief warrior of the Kauravas and whom Duryodhana had made the king of the Aṅgas, a region to the east of Magadha, is the one to defend this territory against Bhīma (II.27.16–17).[52] One wonders if this region would have been included in the Buddhist or Jaina political hegemony of that time; the problem is, when to actually locate *that time*, given that the epic to a great extent represents an unreal

... *purohitāḥ* (the priests worshipped Jarāsaṃdha the king, performing the fire service about him) (II.19.20). Hiltebeitel (2011c, 645–683) has commented at length upon this episode.

[50] At this point in the poem, II.19.1ff., Magadha is physically described by the poets, and it is said that *gautamaḥ ... bhajate māgadhaṃ vaṃśaṃ sa nṛpāṇām anugrahāt* (Gautama apportioned the Magadha clan out of affection for the kings) (II.19.6). Gautama is, of course, one of the clan names of the Buddha.

[51] The listing or catalogue of kings who actually attend the rite similarly supplies the poem with an historical authenticity (II.31.5-16). As an aside, it might be worth noting that A. Agrawal (1989, 128) remarks: "After the extermination of the kings of the Gangetic valley and annexation of their kingdoms, the direct rule of Samudragupta extended up to Mathura region. The republican tribes to the west of Mathura submitted to him either as a result of military pressure or through his diplomatic skill."

[52] As an aside, Duryodhana made Karṇa king of Aṅga (I.126.35–37), and in the sixth century BCE, Aṅga was part of the Magadha empire. When he had been cast away as an infant, Karṇa had floated down the Yamunā and then down the Gaṅgā until he arrived at Campā, the capital of Aṅga, where he was found and then fostered; thus he grew up within the Māgadhan domain.

and wholly literary Bronze Age era? The merging of poetry and historical experience or record is so finely accomplished that any separation of the two elements is methodologically unsound.[53] Just as the epic blends chronologically different religious worlds, so too does it fuse in its story many and various political systems: the poem is a completely compendious work of art that in a way supplies the epic with a unique aesthetic and atemporal quality. This world of the poem is thoroughly *heroic* and not in any way simply 'human'; except until Bhīṣma begins his great address and even then he draws upon a well-founded system of fabulous animal allegory, which is altogether another tradition in the manner of *prosopopoiía*.

With the conclusion of this omni-directional campaign, Yudhiṣṭhira claims that *pṛthivī sarvā madvaśe ... vartate* (all the earth moves in my will) (II.30.18). The warring of these campaigns in every direction has also, of course, brought great tribute into the Indraprastha treasury, which makes possible the vast expense of the *rājasūya*.[54] Such rites are impossible without the sumptuous material wealth that the king is required to give away; the performance of the *aśvamedha* ritual towards the end of the poem makes much of the complex necessity of acquiring wealth *before* the sacrifice becomes feasible. Duryodhana himself describes all this wealth in his own words to his father, and it is the massive ostentation of this property—and one must recall that the conceptual Bronze Age society represented in the poem is a premonetary economy—that really arouses the wrath and envy of Duryodhana (II.47.3–48.31).[55] It is as if the poets ascribe a certain *hubris* to Yudhiṣṭhira at this moment in the narrative, and it is as if his essential decorum has fallen.

At the actual conduct of the rite, if the tributary rulers did *not* offer sufficient wealth, *dvāri tiṣṭhanti vāritāḥ* (restrained, they stood at the gate) (II.48.31). In other words, without a large enough offering to Yudhiṣṭhira, the chiefs were not admitted; this sentence is heard repeatedly, as Duryodhana lists the vast quantities of matériel that were being proffered. The problem is caused by the fact that for a king to be a successful *sacrifice*, and in order to become a paramount ruler,

[53] For instance, in McGrath 2011, I argue that this 'older' world was one that was more indicated in the *Jaya* song of the great Bhārata epic; thus, at IV.5.30, Yudhiṣṭhira curiously supplies himself and his brothers with *guhyāni nāmāni* 'secret names': Jaya, Jayanta, Vijaya, Jayasena, and Jayadbala. Contrary to many current scholarly opinions, I do not view most of the Virāṭa *parvan* as a 'newer phase' of the epic; chariot fighting and cattle raiding are ancient themes in epic poetry.

[54] Oguibénine (1998, 77) succinctly comments: "The warrior's violent deeds are oriented towards the conquest of wealth which is different from that obtained by men from the gods as a compensation for what they sacrifice."

[55] Bhīṣma, in his discourse with Yudhiṣṭhira in the Śānti *parvan*, repeats this expression of envy by Duryodhana verbatim, speaking it dramatically in the first person (XII.124.11–13).

the king *must* act in this fashion: he is required to give away to the *brāhmaṇas* immeasurable amounts of food and goods and other kinds of moveable property. Conquest of territory and the concomitant acquisition of chattels, and the corollary redistribution of wealth in gift form: these are the two necessary conditions of practical and supreme kingship *qua* sacrificer. In a material and completely non-spiritual sense, these two activities are the obverse and reverse of the central practice of a major ritual.

As usual however, Yudhiṣṭhira defers to his ally and joint commander of the Pāṇḍava-Pāñcāla pact:

> anujñātas tvayā kṛṣṇa prāpnuyāṃ kratum uttaman
>
> II.30.22
>
> Authorised by you, Kṛṣṇa, I could accomplish this greatest rite.

It is ironic that Yudhiṣṭhira is here about to perform the dominant rite of universal sovereignty and yet he continues to refer to Kṛṣṇa.[56] This is a most unusual, if not unique, form of kingship, and no other *kṣatriya* in the poem behaves or speaks like this with such persistent deference; certainly neither Duryodhana and Karṇa nor Dhṛtarāṣṭra and Vidura. Even during the battle at Kurukṣetra, Yudhiṣṭhira demonstrates this constant reverence of his ally's judgement.

Yudhiṣṭhira does summon to the occasion his paternal uncle, as well as the *pitāmaha* 'grandfather'.[57] Despite the fact that Dhṛtarāṣṭra is in a senior position to the young prince, and by performing this rite Yudhiṣṭhira is depreciating his authority, the old man attends. Duryodhana is also present along with his brothers, and he is designated to receive the riches the kings offer as tribute at this great appointment; he too is thus accepting of a lesser rank in the establishment of both the ritual and of Yudhiṣṭhira's overall kingship (II.32.8).[58] Such are the strong civilities and protocols of Kaurava politics that dispute is always modulated by manner before it becomes violent. Duryodhana later cynically describes this bringing of gifts or prestations as being:

[56] As I demonstrated in McGrath 2013, as part of this picture Kṛṣṇa continually manifests throughout the epic a strong relationship with the Mahādeva Rudra-Śiva. At one point, Kṛṣṇa even informs Yudhiṣṭhira that *vedāhaṃ hi mahādevaṃ tattvena bharatarṣabha / yāni cāsya purāṇāni karmāni vividhāny uta* (I know the reality of the Mahādeva, O Bharata bull, and of his various ancient deeds) (X.17.8). Kṛṣṇa even describes Rudra-Śiva in this passage as a *creator* figure, like Brahmā or Prajāpati, who *makes* all the creatures—including humans—for the world.

[57] Nominally, Bhīṣma stands in the place of a great step-uncle although he is addressed as 'grandfather'.

[58] At another point in the poem where many kings assemble at one particular court, they are said to be received *yathānyāyaṃ yathājyeṣṭhaṃ* (according to propriety, according to seniority) (II.40.15). Kingship exists within its own known hierarchy, just as there existed a system of *gun salutes* for early twentieth-century Indian princes forming what was known as the Salute States.

upatiṣṭhanti kaunteyaṃ vaiśyā iva karapradāḥ

II.43.25

Like the vaiśyas offer tax to the son of Kuntī.

***

After the proceedings, Bhīṣma, as eldest, determines that of all the attendees it should be Kṛṣṇa who receives the *arghya* 'the guest-offering' (II.33.25), and this decision causes dissension and uproar; for Kṛṣṇa, despite being the most important Pāṇḍava ally is *not* a king, while all the others present are of that standing. Nowhere in the poem is Kṛṣṇa referred to as *rāja*. It is Śiśupāla of the Cedi kingdom who questions this act, saying *hy arājā dāśārho* (for Dāśārha is no king), and he avers that Bhīṣma is thus behaving without propriety or *dharma* (II.34.5). In a way, Yudhiṣṭhira is advancing his ally above his station much as Duryodhana had earlier advanced Karṇa, and this is simply due to *priyakāmya* (the desire of amity) or nepotism.[59] Śiśupāla, through his objection is thus simultaneously putting into question Yudhiṣṭhira's new paramount status; he is also a rival to Kṛṣṇa, in the same way that Duryodhana rivals Yudhiṣṭhira, in that he is a paternal cousin of Kṛṣṇa.[60] Yudhiṣṭhira responds, *nedaṃ yuktaṃ* (this is not correct). The problem is compound, however, for *dharma* is always subject to interpretation, and in this point of time in the *yugas*, right *dharma* is always to be three-fourths inactive and can never be fully achieved: it is an hypothetical state or condition. Bhīṣma rather grandiloquently comments that *kṣatriyaḥ kṣatriyaṃ jitvā raṇe* (a *kṣatriya* having defeated a *kṣatriya* in battle) deserves to be elevated in this manner—implying that Kṛṣṇa is the best warrior present (II.35.7).[61] It was Kṛṣṇa, after all, who arranged the defeat of Jarāsaṃdha, the king of Magadha, even if he did not actually participate in the action.

All this represents the first contention that Yudhiṣṭhira, as a *rāja*, has to deal with if his authority is to retain its new elevation. Bhīṣma speaks to support his position, while the old king Dhṛtarāṣṭra remains silent; nevertheless this discord with Śiśupāla is effective, and the assembled kings plan to reject Yudhiṣṭhira and to violate his royal ritual. Noting this, Yudhiṣṭhira does not act but turns to Bhīṣma, whom he refers to as *pitāmaha*, for advice (II.37.3). Śiśupāla then speaks with extraordinary contumely against Bhīṣma and then against Kṛṣṇa, and he is both offensive and particularly insulting (II.38.18–28). Within minutes, however,

59 Karṇa had been raised into kingship at I.126.35.

60 Kṛṣṇa also comments: *aśvamedhe hayaṃ medhyam utsṛṣṭaṃ rakṣibhir vṛtam / pitur me yajñavighnārtham aharat* (he seized the sacrificial horse [that was] released, surrounded by guards, in the *aśvamedha* of my father, in order to wreck the rite) (II.42.9).

61 Bhīṣma also says that he is *kṣatriyāṇāṃ balādhikāḥ* (most powerful of *kṣatriyas*) (II.35.17).

it is Yudhiṣṭhira's ally and peer Kṛṣṇa who saves the occasion by cutting Śiśupāla down, simply decapitating the delinquent who dies instantly, mid-speech.[62] Once again the audience observes this new power of Yudhiṣṭhira being activated by his ally who *almost* shares this sovereignty. Thus, all opposition to the new king is eradicated—and yet, in a way, Kṛṣṇa has destabilised the ritual propriety and sanctity of the rite; he has unbalanced the *dharma* of the royal ritual.[63]

I would propose that it is this sudden and intensely abbreviated slaying that throws off the efficacy of the ritual causing a sequence of disorder in the kingdom *and* in the poetry that leads to the killing field of Kurukṣetra. There are three effects that occur after the troubled conduct of the latter part of the *rājasūya*. The first stage happens with the disastrous gambling match; the next stage concerns the outcome of the game of dice, the forest exile; and the third stage occurs in the Udyoga *parvan* with the formalities of an exchange of ambassadors between the two presently opposed sides of the clan. It is of course the consequences of these events that cause battle to occur at Kurukṣetra.

***

Firstly, there is no actual description that speaks of the conduct of the rite, and it is as if the poets have no interest in such portrayal and their experience of the event is blank; the *idea* is all that is necessary for the narrative and the name itself is a sufficient signifier.[64] This is because Yudhiṣṭhira, unlike all other kings, will arguably perform a second *rājasūya*, or at least he receives the 'royal unction', the *abhiṣekha*, again, later on towards the end of the poem and his life; that instant stands as a mark of his acquisition of complete kingship, for then the Kaurava moiety are nearly all slain and the king rules from Hāstinapura. This present rite occurs as Indraprastha. There is no dice match at the second occasion of the ritual.[65]

[62] In Appendix I.28 of the Sabhā *parvan*, there is supplied from the Southern Recension (after 2.42.16) a short scene of a hundred lines where Kṛṣṇa and Śiśupāla fight a chariot duel in which the latter is bested. I am grateful for Satya Chaitanya for drawing my attention to this addition to the narrative.

[63] Olivelle (2009, 81) writes: "... in the early texts of this period, especially the Brāhmaṇas and the early Upaniṣads, the term [*dharma*] is used most frequently with reference to Varuṇa and the king. It is likely that *dharma* was part of the specialized vocabulary associated with royalty, especially because of its frequent use within the royal consecration (*rājasūya*). In all likelihood, *dharma* referred to social order and the laws of society that the king was obligated to enforce. *Dharma* thus becomes an abstract concept and entity, a cosmic force that stands above the king; it is called the *kṣatrasya kṣatram*, the power behind the royal power."

[64] The ceremony is simply given cursory mention at II.12.13: *sāmnā ṣaḍagnayo yasmiṅś cīyante saṃśitavrataiḥ* (in which six fire altars were piled with a chant by ones with honed vows); at II.30.26–33.25; and at II.49.5–20. The dice match, however, in its twofold form, receives long and detailed portrayal at II.53–70.

[65] See chapter 3 of the current volume, where we examine the complex and elaborate description the poets supply of this second *rājasūya*. Oldenberg (1988, 249–250) offers a summary picture: "A

With the success and completion of the *rājasūya*, immediate reversal for the paramount king arrives in the form of enmity that is borne by his cousin Duryodhana, who, *dṛṣṭvā pārthivāṃś ca vaśānugān* (having witnessed the submissive princes), becomes jealous, for he has thus been ceremoniously displaced from the Kuru succession; it is as if old Dhṛtarāṣṭra was simply serving as a regent during Yudhiṣṭhira's immaturity (II.43.14). Śakuni, Duryodhana's maternal uncle and a senior member of the *sabhā* or 'court', attempts to raise his spirits by suggesting that, with all the heroes who are loyal to Dhṛtarāṣṭra, he should *jaya kṛtsnāṃ vasuṃdharām* (conquer the entire earth) (II.44.11).[66] Thus, kingship in the poem takes on a new form of contention in which Duryodhana will challenge the recent Pāṇḍava supremacy, and suddenly the narrative leaps to another and more deadly plateau.

When Duryodhana turns to his aged father and complains about his royal station, the old man does not understand, and merely says:

aiśvaryaṃ hi mahat putra tvayi sarvaṃ samarpitam

II.45.8

For great sovereignty is consigned to you, son.

Yet that is insufficient for the young prince who cannot bear to witness his cousin's vast and flamboyant wealth. He, inspired by his uncle Śakuni, plots a gambling match for which Śakuni guarantees victory due to his skill of conniving at dice.[67]

---

solemn function, or to be more exact, sprinkling with water (*abhiṣeka*), initiates the king into his office; a further act, king's coronation (*rājasūya*) elevates him to the plenitude of power. Both ceremonies, not mentioned in the older tradition, must have received their exclusive distinctness only in the later Vedic period ... The celebrations are associated with the Soma-rites ... Thus, there is a raid on a herd of cows, according to another version, arrow-shooting and looting of the less powerful relatives of the king, further a game of dice with a cow as a stake, where the king must be thought of obviously as the winner." Keith (1925, 340–343) similarly describes the procedure of the rite; this description summarises the Aitareya and Kauṣītaki Brāhmaṇas of the Ṛg Veda, VIII.2.5–XXXVII.1ff. In the Taittirīya Saṃhita, Kaṇḍa I, Prapāṭhaka 8 details the liturgical procedure to be followed during the *rājasūya*.

66 Duryodhana, early in the epic, is described by the poets as *gāndhārarājasahitaś* (allied to Gāndhārarāja) (I.1.100). His mother is a daughter of Subala, a king of that Northwestern region; Śakuni is her brother. Both Dhṛtarāṣṭra and Pāṇḍu take wives from that *āryāvarta*, the old and 'sacred land' of the Āryans. The young Aśoka began his political career in that region, and Gāndhāra later became a Buddhist Kuṣāṇa kingdom that flourished in the first five hundred years of the Common Era.

67 As the audience will soon realise, both Duryodhana and Śakuni are fiendish individuals and can perhaps be conceived of as closer to the daemonic world of *dānavas* than to the human domain. Gāndhārī, during her prolonged lamentation in the Strī *parvan*, makes the claim that Śakuni won against Yudhiṣṭhira in the dicing because of his magic; for he was *yaḥ sma rūpāṇi kurute śataśo'tha sahasraśaḥ* (one who makes hundreds and thousands of forms), and *māyayā nikṛtiprajño jitavān yo yudhiṣṭhiram* (one who, dishonest of mind, won against Yudhiṣṭhira by magic) (XI.24.23–24).

Yudhiṣṭhira, of course, is unable to resist the challenge for, like any good *kṣatriya*, he cannot turn away from such a summons, and this is particularly so because of his new status as the matchless king. He says to Vidura, who as step-brother to the old Dhṛtarāṣṭra had been given the office of *dūta* 'messenger', and who visits Indraprastha with the invitation:

> āhūto'haṃ na vivarte kadācit tad āhitaṃ śāśvataṃ vai vrataṃ me
>
> II.52.16
>
> Challenged, I can never turn, that is pledged as my perpetual vow![68]

The remarkable quality about this gaming—for modern readers—is that it is conducted in a manner of great civility and courtesy. There is no hint of violence or of disorder, and the disaster proceeds both lightly and simply, and this is not due to the form of narration but to the culture and protocol of kingship and court life as presented in the poem. There is consensus as to conventional behaviour concerning conduct in a *sabhā* where Draupadī was won *dharmeṇa* 'by right' (II.60.20).[69] This propriety is only exceeded when Draupadī is treated contemptuously and improperly and made abject when she was *rajasvalā* 'menstruant' (II.60.25). Nevertheless, even then there is no overt violence and a certain *etiquette* is observed, such are the complex and specific formalities of *kṣatriya* life where not all action is ruled by the possibility of violence.[70]

It is because the spoken word of a *kṣatriya*, particularly of a king and especially of one who is the *dharmarāja*, is inviolable and forcefully *truthful*, that Yudhiṣṭhira's verbal engagement in the gambling match—staking wealth and kin—stands firm, and the Pāṇḍavas lose their state and status. Conversely, the absolute nature of his losses cause Yudhiṣṭhira to become *tūṣṇīṃ ... acetasam* (quiet, thoughtless) (II.63.8). It is this complete reversal of one who was so recently a sovereign figure of kingship that thoroughly abnegates his position of power, a situation achieved without disorder, but through the exploitation

[68] This sentiment is repeated to Śakuni himself: *āhūto na nivarteyam me vratam āhitam* ("challenged, I would not turn away, that is my pledged vow") (II.53.13). Yudhiṣṭhira himself repeats this sentiment later, in the Kāmyaka wood: *samāhūtaḥ kenacid ādraveti nāhaṃ śakto ... apayātum* ("summoned by someone saying, 'approach', I am not able to depart") (III.6.9). A noble *kṣatriya* is bound to give when asked; Karṇa similarly, when asked to relinquish his earrings and breastplate—although this implies his own death—is morally obliged to accede to the request. The verb √*yac* 'to request' possesses this particular sense of creating the obligation 'to give', such is its customary and formal usage among *kṣatriyas*.

[69] See Sen (2005) on this aspect of Indian culture.

[70] Even in the *sabhā* of the Vairāṭa king, when Draupadī is brutally assaulted in front of Yudhiṣṭhira and Bhīma, they do nothing—much to the disgusted wrath of their wife—not only for fear of losing their disguised status, but also because of court protocol (IV.15.6–26). The assailant is soon violently but discreetly killed, however.

of particular customary manners. It is queen Draupadī herself who saves her husbands with her intelligent words to the old king and thus Yudhiṣṭhira's kingship is strangely retrieved (II.63.27–36).[71] This dramatic scene closes with Yudhiṣṭhira approaching the old king and with great humility, avowing inferiority to the Kaurava patriarch; such is the reversal of the lately superlative *rāja*:

> rājan kiṃ karavāmas te praśādhy asmāṃs tvam īśvaraḥ
> nityaṃ hi sthātum icchāmas tava bhārata śāsane
>
> II.65.1
>
> O king, what must we do for you? Direct us, you are sovereign.
> For always we desire to stand in your command, Bhārata!

As Yudhiṣṭhira is about to depart—without loss—and set off towards his patrimony of Indraprastha, as he is discharged from all that occurred during the match, Dhṛtarāṣṭra speaks with him, addressing him as *rājan* 'king'. The old man explains his actions, why it was that he permitted this situation to arise:

> prekṣāpūrvaṃ mayā dyūtam idam āsīd upekṣitam
> mitrāṇi draṣṭukāmena putrāṇāṃ ca balābalam
>
> II.65.12
>
> This gaming match was deliberately overlooked by me
> Because of a desire to witness the strength, weakness, and allies of my sons.

In other words, the patriarch permitted the crisis to flare in order that the disposition and potential of his sons be revealed, and in this culture the sons of Pāṇḍu are considered to be sons of Dhṛtarāṣṭra; and also he wished to observe who he could consider loyal to them. The old king was, thus, in his words, setting a trial that would test the fortitude and indicate who his successor would be. In terms of narrative exposition, Duryodhana's bellicose excesses and Yudhiṣṭhira's calm and silent dignity, the perfidy of Śakuni and haughtiness of Karṇa, have for the first time all been well displayed. Dhṛtarāṣṭra is right, the event had been both performative and demonstrative, and—in terms of the story—the natures of all the characters, including that of Draupadī with her puissant sexuality and femininity, have all been highly dramatised and exposed. The performing of the *rājasūya* thus incorporates and generates much of the initial drama that surrounds kingship in the poem: this ceremony marks the first act of the story, as it were, and what went before was mere prologue. To sustain this metaphor, the

[71] I have described in detail this super-potency of the queen, and how it is that her presence and language in the poem generates the narrative as well, as much of the political conditioning of the clan (McGrath 2009, chap. IV–V).

third act takes place during the unresolved negotiations of the Udyoga *parvan*, the irresolution of which leads to Kurukṣetra, after the long intermission of forest exile.

Not long after this, Duryodhana has no difficulty in convincing his old father that the Pāṇḍavas are plotting to seize the throne, and Dhṛtarāṣṭra calls back the five brothers for the sake of one more match.[72] Yudhiṣṭhira of course cannot resist a summons or challenge, such is his devotion to *dharma*:

> hriyā ca dharmasaṅgāc ca pārtho dyūtam iyāt punaḥ
>
> II.67.15
>
> The Pārtha, because of attachment to dharma, with shame went to the match again.

He says: *kathaṃ vai madvidho rājā svadharmam anupālayan āhūto vinivarteta* (How, challenged, could a king like me protecting his personal *dharma*, turn back?) (II.67.17).

In the narrative of the poem, the gaming, as it occurs immediately after the *rājasūya* rites that establish Yudhiṣṭhira as the senior of all the cousins, puts his formal authority into crisis, doing so without violence and achieving this with great protocol and manner. Everyone knows that Śakuni is crooked and an adept at skulduggery; yet the *etiquette* of the court is such that formality is everything. Once again, it is as if the poets are manipulating what they have heard of an antique ritual practice they had never in fact witnessed in order that the narrative of the poem might progress according to their own terms.[73] There is a credible situation here, for Yudhiṣṭhira was certainly arrogating his status vis-à-vis his cousins, and in a certain fashion there is a truth to the statement of Duḥśāsana that the Pāṇḍavas:

> balena mattā ye te sma dhārtarāṣṭrān prahāsiṣuḥ
>
> II.68.6
>
> They who were intoxicated with power mocked the sons of Dhṛtarāṣṭra.

[72] Note that it is not simply Yudhiṣṭhira who is invited, but also *all* of his brothers, for this is a fraternal kingship: *punar dīvyāma ... pāṇḍavaiḥ* (we play again with the Pāṇḍavas), says Duryodhana (II.66.17).

[73] See Keith 1925, 342–343. The king, after the consecration, "then sits on a throne placed over the tiger-hide, and takes five dice from the Adhvaryu; the priest gently beats him from behind with sticks of pure trees, doubtless to expel any taint of ill. Before the dicing begins the Purohita hands the king a wooden sword, which he passes on to his brother, and through him it is taken by a man who marks out the place for dicing, where a hut is erected. After the dicing, which is merely formal and which deliberately was so carried out as to make the king a victor, the sacrifice progresses to the normal end ... it is possible to see it [the game of dice] in connexion with the foretelling of prosperity ... in the revenue to be derived from the dicing."

As the Pāṇḍavas take their leave, they—all except Yudhiṣṭhira—extend their arms in a signal fashion and curse their cousins, promising death: *sarve vyāyatabāhavaḥ* (all [are] open-armed) (II.68.46). This is the only hint of violence that occurs in the court, along with Bhīma's repeated threat and outrage.[74]

***

The second stage, after the questionable conclusion of the *rājasūya*, which leads the clan towards the killing field of Kurukṣetra, now occurs when the poem enters into its next act, the *longue durée* of the forest residence for the Pāṇḍavas. This is an interlude of gathering instability before the conflict at Kurukṣetra becomes fully activated.[75] Let us recall the Harivaṃśa once more, where the poet says that:

> mahābhārata saṃhāraḥ saṃbhṛto'gnir iva kratuḥ
>
> 115.19
>
> The Mahābhārata war like a gathered fire was the rite.

The 'rite' refers of course to what was generated by the ill-conducted *rājasūya*; it is as if that royal exercise had ironically established Yudhiṣṭhira as *vanapati* (king of the forest): such is actually the consequence. Let us now examine how this supreme majestic accomplishment became so unravelled.

Thus far in the epic, there have been three princely contests: the *svayaṃvara* (the marriage rite), the *rājasūya*, and the *dyūtakrīḍā* (dice play). There remains the contest of battle, itself a complex rite for *kṣatriyas*, and then the ultimate royal idiom, that of the *aśvamedha* (the horse sacrifice). In all but the final event the Pāṇḍavas are in direct opposition with their Kaurava cousins. It is these five performative acts or ceremonies that establish the nature of Yudhiṣṭhira's active princedom or kingship, each one governed by strict procedural orders; only in the two final rituals is violence permitted.[76]

Just as with the hero Rāma in his eponymous epic, the sojourn in the forest is a period in which a dormant or nascent kingship receives or undergoes further trial and edification before the throne is fully retrieved, as both young kings

[74] Bhīma makes his threatening speech acts at II.61.45, 63.14, and 64.10; all of his oaths eventually have effect. From II.68.20 to 68.46, all four younger brothers vow their revenge. This is the only intimation of violence during this scene at court.

[75] The Āraṇyaka *parvan*, like most of the Śānti *parvan*, is generally a poem of edification and moral discourse with occasional and brief *kṣatriya* interludes.

[76] There is the also rite of abduction of a bride where violence is almost staged, but such—as part of the narrative of the poem—occurs on a secondary register. This is the *rākṣasa* form of marriage rite, appropriate to *kṣatriyas* and kings. Bhīṣma abducted the three Kāṣi girls as brides for Vicitravīrya, for instance. See McGrath 2009, 51–62; Jamison 1996, 218–235.

embrace their unjust ordeal without rancour.[77] In his rustic retreat, Yudhiṣṭhira—as king—is surrounded by his brothers whose functions are characterised as:

> tvaṃ vai dharmān vijānīṣe yudhāṃ vettā dhanaṃjayaḥ
> hantārīṇāṃ bhīmaseno nakulas tvarthasaṃgrahī
> saṃyantā sahadevas tu dhaumyo brahmaviduttamaḥ
> dharmārthakuśalā caiva draupadī dharmacāriṇī
>
> II.69.8
>
> You know the dharmas; Dhanaṃjaya, a knower of battles;
> Bhīmasena, a killer of enemies; Nakula, a grasper of wealth;
> Sahadeva, the controller; Dhaumya, a best knower of prayer;
> And Draupadī, moving in dharma, skilled in dharma and policy.

This is the royal entourage as it sets off towards the forest. Yudhiṣṭhira is said to be *vastreṇa saṃvṛtya mukhaṃ* (having covered his face with a garment), such is the remorse of the king who has brought shame and humiliation upon his brothers and wife (II.71.3). Thus it is that his folly, in fatal combination with the irate delusiveness of Duryodhana, has set on course the movement that will lead to *bheda* 'the partition' of the kingdom and the clan, and the destruction of the lives of many other associated kings. At this instant in the poem the narrative assumes an impetus that is seemingly irreversible.

***

Curiously, at this point the poets then say of Duryodhana and his immediate companions that:

> droṇaṃ dvīpam amanyanta rājyaṃ cāsmai nyavedayan
>
> II.71.32
>
> They believed Droṇa a protector and offered the kingdom to him.

It is suddenly as if *mahārāja* Dhṛtarāṣṭra did not exist, that sovereignty at Hāstinapura was a commodity, and that Duryodhana with his warriors was a broker in this. Droṇa of course rejects the offer, but nevertheless this is a strange line and casts the idea of Kuru kingship into an unusual light. It is as if kingship is something that is almost an independent entity and moves about the various princely or heroic figures at will, such is the mobility of what is essentially and apparently just a sign. Again, this is a fashion that is kindred to what we know of *saṅgha* practice, where an oligarchy supports what is a titular office.

77 The *ṛṣi* Mārkaḍeya comments on this analogy with Rāma when he speaks to Yudhiṣṭhira at III.26.7.

Then the old king's poet and performer of much of the central components of the epic, Saṃjaya, also makes a curious remark. He says (giving strong emphasis to his words by a repetitive display of the term *vasu* 'the earth'):

avāpya vasusaṃpūrṇāṃ vasudhāṃ vasudhādhipa

II.72.3

O lord of the earth, having obtained the earth replete with wealth ...

It is as if the poet is speaking sarcastically and cynically addressing the weakness of the old ruler, for Dhṛtarāṣṭra certainly has acquired nothing except that he might now reclaim Indraprastha.[78] Once again, the actual performance or speech itself is what would project the nuance behind such words towards an interpretative audience, in which the words through the drama become effectively metaphorical. Unfortunately, we, as readers, no longer have access—except occasionally—to that dimension of the poem.

However, what the poets have portrayed is a confusion and lack of focal and controlling authority in this kingdom, where sovereignty is suddenly available to the strange play of protocol and exchange. The three figures involved—the blind old king, his son, and his nephew—are all incapable of monitoring power, no matter what their projects venture in the world; the political culture of Hāstinapura and of the Bhārata Song is such that custom itself diminishes any centripetal and dominant kingship. It is only with the brutality and carnage of war at the field of Kurukṣetra that such indeterminacy is resolved, and by then the Bhāratas as a clan are wrecked, and the Yādavas triumph.

In the Nalopakhyāna (the story of Nala), the young king is foolish enough to allow himself to be intoxicated by a dicing match in which he loses the kingdom and soon loses his wife and mental equilibrium (III.50ff. The micro-narrative is told for didactic reasons as a lesson to Yudhiṣṭhira, and one might infer that the drama that ensues after the *rājasūya* was similarly edifying for whoever composed those early audiences—for such audiences we can presume were fully receptive to both the nuances of myth within the poem and the dramatisation of expression in the poem's living and voiced production.

***

Just as the Kurukṣetra Books and the ritual of war are followed by the edifying discourses of the Śānti and Anuśāsana *parvans*, so too the *rājasūya* leads into

[78] The figure of Maitreya is about to enter the poem and to address the old king; whether he is intended—by the poets or editors—to be the *future* Buddha, the fifth Buddha, or simply a Buddhist personage, is a moot point. He is referred to as *bhagavān ṛṣi* (the lord *ṛṣi*) (III.11.18). Maitreya tells Dhṛtarāṣṭra: *sadā hy abhyadhikaḥ snehaḥ prītiś ca tvayi me* (for my exceeding love and affection are always for you) (III.11.14).

the long duration of the Āraṇyaka *parvan* and its extended teaching: there is a structural similarity here.[79] For a narrative period of twelve years, kingship in *bhāratavarṣa* is simply ignored; the poem pays no attention to what happens to political authority during this interlude and Yudhiṣṭhira remains a curiously recessive protagonist. Yet, almost in counterpoint to the forest situation, there is the situation of Duryodhana during this period of the epic, for while the Pāṇḍavas are in exile, Karṇa addresses his patron and friend as *rājan* and *mahārāja* (III.226.8 and 12).

It is as if the *rājasūya* has suddenly spun awry, and kingship and the integrity of power becomes disoriented and skewed as the poem deliberately obfuscates the location and centrality of king and sovereignty, creating contradictions within the narrative that supply greater complexity to the epic.[80] Aggressive forest *gandharvas* similarly refer to *rājā duryodhana*, and thus the clarity of rule within the poem becomes dispersed and centrifugal, making the progress of the narrative much less dynamic, as power becomes merely ostensible and shadowy.[81] The *dharma* of kingship has become blurred, and this only increases as the poem moves forward; when Yudhiṣṭhira proposes a policy of *jñātidharma* (the *dharma* of kinship), the dissolution of what constitutes correct *rājya* advances even more towards entropy (III.233.2). In the same vein, when Duryodhana, having been thoroughly and ignobly defeated by these *gandharvas*, determines to surrender his position and commit suicide, he tells his brother Duḥśāsana:[82]

pratīccha tvaṃ mayā dattam abhiṣekaṃ nṛpo bhava[83]

III.238.22

Accept the royal unction given by me to you: be king!

79 Sukthankar, in his Introduction to the 1942 Pune Edition of the Āraṇyaka *parvan*, Part 1, p. xiv, comments: "As Pisani has pointed out in his paper on the 'Rise of the *Mahābhārata*,' the bulk of the didactic and episodic matter has been used to fill up the great 'temporal hiatuses' in the narrative, namely, in the first place, the twelve years of exile in the forest (Āraṇyaka), and then the long interval between the end of the Bhārata War and the last adventure of the Pāṇḍavas (Śānti and Anuśāsana) ... In a not different manner Homer introduces often dialogue and episodic stories when he must conceal the flowing of times without noteworthy events ... The episodic material is largely Purāṇic in character." [For Pisani, see *A Volume of Eastern and Indian Studies presented to Prof. F. W. Thomas* (1939, p. 170).]

80 J. P. Sharma (1968, 240), commenting on the *saṅghas*, notes: "The inherent weaknesses of republicanism, clearly noticed by Kauṭilya and the compilers of the *Mahābhārata*, were also chief factors leading to the downfall of the republics."

81 Duryodhana is even referred to by the poets as *dhārtarāṣṭro janādhipaḥ* (the Dhārtarāṣṭra lord of the people) (III.240.44).

82 Aspects of this ritual are described at III.239.16–17.

83 The morbid Duryodhana orders Kṛpa to install Aśvatthāman as *senāpati* 'commander' (at IX,64,40), and the verb is this same term: *drauṇiṃ rājño niyogena senāpatye'bhyaṣecayat* (he anointed the son of Droṇa as *senāpati*, directed by the king).

So the audience perceives an even greater decentralisation of kingship as it founders between the two moieties of the clan. Duryodhana's commission to his brother, as the 'next' king, is to *praśādhi pṛthīvīṃ* (command the world), and *pālaya medhinīm* (protect the land), which are the two fundamental tasks of any ruler (III.238.22 and 25). It is with subtlety that the poets grant princely authority to the person they are presently singing of, and simultaneously disband and emphasise the protean placement of kingship. It is not quite a condition of turmoil, but of mobility, as a labile kingship shifts among characters, a condition that has existed ever since the *rājasūya* went strangely wrong. Instead of empowering the king, the ritual actual completely destabilised Yudhiṣṭhira and also the clan.

All this becomes more reified and precise again when Duryodhana, urged on by his friend Karṇa, decides that his supremacy is such that *he* will have a *rājasūya* performed in *his* own name. When the *purohita* (the domestic priest) arrives, however, to receive this charge, he informs Duryodhana that such is not possible for two reasons. Firstly, Yudhiṣṭhira is still alive, and, since he had already performed this ritual, no one else could accomplish it; and, secondly, the old king Dhṛtarāṣṭra continues to live, implying that Duryodhana was not yet king (III.241.226–227). The priest recommends that Duryodhana have another rite performed, the unconventional *vaiṣṇavo yajña* (the Viṣṇu sacrifice); nevertheless, the poets continue to refer to Duryodhana as *dhārtarāṣṭra mahīpatiḥ* (the Dhārtarāṣṭra great king) (III.241.34). The Pāṇḍavas are invited to attend this *kraturāja* (king of rituals), which involves a *sauvarṇaṃ* ... *lāṅgalaṃ* (a golden plough) that is employed to ceremonially plough a sacred enclosure; this is to be done by the *rājā dhārtarāṣṭro janeśvaraḥ* (lord of the people the Dhārtarāṣṭra king) (III.242.2–3).[84] Duryodhana, now a royal sacrificer himself, accomplishes the sacrifice at which many kings attend, and he then distributes material largesse among the *brāhmaṇas*; so he becomes ritually entitled to assume the office of kingship, even though this rite is uncommon and seemingly *ad hoc*.

Yudhiṣṭhira replies negatively to messengers who arrive in order to invite him to participate at the event since this would have implied his acceptance of his cousin's new title; in his dismissal of them he refers to *rājā suyodhana* (king Suyodhana), a name of Duryodhana, (III.242.11). As the text is all that we have of what was once a performance, we—as readers—are presently unable to judge whether this word *rāja* was spoken in cynical or sarcastic repetition of the language of the *dūta* 'the messenger', or whether the term is employed as a real gesture of formal respect. In the subsequent *adhyāya*, the poets refer to

[84] Allen (2012, 43) has an interesting footnote on this rite: "This recalls the Scythian origin myth, where a golden plough and yoke represent the third function (Dumézil 1966, 446–448)."

Duryodhana as *rājasattamam* (most excellent of kings). Even Arjuna, about to join battle with the Kaurava force in the Virāṭa *parvan*, refers to Duryodhana as 'king': *rājānaṃ nātra paśyāmi* (I do not see the king here) (IV.48.11). However, during the political negotiations that immediately precede war, when Saṃjaya—commissioned by Dhṛtarāṣṭra—visits Yudhiṣṭhira and the latter is formally enquiring as to the well-being of those in the court at Hāstinapura, Yudhiṣṭhira only refers to the old king as *rāja* and never offers this title to Duryodhana, who is merely mentioned in passing as the 'son' (V.23.7–19 and 26.1–28).[85] In the full *sabhā*, however, when Kṛṣṇa acts as Pāṇḍava ambassador, he addresses Duryodhana as *rājan* (V.126.20).

Thus, there actually *is* a precedent or sensibility for how kingship is to be established, and, when the poets sing of Duryodhana being addressed as 'king', this is simply part of the drama of the narrative and not an acknowledgment of hierarchical practice. Such is the depth of the dramatic tension in the poem, where custom is presented in a fashion that also brings emotional modelling to the song.

There are two senses of kingship at work then (or a minimum of two senses of the word): that of custom, and that of poetic tension and theatrical presentation. In the latter usage, the poets modulate this idea in a manner that privileges poetics or aesthetics above the practical usage or application of kingship, and there is no judgement in this since only a theatre of gestural performance exists. They can achieve this because kingship is arguably the one master signifier in the epic that dominates the narrative, acting as a *currency*, as it were, which organises how the characters in this economy of metaphors operate: the trope is constantly being interpreted and reinterpreted and taken on by a spectrum of characters—whomever the poets are speaking of at any particular moment.

The poets close this sequence in the narrative by saying:

> dhārtarāṣṭro'pi nṛpatiḥ praśaśāsa vasuṃdharām
>
> III.243.22
>
> Then the king of people, the son of Dhṛtarāṣṭra, ruled the earth.[86]

Thus, the place of kingship has moved, although ritual priority still remains with Yudhiṣṭhira, the sacrificer, who had performed the *rājasūya*; its initial displacement occurred during the gambling, itself a rite that was aleatory and non-solemn.

The reality and practicality of kingship, or, shall we say, its intrinsic convertibility—what is in fact an aspect of *saṅgha* politics—is such that Duryodhana,

[85] Saṃjaya, however, in his response to Yudhiṣṭhira, does refer to Duryodhana as 'king' (V.25.12).

[86] At V.46.9, Duryodhana is even said to be *kururāja* (king of the Kurus), a powerful and unusual statement.

being forceful and dynamic enough, is able to claim authority without hindrance and rule from Hāstinapura. Duryodhana as *nṛpati* is a sacrificer of a minor impromptu rite that is amplified and given an air of superior magnitude; he is more a figure of ambition and cleverness, though one who works with his maternal uncle, his brothers, and with Karṇa, and he is someone who enjoys an unalloyed success in exploiting ritual protocol. The poets cast *rāja* Duryodhana in such a sharp light, and, as a character to be staged by the poets, he must have been a coruscating figure of unpredictable ebullience.[87]

***

Let us now make a summary digression and turn for a moment to Yudhiṣṭhira's counterpart during this period of the epic, for this is the time of Duryodhana's ascendancy and attempt at the office of kingship. He is an uncommon and slightly *uncanny* character in the poem, and he is—earlier on during the Āraṇyaka *parvan* and unlike all the other heroes in the story—taken down into the *rasātalam* 'underworld' by a feminine daemon, Kṛtyā, who was *mahādbhutā* 'most amazing' (III.239.22ff.). There he was given an underworldly vision and told by the Dānavas about his remarkable destiny and his own unique personage (III.240.1–24). As we shall see, there is something odd, if not unique, about Duryodhana, because he is not quite human and possesses these otherworldly qualities, which appear at times simply as manifestations of mere grandiosity and haughtiness. The question is: are these qualities part of the drama or part of the very *nature* of his identity?

Long after the royal rite and after the years of forest exile, there occurs one particular speech by Duryodhana that more than any other speech by him exemplifies his sense of sovereign office; or, it indicates how the poets are representing Duryodhana as a different *kind* of kingly figure—and possibly even unhuman. The speech occurs in the *sabhā* at Hāstinapura, and the moment is when Saṃjaya, as a *dūta* or 'ambassador', has returned from the Pāṇḍava court and has just reported the verbal exchange that happened on that mission.

Immediately prior to this speech, the poets say that Duryodhana is *atyamarṣana*, 'overbearing' or 'haughty', and that his words are charged with *krodha* 'rage'.[88] I quote this speech at length since it is exceptional and remarkable:

[87] Both the Chopra version of the *Mahābhārata* and the more recent Star TV version of the epic cast Duryodhana as the most dramatic and volatile figure in the whole series.

[88] I think of *krodha* as 'rage', an emotion that is beyond control, unlike *manyu* 'anger', which is a condition that is far more modulated in its discharge. The former cannot be suppressed, whereas the latter can be restrained or resisted until it is finally released in an act of volition. The term *kopa*, also translated as 'anger', is more related to resentment. In the Ṛg Veda, *manyu* possesses a more cosmic sense, as in X.83 where it is almost deified or at least, personified; this quality is lost from the usage of the word in the epic.

yad vā paramakaṃ tejo yena yuktā divaukasaḥ
mamāpy anupamaṃ bhūyo devebhyo viddhi bhārata
pradīryamāṇāṃ vasudhāṃ girīṇāṃ śikharāṇi ca
lokasya paśyato rājan sthāpayāmy abhimantraṇāt
cetanācetanasyāsya jaṅgamasthāvarasya ca
vināśāya samutpannaṃ mahāghoraṃ mahāsvanam
aśmavarṣaṃ ca vāyuṃ ca śamayāmīha nityaśaḥ
jagataḥ paśyato'bhīkṣṇaṃ bhūtānām anukampayā
stambhitāsvapsu gacchanti mayā rathapadātayaḥ
devāsurāṇāṃ bhāvānām aham ekaḥ pravartitā

V.60.10

Whatever the supreme energy by which the celestials are joined,
Know mine as matchless, greater than the deities, Bhārata!
As the world observes, O king, from mantras I shall station
The shattering earth, mountains, and peaks,
I shall calm eternally the terrible and very noisy wind
And stony shower arisen for the destruction
Of the sentient and insentient and of the fixed and mobile,
As the world constantly watches; I, compassionate for creatures.
Soldiers and chariots go on waters stabilised by me,
I alone am the motivator of the being of devas and asuras!

Such claims of magnitude continue further and close with an announcement that:

parā buddhiḥ paraṃ tejo vīryaṃ ca paramaṃ mayi
parā vidyā paro yogo mama tebhyo viśiṣyate

V.60.27

High wisdom, high energy and high heroism in me,
High knowledge, my high yoga, are distinguished from them ... [—the Pāṇḍava alliance].

The poets are here supplying Duryodhana with a supernatural omni-competence and omnipotent position in the universe, giving him this voice of divine force.[89] These are not words—unlike the occasional theophanic pronouncements

[89] Malinar (2012, 62–63) explains this action that Duryodhana claims about the 'waters' by saying: "The first passage [in the PCE Appendix] deals with the ideal king and cultural hero Pṛthu Vainya ... One of his fundamental life-procuring deeds is the 'stabilisation' of the waters, which here means that he lays down their course toward the ocean (*saṃstambhayann āpaḥ samudram abhiyāsyataḥ*, Mbh. 7, App. I, No. 8, line 779). Duryodhana near the end of his speech will announce that he will destroy his enemies, whom he compares (5.60.24d–25) to rivers that meet their end in the ocean." Malinar (2012, 63–68) examines at length Duryodhana's connection with images of water throughout the epic; and closes her beautiful essay by saying that Duryodhana is a "spellbinder of royal power" (77).

of Kṛṣṇa—that are informed by any *vaiṣṇava* position. In fact, this is a voice that is almost primaeval and pre-brahminical, and it is as if Duryodhana speaks like a *shaman* in a manner that is even pre-Vedic.[90] These are mere reflections, though, for we possess no real material evidence to continue with such a line of inference.[91] He does mention the *prajāḥ* 'populace' who live *viṣaye ... me* (in my kingdom), and one should recall that he delivers this speech in the full plenum of the *sabhā*, among all the assembled kings and allies, the aristocracy of *bhāratavarṣa* (V.60.16–17). One can imagine the poets playing such a speech with great metaphorical theatricality and histrionic stress.

Is this simply the proud and magniloquent boasting of a maniac? Or is the audience being guided toward the perception of a truly universal figure? Remember that these are the words of a great ruler—if they possess even mythical veracity. Duryodhana also announces that whatever he directs his attention towards actually happens and occurs; the word he uses is *abhidhyāmy ahaṃ* (I intend). However, it is in a conceptual or mental sense, and he says that *bhaviṣyatīdam iti vā yad bravīmi* (whatever I say, it becomes), which is actually magical thought; and he adds that *satyavāg iti māṃ viduḥ* (they know me as the truth-speaker) (V.60.21–22).[92] Is it simply that the poets are demonstrating that it is Duryodhana who has *won* the true consequences of the *rājasūya* from his cousin and presently considers himself superbly paramount? This period in the poem between the *rājasūya* and the battle of Kurukṣetra is a strangely amorphous and polysemic period in the narrative, which is possibly what the poets intended. Whatever the place or function of this unique speech in the epic, old Dhṛtarāṣṭra later confesses to the *ṛṣi* Nārada—despite his completely superior position—that *na tvīśo bhagavann aham* (I am not powerful, sir) (V.122.1). Duryodhana has thus managed to confound and emotionally overpower the old man, as well as bedazzle the allies and court in the assembled *sabhā*.

One of the problems in attempting to analyse a point or theme in the *Mahābhārata* is that—because the poem is so syncretic and compounded of

90 Solely in terms of the narrative, his *hauteur* is akin to that of Yayāti in the Ādi *parvan* (I.83.2).

91 Towards the end of the Udyoga *parvan*, when the two armies are being described, as they prepare to assemble at Kurukṣetra, it is the army of Duryodhana, depicted at V.152.1ff., that appears more 'archaic' than that of the Kauravas, which is portrayed at V.149.52ff. In the army of Duryodhana, for instance, there is much technical emphasis given to chariots and to charioteers: *caturyugo rathāḥ sarve* (all chariots yoked with four horses) (V.152.9–12).

92 Perhaps as an another aspect of this mantric capacity, when Duryodhana is being addressed by the *ṛṣī* Maitreya, the poets describe him as *kṛtvā caraṇenālikhan mahīm* (having marked the earth with his foot) (III.11.29). One wonders what these marks would indicate for Duryodhana? We should also recall that in the newly constructed palace at Indraprastha, when Duryodhana visited, he was easily easily deluded by *trompe l'oeil*, and was subject to optical error (II.46.26–35). Perhaps this too is another element that indicates the *otherworldly* nature of his senses.

many different components and sources, however well integrated these elements might be (meaning any one point in the text can be overridden or ignored at other points in the epic)—there is no uniform and unified judgement (or even formulation) of events or even values as words shift in their interpretation and metaphorical perspective. It is not a synoptic text. For instance, not long after this scene in the *sabhā*, the poets report in direct speech what the *kuravaḥ saṃgatā* (the assembled Kurus) say among themselves about Duryodhana:

pramūḍhā pṛthivī sarvā mṛtyupāśasitā kṛtā
duryodhanasya bāliśyān naitad astīti cābruvan

V.135.26

All the foolish earth is made noosed by death
Because of the thoughtlessness of Duryodhana; and it is not right, they said.

Once again the poets or the editors allow an unspecific and popular voice in the poem to comment upon the situation of kingship or putative kingship. Such a communal voice *only* appears vis-à-vis the place and function of a king as it appears and recedes in the poetry. The audience does not hear of this social persona otherwise or elsewhere for it arises and vanishes and takes on no enduring characteristic, yet it is constantly intrinsic to any functioning of the epic polity. The one exception is in the kingdom Bhīṣma later portrays, which—as we shall see—refers to a thoroughly different political scenario.

As another element of this oddly archaic nature that often seems to encompass the figure of Duryodhana, in the great Droṇa *parvan*, Droṇa, as *senāpati* (commander of the army), at one point binds onto his king an unusual and invulnerable armour so that he becomes invincible:

eṣa te kavacaṃ rājaṃs tathā badhnāmi kāñcanam
yathā na bāṇā nāstrāṇi viṣahiṣyanti te rāṇe

VII.69.35

As I bind this golden breastplate to you, O king,
So no arrow nor missile shall overpower you in battle.

Droṇa—with potent incantations and *mantras* functioning as a speech act—charges this armour with a miraculous tenacity that had originally derived from the Mahādeva Śiva himself. Once again, Duryodhana, unlike his rival and counterpart Yudhiṣṭhira, is shown in a peculiarly outlandish light.[93] Certainly,

[93] We shall later review a scene where Yudhiṣṭhira finally makes his victorious entry into Hāstinapura and a *rākṣasa* 'demon' figure appears and verbally arraigns him. The poets say, *eṣa duryodhanasakhā cārvāko nāma rākṣasaḥ* (This *rākṣasa* named Cārvāka, a friend of Duryodhana) (XII.39.33). Again, there is this uncanny association between the daemonic and Duryodhana.

Yudhiṣṭhira is only half-human, for his paternal genealogy is divine, while Duryodhana is fully mortal; yet the latter often manifests ancient and supernatural qualities, whereas *rāja* Yudhiṣṭhira behaves in a fully human manner.

One should recall that at the end of his life, in the Śalya *parvan*, Duryodhana enters a pond or lake and remains submerged beneath the waters that he had caused to become stiff or stationary: *astambhayata toyaṃ ca māyayā* (and he hardened the water with magic) (IX.28.52).[94] On arriving at this lake, Yudhiṣṭhira remarks to Kṛṣṇa: *paśyemāṃ dhārtarāṣṭreṇa māyām apsu prayojitām viṣṭabhya salilaṃ śete* (Look at this enchantment employed by the son of Dhṛtarāṣṭra! Having made firm the water he lies in the waters!) (IX.30.3). This is, he adds, *daivīṃ māyām* 'divine magic', and he says to his opponent:

> śūramānī na śūras tvaṃ mithyā vadasi bhārata
>
> IX.30.25
>
> Boastful of heroism, you are not a hero: you speak vainly, Bhārata!

There is something more than exuberant and primitive about Duryodhana that makes him exceptional; he is not simply the grandiose *kṣatriya* who is adept at being brazen nor is he merely a fractious and quarrelsome prince who is intent on power and war. It is for these reasons that he is able to transform the empowerment of the *rājasūya* rite through the *vaiṣṇava* ritual into something personally overbearing and almost cosmic. The preliterate tradition of *Mahābhārata* poetry coalesces so many differing genres into the single epic—Vedic, pre-Hindu, Hindu, even Jainism and Buddhism—that it is impossible now for a reader to isolate and identify such ancient patterns specifically and precisely.[95] These uncanny qualities of Duryodhana stem from particularly Śaivite traditions, what later came to be known as *tantra*. Whatever the source of these cultural paradigms, they nevertheless remain integral to the nature of Duryodhana's demonstration of kingship.

Then, when Duryodhana does finally succumb and collapses, towards the end of the Śalya *parvan*, the whole cosmos reacts, with winds and seismic movements, meteors and showers of dust, drums, conches, and animal sounds; all

[94] At X.19.14, Śiva is similarly immersed and hidden in the waters and performing *tapas*. In the Sauptika *parvan*, Kṛṣṇa tells of how Rudra Mahādeva, commanded by Brahmā to create creatures, submerged himself in the waters in order to make these beings (X.17.14–20). Duryodhana also makes the unusual and unique simile in an early argument with his father, where he accuses the elder of being *nāvi naur iva saṃyatā* (like a boat enclosed in a boat)—the image being that the father is hindering the son (II.50.10).

[95] By pre-Hindu I think of all those indigenous elements of early Indian religious culture that preceded the Indo-Āryan migrations and that might or might not have been part of Indus civilization. See Klostermeier (1984), for instance.

these are heard and unearthly creatures are observed (IX.57.46–59). It is as if the universe itself cries out in anguish, such is the strange and almost inhuman quality of this heroic Kaurava king.[96]

> nadyaś ca sumahāvegāḥ pratisrotovahābhavan
>
> IX.57.55
>
> And fast rivers were bearing backwards.

Sometime later, as Duryodhana lies dying upon the earth, the poets describe that *gandharvas*, *siddhas*, and *apsaras* were heard singing in the sky while fragrant breezes moved, and:

> apatat sumahad varṣaṃ puṣpāṇāṃ puṇyagandhinām
>
> IX.60.51
>
> A very great shower of auspiciously smelling flowers fell.

Such is both the preternatural and natural registry of Duryodhana's kingliness, despite all of his wrongdoing and follies, and, unlike any of the Pāṇḍavas, he dies a hero's death. The universe recognises his sacral kingship, which is deemed divine in origin, a kingship that originated from the moment that Yudhiṣṭhira determined to gather the obligatory wealth that would allow him to celebrate the 'royal unction'. Duryodhana's single egregious error was to offend and insult in such deprecatory manner the menstruating Draupadī; the wrath generated thereby became the fuel that drove the Pāṇḍavas—thanks to the direction of their ally Kṛṣṇa—to destroy the Kaurava prince. Also, Duryodhana's strange and uncanny shamanistic qualities necessarily put him on the margins of this narrative about Kuru society.

***

The third and final stage in the effects of the troubled *rājasūya* occurs during the formalities of the Udyoga *parvan*. When Kṛṣṇa as *dūta* or 'ambassador' arrives at Hāstinapura with a commission from Yudhiṣṭhira to secure some recognition of Pāṇḍava status, he makes four visits before he actually delivers his message. Firstly, he visits the *gṛha* 'house' of Dhṛtarāṣṭra, where he is received *yathānyāyaṃ* 'appropriately' (V.87.19), and there *govindaḥ sarvān parihasan kurūn āste* (Govinda was laughing with all the Kurus). Then he visits his *pitṛṣvasaraṃ*, his 'paternal aunt', Kuntī, where he is met with great affection to which he responds similarly as he listens to his aunt's lengthy inquiry about her sons and their wife. Next, he goes to the *gṛha* of Duryodhana who is surrounded *rājasahasraiś ca kurubhiś ca*

[96] Gitomer (1992) has carefully examined these unearthly, if not divine, aspects of Duryodhana and the benign aspect of his death.

(by thousands of kings and by the Kurus); Duryodhana is said to be *ādīnam āsane* (sitting on a stool) (V.89.4). There Kṛṣṇa rejects all formal and ritual hospitality and soon repairs to the dwelling of Vidura, the half-uncle of Duryodhana, where he accepts refreshment and stays for the night.

In this progression, one can discern a certain ranking of political stature, where Kṛṣṇa places his paternal aunt above Duryodhana, and where he only really accepts the hospitality of Vidura, the half-brother of Dhṛtarāṣṭra (V.89.39–92.6). Diplomacy, even in these archaic and ostensibly Bronze Age times, was as subtle and as nuanced as it is today, where manner and implication or even gesture are more profoundly communicative and telling than actual speech. Kṛṣṇa, in conversation with Vidura, here refers to himself as *mitra* 'friend', which is an ancient term and one that corresponds with a sense of 'alliance' and 'right'. He says:

> jñātīnāṃ hi mitho bhede yan mitraṃ nābhipadyate
> sarvayatnena madhyasthaṃ na tan mitraṃ vidur budhāḥ
>
> V.91.15
>
> When a false friend—stationed midway—does not endeavour with all effort
> In the mutual partition of kin, the wise know that he is no friend.

It is this friendship that surrounds the tenacity and formality of a king and all his activity.[97] This idea of *mitra* is not simply emotional, but is also deeply formal and political, and is, in fact, constitutive of kingship; in terms of the Pāṇḍava, it is specifically constituted by his brothers and at large by his *saṅgha* or clan 'association'.

It is only on the next day that Kṛṣṇa delivers his message, and there the old king Dhṛtarāṣṭra is treated as the sole and senior authority or power. Kṛṣṇa addresses him thus:

> tvaṃ hi vārayitā śreṣṭhaḥ kurūṇāṃ kurusattama
>
> V.93.8
>
> For you, O best of the Kurus, are the best protector of the Kurus![98]

He says to him that, after the *rājasūya*, Yudhiṣṭhira *na ca tvām atyavartata* (did not exceed you) (V.93.56). More specifically, Yudhiṣṭhira respected the old king's primacy and superior standing in the kingdom. Now, this is not exactly true, not if he had just performed the paramount royal ritual. It is interesting how the

97 See McGrath 2013 on the dynamic importance of "friendship" in epic *Mahābhārata*.

98 *Vārayitā*, from √*vṛ* 'to restrain', which concerns a king's fundamental control of *all* violence in a polity, the sole right to the *daṇḍa*.

poets rarely make a moral judgement about the figures in the poem, but represent the character or the speeches from the speaker's point of view, leaving the audience to bear judgement as to both meaning and veracity.[99] We tend to forget that the poets were *actors* who did not simply state their words but *demonstrated* their interpretations of such language. This—as in this instant—can even reach to the extent of either misdirection or untruth, leaving the audience in the place of critical appraisal. Such a form of poetics reveals how dramatic the poetry was, and not simply in a performative manner, but also substantively: the *truth* of the poets is not only literal nor mimetic but must always be interpreted, just like metaphor.[100]

***

The narrative style of the epic is such that, when a crucial situation arises, there is often a pause in the movement of the poem and someone tells a story, illustrating the *dharma* or likely 'moral' of the moment.[101] After Kṛṣṇa's speech to the Kauravas in the *sabhā*, and after Duryodhana had walked out of the assembly *mahānāga iva śvasan* (sighing like a great snake), the ambassador tells his audience that:

> bhojarājasya vṛddhasya durācāro hy anātmavān
> jīvataḥ pitur aiśvaryaṃ hṛtvā manyuvaśaṃ gataḥ ...
> āhukaḥ punar asmābhir jñātibhiś cāpi satkṛtaḥ
> ugrasenaḥ kṛto rājā bhojarājany avardhanaḥ
>
> V.126.36

99 The exception to this is, of course, Saṃjaya's constant critical refrain where he judges his old king and patron Dhṛtarāṣṭra in a negative light, always blaming him for the downfall of the clan; so many of his speeches to the old *mahārāja* begin with such a statement. See McGrath 2011 for the poetics of Saṃjaya.

100 As an aside here, one should note that Sātyaki is once glossed as *iṅgitajñaḥ kaviḥ* (one who is knowing of signs or covert purpose, gifted with insight) (V.128.9) *Kavi* is also a noun that indicates a 'poet', someone who is a 'knower'.

101 Just prior to these words of Kṛṣṇa there occurs a peculiar instant in the poem where two speakers are heard to declaim a speech of seventeen *ślokas* (V.124.1). This happens when Bhīṣma and Droṇa simultaneously respond to the words of Dhṛtarāṣṭra, who is encouraging his son to act in accord with the ambassador Kṛṣṇa. The poets say: *bhīṣmadroṇau ... duryodhanam idaṃ vākyam ūcatuḥ* (Bhīṣma and Droṇa both spoke this speech to Duryodhana). The dual inflection of both subject and verb indicates that the language is spoken by *both* heroes simultaneously, perhaps for emphasis and effect. It is, to my present knowledge, completely unusual for this to occur, and one wonders how the poets achieved such a dramatic moment; this rare *duo* lasts for several minutes. There is one similar instance at V.94.21, where Nara and Nārāyaṇa speak jointly, and the poets refer to this by saying *ūcatuḥ*, but they are technically *one* person. Does a single poet speak *as if* joining both persons, in which case the duals simply signify this action; or, were there actually *two* poets who joined their words together vocally in order to achieve such an end? There are many occurrences in the poem of two speakers acting together in *duo*, but there is no other occasion where two speakers sing their lines jointly.

The unconstrained and bad [son] of old king Bhoja,
Overtaken by anger, having seized the sovereignty of his living father ...
Ugrasena Āhuka the good [father], thriver of the Bhoja kṣatriyas,
by us and the kin was made king again.

As we have observed above, Duryodhana brings counterpoint to the picture of kingship with which the poets delineate *rāja* Yudhiṣṭhira. Here, in this small anecdote there is given—in allegorical form—an account of a belligerent son who ousts his father and who is then himself ousted by his *kṣatriya* kin and the former sovereignty reestablished. Kṛṣṇa then urges the members present in the assembly to 'bind' Duryodhana and his gang and so maintain the ascendance of the old king. Kingship in the *Mahābhārata* almost always seems to be modulated by clan, by the senior members of that *kṣatriya* group that constitute a *saṅgha*. Kingship is not absolute in the Mauryan sense, although later, during the discourse of Bhīṣma, it certainly appears to approximate to such a state.[102]

Gāndhārī is then drawn into the *sabhā* where she speaks critically of both her irate son and her husband. She comments on the folly of the old king: *rājyapradāne muḍhasya ... dhṛtarāṣṭro' śnute phalam* (Dhṛtarāṣṭra obtains the fruit of the donation of the kingdom to a fool) (V.127.13). *Rājyapradāna* is a technical term that denotes the handing over of kingship to another—typically the son—by an extant king who has attained the age of wishing to enter into a renunciant life of *vanāśrama* 'forest retreat', which is desirable and recommended for those who are elderly and whose grandchildren have appeared in the world.[103]

As a curious coda to all this formal activity, during their dialogue on a chariot towards the end of the Udyoga *parvan*, Kṛṣṇa, whether honestly or rightfully, seeks to convince Karṇa—who is his maternal cousin, let us not forget—that he should be the paramount Kuru king, one whom both Pāṇḍavas and Dhārtarāṣṭras will honour in his consecration and rule. Kṛṣṇa even concludes his speech by addressing Karṇa as *kaunteya* (son of Kuntī) (V.138.8–28). Karṇa responds quite simply by saying:

yadi jānāti māṃ rājā dharmātmā saṃśitavrataḥ
kuntyāḥ prathamajaṃ putraṃ na sa rājyaṃ grahīṣyati

V.139.21

[102] One wonders how Nīlakaṇṭha conceived of kingship, given that he lived and flourished in the latter years of Moghul dominion in Northern India; and with what knowledge did he view the extremely distant and ancient past?

[103] A similar custom perhaps explains why old king Laertes in the *Odyssey* had retreated from a position of kingship to live a simple and rural life away from the town in Scrolls xi.187 and xxiv.

If the Dharmarājā, whose régime is sharp, knows me
The first-born son of Kuntī, he will not take the kingdom.

This unique scene takes the model of Kuru kingship—as expressed by the poem—even one step further, removing it from the domain of either Yudhiṣṭhira or Duryodhana. Again, an audience hears how the poets are constantly representing differing points of view concerning this focal motif of the epic, for there is no one single narrative dimension or position. Kingship is an idea that is constantly in motion. It is friable and variable, both conceptually and practically. There is no 'gold standard' as it were, for kingship, and the nature of the office is that it is something to be constantly negotiated or performed as if it were a diagram being passed from hand to hand among a group of associates or company and needs constant reinterpretation. Kingship has, in this view, no fixed value.

Gāndhārī, however, speaking to her son in the *sabhā* towards the close of this *parvan*, moves the argument or focus one more time, when she says:

rājyaṃ kurūṇām anupūrvabhogyaṃ kramāgato naḥ kuladharma eṣaḥ

V.146.29

The kingdom of the Kurus is to be enjoyed by succession, our inheritance is this clan-dharma.

Kingship is here to be subject to the judgement of the clan, she claims.[104] Then she follows up her interpretation by adding:

rājyaṃ tu pāṇḍor idam apradhṛṣyaṃ
tasyādya putrāḥ prabhavanti nānye

V.146.32

This kingdom of Pāṇḍu is inviolable.
The sons of him now rule, not anyone else.

This is the view of the queen at Hāstinapura, so unlike that of her husband or her eldest son. Again, the audience perceives this multidimensionality of what goes to constitute active kingship: it is something to be arrived at by contest and is thereafter highly unstable and mutable. It is also subject to many simultaneous perceptions, and, as we have noted, even after the magnificent *rājasūya*, kingship is in no way made permanent or certain. Simply in terms of the poetry alone we can observe all these constantly varying messages as to what kingship is or how it is to be conducted. One considers a *rājasūya* to be indubitable or unconditional,

[104] At III.232.2, Yudhiṣṭhira cites *jñātidharma* (the *dharma* of caste).

when in fact it appears to have caused the completely opposite effect and to have actually detonated practical kingship at Hāstinapura. The ensuing instability of both the institution and the title of kingship takes its origin from that moment.

***

In sum, after the *rājasūya*, the equilibrium of the clan and of their poetry goes horribly awry, and the poets are thus heard constantly displaying many competing interpretations of what should or *could* constitute right kingship.[105] Consensus in the kingdom vanished after the *rājasūya*, and if Yudhiṣṭhira had not accomplished this rite, that former stability might have remained, for the performance of the rite engendered a pernicious and destructive envy. Gāndhārī says that this injunction of hers—proposing that Yudhiṣṭhira be supported by her husband—be implemented by the king-maker Bhīṣma (V.146.35).[106] Dhṛtarāṣṭra is soon heard to comment: *yudhiṣṭhiro ... nyāyāgataṃ rājyam idaṃ* (Yudhiṣṭhira has rightfully acquired this kingdom) (V.147.31).[107] It is as if the poets—or whatever editors arranged this text that we have received of the poem—are presenting every possible aspect and dimension of potential succession or claim to the kingdom; there is no single moral nor one just message as to who owns true right to the throne. Kingship in this light is a voucher or sign that is subject to the argumentation of an inner group composed of family, their clan companions, and the local elite populace. It is as if it were an object being passed from hand to hand, and each time was being used for a different purpose, being constantly subject to further revaluation.

2. War As Royal Rite

As we have seen, kings in this epic poetry are traditionally the sponsors of sacerdotal rituals, and in this they offer to the *brāhmaṇas* who are performing the rites great quantities of mobile wealth. In the poem there is little reference to wealth, except on the occasion of such sacrificial moments, or on the occasion of a

105 Heesterman (1993, 3) writes: "If sacrifice is catastrophic, ritual is the opposite. It is called upon to control the passion and fury of the sacrificial contest and to keep such forces within bounds. Sacrificial ritual presents 'the rules of the game.' However, there is no guarantee that the rules will hold ... the epic starts with the orderly arrangements of a sacrifice that develops into a nightmarish devastation."

106 Bhīṣma is also the matchmaker for this side of the clan in that he often secures the brides.

107 Allow me to add the significant note here that these speeches of the royal old couple are being spoken or sung by Kṛṣṇa as he reports to his ally Yudhiṣṭhira what ostensibly occurred during his ambassadorial mission to Hāstinapura. The speeches the audience heard during that session did not contain any of these words; Kṛṣṇa is being either poetic or wily, or there is simply an editorial divergence in the text as we have it today.

princely marriage; the culture that is represented in the *Mahābhārata* is premonetary, and there is no coinage.[108] Immediately prior to the battle at Kurukṣetra, the poets says:

> tataḥ sa vastrāṇi tathaiva gāś ca phalāni puṣpāṇi tathaiva niṣkān
> kurūttamo brāhmaṇasān mahātmā kurvan yayau śakra ivāmarebhyaḥ
>
> VI.22.8
>
> Then the great souled best of the Kurus, making presentations
> To the brāhmaṇas—gold ornaments, flowers, fruit, and cows and also cloth—
> Went, like Śakra towards the immortals.

This marks the commencement of what is referred to as the *śastrayajña* (rite of weaponry) or battle, in which the death of warriors, the *kṣatriyas*, is ideally the offering that is to be made, and it is their bloodshed that causes a *nadī*, a 'flood', towards the domain of Yama, the deity of death, while their released spirits go towards the *indraloka* (the world of Indra).[109] The emotion engendered by so much death is, of course, grief, and, unlike the two other great rites performed by king Yudhiṣṭhira, grief is what colours the performance of these four Kurukṣetra Books (that is, from an audience's point of view). Let us now turn to this central section of the epic and attend to how kingship is here represented and observe how Yudhiṣṭhira fulfils this office.

Towards the end of the Udyoga *parvan*, where Kṛṣṇa and Karṇa converse together on a chariot, Karṇa closes the exchange by saying: *brāhmaṇāḥ kathayiṣyanti mahābhāratam āhavam samāgameṣu ... kṣatriyāṇāṃ* (*Brāhmaṇas* will tell the great Bhārata sacrifice among the associations of *kṣatriyas*) (V.139.56). What is remarkable is that—for Karṇa—it is not *kṣatriya* poets, the *sūtas*, who will sing the epic, but *brāhmaṇas*, and also that the poem—for Karṇa—possesses this quality of cosmogonic ritual, a 'sacrifice'. Ritual, of course, is a means for inducing equilibrium in the cosmos, for the balancing of order in the supernal and mundane worlds. Karṇa had said before of this, *dhārtarāṣṭrasya ... śastrayajño bhaviṣyati* (there will be a sacrifice of weapons for the son of Dhṛtarāṣṭra); that is, the rite is to be sponsored by Duryodhana *as king* whom Karṇa considers—in

[108] From the early days of coinage, kingship was always linked to the image that was impressed upon the metal of the coin.

[109] See Hiltebeitel 1976. Following him, Feller (2004, 6:281) discusses this formulation of battle as a ritual of sacrifice and especially the associated *parvan*, the Sauptika, where, "Aśvatthāman, after praising Śiva ... being 'possessed' by him, proceeds to slaughter the sleeping warriors, but in a peculiar manner, kicking them and mutilating them, 'like *paśus*' (10.8.18 & 12.20), in the same manner as Śiva at Dakṣa's sacrifice." A *paśu* is the bovine 'victim'.

terms of the metaphor of the *ritual* of war—as *dīkṣita* 'the initiated' (V.139.29).[110] This is also the instant of time—according to the poem—where the *yuga* transits from the *dvāpara* to the *kali* cycle.

For *kṣatriyas*, war is a ritual leading either to death and fame or to victory and rule, and the king, as the 'best' of the people, is the figure who proposes and materially supports the practice of such ritual. The *nadī* is a major simile of battle in the epic and occurs frequently during the Kurukṣetra scenes; it is a *saṃgrāmanadī* (a river of battle) (VI.108.29). The fighting of the heroes in the conflict is also often likened to qualities of fire, the element that lies at the focus and centre of orthoprax rite, and this is a vital part of the store of similes that are engaged in the four Kurukṣetra Books.[111] Sustaining this trope, at the outset of the Karṇa *parvan*, the poets make the observation about the Kaurava heroes:

> teṣāṃ niśamy eṅgitāni yuddhe prāṇāñ juhūṣatām
>
> VIII.6.11
>
> Having observed the gestures of those desiring to pour their lives into battle ...

The icon is that of warriors being considered as libations made into a sacrificial fire of war, an image that is constantly repeated throughout the Kurukṣetra Books.[112] When Karṇa, in the Udyoga *parvan*, describes the *śastryajña* to Kṛṣṇa, he says especially of Yudhiṣṭhira that:

> japair homaiś ca saṃyukto brahmatvaṃ kārayiṣyati
>
> V.139.34
>
> Engaged with prayers and libations he will perform the office of the brahman.

The *brāhmaṇa* at the solemn rite is chief priest, one who says nothing unless there is an infringement or error in the procedure; he oversees the propriety

[110] Duryodhana himself, at V.57.12, had described how he would conduct this ritual when he said: *yudhiṣṭhiraṃ paśuṃ kṛtvā* (having made Yudhiṣṭhira the victim).

[111] A third key simile and motif of this part of the epic is the image of the hero as a tree: a beautiful and sometimes flowering tree, or a tree that is toppling having been felled. River, fire, and tree are essential and repetitive elements, serving as both similes and as metonyms in these core books of the poem; they are key signs in the poets' hoard of words.

[112] XII.25.26–27 neatly summarises *in extenso* this simile of weapons and sacrificial instruments. At XII.99.15–46, the poets enjoin this image in a more complex form by combining it with the simile of the *nadī*. These words, which give details of the metaphorical system of the *yuddhayajña*, are sung by Indra in the voice of Bhīṣma; it commences with the phrase: *ṛtvijaḥ kuñjarās tatra* (there the elephants are the priests). All the paraphernalia of the solemn ritual are expressed as elements of battle—including the sounds—and the armies.

of the ritual, and this is a metaphor that fits Yudhiṣṭhira nicely. It is notable that Karṇa refers to this bloody ritual as belonging to or being sponsored by Duryodhana, and it is *not* Yudhiṣṭhira who is commissioning the ritual but his rival (for only a king can be the sponsor). The poet Vaiśaṃpāyana recounts the words of Saṃjaya—which reverses this form—to the old king Dhṛtarāṣṭra when they are back in the palace at Hāstinpura after the battle of Kurukṣetra is finished. Saṃjaya there speaks about the *jvalitah pārthapāvakaḥ* (the blazing Pārtha-fire) into which his sons had been poured as libations (XI.1.33–34).[113] As the old Bhīṣma later states concerning the king in war: *ātmānaṃ yūpam ucchritya sa yajño* (he the sacrificer having raised himself as the sacrificial stake) (XII.98.10).[114] In other words, the king is a metaphor of the *yūpa* himself, the central pole of the Vedic ritual upon which the victim is immolated. Again, we observe how different poets *and* different voices or characters project changing points of view; the poetry presents no single narrator or narrative perspective, and hence there can be no judgement by those who *speak* the poem. All that the poets can do is enact a certain kind of emotion (with their tone of voice and expression as they perform), which is a secondary form of interpretation if not judgement.

Let us proceed through the details of these four *parvans* and see how the poem's understanding of kingship activates and is activated by this *kṣatriya* rite of war and its poetic conceiving. What kind of ritual is this really? And what does the ceremony accomplish in the cosmos?

***

The Kurukṣetra *parvans* (VI–IX) are poetically the most integrated and stylistically uniform of all the *Mahābhārata parvans*.[115] They arguably represent the older *kinds* of poetry in the epic, although this does not necessarily mean that they are chronologically older.[116] More specifically, these *parvans* present a

[113] Concerning the focus of orthoprax sacrifice, the fire, let us recall that Draupadī was born from a ritual fire (I.61.95); Arjuna receives his chariot and bow at the command of Agni (I.216.5); and that Arjuna, Bhīma, and Kṛṣṇa are described as *traya ivāgnayaḥ* (like three fires), as they prepare to destroy Jarāsaṃdah of Magadha. Heroes frequently receive this metaphor or simile during the Kurukṣetra Books, and thus the ritual of battle is figuratively magnified.

[114] This is repeated at XII.99.26. Nīlakaṇṭha glosses this line as: *ātmānaṃ dahayūpaṃ yajñastaṃbhaṃ utsṛjya ucchritya yajño yuddhayajño* (the sacrifice of war is the sacrifice/r, having raised the sacrificial stake—having given up himself as the burning pole) (XII.97.10).

[115] The seasonal setting of the battle is that of winter, a time when the sun is in the south (VI.114.96). This is a time after the rains and after the harvests.

[116] In McGrath 2011, I proposed arguments towards such a statement. At present we are unable to actually *prove* that certain elements of the great Bhārata are 'older' than others, except in the sense of being stylistically or developmentally—and I would not say historically here—more *fundamental* to the text of the poem. We might hold opinions as to the relative age represented by parts of the epic, but it is at present difficult to make any sound inference or to construct any firm hypothesis confirming such

fashion of poetry or kind of verse medium that displays an archaic pattern of warrior culture, where chariot battle is more a venue for heroes than it is for kings.[117] Kurukṣetra itself is glossed by the poets as *tapaḥkṣetra* (a field of bodily ordeal), implying a sense of profound spiritual devotion (VI.1.2). Saṃjaya's Kurukṣetra Song begins with the words: *bhrātṛbhiḥ sahito ... putro duryodhanas tava* (together with the brothers, your son Duryodhana) (VI.42.2). It is as if Duryodhana is the star hero of this performance of Saṃjaya's; he is certainly the one to receive an heroic death, unlike Yudhiṣṭhira.

When Bhīṣma has made the first kill at Kurukṣetra and the first of the heroes, Uttara, the young son of king Virāṭa, has fallen—felled by Śalya at VI.45.39—Yudhiṣṭhira is soon heard telling his closest ally, Kṛṣṇa, about his despondency and dismay at the approaching mayhem (VI.46.4). The poets say that he is *śokārtaṃ ... duḥkhena hatacetasam* (mindless with sorrow, pained by grief); this is a tone or mood that he displays throughout much of this period of warfare, and the guilt and shame from this especially inhabit the later *parvans* (VI.46.26). As the chief *sacrificer* in this ritual, the king should *not* be mourning for those immolated by his rite. In no way is Yudhiṣṭhira a truculent and profligate warrior-king, and it is his sovereign-double, the super-hero Kṛṣṇa, who is the one to be in command, proposing both tactics and strategy. The *senāpati* 'army commander', Dhṛṣṭadyumna, is a third figure of authority and determination, but his decisions are generally nugatory.

The *bhāga*, or 'appointed opponent', of Yudhiṣṭhira is Śalya, the king of Bālhīka in the northwest, who is in fact Yudhiṣṭhira's nominal maternal uncle, being the brother of Pāṇḍu's second or co-wife Mādrī.[118] Yudhiṣṭhira does participate in the fighting at Kurukṣetra, but not excessively, and he does eventually kill his *bhāga*; while Duryodhana, who is *not* his formal opponent, does participate frequently in the combat and at one point even duels with Arjuna (VII.78.1).[119] The audience sometimes hears a single *śloka* about how Yudhiṣṭhira

a surely temporal view. For instance, the term for 'you' in the *tvam* form is arguably of an older usage than the *bhavān* form, the latter being a more classical practice of address. I am grateful to Thomas Burke for this observation.

117 By 'older' here we can think in synchronic terms, in terms of morphology rather than the temporal. In this light, in McGrath 2004 and 2013, I examined two particular heroes in terms of their martial endeavour, their mental vigour, and their patterns of speech.

118 All the heroes at Kurukṣetra who figure significantly in the narrative have their appointed *bhāgas*, such is the nature of fixed duality for *kṣatriyas* in battle. The convention is that a warrior should *not* kill another's *bhāga* although he may fight with him.

119 Duryodhana's *bhāga* is Bhīma. There is a condition of asymmetry here whose reasoning is not explicit.

had pursued Śalya and struck him with arrows, but that is all.[120] There is no symmetry between these two chiefs in the poem apart from the fact of their equal and opposing kinship status.[121] This is despite the fact that individual combat should, by *kṣatriya* custom, only occur between warriors of like rank. Thus Bhīṣma reminds Duryodhana in battle that:

> rājadharmaṃ puraskṛtya rājā rājānam ṛcchati
>
> VI.91.12
>
> Having observed the dharma of a king, a king goes to a king.

Never in the battle however do Duryodhana and Yudhiṣṭhira come together in order to fight, except in the Karṇa *parvan* where the two briefly engage and Duryodhana is soon vanquished (VIII.19.36). (This modicum of contact is due to these two warrior chiefs being the main sponsors of the *sacrifice of weapons*.) This particular scene is an extremely formulaic instant, however, and conveys little of significance or development; in fact most of Yudhiṣṭhira's mentions in the Kurukṣetra Books are formulaic and cursory in nature, and he is *not* a significant warrior. The duel is renewed in the next *adhyāya*, and once again Yudhiṣṭhira triumphs, only to be reminded by Bhīma not to destroy his set opponent—for he has vowed to fell Duryodhana himself, and the avowal or promise of a *kṣatriya* is inviolable and intractable. Yudhiṣṭhira accepts this counsel.

Again, most of this scene is thoroughly formulaic, apart from the few words of Bhīma, and contributes little of character or transition to the narrative

[120] Yudhiṣṭhira engages Śalya at VI.67.19 *sahaputrāḥ sahāmatyāḥ* (with [his] sons and ministers); and at VII.71.29. Yudhiṣṭhira is said to assail Droṇa at VII.81.18, VII.85.19, and VII.132.22; at VII.136.1, he attacks Droṇa's son; at VII.137.36, he is assaulted by Droṇa; at VII.140.5–41, he encounters Droṇa, but is then bested by Kṛtavarman and made to flee, having lost his *kavaca* 'cuirass'. After the death of Ghaṭotkaca, Yudhiṣṭhira sets out to attack Karṇa at VII.158.48. At VIII.39.12, he encounters Aśvatthāman. At IX.21.13, he is again mentioned in a cursory manner, as at IX.22.6 and IX.24.33. These mentions are all thoroughly formulaic and do not contribute to any transition or progression in the narrative. Occasionally Yudhiṣṭhira is simply mentioned by name, but this is merely in passing, and no activity is described.

[121] In the Bombay text, Yudhiṣṭhira's chariot is described as having: *mṛdaṅgau cātra vipulau divyau nandopanandakau / yantreṇāhanyamānau ca susvanau harṣavardhanāu* (There, two divine broad kettle-drums, Nanda and Upananda, being struck by a device [gave] beautiful and joy-thriving sound). No other chariot is said to be endowed with such instruments (VII.24.85). On this vehicle the *dhvaja* 'battle-standard' of Yudhiṣṭhira is pictured as *sauvarṇaṃ somaṃ grahagaṇānvitam* (a golden moon accompanied by a crowd of planets) (VII.24.84). Solely as an intriguing point of interest, let us make note of the fact that Candragupta Maurya ruled from 320 to 298 BCE, and Candragupta II, during the Gupta dynasty, ruled from 380 to 415 CE; both names of course indicate someone who is literally 'a protector of the Moon', or 'protected by the Moon'. Candragupta Maurya is by tradition said to have died as a Jain, a follower of the *guru* Bhadrabahu. The *dhvaja* of Duryodhana is said to be *nāgo maṇimayo ... kanakasaṃvṛtaḥ* (an elephant made of jewels surrounded by gold) (VII.80.26).

(VIII.20.6-32). Warfare is the domain of heroes and not of kings, even on the level of myth where battle is considered as a blood rite.

***

Yudhiṣṭhira, due to the Pāṇḍava failure to kill Bhīṣma, the leader of the Kaurava army, during a conference of the best of the heroes one night proposes to withdraw from the contest and to adopt the renunciant life of a forester; he says to Kṛṣṇa, *vanaṃ yāsyāmi durdharṣa* (O invincible one, I shall go to the forest) (VI.103.19). This is a sentiment on the part of the king, uttered in times of duress when success evades the brothers, which the audience repeatedly hears throughout the poem. Its occurrence provides a strongly quiescent quality to Yudhiṣṭhira's kingship, echoing what he said during the Āraṇyaka *parvan* when in discourse with Draupadī he had refuted her desire for anger and vengeance with the proposal of *kṣama* ('mildness' or 'patience') (III.30).

Duryodhana, too, at times, expresses a similar yearning to withdraw from his position and public life, and at one point, having been bested by the Pāṇḍavas in a fight, announces his intention to end his own life.[122] After Bhīṣma, Bhūriśravas, and Jayadratha have all been felled, and after Bhīma has slain thirty-one of his brothers (VII.122.16), Duryodhana himself—speaking to Droṇa—again threatens to retire from the world and life itself: *so'ham adya gamiṣyāmi yatra te ... hatā madarthaṃ saṃgrāme* (today I shall go to where they are [who] were slain for my benefit in battle) (VII.125.32). There is the implication here, by both these rival cousins, that if the king is unsuccessful in his endeavours or ideals, he is customarily justified in removing himself—either by ritual suicide or by taking on the life of renunciation—from the political arena and authority, and there would be no political stigma attached to such a withdrawal. There is no indication, however, of the significance of the king—as sponsor of the *śastrayajña*—removing himself from the office of this rite; for, as we shall see, this is ritual only in terms of the *myth* and not in terms of a pragmatic sacrifice.

Despite this recurrent diffidence on the part of Yudhiṣṭhira, he remains the focal point in the Pāṇḍava allegiance; during the Droṇābhiṣeka sub-*parvan*, Droṇa, now in command of the Kauravas, requests that Duryodhana somehow cause Arjuna to be removed from the battle so that he, Droṇa, might capture Yudhiṣṭhira (VII.11.26).[123] Implicit here is the statement that, with the seizure

122 The words are *prāyam upāsiṣye* (I shall engage in meditative suicide) (III.238.19).

123 Since Arjuna is guarding his brother, Yudhiṣṭhira, Droṇa needs to distract the hero from the king's presence. The Trigarta brothers, along with some others, pledge to remove Arjuna from the battle and so form the *saṃśaptakās*, a 'sworn band'. As part of their initiation into this *kṣatriya* unit, they perform a strangely archaic rite: *tato jvalanam ādāya hutvā sarve pṛthak pṛthak / jagṛhuḥ kuśacīrāṇi citrāṇi kavacāni ca / te ca baddhatanutrāṇā ghṛtāktāḥ kuśacīriṇaḥ / maurvīmekhalino vīrāḥ* ... (All the warriors,

of the king, the Pāṇḍavas will capitulate—a strategy that reveals the valence of a king's symbolic centrality in this war-polity.[124] Yudhiṣṭhira is a complex amalgam of many contradictory elements that supply his kingship and his character with drama, sophistication, and a reserved yet robust confidence; he is stealthily enigmatic, and yet ferociously ambitious, but lacks the warrior passion that would make him a great emperor of the likes of Candragupta Maurya or Aśoka. Yet, despite not being a superb warrior, he remains—as *rāja*—at the heart of the army, and in that sense the king is the key signifier or sign regardless of how he acts or does not act: *he* being the main sponsor of the rite of battle, even if only in a titular sense. This is an essential aspect of Yudhiṣṭhira's kingship: he is without doubt central within his political galaxy, and yet the practice or function of kingship within that sphere is profoundly de-central in action.

***

Grief is the emotion that governs, or is attached to, this *kṣatriya* rite, and when the young warrior Abhimanyu, in one of the most valiant scenes of the war, is ultimately struck down after his terrific *aristeía*, the allies, kings and heroes are described as:

> upopaviṣṭā rājānaṃ parivārya yudhiṣṭhiram
>
> VII.49.2
>
> Having taken seats, having surrounded the king Yudhiṣṭhira ...

The king then begins to formally declaim, publicly lamenting for his fallen nephew, beginning: *abhimanyau hate vīre* (when Abhimanyu the warrior was slain). He recapitulates the great deeds of the youth and then draws upon the usual formulae that are sung on such occasions; the performance continues for eighteen *ślokas*. There is something grimly prescribed about this archaic scene with the central king conducting the lament for a courageous adolescent as he is encompassed by his men, both warriors and companions. The picture is forbidding and stern, that of a chief leading a threnody in the company of his armed champions. For a *kṣatriya*, there is no death like the death of a son, this being

---

one by one, having brought fire, took fine *kuśa* grass garments and breastplates; armour bound, the *kuśa* grass anointed with ghee, wearing a bow-string as girdle ...) (VII.16.22–23). They vow either to succeed or to die, and this ritual establishes that avowal. This is a rite embedded within a larger rite, as it were.

[124] Allow me to add, however, that the model of war in this central part of the epic is not that one army or force defeats another but that one army destroys and incapacitates the other army's leader. This is arguably a thoroughly Indic view of warfare, where the leader—either king or hero—is the sign representing a whole force. Victory in the *Iliad*, for instance, turns upon the defeat of all an enemy's assembly: it is symmetrical.

the most important kinship relation for a hero.[125] Lamentation—especially as it will be manifest in the Strī *parvan*—is an essential secondary component in this liturgy of battle; and here, as also at the close of Book Eleven, Yudhiṣṭhira, as chief agent of the rite, takes the leading voice in the mourning.

When Ghaṭotkaca, the *rākṣasa* nephew of Yudhiṣṭhira, is killed by Karṇa, Yudhiṣṭhira is portrayed as:

aśrupūrṇamukho rājā niḥśvasaṃś ca punaḥ punaḥ

VII.158.22

The king, his mouth full of tears and sighing repeatedly.

Nevertheless, despite his repeated grief or despondence, Yudhiṣṭhira always manages to maintain a decorum and resilience; he is not a hothead like his cousin Duryodhana. So Yudhiṣṭhira is possessed by grief once again for this nephew even though he was a *rākṣasa*; Vyāsa, his lineal grandfather but not his genetic grandfather, appears from the outer frame of the poem in order to console him.[126] Vyāsa reassures Yudhiṣṭhira of the clan's future and its success, and says:

mā krudho bharataśreṣṭha mā ca śoke manaḥ kṛthāḥ

VII.158.59

Best Bharata, do not be wrathful and do not make your mind grievous!

The *ṛṣi* informs his grandson that:

pañcame divase caiva pṛthivī te bhaviṣyati

VII.158.60

So in five days the earth will become yours.

He specifically instructs Yudhiṣṭhira *not* to pursue Karṇa in order to find revenge for the death of Ghaṭotkaca, although revenge often appears to be an intrinsic action in this sacrifice of weaponry, just as grief is an implicit emotion of the rite.

Vyāsa is a mysterious *magus*-like figure in the *Mahābhārata* being the putative original poet who once sang the 'first' Bhārata Song; he is two

[125] See McGrath 2004, 5:1. The picture that we have of Arjuna and Kṛṣṇa, hero and charioteer, portrays an even deeper warrior emotion, but they are unique. See McGrath 2013.

[126] Let us recall that it is the seed of Vyāsa that generates the conception of Pāṇḍu and Dhṛtarāṣṭra, the two kings who stand at the commencement of the Bhārata Song (I.100.1ff.). He also assisted Gāndhārī in the gestation of her hundred sons (I.107.18).

generations away from Yudhiṣṭhira who is in turn Janamejaya's great-great-half-uncle.[127] Vyāsa, who is older than Bhīṣma, comes and goes in the poem and the generations like an unworldly prophet and sage; his consciousness is the timeless matrix that generates the poetry. The almost co-equal presence of Nārada in the poem and the knowledge that Nārada demonstrates about the presence and future of the narrative make him appear at times to possess an overall intelligence and cosmic foresight that is identical to that of Vyāsa. Hence the intellectual relationship between these two semi-divine figures is blurred, although the poets claim that it is Vyāsa who is the true master of the narrative. When Vyāsa appears, as he does now in the *śastrayajña* with Yudhiṣṭhira, it is always to advise and gently direct with words, and he stabilises the ritual, as it were; he never performs in this manner with Duryodhana, and only on a couple of occasions does he appear and address—and then usually to admonish—the old king Dhṛtarāṣṭra. It is as if Yudhiṣṭhira has this special direct contact and impulsion from the proto-poet, the biological *and* nominal progenitor of the clan; it is this connection or transmission that distinguishes him as the true *king* of the epic.[128] One should recall that it was to Kuntī, when she was roaming the countryside alone with her sons, that Vyāsa had once said:

> jīva putri sutas te'yaṃ dharmaputro yudhiṣṭhiraḥ
> pṛthivyāṃ pārthivān sarvān praśāsiṣyati dharmarāṭ
>
> I.144.13
>
> Live, daughter! This, your son, the son of Dharma, Yudhiṣṭhira,
> Shall rule all the princes on earth as King Dharma!

The *ur*-poet and *manipulator* of the poem—if not the arch-priest—thus maintains a continual tutelage of the moral and political trajectory of his nominal grandson in this poetic movement towards paramount supremacy, as it concerns battle. Not mortal, yet not quite divine, Vyāsa is a unique figure in the epic, and he is always close to Yudhiṣṭhira in a narrative sense; therefore, if one is examining kingship in the epic *Mahābhārata* it is to Vyāsa that we should always first direct

[127] In McGrath 2011, I examined the poetic valence or *mise en abîme* of Vyāsa at length, particularly as he makes the poem *work* in the company of his *therápōn* 'assistant', Saṃjaya. From Śaṃtanu to Janamejaya, inclusive, there are seven nominal generations of heroes and kings: this is the central narrative sequence of epic *Mahābhārata*, the core of which focuses on the world of Yudhiṣṭhira and his kin. There is the rider, however, that Śaṃtanu has no genetic descendants, and it is Vyāsa, son of Parāśara who continues the lineage—all of whom perish in the poem.

[128] We should perhaps reiterate that Yudhiṣṭhira has *no* genetic connection with Vyāsa, whereas Duryodhana stands very much within that strain of the patriline as the great-grandson. (Parāśara > Vyāsa > Dhṛtarāṣṭra > Duryodhana.)

our attention, for he is the progenitor not only of many of the heroes, but also of the song itself, which is the vehicle of these heroes.[129] Just as Kṛṣṇa stands beside Yudhiṣṭhira the king as his partner in practical direction, so too does Vyāsa appear and intervene in order to indicate how the present war narrative is to proceed.

***

Yudhiṣṭhira is the principal sacrificer of this violent ritual. When Yudhiṣṭhira, in order to expedite the removal of Droṇa from the battle and so facilitate his death, verbally compromises himself with a deceit about the demise of Aśvatthāman, the beloved son of Droṇa, there ensues a crisis in *dharma*: for the incontrovertible truthfulness of Yudhiṣṭhira, the veracity of his speech, and the moral flawlessness of the king is shattered. He had lied to Droṇa about the death of his son, and Droṇa, knowing that Yudhiṣṭhira never spoke an untruth, in his despair and sorrow gave up the fight in order to enter *prāya*, in which state he was quickly decapitated. Apart from an occasional moment of animus in the Karṇa *parvan*, this is the only instant in the poem where Yudhiṣṭhira compromises himself with such *upāya* 'expedience', where the moral benefit of an end justifies the amorality of the means. Note, however, that in the *kali yuga* almost all 'moral' action—at least three-quarters of it—is actually in the manner of such expedience; in fact, as we know, moral propriety is *only* possible then in a mere quarter of all human experiences, as human beings become almost universally adharmic. As Draupadī remarks:

> kartavyaṃ tveva karmeti manor eṣa viniścayaḥ
>
> III.33.36
>
> Action is to be done, this is the mandate of Manu.

Thus, most of human activity and accomplishment during this time is necessarily to be without *dharma*, and at best only a sense of moral dilemma rather than of full conviction.

Yudhiṣṭhira had practically covered over his mendacious lapse by whispering—when he had made the statement—that Aśvatthāman was not in fact Droṇa's son but merely an elephant with that same name:[130]

[129] At I.157.15, Vyāsa directs the Pāṇḍava brothers to attend the *svayaṃvara* of Draupadī. Then, later, when she has become their bride, he privately informs her father, Drupada, about the myth that lay behind this unusual practice of polyandry (I.189.1). At III.37.27, Vyāsa, in an aside, secretly imparts *vidyāṃ pratismṛtim* 'magical knowledge' to Yudhiṣṭhira: *yogavidyām* 'yogic knowledge' (I.37.34). He appears and speaks encouragingly to Yudhiṣṭhira during the forest years (III.91.17 and 245.8).

[130] Yudhiṣṭhira recalls this untruth and the anguish it causes for him at XII.17.15–16.

avyaktam abravīt rājan hataḥ kuñjara ity uta

VII.164.106

O king, he said indistinctly: "the elephant is killed."

The truth here concerns not so much the validity of the expressed statement, but the effect and consequence of the received statement: veracity is objective and not subjective in the world insofar as it concerns the movement of signification and not merely the static quality of a statement. Truth is practical and not simply linguistic, and illusions possess consequences and generate action: for something that does not exist can cause an effect if the source of the illusion is considered truthful in itself.[131]

As a result of this minor, yet profound, deceit, the poets say of Yudhiṣṭhira that:

tasya pūrvaṃ rathaḥ pṛthvyāś catur aṅgula uttaraḥ
babhūvaivaṃ tu tenokte tasya vāhāspṛśan mahīm

VII.164.107

His chariot was previously four fingers above the earth,
But the utterance was such—his vehicle [now] touched the ground.

This account of Yudhiṣṭhira's infidelity is repeated by the poets on two subsequent occasions, and it is as if the message is being amplified for the benefit of the poem's audience: the king or princes who were the patrons of this epic performance.[132]

To make a brief digression on this morally charged *motif* of truth in the poem, there are two other occasions of overt *anṛta* 'untruth' that I have so far encountered as being made by a hero. At I.181.19, Arjuna, speaking to Karṇa, says that *brāḥmano'smi yudhāṃ śreṣṭhaḥ* (I am the best of fighters, a brahmin). Karṇa immediately withdraws from the attack for it is incorrect of a *kṣatriya* to offend a *brāhmaṇa*, and the poets say that he is *śaṅkite* 'alarmed'. Similarly, Karṇa, in order to secure a divine and magical weapon from the martial *guru* Rāma Jāmadagnya, lies that he is a *brāhmaṇa* at V.61.2.

In the Virāṭa *parvan*, the Pāṇḍavas and Draupadī inform the king and queen that they are menials, so sustaining their necessary disguise; yet this is not so

[131] This condition is similar to the exemplum in philosophy where the validity of a perception that is actually invalid generates valid knowledge: the strand of rope that is perceived as a snake, for instance, which causes fear; as in *viparyaya*, the 'misapprehension' of Nyāya philosophy.

[132] This happens in the words of Kṛpa to Aśvatthāmam himself at VII.165.115–116; and by Arjuna at 167.34.

much an untruth as the continuation of what is in fact their condition or social status at the time.[133] Likewise, in the Udyoga *parvan*, Saṃjaya and Kṛṣṇa, who both act as *dūtas* or messengers, ostensibly recite speeches that have not—as far as the audience in our present text are aware—been previously spoken. This is not exactly lying, however, and might simply be an aspect of the preliterate tradition insofar as the earlier speeches had been somehow elided from the poem.[134] Thus, Kuntī as an important 'speaker of truth' in the poem is profoundly concerned with the certainty of her words when she inquires: *mucyeyam anṛtāt katham* (how might I escape untruth?) (I.188.17).[135] Lying, or the verbal practice of untruth is rare in the poem, and 'truth' *satya*, is a vital motif in the epic, and its bearing is essential for right *kṣatriya* conduct.[136] Karṇa, for instance, gives absolute priority to the valence of truth in all that he says or does, and it is telling that at the moment when Arjuna—in the scene just mentioned—appears disguised as a *brāhmaṇa*, it is not his true self that speaks with such mendacity but his pretended self.

For a literary work to become what is often known as the 'Fifth Veda' there cannot be any falsehood, fraudulence, or untruth in its communication, and if such does occur—as in these two instances—there is an implicit and coded reason for such expression. Bhīṣma, at XII.156.3, in answer to a question of Yudhiṣṭhira about the nature of *satya*, speaks at length upon this topic: first he uses the word itself thirteen times; then he makes a gloss of *satya* with thirteen other homologous words; and then he extemporates upon each of these thirteen nouns. The purpose of Bhīṣma's explication of 'truth' is to demonstrate that truthfulness, or human veracity, concerns not simply verbal action but a complete manner of *being* human, of performing in life and the world in a fashion that does not compromise one's belief or vision; this is *truth* in the European renaissance sense of *virtù* and is the same sense of 'truth' that Gandhi enjoined in his Autobiography, truth being in this sense not simply a just statement that is logically defensible.[137] It is this usage of the term that underlies the

[133] The name that Yudhiṣṭhira assumes in the kingdom of the Virāṭas is Kaṅka. This is the name of a bird, the kind of bird which Yudhiṣṭhira's father, Dharma, disguised himself as—in the form of a *yakṣa*—in the Āraṇyaka *parvan* (III.297.66 and IV.1.20).

[134] See McGrath 2011, chap. 3 and McGrath 2013, chap. 5.

[135] See McGrath 2009, chap. V on women heroes in the epic as "speakers of truth."

[136] There is an historical distinction between the terms *an-ṛta* and *a-satya* where the former is of a much older usage and concerns cosmic 'right', and the latter is more concerned with the moral demonstration or evidence of truthfulness.

[137] Gandhi 1927.

force or moral validity of the *Mahābhārata* as a primary human document and treasury of human experience.

Returning to our thread, the medium here of culpability that signifies the immaculate and complete quality of Yudhiṣṭhira's kingship—in its generation of truth within the world and kingdom—is that of the *ratha* 'the chariot', that old-fashioned vehicle of the Bronze Age warrior world.[138] The *ratha* is the medium of truth, and it is fitting that the Gītā of Kṛṣṇa—the central message and initiation into cosmic truth and its theophany—was performed on a chariot. This is a key and crucial symbol in *kṣatriya* literature, and it is thus appropriate that Yudhiṣṭhira's single falsehood is so marked by such a vehicle.

Yudhiṣṭhira becomes distraught reflecting on what he had done, and once more he becomes desperate and is full of anguish. As the principle *sacrificer*, he should not have so compromised himself, both verbally and morally; the *rājasūya* had been morally diverted, and now too, the *śastrayajña* is to become tainted. He says:

> ahaṃ hi saha sodaryaiḥ pravekṣye havyavāhanam
>
> VII.170.28
>
> For I, with brothers, shall ascend the funeral pyre.

Such is the moral guilt attached to a betrayal of a *guru* by the telling of a solitary lie. Once again, however, the audience perceives the fraternal involvement of this king: he does not exist alone as a solo and remote *rāja*, but only acts in the company of his four half-siblings. Certainly neither Arjuna or Karṇa responds in this fashion when their spoken *anṛta* has been uncovered. In later centuries in India, when heroes became objects of hero cult and of worship, this quality of truth—in terms of the fiction of a hero who existed only in the songs where such figures lived and died—takes on a spiritual or supernatural potency.

***

Soon Yudhiṣṭhira and Karṇa engage with each other in a duel in which the king is bested and turns to flee. It is fitting that these two assail each other because Karṇa is *the* Sanskrit hero, as I have previously argued.[139] As Karṇa is the *best of the Kurus*, it is appropriate that Yudhiṣṭhira, the best of the kings, encounters this warrior on the field; there is a particularly tragic morphology about this engagement because Karṇa is of course Yudhiṣṭhira's elder half-brother and

[138] See McGrath 2013 for a description of how chariots figure in the *Mahābhārata*.

[139] In McGrath 2004.

should—or could—in fact be *rāja* himself.[140] This is the first real duel in which Yudhiṣṭhira is an active participant, and the account lasts for more than thirty *ślokas* (VIII.33.8–40). Karṇa, of course, triumphs, but recalling his promise to his mother Kuntī in which he vowed *not* to kill his brothers, he does not slay the king.[141] What Karṇa does is:

tam abhidrutya rādheyaḥ skandhaṃ saṃspṛṣya pāṇinā

VIII.33.36

Rādheya, having run up to him, touched his shoulder with a hand.

This, by *kṣatriya* convention, is a manner for claiming prestigious dominance and victory over an opponent without bloodshed, and, as a consequence, Yudhiṣṭhira—humiliated—turns and flees.[142]

Having heard from Bhīma that Yudhiṣṭhira had fled the field after being overwhelmed by Karṇa, Arjuna urges his driver, Kṛṣṇa, to go towards the camp of the king (VIII.45.58). What follows is a unique occasion where Yudhiṣṭhira loses his temper and angrily reprimands his brother:

hatam ādhirathiṃ mene saṃkhye gāṇḍīvadhanvanā

VIII.46.1

He thought the Ādhiratha [Karṇa] killed in battle by the bearer of the Gāṇḍīva bow [Arjuna].[143]

Karṇa had always been a source of great anxiety for Yudhiṣṭhira due to his extraordinary heroic prowess, hence the king's joy at the prospect of his demise:

140 In general, kinship in the *Mahābhārata*—in terms of speech—compounds the cognate, agnatic, and the affiliate, and there is often no distinction between these kinds of relationships. Similarly, the terms for individual parents or for siblings and children are often extended beyond the immediate genetic connection. For example, Yudhiṣṭhira might refer to Gāndhārī as his 'mother', or to Bhīṣma as his 'grandfather', or to the son of Arjuna as his own 'son'. The irony of Karṇa's position is that only he, his mother, and Kṛṣṇa are aware of his true kinship status. The inner workings of clan are often so reductive in their kinship terminology and relations; in contemporary Western Gujarat, I have often noticed this verbal occurrence in simple family relationship terms where there is commonly such nominal aggregation.

141 At V.144.25.

142 In the Native American warrior tradition, this kind of act was referred to as *counting coup*. To count coup was to win higher status than to kill an opponent or to receive a wound. See Parkman 1849.

143 This strange bow is presumably a composite recurve bow and fabricated of valuable *gāṇḍi* or 'rhinoceros horn'. Composite recurve bows were typically of a central Asian provenance, and thus this might indicate that Arjuna's bow is part of the world of the Kuṣāṇas who flourished in the subcontinent during the first two centuries of the Common Era; for a while their capital was at Mathurā, once a town of Kṛṣṇa's clan and later a great centre of Buddhist culture.

trayodaśāhaṃ varṣāṇi yasmad bhīto dhanaṃjaya
na sma nidrāṃ labhe rātrau na cāhani sukhaṃ kvacit

VIII.46.16

Because, Dhanaṃjaya [Arjuna], I was fearful for thirteen years,
I had no sleep at night and no happy days ...

Karṇa was always strangely more baneful to Yudhiṣṭhira than Duryodhana ever was, and, in their brief and formal engagements on the battlefield, it was Karṇa who always bested his sovereign half-brother. Yudhiṣṭhira now sings a long quasi-eulogy for the Karṇa whom he presumes to be dead, praising his heroism and expressing his own fears of that warrior; again we observe the figure of the priest-king as chief mourner in the liturgy of battle (VIII.46.4–47). He says of Karṇa that he was like Indra or Yama or Rāma:

paśyāmi tatra tatraiva karṇabhūtam idaṃ jagat

VIII.46.19

Here and there, wherever I see this world, it is the spirit of Karṇa!

There is nothing vindictive about Yudhiṣṭhira, and he recognises and pronounces the greatness of Karṇa; just as when Duryodhana had been made captive in Book Four, Yudhiṣṭhira was the one to send his brothers to the rescue.[144] This speech is the longest verbal performance by Yudhiṣṭhira in the Kurukṣetra Books, and thus the poets are making much of his illusion or misdirection at this moment and of his subsequent rage when he discovers that Arjuna has in fact *not* felled Karṇa. At this point in the poem, Yudhiṣṭhira is unaware that Karṇa is his half-sibling, yet this rivalry is practically much stronger in fact than what he bears with his cousin Duryodhana. Yudhiṣṭhira has *no* fear of the cousin. Karṇa however, is aware of his kinship priority, but he makes little of the fact due to his inflexible loyalty to his patron, Duryodhana. In performance, this speech, which concludes by blaming Karṇa for much that happened in the *sabhā*, must have been freighted with ironic drama, especially as the dialogue between the king and Arjuna is about to explode into terrific mutual insult.

***

[144] It is extremely rare in the *Mahābhārata* for captives to be mentioned; it is as if a *kṣatriya* only knows the possibility of victory or of death, which is so unlike the culture of warfare represented in the Homeric *Iliad* where prisoners are an important source of *āpoina* 'ransom' and significantly figure in the larger economy of war. Karṇa dismisses the Pāṇḍava brothers in the Karṇa *parvan*, and Bhīma, at III.256.9, submits Jayadratha to ritual humiliation after a defeat—but in general the poem avoids all mention of captives or the vanquished.

Arjuna corrects Yudhiṣṭhira's misapprehension and the latter becomes profoundly *kruddhaḥ* 'irate', still emotionally burning with the physical wounds from Karṇa's arrows. The king verbally excoriates Arjuna for the failure to live up to his promise that he would destroy Karṇa, an avowal that he had been making during all the years that they were in exile.[145] To question a *kṣatriya's* verbal integrity, as well as his martial competence, is not only to insult him, but also to convey an expression of his lack of moral vigour. Yudhiṣṭhira recapitulates all of Arjuna's boasts and pledges, and then says: *karṇād bhīto vyapayāto'si* (you retreated from Karṇa, fearful) (VIII.48.13).[146] He then berates the weapons of his brother, saying that he is *durātman* (a wicked soul), and that *na ... garbho'py abhaviṣyaḥ pṛthāyāḥ* (thus you will not become the womb of Pṛthā), their mother (VIII.48.15). This latter expression is an awful insult, and the effect is immediate and super-tensioned, as Arjuna:

> asiṃ jagrāha saṃkruddho jighāṃsur bharatarṣabham
>
> VIII.49.1
>
> The furious one seized his sword wanting to kill the Bharata-bull.

He also, with an air of the tragic, says:

> pratijñāṃ pālayiṣyāmi hatvenaṃ narasattamam
>
> VIII.49.11
>
> I shall protect the vow having slain this best of men!

Kṛṣṇa manages to appease this incipient violence of Arjuna, but the latter continues to vilify Yudhiṣṭhira, commenting on how far from actual battle the king is presently stationed and how he *draupadītalpasaṃstho* (sat upon the bed of Draupadī); he is contemptuous of Arjuna's combat and violent ordeals (VIII.49.83). Arjuna rudely and offensively blames Yudhiṣṭhira for all their trials, beginning with the gambling session.[147]

145 In McGrath 2013, VI:3, I examined this vicious argument in more detail.

146 Such *ātmastava* (self praise, boasting) is typical of heroic speech prior to engaging in a duel; this is usually spoken to the charioteer. Before Arjuna finally sets off to fight with Karṇa in the most important duel of the poem, he—in response to his charioteer's grandiloquent praise—sings such vivid poetry, that it in effect is—or becomes—a speech act. At VIII.52.30–33, this *ātmastava* is specifically signalled and given in irregular *triṣṭubhs*; all of the fifty-second *adhyāya* is in fact a great and violent vaunting by Arjuna, both terrible and threatening. For a hero to make such boasts and to fail in their accomplishment as well as to remain alive—which is what Yudhiṣṭhira has been referring to—is intolerable.

147 It is remarkable that for much of this virulent exchange—which is given in irregular *triṣṭubhs*—the scholiast Nīlakaṇṭha offers the reader no commentary. This would imply that his text or texts of the poem did not possess these archaic elements or sections of the *Mahābhārata*, what M. C. Smith (1992) calls its "warrior code." This phenomenon is often the case in the Karṇa *parvan*.

It is only the intercession of Kṛṣṇa that conciliates their mutual and despicable wrath, and, once mollified, the two resolve their difference and admit their love for each other, and the crisis passes. Yet here the distinct expressions of a king and a hero are well and briefly exposed: the disagreeable contention between a warrior and the figure of policy, between the *act* and the *idea* of violence. It is the heroes who win the earth for the kings, but the kings remain the ones who establish what is termed *right* in behaviour and conduct. Yudhiṣṭhira, *utthāya ... śayanād* (having risen from rest), confesses his own error as Arjuna similarly admits his wrong, and the two reconcile. Yudhiṣṭhira is depicted thus:

> babhūva vimanāḥ pārthah kiṃcit kṛtveva pātakam
>
> VIII.50.1
>
> The son of Kuntī became listless, having thus made a small error.

Arjuna bends to touch his brother's feet with his head and the two of them weep together and make admissions of affection (VIII.50.9–24). In customary *kṣatriya* manner, they both vow to die if Karṇa is not felled. *Ehy ehi ... māṃ pariṣvaja* (come, come, embrace me), says the elder to Arjuna; *ahaṃ tvām anujānāmi jahi karṇaṃ* (slay Karṇa, I command you!) (VIII.50.26–27).

So closes this brief and electric interlude in the ritual of battle where *rāja* Yudhiṣṭhira is shown to drop his emotional guard and austere dignity with the one person with whom he is probably closest, although this is not intimate.[148] Yudhiṣṭhira does not really demonstrate qualities of friendship with anyone, and human love is not part of his portrait or of the epic's emotional spectrum. Certainly he does occasionally speak of Draupadī with fondness, and he does demonstrate—as here—a certain dear feeling for his brother, but such detailed affective manifestations are rare indeed. Such *realism*, in a modern narrative sense, is unusual in the epic for this is a literature of *kṣatriyas*, of warriors, and of a particular court, that of Samudragupta, say. Much, however—as it concerns intimate feelings of love or pity or distress—would depend upon the particular performance of a poet; it would be his theatrical and histrionic skills that brought to life and vivacity this poetry of war, violence, death, and the complex varieties

[148] Certainly, with Kṛṣṇa, Yudhiṣṭhira has a close relationship, but it is founded on power and decision and not on mutual emotion. Apart from the profound and intense friendship that is demonstrated between Arjuna and Kṛṣṇa, there is little other emotional intimacy or amity displayed by the epic poets. Grief at the death of kin is the occasion for the most significant emotional expression in the poem. Even when a male figure is caused to ejaculate his semen at the sight of a beautiful feminine character—in an instant of nympholepsy—the poets do not make anything of the emotions that might be engaged by the scene. Lyrical expressions of human desire are likewise formulaic and impersonal. Anger and grief are the signal affects of epic *Mahābhārata*; for a *kṣatriya* the intimacy of death is far greater than the intimacy of love.

of human suffering and rare desire. It is the poet's task and skill to animate and inspire life into these verbal metaphors via enactment during performance. What the audience has heard is an intermission in the battle where human passion is revealed in a positive manner rather than in the colours of destruction and bloodshed. For a poet to perform this charged scene would require an artist of enormous theatrical and thespian gifts, for the transitions from voice to voice—without losing the stress of emotional suspense—would be difficult in itself. Arjuna is about to kill his brother, Yudhiṣṭhira, one should remember; while Yudhiṣṭhira is overwhelmed by despair, remorse, and opprobrium.

Arjuna's final words as he sets off again on his chariot—having once more avowed the slaying of Karṇa—are:

> iti satyena te padau spṛśāmi jagatīpate
>
> VIII.50.34
>
> By truth I touch your feet, O lord of the world!

There is a single *śloka* that acts as a rider to this scene, which comes later when Arjuna has proceeded towards his final great duel with Karṇa, the most important duel of the epic. Arjuna encounters Bhīma on the field, and, while they are surrounded by carnage, destruction, bloodiness, and wounds, he pauses with him for an instant:

> samāgamya sa bhīmena mantrayitvā ca phalgunaḥ
> viśalyam arujaṃ cāsmai kathayitvā yudhiṣṭhiram
>
> VIII.58.21
>
> Phalguna having encountered Bhīma and having consulted,
> Told him that Yudhiṣṭhira was painless and unwounded.

It is these small verbal images that always break the extensively formulaic variation of the Kurukṣetra Books: suddenly the narrative tempo, the long *recitative* of fighting and combat, and all the endless metaphor of death is rent, and it is as if the camera manages to catch a minute of ordinary and mundane humanity via such an open window.

***

The Karṇa *parvan*, which lies at the very centre and focus of the ritual of weaponry, closes with what appears to be another ironic touch on the part of the poets; for after the most terrible and lengthy duel in the whole poem, between Arjuna and his *bhāga*, which terminates with the beautiful death and subsequent beautiful corpse of Karṇa, the two heroes—Arjuna and his driver Kṛṣṇa—return from the field in order to inform the king of their victory. The poets say:

govindo dadarśa ca yudhiṣṭhiram śayānaṃ ... kāñcane śayanottame (and Govinda saw Yudhiṣṭhira lying upon a fine golden couch) (VIII.69.9–10). The counterpoint between this image of repose and luxury with the hundreds of *ślokas* that precede this moment depicting the ferocity of aggression prior to the protracted death of *the* greatest *Mahābhārata* hero is one of high distinction. Why the poets should make such a point though is curious: why would they depict the king in such a lenient and luxurious light in contrast to the cruel and fierce drama of the recent duel to the death? It is as if they wished to portray Yudhiṣṭhira as unheroic, and, certainly, in contrast to Duryodhana, who is often to be heard of fighting on the field, Yudhiṣṭhira is *not* a powerful combatant or a great warrior. He is a king only.

This particular scene where the heroes return to the presence of their sovereign is an infrequent occasion in the poem in which the poets allow themselves some degree of innuendo or nuance concerning Yudhiṣṭhira. This quality of communication—a metaphor of enactment that an audience must interpret—rarely happens so explicitly in the epic, and one wonders why, given the greatness of Karṇa and the terrific majesty of his *dvairatha* 'duel' with Arjuna, this instant in the progress of Yudhiṣṭhira receives such an ambivalent and ambiguous rendering? Again, it is as if the demise of Karṇa is being covertly endued with a tragic air; this emotion though is not given overtly—and the audience must receive the message only by virtue of their own interpretation—for it remains coloured by the fine chiaroscuro artistry of the poets.

Having gone to the field in order to view the decapitated corpse of Karṇa, Yudhiṣṭhira says:

> adya rājāsmi govinda pṛthivyāṃ bhrātṛbhiḥ saha
>
> VIII.69.31
>
> Govinda, now I am king in the world, together with my *brothers*.

It is noteworthy that the king refers to himself—and we frequently hear such a statement—as *rāja* only in cohort with his brothers. Kingship for the *dharmarāja* concerns his immediate kin and *never* just himself, for they are his immediate *gaṇa* 'the companions'. This sensibility for kin, underlying the vicious verbal contest that the audience has just listened to between king and hero, only sharpens the emotion of those moments. Yudhiṣṭhira is never without his brothers, and in this *śastrayajña* they function as his subsidiary priests, in terms of enactment and of the myth. As we shall see later in the poem, during the pedagogy of the Śānti *parvan*, the singular and solitary king is a manifestation of a much more literate culture than what we have so far been reading; in the earlier half of the poem the society is what I would argue is thoroughly preliterate.

***

Yudhiṣṭhira's *aristeía*, as brief as it is, marks the essential closure of the *śastrayajña* that finally occurs when he at last enters the field and encounters and slays his *bhāga*, Śalya, whom Yudhiṣṭhira refers to as his *mātula* 'maternal uncle'. In matrilineal society, the maternal uncle often bears the functions of a paternal figure, and the genetic father is of lesser significance. Thus, in the context of this duel, Yudhiṣṭhira is bound to kill someone who is of vital importance and dearness in his kinship relations, which is morally reprehensible.[149] As *dharmarāja*, such an act is heinous, although as the *kali yuga* has commenced, such improper behaviour is inevitable. The engagement begins at IX.10.18, although the actual events are scarcely even mentioned *en passant* until the fight becomes a duel to the death. Nakula, Sahadeva, Bhīmasena, and also Sātyaki assist the king by wearing down the temerity of Śalya until Yudhiṣṭhira can himself deliver the final coup. It is as if the poets are casually indicating to the audience how un-formidable the elder Pāṇḍava is because he requires to be so protected.[150] At one point the poets coyly observe that:

> dharmarājapurogās tu bhīmasenamukhā rathāḥ
>
> IX.12.45
>
> The Dharmarājā as leader, the chariot led by Bhīma ...

The king is thus not excelling in his valiance, and yet *kṣatriya* custom requires that he fell his allotted opponent. At this point, Yudhiṣṭhira appoints Arjuna, Bhīma, Sātyaki, Dhṛṣṭadyumna, Nakula, and Sahadeva to guard his chariot, and it is not as if he is entering the *dvairatha* 'the duel' in a solitary and unassisted manner. As the fight increases, the poets comment more correctly about Yudhiṣṭhira the fighter:

> purā bhūtvā mṛdur dānto yat tadā dāruṇo'bhavat
>
> IX.15.47
>
> Having been before gentle and mild, then he became pitiless!

[149] Just as Arjuna slays his *guru* and significant elder, Bhīṣma, as well as—unknowingly—his half-brother, Karṇa, and Bhīma fells his nominal cousin, Duryodhana, all these acts are accomplished in a morally tarnished fashion. The king and his two closest brothers are shady characters when it comes to the question of ends and means.

[150] In the fighting against the *gandharvas* in the Goṣayātra *parvan*, Yudhiṣṭhira does not engage in combat, but sends his four siblings to do the work (III.233). When the Pāṇḍavas assault Jayadratha in the forest, it is said that Yudiṣṭhira kills a hundred Sindhis (III.255.9). During the fighting at the end of Book Four, the Goharaṇa sub-*parvan*, which is mostly a battle of chariots, Yudhiṣṭhira does fight well, albeit briefly (IV.32.24).

This is an aspect of the king that the audience has never before witnessed, the warrior in his deathly combat rage, the *berserker* who destroys with a massive discharge of innumerable arrows.[151] Śalya's driver is killed by Kṛpa (IX.16.23), his horses are destroyed by Bhīma who then cuts away his armour (IX.16.26), and Śalya is left with little; finally Yudhiṣṭhira delivers the death-blow 'like Rudra' (IX.16.47). Śalya, fallen upon the earth, receives the unusual simile that portrays him:

> priyayā kāntayā kāntaḥ patamāna ivorasi
>
> IX.16.54
>
> Like a husband falling onto the breast of a devoted lover.

Enraged and reckless, inspired by bloody violence, Yudhiṣṭhira then rampages among the Kauravas, killing the younger brother of Śalya (IX.16.65); the theatre of war is thus essentially concluded, even though Duryodhana remains at large. Yudhiṣṭhira has not only won his duel, but also the battle and hence the kingdom, and it is as if the poets have given the king this *coup-de-grâce*, which both terminates the fighting and brings *jaya* or 'victory' to the Pāṇḍavas: the heroes win the battle and the king wins the kingdom, and Śalya's death blurs this distinction. So the ritual of weaponry is almost terminated as the *yajña* 'sacrifice' receives its concluding gesture from the principal *sacrificer*. The obsequies for the dead will conclude this rite, and Yudhiṣṭhira will also terminate that part of the liturgy. Both the death of Karṇa and the death of Śalya, insofar as these heroes are in fact close kin to Yudhiṣṭhira, only cloud the moral dignity of the king.

***

As a postlude to the gory rites of Kurukṣetra, when the Kaurava army has been annihilated and Duryodhana retreats beneath the waters of a lake in ritual *katábasis*, Yudhiṣṭhira with his entourage approaches the place and challenges his enemy:

> uttiṣṭhottiṣṭha gāndhāre māṃ yodhaya suyodhana
>
> IX.31.31
>
> Rise, rise, O son of Gāndhārī! Fight me, Suyodhana!

There is of course no question that Yudhiṣṭhira would ever fight such a hero as Duryodhana; this is simply the rhetoric of battle.[152] The *rāja* even—foolishly—offers

[151] This is from the Old Norse *berserkr*. The warrior's *lussa* in Greek is a violent 'wolfish rage', and in the Old Irish epic tradition this is *ríastrad*.

[152] However, it is said that *rājñā rājaiva yoddhavyas tathā dharmo vidhīyate* (A king should fight a king, so *dharma* intends) (XII.97.7).

Duryodhana the chance of kingship once again, if he is victorious in this individual encounter; such is the reckless magnanimity of Yudhiṣṭhira who always remains elevated and uncannily great. His greatness is strange, though, muted and almost unstated; yet he retains this impeccable sense of personal superiority, but without grandiosity. When Bhīma has finally struck down Duryodhana and begins to kick the weak and wounded body, Yudhiṣṭhira intervenes to prevent this, commanding his brother:

> rājā jñātir hataś cāyaṃ naitan nyāyyaṃ tavānagha
>
> IX.58.15
>
> He a king, a kinsman, and this one is struck! That is not proper of you, O rightful one!

There remains something about the inherent and *natural* quality of kingship that the tearful Yudhiṣṭhira cannot bear to see abused like this by his brutal and vindictive brother, and *vilalāpa ciraṃ* (he sobbed at length).[153] Yudhiṣṭhira, when Kṛṣṇa attempts to justify Bhīma, then responds further, saying: *na mamaitat priyaṃ yad rājānaṃ vṛkodaraḥ padā mūrdhny aspṛśat* (it does not please me that Vṛkodara touched the king on the head with his foot) (IX.59.31). It is never quite clear how protocol functions between the brothers, and Bhīma replies to his brother: *tavādya pṛthivī ... tāṃ praśādhi mahārāja* (now the earth is yours, rule it, Mahārāja!) (IX.59.39). It is remarkable, though, that after so much death, destruction, and vicissitude, Yudhiṣṭhira refers to and treats the dying Duryodhana with such reverence and esteem, and this small instant encapsulates the profoundly *good* quality of the *dharmarāja*. There is a thorough absence of malice about his person, which is how contemporary twenty-first century Indian culture views this character. In my experience of contemporary Indian modernity, Yudhiṣṭhira is always pictured as mild, dignified, and sincerely blameless, and he remains a cultural model for so many aspects of present-day society.

***

As a ruthless and vengeful epilogue to the battle, or as an *exeunt* to the ritual, Aśvatthāman and his two companions create carnage during the following night, as depicted in the Sauptika *parvan*, and the five sons of Draupadī are among the

[153] To repeat from earlier, when in the Āraṇyaka *parvan* Duryodhana is vanquished by the *gandharvas*, Yudhiṣṭhira is the altruistic one to instruct his brothers to free their cousin (III.232.1–19). Again the audience perceives how well the young king treats his opponent. He says, *bhedā jñātīnāṃ kalahāś ca* (despite 'the partition of kin and the strife'), *jñātidharmo na naśyati* (the *dharma* of kin does not perish) (III.232.2). Yudhiṣṭhira's practice of kingship is thoroughly kin-oriented and *not* autarchic.

victims.[154] Arguably, the *śastrayajña*, just like the *rājasūya*, has become a rite that has gone wrong, presumably because of the careful amorality that secured the deaths of Bhīṣma, Bhuriśravas, Abhimanyu, Ghatoṭkaca, Droṇa, and Karṇa. When Yudhiṣṭhira learns of the death of the Draupadeyas, *papāta mahyāṃ* ... *putraśokasamanvitaḥ* (full of grief for his sons he fell on the ground) (X.10.7). He exclaims: *jitvā śatrūñ jitaḥ paścāt* (having conquered enemies, I am conquered afterwards); victory has turned into defeat, despite all those—kinsmen and friends and allies—who perished in the endeavour. He sings a monody of seventeen *ślokas*, anguishing over their pyrrhic triumph, which has become so useless and futile, and then sends Nakula to escort Draupadī to their presence.[155] Yudhiṣṭhira proceeds to the field of slaughter in order to view the five decapitated and mutilated bodies, a sight that causes him once more to weep and to collapse, and Draupadī threatens to enter *prāya* and die unless the king is able to secure immediate and bloody revenge and to punish the slayer (X.11.15). Again, grief is very much the central *bhāva* or 'emotion' of the Bhārata Song, and there is little that is lightly joyous in these *kṣatriya* parts of the poem.

Bhīma soon returns from finding Aśvatthāman, bearing the jewel that Aśvatthāman had borne on his head.[156] Draupadī offers this to the king and relinquishes her vow of entering *prāya*; he accepts the jewel and places it on his own head:

> tato divyaṃ maṇivaraṃ śirasā dhārayan prabhuḥ
> śuśubhe sa mahārājaḥ sacandra iva parvataḥ
>
> X.16.35
>
> Then the majestic one bore the divine best jewel on his head.
> The great king shone like a mountain with a moon.[157]

[154] Aśvatthāman is a *brāhmaṇa* and son of Droṇa; the elder was not born of a woman but simply of male semen in a pot. Aśvatthāman was a devotee of the Mahādeva Śiva, and in Book Ten, *paśumāram amārayat* (he killed as if slaughtering a sacrificial victim) (X.8.18). One of his victims is Śikhaṇḍin, and, appropriately—because he was changed from woman to man—*dvidhā ciccheda so* (he cut him in two parts) (X.8.60).

[155] Unlike her kingly husband, she appears without overwhelming grief, just like a tough and doughty *kṣatriya* matron should be (X.11.10).

[156] Like Karṇa, Aśvatthāman possessed innate jewelry; Draupadī says, *droṇaputrasya sahajo maṇiḥ śirasi me śrutaḥ* (I have heard of the innate jewel on the head of the son of Droṇa) (X.11.20). She demands to own this.

[157] As a note, it might be worth recording that the deity who is often portrayed with the moon in his hair is the Mahādeva Śiva or Rudra. Also, this particular jewel that Yudhiṣṭhira now bears on his head—perhaps on his forehead—comes from Aśvatthāman who was a strong devotee of the lord Śiva. The two final *adhyāyas* of this *parvan* are full of verses that praise the Mahādeva (X.17–18). Kṛṣṇa, who speaks most of these two chapters, in his address to Yudhiṣṭhira, closes the speeches with the statement

The war—and the *śastrayajña*—then receives its formal termination in the obsequies for the fallen, which are given in the Strī *parvan*, where the women—mothers, wives, and sisters—enter the field of the Kurus to identify and lament for their fallen male kin, for all the *kṣatriya* men are now dead. This book, along with the solely ritual parts of the Āśvamedhika *parvan*, concludes what I consider to constitute the *epic Mahābhārata*, a song that began with the *svayaṃvara* of Draupadī, when she selected and affirmed her choice of husband and brother of the future king.[158]

The *parvan* begins with Yudhiṣṭhira's victory and triumph being glossed by the poets as:

nirjaneyaṃ vasumatī śūnyā saṃprati kevalā

XI.1.6

This earth is unpeopled, entirely and completely empty.

The Pāṇḍavas have won their kingdom and found revenge for Draupadī's outrage, but it is a place of desolation; kingship now overlooks a barren, unmanned, and widowed world. King Dhṛtarāṣṭra has lost his ninety-nine sons, king Duryodhana is dead along with all his great heroes, including Karṇa, who himself possessed an unspoken and unresolved claim to kingship; and king Yudhiṣṭhira is now met with a vast hollow sound of horror and destitution to which he will contribute his own protracted and shameful expression. It is this anguish that colours and inhabits the reality of Kuru *jaya* 'victory', at least for the Pāṇḍava.

Yudhiṣṭhira is present during the performance of the Strī *parvan* where Gāndhārī sings a long and mournful dirge lamenting the dead heroes and kings who lie upon the field. At the end of this book, he converses with the aged Dhṛtarāṣṭra, and, in response to the old ruler, he makes the claim that, during his forest exile, from the divine *ṛṣi* Lomaśa:

---

referring to how it was *not* Aśvatthāman but Śiva who caused the recent deaths: *mahādevaprasādaḥ sa kuru kāryam anantaram* ([it was] the approbation of the Mahādeva! Do your duty immediately!) (X.18.26).

[158] By epic *Mahābhārata*, I mean that main part of the poem that is in the genre of *kṣatriya* poetry; this would put aside the books subsequent to the Strī *parvan*; these later books I think of as being drawn from another *kind* of poetic tradition. However, these two combined elements of the poem as we know them now, I nevertheless consider a successful, coherent, and finely integrated work of art. The eventual transcription of the poem into writing is when I consider these two components to have been so closely integrated. The two bodies of the poem are not absolutely exclusive for there occur elements indicative of the other in each of these two parts—as in the Āraṇyaka *parvan* and in the Āśvamedhika *parvan*, for instance.

divyaṃ cakṣur api prāptaṃ jñānayogena vai purā

XI.26.20

Once then, divine vision was obtained by [my] yoga of knowledge.[159]

The audience hears little about this gift, and Yudhiṣṭhira is possibly once again speaking in a slightly mendacious manner in order to assuage his guilt towards the old king; this verse could be drawn from another poetic tradition in which the *dharmarāja* played a different role.

Yudhiṣṭhira commands that pyres be made to incinerate the myriad dead, the kings, the heroes, and the unspoken nameless ones. This is his first order as Kururāja (XI.26.24–26). Then, when Kuntī has sung a long formal lament for her eldest son, Karṇa, Yudhiṣṭhira—now ostensibly enlightened as to Karṇa's primogeniture—himself sings a lament responsively to his mother.[160]

tataḥ śataguṇaṃ duḥkham idaṃ māṃ aspṛśad bhṛśam

XI.27.19

This hundredfold grief touched me vehemently.

This is the effect of the ritual of war. In fact, this grief is greater, he says, than what he endured at the death of Abhimanyu and at the death of Draupadī's sons.[161]

na ca sma vaiśasaṃ ghoraṃ kauravāntakaraṃ bhavet

XI.27.20

Truly, the terrific calamitous end-of-the-Kurus should not occur.

[159] There are two other mortal humans who possess such a sense of divine vision in the poem, Saṃjaya and Gāndhārī, both of whom received their gift from Vyāsa. This ability to visualise, as I have shown in McGrath 2010, is an intrinsic skill in preliterate poetry, particularly as the poets *visualise* the poem for the audience. It is also said that Vyāsa verbally imparted to Yudhiṣṭhira *yogavidyām anuttamāṃ* (the utmost knowledge of *yoga*) (III.37.34). There is never any real indication, however, that Yudhiṣṭhira possesses esoteric learning or such a capacity for influence. He tells Arjuna that *tayā prayuktayā samyag jagat sarvaṃ prakāśate* (by this pronouncement [what Vyāsa imparted] the entire world is completely visible) (III.38.9). Again, this statement never receives any amplification or effect. It bears no consequence in the narrative; the poets only say that Yudhiṣṭhira conveyed this *vidhi* 'method' to Arjuna so that his brother might be able *draṣṭuṃ* 'to see' the deity Indra (III.38.14–15), although Arjuna had no difficulty *seeing* deities on previous occasions. At VI.33.8, Arjuna receives momentary divine vision from his charioteer Kṛṣṇa so that he might fully experience the latter's theophany.

[160] Kuntī announces: *sa hi vaḥ pūrvajo bhrātā* (for he is your elder brother) (XI.27.11).

[161] He is therefore favouring the sanguine relationship with the mother more than the lateral and affiliate relationship with the spouse.

Along with all the mourning women and the kinfolk of Karṇa, and his own brothers, Yudhiṣṭhira performs the funereal rites standing in the Gaṅgā, and then, once more, he collapses unconscious, this time upon the riverbank. It is as this point in the narrative thread of the Bhārata Song that the Āśvamedhika *parvan* later recommences—after the immense interlude of the Śānti *parvan* and the Anuśāsana *parvan*—with the fallen king and Kṛṣṇa attempting to restore some gravity or dignity to the moment (XIV.1.1–4).[162] Even old Dhṛtarāṣṭra remonstrates with him in attempt to change his mood and be more kingly; the poets play with the word *kuru* here—the name of the clan and the imperative:

uttiṣṭha kuruśārdūla kuru kāryam anantaram

XIV.1.7

Arise, O tiger of the Kurus. Perform the tasks immediately!

Mourning, remorse, and the anguish at the human cost of his kingship will now entirely colour Yudhiṣṭhira's reign. As he is the primary agent and benefactor of this *śastrayajña*, the poem subsequently deals with how it is that the king is made to forget the human and moral cost of the ritual. The plaintive and melancholic Strī *parvan* closes with *rāja* Yudhiṣṭhira performing a formal lament for the deceased Karṇa when he has learned that the hero was in fact his nominal elder half-brother. This is where the *śastrayajña* finds its closure, and, in a metonymical sense, it is Yudhiṣṭhira's song for all those who perished—including Karṇa (who died in order to secure his title and its terrain)—that terminates this violent ceremony. Yudhiṣṭhira is the one who officiates as leading sacrificer, and it is his words for Karṇa that end the rite; the efficacy of this ritual is actually—in the long term, as we noted at the beginning of this book—concerned with the Yādava clan rather than with the family of the sons of Pāṇḍu. The immediate sorrow leaves king Yudhiṣṭhira in desperate need of consolation or what is called *śānti* 'pacification'.

[162] Why the editors of the poem chose to introduce the Śānti and Anuśāsana *parvans* after the Strī *parvan* and before the Āśvamedhika *parvan* is an important question: why would they determine to break the tempo and movement of the narrative with a vast and highly literate text that is more didactic and more like *śāstra* than the rest of the Bhārata Song? Certainly the continuity of performance is broken by the introjection of these two edifying narratives. The Āśvamedhika *parvan* itself experiences a similar disjunction, for by the fourth *adhyāya* the narrative enters on a long divagation about sacrifice and wealth, followed by the Anugītā, that continues to the end of the fiftieth *adhyāya*, and only then does the poem resume the account of the *aśvamedha* rites. The reasoning behind such a *bricolage* of varying and profoundly diverse elements of style in the epic remains opaque. The questions are: How would such evolutions occur in performance? And what was the purpose for such a sequencing of so many disparate kinds of poetry? The arrangement is certainly literary rather than preliterate, yet how this came to be remains a mystery.

***

To bring a close to the *śastrayajña*, this long eighteen-days of human immolation, Yudhiṣṭhira speaks about the battle and refers to Bhīṣma. It is a significant question whether the 'rite of weaponry' or 'sacrifice' was viewed by the audience simply in terms of simile—a series of images that relate to sacrificial scenes along with the other kinds of serial tropes where heroes are *like* trees, or the image of battle generating a *nadī* or a flood of human blood and war detritus—or whether this icon of the *yajña* is actually drawing into the narrative a system of *myth* in which battle and war are considered as an action on a universal or cosmic level that have material effects in the world. Is this more a situation of poetry and simile? Or have the poets actually been portraying an effective rite that does possess practical consequence in the mundane world, just like any other sacrifice is putatively considered?

Yudhiṣṭhira says:

dhvajottamāgrocchritadhūmaketuṃ śarārciṣaṃ kopamahāsamīram
mahādhanur jyātalanemighoṣaṃ tanutranānāvidhaśastrahomam
mahācamūkakṣavarābhipannaṃ mahāhave bhīṣmamahādavāgnim

X.10.20

The best banner raised at the top—a standard of smoke, flames of arrow, a great wind of anger,
The great bow, noise of hands on bow-strings, the libation—of various weapons and armour,
The great army—assisted by the finest dry-grass in the vast battle—a great burning forest of Bhīṣma!

Such endless *secco recitative* of verses in the four Kurukṣetra Books are often made on such a tempo of simile: these are *pictures* taken from the fire sacrifice, images of trees and forests (and sometimes mountains), and the metonymical repetition of the 'river of blood' composed of war paraphernalia. These visual images convey an almost musical quality to the poem by supplying a steady and constant refrain and metonymy in what is actually a long, dense narration of violence and death, and scenes of horrific bodily and mortal carnage; thus, cruelty, brutality, and death are made lovely and beautiful.[163]

Whether such images enjoin a particular *myth*, however, invoking another activity that is being represented by all this destructive behaviour, is a worthy question. In a sense, myth *explains* something that exists or occurs in human experience, whereas a metaphor of enactment embellishes in order to transform

[163] I have discussed the image of the *nadī* in McGrath 2004, VI:1; and in McGrath 2011, 79–81.

the experience into an aesthetic and emotional condition. Myth, ideally, generates truth, whereas metaphor is creative of pleasure and its sentiment. (To repeat what we stated earlier in this book, myth occurs in narrative form, while enactment—in this point of view—is performative or theatrical, and affective.) As we observed with the *rājasūya*, what was an old-time myth was drawn upon by the poets who had obviously heard of such a ceremony, but had little experience of the event, and the rite thus became a metaphor within the context of the epic narrative—an occasion they *had* to enact dramatically because they had *no* experience enabling them to actually describe it.

Similarly, the *śastrayajña* is more a rite where signifiers are exchanged among *kṣatriyas* in an economy of metaphor: death is exchanged with *kīrti* 'fame' and *yaśas* 'glory', so that by mentioning *fame* we understand *death*. The myth, in whose telling the supernal orders find temporary equilibrium with the sublunary and human register of being, does not actually occur; therefore, the *śastrayajña* cannot really and truly be considered a *rite* at all, unlike the *rājasūya* or the *aśvamedha*.

However, the performance of the poem itself—*qua* ritual—possesses consequences for an audience, and I would here propose that one of the effects of epic declamation or singing is the assuaging—a *kátharsis*—or sedation of grief and the despair caused by participation in violent behaviour, that is, war.[164] Only in this latter sense, of the poem being a ritual in itself and during performance, can we view these four Kurukṣetra Books as a depiction and a script for the *śastrayajña*. By the word ritual here I do not simply mean a closed and self-referential system of communicative behaviour and speech, but more a manner of formal enactment that engages the divine and cosmic world with the human order so that some form of temporary and harmonious equilibrium is caused. I use the term 'ritual' in this latter sense of ideally possessing universal and worldly efficacy, if it is successfully accomplished.

It is the metaphors in the speech of the poets that allows the *kṣatriya* audience to find relief or discharge for their own personal emotions of mourning and ignominy, emotions coming from violent warrior behaviour.[165] As we have said earlier, in this telling, myth is the vehicle and enactment is the expression: the former concerns kinship, while the latter concerns declamation itself and acting. The poets in their expressiveness, and through their dramatic skill, supply

[164] Hence the dominant aesthetic tone of the poem, its *rasa*, is that of *śānta* 'pacification'. See Shay (2002) on warriors and the necessity of grieving in a post-war situation.

[165] To repeat an earlier note, the metaphor of fire, as a sign of either the warrior in combat or of the hero as he offers his body to the conflagration of war, is a constant motif in the Kurukṣetra Books. Battle thus receives a sacrificial and ritual attribute.

these metaphors with verve and life, thus invigorating the poem and (of course) the audience. Therefore, we see a constant oscillation between what constitutes myth and what goes to make the dramatic metaphors at work in the poem as it is performed. For us today, as twenty-first century *readers*, in order to re-form what must have occurred during the enactment of the poem requires careful and detailed perception—via precise and slow reading—in order to achieve a retrieval of those long-vanished voices. This is a key component in the act of close reading, the being able to identify those affective nuances of language in the poem that derive, not from its substance, but from its old-time performances: *how* it is that the poets once infused emotion and significance into their words, an experience that was then received by an audience.

***

To reemphasise, in closing, for preliterate epic, myth is the story of kinship, while enactment is the simultaneous interpretation of qualities by both audience *and* the poets. For instance, the poets must communicate to their listeners and viewers a vast range of human affect: the profound *diapason* mood of feminine voices in the lachrymose Strī *parvan*, the cynical offensive words of Draupadī, the often jejune aridity of Vidura, and the weary *pathos* of old Dhṛtarāṣṭra, the virulent bombast of Duryodhana, and the tough doughty words of Arjuna, as well as the terse brittle anger of Yudhiṣṭhira in the scene we examined above, and many more instances simply of irony and poetic insinuation.

Emotion, as a signifier and just like metaphor, requires interpretation as well as expression, and this is a fundamental requisite for any successful and skillful dramatic performance; in a sense the poets must possess an excellent critical faculty and judgement concerning *how* they intend to perform the work. There is the poem in a literary or textual sense, there is its performance as a song, and thirdly, there is the poem as a ritual that possesses—like an effective rite—a certain universal efficacy that bears worldly consequences. The first concerns the editors of the poem, the second quality is the concern of the poets themselves, and the third aspect has relevance for an audience.

The putative efficacy of this third form, what I have argued as a rite of grief—which is how I understand epic *Mahābhārata*—is a ritual the poem itself states as possessing tremendous moral and cosmic effect. The poem also, especially at the close of the Svargārohaṇa *parvan*, speaks of how morally and spiritually effective the poem is for human life *qua* the rites of its performance, as, for instance:

> imāṃ bhāratasāvitrīṃ prātar utthāya yaḥ paṭhet
> sa bhārataphalaṃ prāpya paraṃ brahmādhigacchati

XVIII.5.51

Having risen at dawn, whoever would recite this Bhārata-verse,
Having obtained the fruit of the Bhārata, that person would go towards the highest Brahmā.

The delicacy of how the three moments of force that make up the totality of the epic—text, performance, and ritual audition—has cohered during millennia of time. How this became arranged is in fact the focus of all my *Mahābhārata* studies. We treat the poem as a single and integral written document that took its origin at a certain point in time, but we must not exclude the vast, complex, and rich antecedence that led to the production of that beautiful monument. To quote from Olivelle, "Philology must not simply look at the web but at the spider also."[166] The problem for us today is that the web was developed during a period of many centuries by *many* spiders before it became formally and materially articulated in written and documentary form.

3. The *Aśvamedha*

The fourteenth *parvan* of the poem is in part devoted to a portrait of this rite.[167] This is a *parvan*, which for the main, is unusually *whole* and well fitted with the earlier and more central *parvans* of the poem. It also appears to carry on directly after what occurred at Kurukṣetra without regard for the intervention of the Śānti and Anuśāsana *parvans*, for it continues very much in that *heroic* tradition. Along with the *digvijaya*, which preceded the rite of the *rājasūya*, and the recounting of *tīrthas* in Book Three, this is one of those parts of the epic collection that deals in some geographical detail with *bhāratavarṣa* (the territory of the Bhāratas)—the picturing of topography serving as an important aspect of what makes for a literary 'classic.'[168] Yudhiṣṭhira's firm adherence to an ideal of

[166] Olivelle 2009, 85.

[167] Much of the early part of the Tīrthayātrā sub-*parvan*, III.80–83, quantifies the spiritual valence acquired by the particular pilgrimages described; one of the ways of calibrating such valence is by equating it with the heavenly value earned for a king by the sponsorship of a horse sacrifice. In the ritual economy of *bhāratavarṣa*, the *aśvamedha* possesses extremely high worth; it is even more significant in its merit for a king than the *rājasūya*. The rite of immolating horses has a long-standing history and was not an uncommon mode of conducting a sacrifice; see Stark, in Stark et al. 2012, 107: "Powerful elites—cultivating a military lifestyle, displaying social status via large-scale horse sacrifices, and expressing their worldview in a distinctive artistic language ... emerged in the Eastern Eurasian steppes as early as the Late Bronze Age." What was possibly unique about the *aśvamedha* was the ceremonial pursuit of the wandering animal and the formal battles that occurred during that journey.

[168] The *digvijaya* occurs at II.23.12–29.19; the *tīrthayātrā* commences at III.80.12; Saṃjaya describes in catalogue form the geography and political society of *bhāratavarṣa* at VI.10.5–68.

clan polity came with a terrible price: that of almost complete destruction of the menfolk of the land, all killed at Kurukṣetra in an horrific and totally pyrrhic, internecine war.[169] What would be the message here or the *judgement* of the poem—as far as an audience or the king are concerned—when so much was annihilated in order to achieve so little? And what valence is attributed to the securing of kingship on these terms? The ritual pursuit of the sacred horse by Arjuna and his force during this *parvan* is through the various clan and family lands of those who survived the battle. This ceremony—as both rite and a material demonstration of martial power—finally stabilises the Kuru kingdom after years and years of bloody disaffection.

The Āśvamedhika *parvan*—the fourteenth book—brings formal and ritual closure to the epic following on from where the Strī *parvan* ended.[170] The idea for a great sacrifice comes from Kṛṣṇa, who at this point still remains moderately close to Yudhiṣṭhira although the former duality of power has lapsed. He says, *yajasva vividhair yajñair bahubhiḥ* (sacrifice, with appropriate and large sacrifices!).[171]

> devāṃs tarpaya somena svadhayā ca pitṝn api
>
> XIV.2.3
>
> Satisfy the deities with soma and then the ancestors with portions!

It is notable that a certain archaism creeps into the poem here with the mention of *soma* and also with the intention to perform the ancient horse sacrifice, which Vyāsa, Yudhiṣṭhira's timeless and unearthly nominal grandfather, also proposes

[169] Witzel (2012, sec. 3:11) situates such a moment in the tradition of Laurasian myth.

[170] If one excludes the Śānti and Anuśāsana *parvans* from the epic sequence, then the Āśvamedhika *parvan* is the twelfth book. In the Javanese version of the Great Epic, translated towards the end of the eleventh century, the Śānti and the Anuśāsana *parvans* are absent; see the Introduction to Belvalkhar's 1959 edition of the Pune Āśramavāsika *parvan*, p. xxix. Karmarkar, in his Introduction to the 1960 Pune Edition of the Āśvamedhika *parvan* (pp. xxiii–xxiv) notes: "the Parvasaṃgrahaparvan ... makes no mention of the Anugītā ... The Parvan though named the Āśvamedhika actually does not say much about the Aśvamedha. There is another work called the 'Jaimini-Aśvamedha,' supposed to have been written by Jaimini, one of the pupils of Vyāsa himself. Tradition also says that Jaimini wrote a *Mahābhārata* (all of the five pupils of Vyāsa, Paila, etc. are also credited with having written the *Mahābhārata* independently) but as the Pāṇḍavas were there shown in an unfavourable light, it was never published; only the Aśvamedha portion of it has survived, where, however, the Pāṇḍavas and Kṛṣṇa do cut a sorry figure throughout ... The 'Jaimini-Aśvamedha' is obviously a later work, completed possibly before or about the beginning of the Christian era."

[171] One should recall that it was Nārada who inspired and impelled Yudhiṣṭhira towards fulfilling the *rājasūya* rite. Yudhiṣṭhira is always dignified and firm, yet he is not an initiator; he always responds to his *gaṇa*—which is so unlike the paradigm of kingship pictured and related by Bhīṣma is his discourse on *rājadharma* in Book Twelve.

when he appears; Vyāsa instructs the new *rāja* to be more kinglike and not to allow terrible mourning to dominate his psyche. Once again we can see how the poets arrange this artifice of Bronze Age society, and archaic kingship drawing upon the *heard* traditions of the past. The Gupta dynasty similarly attempted to retrieve and revive this ancient rite as a means of legitimising power, for an idealised past is a source of great durability and historical connectivity if correctly reformulated and dramatised.

The situation at the outset of the *parvan* concerns the visceral grief and remorse of the king for all the death and violence he had overseen at the battle. Addressing the king's sorrow, Vyāsa says:

> maivaṃ bhava na te yuktam idam ajñānam īdṛśam
>
> XIV.2.18
>
> Do not be so! This is not correct, such ignorance!

Everyone is appalled by Yudhiṣṭhira's continuing and inappropriate sorrow, and Vyāsa too is soon to encourage the new king in the production of this major rite. Yet Yudhiṣṭhira continues to feel totally culpable for the vast and devastating annihilation of life and wealth that occurred at Kurukṣetra, and he says of himself: *imaṃ jñātivadhaṃ kṛtvā sumahāntaṃ* (having accomplished this very great destruction of kin), he now possesses no wealth to perform such a complex and sophisticated rite as the horse sacrifice (XIV.3.12). The main task of a king as sacrificer is not simply to accomplish the ritual successfully, but simultaneously to distribute great quantities of moveable wealth to the *brāhmaṇas*, as well as feeding them during the festival of the rite. He adds, *vināśya pṛthivīṃ yajñārthe* (having ruined the earth for the sake of a ritual), there remains no wealth: both *rājasūya* and *aśvamedha* require vast disbursements of supplies and also copious distributions of food.[172] Therefore, a king acquires wealth through his campaigns and prestations, and then returns the substance on the occasion of a formal sacrifice; in a premonetary economy the circulation of wealth is founded upon this kind of massive exchange or transmission of matter and services that vitalise the economy.[173]

[172] See Anthony 2007, 331: "The speakers of Proto-Indo-European followed chiefs (*weik-potis*) who sponsored feasts and ceremonies and were immortalised in praise poetry." "Proto-Indo-European contained a vocabulary related to gift giving and gift taking ... the public performance of praise poetry, animal sacrifices, and the distribution of meat ... were central elements of the show." Ibid., 343.

[173] In McGrath 2009, I argued that in the epic's premonetary economy the mention of moveable wealth occurred on the occasion of marriages and sacrifices. I proposed that women and the movement between households or clans constituted the 'standard' for a calibration of value. Byrne (2001, 33) notes similarly: "The *cumal* (literally 'bond-woman', in Hiberno-Latin, *ancilla*) was the highest unit of value in the pre-monetary Irish economy ... worth three milch-cows, or sometimes rather more [and] also used as a land-measurement. Seven *cumula* is a common figure of higher values."

As we have already observed, in this sense the *śastrayajña* was not a true sacrifice except on the level of metaphor. Certainly in an orthoprax and orthodox sense, the 'rite of weaponry' is no more than a metaphor because in high brahminical terms *all* rituals, and especially the sacrifices, are absolutely controlled and precise in their performance; otherwise they lack efficacy in commanding balance between the earthly and the heavenly forces. Heroes as libations being offered into the fire of battle are similes only, and sometimes this trope translates into another expression, that of the *nadī*, the 'river', of heroic blood that flows downward towards the domain of Yama.[174] All these rituals taken from late Vedic times are simply a manner by which the poets paint their epic account of how it is that they view and review a former heroic era, one projected upon an ancient almost pre-discursive time. This retrospective vision—performed as an epic song—is a medium for how the poets and editors illustrate their scheme about the nature and operation of kingship and about the conception of material terrain and topography.

***

Before the rite of the horse sacrifice begins to be arranged, there occurs what is called the Anugītā, another disjunction in the narrative process and what is in fact a long esoteric peroration sung by Kṛṣṇa in the voice of an anonymous *brāhmaṇa* who once initiated him into the mysteries; this commences at XIV.16.16 and runs until 50.41. Arjuna had requested his friend to teach him once again, since he had forgotten what he had been told and initiated into during the performance of the Gītā. Kṛṣṇa is troubled by this lapse of memory and says (concerning that first pronouncement):

abuddhvā yan na gṛhṇīthās tan me sumahadapriyam
nūnam aśraddadhāno'si durmedhāś cāsi pāṇḍava ...
na śakyaṃ tan mayā bhūyas tathā vaktum aśeṣataḥ
paraṃ hi brahma kathitaṃ yogayuktena tan mayā

XIV.16.10

Since—having not been aware—you did not grasp that: it
displeases me;
Now, O Pāṇḍava, you are foolish and you are faithless,
So I am not able to retell completely
For the ultimate Brahma that was told by me was enjoined by
yoga.

[174] Except, of course, as we noted above, unless we take the performance of epic singing as a rite that possesses its own social and spiritual efficacy. After all, the battle *only* occurs in fact in the performance of the epic, and there is no *real* battle; that is the myth.

Since that yogic inspiration is not with him now, there follows another long discourse, ostensibly for the ears of Arjuna, but in fact the audience is the true recipient as would be the actual patron of the performance; for one presumes that epic *Mahābhārata*, at this point in time, was a medium that was performed before kings or young princes. Just as the singing of the Gītā preceded the great battle, so now the recitation of the Anugītā precedes the fighting Arjuna will engage in as he pursues the sacred horse about the kingdom. It is as if, before entering combat, an elite *kṣatriya* is to receive philosophical and yogic instruction so that, conceptually, he is prepared to do battle. Kṛṣṇa does not speak of his own vision and experience on this occasion, but recalls the mysteries into which a *brāhmaṇa* once initiated him.[175]

***

The account of the rite formally opens with king Yudhiṣṭhira setting off in high style with his army towards the mountainous north in order to acquire the wealth such a ceremony requires. He is described as:

> saṃstūyamānāḥ stutibhiḥ sūtamāgadhabandibhiḥ ...
> pāṇḍureṇātapatreṇa dhriyamāṇena mūrdhani
> babhau yudhiṣṭhiras tatra paurṇamāsyām ivoḍurāṭ
>
> XIV.63.2
>
> Being praised with hymns by poets, eulogists, and songsters,
> With a white umbrella being borne above his head,
> Yudhiṣṭhira shone there like a king of stars on a full moon night.

This great moon, as we have seen before, is the king's personal emblem and standard.[176] Vyāsa is the director of the proceedings and Yudhiṣṭhira defers to his judgement; the rite was partly his conception, and it was also Vyāsa who suggested that the king make his journey in order to acquire the necessary wealth.[177] Once all is prepared, Yudhiṣṭhira says to his nominal grandfather, *anujñātum icchāmi bhavatā* (I desire to be authorised by you) (XIV.70.14). The elder responds, *anujānāmi rājaṃs tvāṃ ... kriyatāṃ* (I permit you, O king ... let it be done).

[175] See McGrath 2014 for further comment on the Gītā and the Anugītā.

[176] The Kurus, like the Yādava clan, are part of the *candravaṃśa* (the lunar dynasty) for those born of Soma. The Rāmāyaṇa tells of the *sūryavaṃśa* (the solar dynasty), referring to those born of Agni.

[177] The poets say: *tataḥ saṃcodayāmāsa vyāso dharmātmajaṃ nṛpam / aśvamedham prati* (Then Vyāsa urged the king, the son of Dharma, to perform the Aśvamedha) (XIV.61.18).

yajasva vājimedhena vidhivad dakṣiṇāvatā

XIV.70.15

Sacrifice with the horse-rite appropriately, with gifts!

These are the two figures propelling the ritual, the *ṛṣi* and the *rāja*: the former directs and the latter causes the ceremony to be performed and then shares property among *brāhmaṇas* in the old Indo-Āryan manner. The sacrifice is viewed almost as a propitiation for the horrors and complete disorder that eighteen days of absolute war generated.

Then the king turns to his other advisor, heroic Kṛṣṇa, and requests his confirmation of the rite, saying: *dīkṣayasva tvam ātmānaṃ* ('consecrate yourself' or 'initiate yourself') for the rite. It is as if at this point in narrative time Yudhiṣṭhira regards these two figures—both of whom bear the title of Kṛṣṇa—as the mentors of his kingship: one who generated the ideas behind the clan (i.e., the priestly) and one who generated the practical and martial policies that conduced to the clan's victory (i.e., the heroic).[178] Kṛṣṇa tells the king:

tvaṃ cādya kuruvīrāṇāṃ dharmeṇābhivirājase ...
yunaktu no bhavān kārye yatra vāñchasi bhārata

XIV.70.23

And now you are radiant with dharma among the Kuru warriors ...
O lord, yoke us in the rite where, O Bhārata, you strive![179]

The horse is selected, and the poets and priests commissioned, and the animal is sent off to wander the earth and so to establish the king's order and ways, the horse being the icon of kingly *regime*. Arjuna is appointed to escort the horse on its peregrination about the landscape so actually reifying the material presence and literal force of that metaphor. Vyāsa says of Arjuna that *yathāśāstraṃ ... cārayiṣyati te hayam* (he will make your horse roam according to the *śāstras*) (XIV.71.17).[180] In that progress, he both symbolically and really fights with the

[178] Kṛṣṇā Dvaipāyaṇa Vyāsa and Kṛṣṇa Vāsudeva. Kṛṣṇā Pāñcālī, or Draupadī—whose outrage generates the Pāṇḍava wrath—is the third to bear this 'dark' epithet.

[179] On a technical note, both Vyāsa and Kṛṣṇa tell Yudhiṣṭhira, *yajasva* (perform the sacrifice); whereas Yudhiṣṭhira says to Kṛṣṇa, *dīkṣayasva* ('initiate the sacrifice' or 'commence it') (XIV.70.15 and 24; and at 21). The ongoing political intimacy of the king and his chief ally Kṛṣṇa are thus portrayed even in a ritual setting.

[180] *Haya* is a Ṛg Vedic name for a horse, from √*hi*. *Vājī* is another Vedic word for 'horse' that is employed by the poets in this *parvan*. It is as if they are attempting to recreate that ancient and archaic world by the use and artifice of such old terminology.

descendents of the kings and heroes who fell at Kurukṣetra; the wandering of the animal, thus, in an ideal sense, establishes the reach of the new king's political *dharma* by reconnecting all those old clans and lineages on a nominal level with the new *rāja*. As the horse is consecrated, Yudhiṣṭhira—who is no longer likened to Indra but to Prajāpati, the divine creator and proto-sacrificer—is pictured:

hemamālī rukmakaṇṭhaḥ pradīpta iva pāvakaḥ ...
kṛṣṇājinī daṇḍapāṇiḥ kṣaumavāsāḥ sa dharmajaḥ

XIV.72.4

The Dharma-born, alight as if fire, with a gold collar and golden necklace,
With a black-deer skin, staff in hand, wearing a linen garment ...

I like to think of this customary event as the sacrosanct horse sets off on its journey as a formalised folk-recapitulation of the equine and nomadic migrations of the ancient Indo-Āryans, a migration that established the *ṛta* 'order' of those early Vedic speaking peoples in the northern subcontinent. The poets in fact actually do describe some of the encounters that Arjuna enters into—as he accompanies the consecrated animal—as being composed of:

āryāś ca pṛthivīpālāḥ prahṛṣṭanaravāhanāḥ

XIV.72.25

Āryan kings, possessing vehicles drawn by joyous men.

It is as if the poets are trying hard to revision that ancient *Āryan* world insofar as that would be a source of rightful authority for the new king. This would be particularly applicable if the performance of the poem occurred at the court of a Gupta ruler who was attempting to remaster that old ritual ideology in the service of his new governance.

Yudhiṣṭhira interdicts Arjuna from killing any of those who had kin that perished at Kurukṣetra, and thus many of the ensuing fights are more like theatrical, or ritual, chariot skirmishes than deadly encounters. The king had instructed him: *hatabāndhavā na te ... hantavyāḥ* (you are not to kill those whose kin were slain) (XIV.73.7). The poets say of Arjuna:

punar evānvadhāvat sa taṃ hayaṃ kāmacāriṇam

XIV.77.43

Thus again he pursued that horse—wandering as it desired.

The travels of the sanctified horse encompass all of Northern India, from Sindh to Aṅga and up to Gāndhāra; a huge amount of terrain is referred to by the poetry (XIV.73ff.).[181] The wandering of the horse is a prelude to the praxis of the rite, and, when the animal returns towards Hāstinapura, Yudhiṣṭhira invites many kings to the ceremony and has costly structures, arches and buildings, prepared, as well as *yūpas* 'sacrificial stakes' that are decorated with gold; enormous wealth is employed in these proceedings as part of the feasting and hospitality (XIV.87.5). The sacrifice itself occurs on the full moon in the month of Caitra, which takes place around the spring equinox. Kṛṣṇa is said to remind the king about the killing that occurred at the *rājasūya* rite—concerning the gift that Yudhiṣṭhira had offered him—and he advises the king to be careful on this occasion and not to tarnish the rite with human bloodshed; we have noted how the *dis*-order subsequent to the *rājasūya* was ostensibly caused by Kṛṣṇa himself (XIV.88.16–17). There is no mention by the poets that the death of Śiśupāla had contaminated the *rājasūya* and that the *bad* ritual had in fact led to the horrors of total war. Nevertheless, ritual efficacy and ritual propriety were understood *always* to possess a causal relation vis-à-vis the framing society. Once again we see Kṛṣṇa supplying his ally with crucial advice.

It is Vyāsa who announces the opening of the ritual: *yajasva*, he commands, 'sacrifice!' (XIV.90.12).[182] All the procedures, ordinances, and directions are sustained, but this is mentioned only cursorily, and it is as if the poets are familiar with the concept and lexicon of the event. Yet concerning the actual details they are vague: it is something that they have merely *heard* about in the old past but never personally *seen*; and as a result the descriptions bear a *recherchés* semblance that seems quaintly anachronistic.[183]

[181] As with the *yātrā* or 'pilgrimage' as related by Rāma (IX.34), or the song of the *tīrthas* 'sacred fords', as told by Nārada and Lomaśa (III.80), or the ritual journeys the Pāṇḍava brothers performed as an integral prelude to the *rājasūya* ceremony (II.24), almost all of the geography of the northern subcontinent—including as far west as what we now know as Afghanistan and Pakistan—is depicted in the *Mahābhārata*. As we have already observed above, this is the famed *bhāratavarṣa*, the terrestrial ground of the poem. This literary impulse to classify and catalogue topography is typical of what I consider to be a 'classical moment.'

[182] Keith (1925, 343–47) describes the elements of the rite, one of which is said to be: "During the period of its [the horse's] absence the priests and the sacrificer sit on golden thrones: the Hotṛ begins the telling of the cyclic narrative—*there is nothing of sequence in the several narratives* [my emphasis]—Pariplava Ākhyāna, the telling of tales, Ākhyānas, of ancient kings, which last by for series of ten days for the whole year." The liturgical directions for this rite are supplied in detail by the Taittirīya Saṃhita. Perhaps this lack of 'sequence' is in fact akin in practice to what we have been referring to as *bricolage* on the part of the poets?

[183] It is said that the *dīkṣā* 'initiation', the *pravargya* 'the milk rite', the *soma* rite, and the *savana* 'pressing' all occur (XIV.90.17–21). However, these actions are mentioned *en passant* in a manner that lacks real liturgical sensibility, and it is as if the poets are simply referring to what is generally 'known' rather than portraying a rite they had properly witnessed.

yūpeṣu niyataṃ cāsīt paśūnāṃ triśataṃ tathā

XIV.90.34

Then three hundred victims were attached to stakes.

The sacrificial horse is one of these animals. Then it is said that:

gandharvā gītakuśalā nṛtteṣu ca viśāradāḥ
ramayanti sma tān viprān yajñakarmāntareṣvatha

XIV.90.39

Gandharvas, adept in song and skilled in dances
Then entertained those brāhmaṇas in the intervals of the rite.[184]

This expression is curiously reminiscent of what is reported in the Ādi *parvan*—the most difficult and complex book of the whole epic—where of the poet Vaiśaṃpāyana it is said: *śravayāmāsa bhāratam karmānteresu yajñasya* (he recited the Bhārata Song during the intervals of the rite) (I.1.58). The phrase is also repeated at XVIII.5.26, when that first performance of the Bhārata Song is again mentioned. Whether this is simply a formulaic expression or a description of customary practice, or whether this is actually an indication of the first performance of the *Mahābhārata* as we know it today at one of the *aśvamedhas* of Samudragupta, we might only surmise.

The victims are immolated, *śamayitvā paśūn*, including the sacred horse who is then dismembered; concerning Draupadī, it is said that *upasaṃveśayan ... tām* (they caused her to lie [beside the victim]) (XIV.91.2). Parts of the creature are burned after Yudhiṣṭhira has inhaled *vapādhūmagandhaṃ* (the sweet fumes of the omentum), and he disburses huge wealth to the *brāhmaṇas*. Then it is said of Yudhiṣṭhira, *prādāt ... vyāsāya tu vasuṃdhāram* (he gave the earth to Vyāsa). Vyāsa accepts and equally reciprocates, stating: *pṛthivī bhavatas tv eṣā saṃnyastā* (this earth of yours is relinquished [or returned]) (XIV.919). Such a gesture of totality in the surrender and return of the kingdom was a crucial element in the rite. Thus, the relationships between king and queen, king and *brāhmaṇas*, and king and the one who is behaving as chief priest, are all correctly confirmed and reconstituted. Arjuna as the king's hero is affirmed as the most active warrior, and the terrain of *bhāratavarṣa*, according to the roaming of the horse, is acknowledged as coming under the regime of Pāṇḍava Yudhiṣṭhira Kururāja.

[184] One wonders what it was that such dancers represented with their movements and if their steps and gestures were in any way mimetic or dramatic in how they expressed what was being simultaneously sung during the great sacrifice. Perhaps there was a dance tradition, more than balletic, that sometimes accompanied the performance of epic?

Contrary to what happened at the closure of the *rājasūya*, Yudhiṣṭhira (speaking of himself here and enjoining the others) now announces:

vanaṃ pravekṣye viprendrā vibhajadhvaṃ mahīm imām

XIV.91.12

I shall enter the forest! O brāhmaṇas, apportion this earth!

Unlike the triumphalism of the *rājasūya*, Yudhiṣṭhira now remains full of remorse after the holocaust of Kurukṣetra and the death of all his male heirs, and he still wishes to renounce the political world and his kingship. His wife and brothers affirm this vocation and a voice in the sky is heard to declaim, *sādhu sādhu* 'bravo, bravo'. Yet Vyāsa, the arch-patron of the clan and of the poem itself, reiterates that the king must retain his kingdom and simply give away wealth to the *brāhmaṇas*. Once again, the audience observe how Yudhiṣṭhira is directed:

dattaiṣā bhavatā mahyaṃ tāṃ te pratidadāmy aham

XIV.91.17

This given by you to me, I return that to you.

Kṛṣṇa Vāsudeva, who is present, confirms this expression of Vyāsa, who gives back the formal offering.[185]

The dicing match that ensued after the *rājasūya* was a comparable drama of reciprocal exchange played out in game form rather than verbally or symbolically, and yet that game went horribly wrong, due—arguably—to the *daemonic* influences of Duryodhana and Śakuni. It is the sacrificer who suffers in such circumstances insofar as the rite *belongs* to him. The *aśvamedha*, however, does purify and bring atonement to king Yudhiṣṭhira for all—as far as he himself considers—the wrong he performed at Kurukṣetra, and he is said to become *dhūtapāpmā* and *vipāpmā*, ('free of wrong' or 'without wrong') (XIV.91.22 and 41). The ritual has formally cleansed him and his brothers of all the moral contamination and spiritual pollution that the cruelty, violence, shame, and death of battle had brought to them and to the kingdom.[186] All that remains is the ritual bathing of the king, the *avabhṛtha* 'ceremonial ablution', which finally

185 These three figures, the priest, the king, and the hero—or grandfather, nominal grandson, and cousin—represent the lineal and lateral kinship pattern of the clan of Pāṇḍu, both patriline and matriline.

186 Faust (2008, 36) comments on the "frightening transformation" that occurred during nineteenth-century battles, where it was reported that: "Men lost their semblance of humanity ... and the spirit of the demon shone in their faces. There was but one desire, and that was to destroy." The recollection of this 'desire' can itself become polluting and deranging.

frees the new *rāja* of moral stain and ideally returns the kingdom to harmony (XIV.91.29). *Kṣatriyas* require that the taint and guilt of violent bloodshed—like filth—be somehow washed away and that their ethical standing be renewed after so much terrible warfare. The day closes with the poets saying:

> vipāpmā bharataśreṣṭhaḥ kṛtārthaḥ prāviśat puram
>
> XIV.91.41
>
> Purified, the best of the Bharatas, his purposes fulfilled, entered the city.[187]

It is as if the rite of the *aśvamedha* has been personally employed in order for king Yudhiṣṭhira to secure atonement for all the horror he had led the *kṣatriyas* into in order to secure his kingdom. The personal loss of the Pāṇḍava heirs, the sons of Draupadī and the son of Arjuna, only made this atonement more necessary for the new king, and in that sense the ritual was a success. It also politically and militarily established the brothers in their new domain as paramount rulers. As Bhīma says to Yudhiṣṭhira, early on in the poem and long before war is engaged:

> yad enaḥ kurute kiṃcit rājā bhūmim avāpnuvan
> sarvaṃ tan nudate paścād yajñair vipuladakṣinaiḥ
>
> III.34.75
>
> Whatever wrong a king does obtaining the earth,
> He removes all that later with sacrifices and broad distributions.

Hence the four books that follow the horse sacrifice depict Yudhiṣṭhira in an altogether different light.[188]

[187] One might argue that epic *Mahābhārata* closes with this line.

[188] I have previously argued, in McGrath 2010 and 2013, that the performance of epic song—in terms of its *pathopoiía*—is a medium designed to assuage the guilt and grief or the *trauma* of warriors for all the violence and horror experienced during warfare. By making violence and death beautiful, or pleasurable—via metaphor—the poets intensify that emotion of horror, thus enabling a spectating audience to participate in a *re*-experience of those sufferings caused by gruesome and savage death, a transference that facilitates the purging of such trauma. To quote from Bellavia (2007, 113): "Combat is a descent into the darkest depths of the human soul. A place where the most exalted nobility and the most wretched baseness reside naturally together. What a man finds there defines himself for the rest of his life. Do we release our grip on basic humanity to be better soldiers?" For an audience, epic performance, in this sense, brings catharsis; it is therapeutic. To repeat what we stated earlier—hence the notion that the governing or master *rasa* ('taste' or 'mood') of the epic is that of *śānta* 'pacification'—what is being pacified is the terrific sorrow and shame caused by excessive violent conduct and the experience of brutal death. See Ānandavardhanācārya IV.5.572 in the 1965 edition of the Dhvanyāloka: *tataś ca śānto raso rasāntair mokṣalakṣaṇaḥ puruṣārthaḥ puruṣārthāntarais tad upasarjanatvenānugamyam āno'ṅgitvena vivakṣāviṣaya iti mahābhārata tatpāryaṃ suvyakam evāvabhāsate* (It clearly appears that the ultimate meaning of the *Mahābhārata* is *śānta rasa* and the human goal characterised as *mokṣa* is the principle subject, with the other *rasas* subordinate to it.). I am grateful to P. Banos for his assistance in understanding the orthography of this sentence, which, in the 1965 text, was corrupt.

***

To close this chapter on the king as sacrifice, let us turn to a unique moment in the epic where the regal deities are mentioned. Nowhere else in the poem are such figures described, and this instant occurs immediately prior to the fall of the elder of the clan, Bhīṣma.[189]

devatāyatanasthāś ca kauravendrasya devatāḥ
kampate ca hasante ca nṛtyanti ca rudanti ca

VI.108.11

The images of divinities standing in the temple of the Kaurava:
They shake and laugh and dance and weep.

The word *devatā* possesses qualities that indicate 'figures' or 'statues', objects that in the eighteenth century were sometimes referred to by Westerners as 'idols'. Such mentions of material icons are extremely rare in the poem, and here they are said to belong to the temple of the Kaurava king, signifying Dhṛtarāṣṭra. These images—as the imminent fall of Bhīṣma, the *ancient* of the family, is about to occur—being so spiritually attached to the clan respond physically and eidetically to this terrible earthly event. Here, the audience perceives the divine correlation between kingship and deity, and one wonders whom these figures represented, what particular deities would Dhṛtarāṣṭra approach in the family temple in order to worship? Perhaps these figures were not of divinities, but of ancestors and revered heroes and served as the material objects of hero cult and similar commemorative worship?[190] This scene, so lightly accentuated, is quite unlike the aniconic world of the Vedic and pre-Hindu culture as we know it today; for the first identifiable stone statuary in the subcontinent were Buddhist objects and were fabricated during the era of Aśoka. In fact, those initial manifestations of mineral statuary were not actually human figures or representations of deities, but of *yakṣas* and of animals taken from the natural world.

It is odd that such representations of the clan deities are so completely absent from all the various ceremonies and rituals the *rāja* as sacrificer is obliged to perform in order to sustain the cosmic equilibrium of his kingdom; this in

[189] Certainly, Vyāsa is the eldest male member of the clan, but he is not mortal. Also, his mother, Satyavatī, is supposedly still alive.

[190] On the figurative evidence for hero cult in the epic world, see McGrath 2004, 215. Rosenfield (1967, 149–153 and 168–169) regards the *devakula* 'house of images' as an Iranian-influenced innovation in India. Sītā, in the Uttarakāṇḍa of the Rāmāyaṇa, is figuratively represented, although in this case the ritual function of the statue is different from the usual purpose of cult statuary.

itself points to an archaic form of culture.[191] Similarly, apart from the reference just cited, there are no mentions of ritual architecture, formal stone structures where worship occurs; the *sabhā* that is divinely constructed at Indraprastha by Maya is certainly not a building where devotions are made. In that sense, the poem remains exclusively literary, if not courtly, and it is as if there is a conscious effort at work on the part of the poets or editors to specifically elide or exclude any such devotional reference while simultaneously including as much of known and remembered North Indian religious culture as it possibly can into one syncretic master narrative, as well as a nominal mention of the physical territories.[192] This is because stone sculpture at that time was a solely Buddhist or Jaina phenomenon.[193] Similarly, one thinks of the absence of deities in any form of plastic representation in the Homeric epics, poetry that, like the *Mahābhārata*, was also both centralising and totalising in its vision.

[191] In the Droṇa *parvan* of the Bombay Edition of the epic, however, it is said: *pañcānāṃ draupadeyānāṃ pratimādhvajabhūṣaṇam / dharmamārutaśakrāṇām aśvinoś ca mahātmanoḥ*, and the verb, carried on from the previous-but-one *śloka*, is *apaśyāma* (we saw ... the decorated standards with their images—of both great-souled Aśvins, of Śakra and a son of the Māruts and of Dharma—of the five sons of Draupadī) (VII.23.88). This *adhyāya* visualises the horses and standards of the best of the heroes and is much abbreviated in the PCE. The word *pratimā* signifies 'image, symbol, picture', indicating, one presumes, depictions of statues of these five deities, which were painted or sown onto the banners. The text says, *pate citram ivārpitam* (like a picture drawn on a cloth) (VII.23.97 BE). In the Pune Critical Edition there is a variant of this line, appearing at VII.39.16: *dharmamārutaśakrāṇām aśvinoḥ pratimās tathā / dhārayanto dhvajāgreṣu draupadeyā mahārathāḥ* (The great charioteers, the sons of Draupadī, bearing on the uppermost part of their banners images of the Aśvins, of Śakra, of the son of the Maruts, and of Dharma).

[192] There does occur the famous statement of Kṛṣṇa during the Gītā that—textually—marks the origins of what we nowadays describe as *pūjā*: *patraṃ puṣpaṃ phalaṃ toyaṃ ya me bhaktyā prayacchati* (Whoever offers me, with devotion, water, fruit, a flower, a leaf ...) (VI.31.26). He adds that (even if this is performed by non-*brāhmaṇas*): *striyo vaiṣyās tathā śūdrās te'pi yānti parāṃ gatim* (Women, vaiṣyas also, even *śūdras*, they go to the ultimate goal) (VI.31.32). I would strongly aver, however, that this is a classical or 'later' aspect of the epic, such devotional activity not beginning until Buddhist or Jaina times.

[193] Perhaps analogously, there is virtually no mention of any mortuary or memorial tradition in the poem—apart from a rather occasional and cursory custom of cremation—after which the deceased, either as heroes or as ancestors or past kings, go on to receive forms of devotion or worship.

3

Ideals of Kingship

The figure of Indra, king of the deities, is the primary ideal of universal rule in the poem; ideally he is also the warrior deity. As the epic progresses, however, this standard is modulated by other than *kṣatriya* ideals of kingship, and the office is depicted in pragmatic, rather than mythical or martial, terms. The divine and heroic monkey Hanūmān is the first to speak of *kṣatradharma* in the poem, in a form that anticipates the rational catalogue of *arthaśāstra* (III.149.37–49). This mode of discourse reaches its ultimate expression in the vast and dramatic pronouncements of the supine Bhīṣma in the Śānti and Anuśāsana *parvans*, which themselves echo and magnify what the audience has already heard the *ṛṣi* Nārada express to the *dharmarāja* in digest form at the opening of the Sabhā *parvan* (II.5.7–116).[1] The Gītā is not addressed to a king, nor does it propose or advocate any activity relating to kingship; it is a discourse directed towards a hero and thus does not adhere to this model of being a *principum specula* (mirror for princes).[2] In this chapter, let us examine how epic *Mahābhārata* expresses

[1] As we have already noted, the most influential of *Mahābhārata* scholars, the brilliant Sukthankar, argued that the Bhārgava Clan were central figures in the reworking of the older Bhārata songs in their reformation of the text. He comments: "Now it happens that Dharma and Nīti are just the two topics in which the Bhṛgus had *specialized* and with which their names are prominently associated ... One has only to recall that, according to a tradition preserved in the work itself, our Manusmṛti, the most famous and popular of ancient Indian works bearing on the Dharmaśāstra, is the ancient Code of Manu in the form in which it was communicated to mankind by Bhṛgu and it is therefore even commonly known as the Bhṛgusaṃhitā ... The opinions of Manu have been frequently cited in our *Mahābhārata*, (*ity evaṃ Manur abravīt*). According to Bühler's computation, there are about 260 stanzas of the Manusmṛti, that is nearly 10 percent of the total, which are again found verbatim (or with only slight variations) in *parvans* 3, 12 and 13 alone of the Great Epic." Sukthankar (1944, 335), quoting Bühler, *The Laws of Manu*, S.B.E., 25:lxxx.

[2] Before he departs for the forest, the old king, Dhṛtarāṣṭra, advises his successor, Yudhiṣṭhira, as to the good conduct of kingship (XV.9.7–12.23). These are all common and formulaic maxims of the *nītiśāstra*, or 'mirror for princes', kind that Vidura sometimes repeats (V.33.16 to 45.28). Similarly, the *ṛṣi* Nārada, on visiting *rāja* Yudhiṣṭhira at his new palace at Indraprastha, summarises precisely the duties of kingship at II.5.7–99.

kingship explicitly in terms of practical ideals rather than through metaphors of action; that is, how it is that a good and strong king *should* behave. Since Yudhiṣṭhira, due to the onset of the *kali yuga* and to the inconsolable insistence of *adharma* in the human world, is perpetually beset by dilemma, how can he possibly conduct himself in a dharmic fashion? He is thus constantly imbued with sadness or melancholy as to this great irony that confronts someone intent on moral probity in all that he says or does or has done. At one point he inquires of Bhīṣma:

> kathaṃ dharme sthātum icchan naro varteta bhārata
>
> XII.110.1
>
> How should a man desiring to stand in dharma behave, O Bhārata?

This is not obvious, despite an understanding of *śāstra* (moral and ritual learning). He asks Bhīṣma to instruct him in the ways or manners of *ṛta* 'cosmic order'. Bhīṣma responds only by adjuring his devotion or apprehension to *satyam* 'truth', but the nature of this super-veracity is not actually indicated—it is simply said to be the 'ultimate': *na satyād vidyate param* (nothing is found more ultimate than truth) (XII.110.3).

***

To begin, on several occasions Yudhiṣṭhira's close family admonish him towards such ideals of kingly behaviour; then it is the dying arch-hero who speaks at colossal length on the subject of how kings should act and think. Between these two kinds of verbal events occurs the *rāja*'s entry into his capital town, at last, and the poets offer to their audience a wonderfully intimate and vivid scene detailing all the regal activities that occupy this princely moment. Let us now turn our attention to these three instances: to the family, to the installation, and to the words of the ancient hero. As we shall soon see, the last of these scenes completely changes or redirects the form of the epic, not simply in narrative, but also in concept.

i. Archaic Ideals

The question of goodness and the practice of kingship in the poem as a topic worthy of discussion initially arose when Draupadī and her husband Yudhiṣṭhira are caught up in an exchange—in fact a series of three sequential arguments—on the nature of power and kingship; this occurs early on during the forest sojourn.[3]

[3] I have examined this exchange from Draupadī's point of view (McGrath 2009, V:3).

The counterpoint in their discourse here derives from the wife taking a strict and tough point of view, while her husband favours a policy that is more tolerant and accommodating. Draupadī questions why, given what happened in the *sabhā*, that his *manyu* 'anger' was not ignited; she repeats this word three times as she makes her demand (III.28.32–34). Then Draupadī draws upon the word *tejas* 'majesty', questioning his timid lack of this quality and condemning his practice of *kṣamā* ('patience' or 'submissiveness') (III.28.35–37).

Yudhiṣṭhira's response is to say that *krodho hantā manuṣyāṇāṃ* (rage is the destroyer of humans) (III.30.1). He is responding to her point, but he uses a different word, substituting *krodha* for *manyu*, a term that indicates a much stronger emotion signifying 'rage' rather than simply 'anger': it is the heroic emotion. Draupadī proposes that a good king be potent in his wrath, whereas Yudhiṣṭhira responds with a picture of kingship that is more moderate and evenly tempered: these are two distinct ideas in the manner of rule. For Yudhiṣṭhira, *krodha* is a despicable quality, and he says that *tyajet krodhaṃ puruṣaḥ* (a man should abandon rage) (III.30.23); whereas his wife's view of kingship esteems this emotion in terms of high worth for a king.[4] Draupadī replies to his claims by insulting a policy of pusillanimous *kṣamā* since it is a policy that has led to their forest exile.

Draupadī speaks a second time, cynically and sarcastically condemning him for his inert manner in passively accepting all that the universe ordains:

> namo dhātre vidhātre ca yau mohaṃ cakratus tava
>
> III.31.1
>
> Praise to Dhātar and Vidhātar who have made your delusion![5]

Yudhiṣṭhira makes his response to this by saying, *nāstikyaṃ tu prabhāṣase* (you speak as an unbeliever) (III.32.1).[6] Models of kingship at this point in their argument—and this is *not* a debate—have suddenly become universal in their modulation, and they are both propounding a different kind of princely *dharma*. He says that *aphalo yadi dharmaḥ syāc ... nirvāṇaṃ nādhigaccheyur* (if *dharma* were fruitless they [people] would not acquire *nirvāṇa*) (III.32.23–24). Bhīma comes to the support of Draupadī, as he always does in the poem, and joins in her criticism of his elder brother's conduct, going so far as to call his brother's kingship *klība* 'emasculated' (III.34.13). Bhīma tells Yudhiṣṭhira:

4 In this speech, beginning at III.30.1, a strong rebuttal of what Draupadī has just been claiming, Yudhiṣṭhira engages the word *krodha* and its related terms for 'anger' seventeen times; such is the force of his statement and his rejection of such an emotion, an emotion that thoroughly possesses his chief wife.

5 These are cosmic forces of destiny and determinism.

6 *Nāstika* is often translated as 'atheist', and its usage is pejorative.

anubudhyasva rājendra vettha dharmān sanātanān[7]
krūrakarmābhijāto'si yasmād udvijate janaḥ

III.34.52

O great king, awake! Know the eternal dharma.
You are born to cruel action, from which people tremble.

He extols the *kṣatriya* virtue of dynamic action, and says, *savituḥ sadṛśo bhava* (be like Savitur [the impulsive sun]) (III.34.69). He then says, *ratham āsthāya* (mount the chariot) and attack Hāstinapura just like Indra would (III.34.80–85). Bhīma continues in this urgent vein, admonishing his brother towards strong and potent activity; at one point he makes the unusual observation:

aśrauṣīs tvaṃ rājadharmān yathā vai manur abravīt

III.36.20

You have heard the dharma of kingship as Manu declared.

One wonders exactly what it was of the tradition of Manu that the poets are here indicating with this reference.[8] It is a good point though: Why was it that king Yudhiṣṭhira waited thirteen years before assembling a coalition to attack the Dhārtarāṣṭras? Was he simply keeping to the agreement?

Apart from the edifying discourses spoken during this long forest exclusion, the poets supply few events that describe this time for the Pāṇḍavas, and certainly there is virtually no mention of life at Hāstinapura during these years, or of Kṛṣṇa's life. In the more 'original' tradition of epic *Mahābhārata*, the poem could have moved simply from the Sabhā *parvan* directly to the events of the Virāṭa and Udyoga *parvans*. In terms of the narrative movement, this forest period in the poem is a strange *educational* hiatus;[9] that is, apart from the two instances when Arjuna acquires weaponry from the deities Śiva and Indra.[10] As we have already observed, both the Āraṇyaka *parvan* and the Śānti and Anuśāsana

7 The expression *dharmaḥ sanātanaḥ* appears in the Mānava Dharmaśāstra at I.138; here the words are employed in relation to speaking *satyam* 'truth'.

8 The poets or editors of the Śānti *parvan* are well aware of the *dharmaśāstra* tradition. Chapter VII of the Manusmṛti concerns kingly right: *rājadharmān pravakṣyāmi* (I shall pronounce the *dharmas* of a king) (VII.1). Manu is also the name of a mythical ancestor of the lineage of that title: *manor vaṃśo mānavānāṃ tato'yaṃ prathito'bhavat* (then this lineage of Manu was known of humans) (I.70.11)

9 Perhaps the exclusion of young men from society recapitulates a folk memory of when unmarried youths were sent away from the community and made to survive in unorthodox fashion. These are the *vrātyas*, young "Āryans outside the sphere of Brahmin culture." (See MacDonell and Keith [1912] for that definition.) They are given voice in the Atharva Veda XV. See Vidal-Naquet (1981) on the Greek model of such a convention.

10 At III.41.13; and at III.44.23.

parvans are lengthy pedagogical texts that suddenly cause the epic narrative to pause in order that certain characters can perform their didactic narrations; then the poem continues in its former warrior fashion.[11] Thus, these three books serve as compendious and learned digressions from the overall aesthetic force of the poem.

***

Continuing with this image of the family as it informs and influences the discourse surrounding Yudhiṣṭhira's ideals of kingship, the Śānti *parvan* opens with a domestic gathering of the royal household when the timeless *ṛṣis*, Nārada, Kaṇva, and others, are visiting Yudhiṣṭhira upon the shore of the Gaṅgā in order to temper his *śokavyākulacetasam* (mind confounded with sorrow) (XII.1.8). These early *adhyāyas* in the book address the awful anguish of the king for his deceased kin and the moral introversion this causes him. This is the situation of the Śānti *parvan*: the appalling despair of the king caused by the destruction he had campaigned for at Kurukṣetra, what in fact composes the *price* of his kingship, and the exchange he had made in order to become *rāja*. As Bhīṣma later tells Yudhiṣṭhira, during the long session on *rājadharma*:

eṣa rājñāṃ paro dharmaḥ sahyau jayaparājayau

XII.107.27

This is the supreme dharma of a king: defeat and victory are to be endured.

In other words, there can be no joy for a king who challenges and goes to war, which is paradoxical, and for a rare moment Bhīṣma captures the loneliness or ultimate fruitlessness intrinsic to kingship. It is this thankless, if not sterile, quality of rule that constantly irks Yudhiṣṭhira, and it is the emotions concerned with this that qualify Yudhiṣṭhira as a character, particularly at this moment when he faces the triumphalism of his brothers and wife.

Unlike so many others in the poem, such as Dhṛtarāṣṭra, Yudhiṣṭhira does not claim that adversity is caused by *daiva* 'divine destiny', but he actually accepts his own responsibility, and, at this point in the poem, he desperately seeks to atone for the wrong and the pollution of so much violent death. He is unique in this respect insofar as he attributes his actions to no other source than his own personal volition and active autonomy; Yudhiṣṭhira is unusual here, and in this he makes a perfect audience for Bhīṣma's words for there exists no devolution of moral agency as far as Yudhiṣṭhira is concerned. Certainly, this was not the case

[11] Sukthankar (1944, 313) comments on the Śānti *parvan* that it was "compiled in the peculiar pedagogic technique developed by the redactors of the Great Epic for the edification of the people combined with their entertainment."

for Dhṛtarāṣṭra and his leading son, nor for Karṇa or Kṛṣṇa, and not even for Draupadī, all of whom, at some point or other in the poem, make claims upon *daiva* or some such cosmic force. Also, the rituals of obsequy were profoundly insufficient in clearing Yudhiṣṭhira's own ethical and emotional debt, as he sees it.

Nārada says to the king, *bāhuvīryeṇa ... jiteyam avaniḥ kṛtsnā dharmeṇa ca* (this earth is entirely conquered by a warrior's arms and by *dharma*) (XII.1.10). Yudhiṣṭhira ignores such a statement and merely responds by speaking of his grief for Abhimanyu and the deceased five sons of Draupadī, and also for his elder half-brother, Karṇa. Nārada then recapitulates the life of Karṇa for the king: he was one who was a great *kṣatriya*, who was *śastrapūtam* (purified by weapons), and he was the ideal of every warrior (XII.2.4).[12] Then Kuntī appears and tries to mollify her son's desperation concerning Karṇa, but the king only rebukes her for keeping Karṇa's true fraternal status secret. In his anger, the poets say of him: *śaśāpa ... sarvalokeṣu ca striyaḥ* (and he cursed women in all the worlds). He states: *na guhyaṃ dhārayiṣyanti* (they will bear no secret!) (XII.6.10). Such is the visceral emotion that his mother's secrecy causes him, and this is another rare instance of Yudhiṣṭhira's capacity for ire, an emotion that is directed at members of his family rather than at his adversaries.

In these early *ślokas* of the Śānti *parvan*, the poets make much of this almost demented melancholy of the king, and the audience hears of his mood repeatedly.

> dhig astu kṣātram ācāraṃ dhig astu balamaurasam ...
> sādhu kṣamā damaḥ śaucam avairoghyam amatsaraḥ
> ahiṃsā satyavacanaṃ nityāni vanacāriṇām
>
> XII.7.5
>
> Damn kṣatriya conduct! Damn its innate power!
> Good for the patient, the self-controlled, the pure, the unimpassioned, the disinterested,
> The pacific, the honest, the perpetually forest-going ...

The king adds, addressing Arjuna:

[12] This *karṇacarita* (life of Karṇa) in micro-narrative form omits his conception and birth, but does relate his experience with the teacher Rāma. Nārada tells of how—and this is heard nowhere else in the epic—Karṇa aided Duryodhana to win a Kaliṅga bride at a *svayaṃvara*. In this rite, a *kṣatriya* marital rite, usually the hero must be alone in a chariot, but in this telling Karṇa assists Duryodhana, which is unusual, and defends his patron when the other kings attack him (XII.4.15ff.). The audience also hears in this account of how Karṇa fought with Jarāsaṃdha of Magadha and defeated him, which pleased the Māgadhan, who said: *prīto'smīti* (I am pleased); and he gave Karṇa a city. Nārada then says that *aṅgeṣu ... rājāsīt* (he was king among the Aṅgas) (XII.5.5-6). This summary of Karṇa's heroic life projects a slightly different point of view from what the audience knows of him from the epic poem and thus perhaps draws upon another Song of Karṇa or *karṇakathā* tradition.

vayam evāsya lokasya vināśe kāranaṃ smṛtāḥ

XII.7.21

Thus we are remembered as the cause in the destruction of the world.

Yudhiṣṭhira proceeds for thirty-seven *ślokas*, decrying his own policy and the delusions of Duryodhana in a plaintive tirade of anguish and despair.[13] He says that the Pāṇḍavas are:

pradahanto diśaḥ sarvās tejasā bhāskarā iva

XII.7.30

Burning all the directions, like the sun with energy!

He only sees and thinks of the negative, for the kingdom offers neither delight nor pleasure to him: *hatāḥ śūrāḥ kṛtaṃ pāpaṃ* (the heroes are dead, wickedness has been done). One should remember that the great rite of the *aśvamedha* has neither been proposed nor implemented as yet, and there is nothing for Yudhiṣṭhira to find happiness in at this time. The ostensible purpose of the Śānti *parvan* is the allaying of the overwhelming remorse the king continues to endure due to the deaths of his immediate kin during the later days of the war; hence the title of *śānti* ('peace' or 'pacification').

Arjuna's response is super-critical and insulting, calling his brother *klība* 'emasculated' and saying that he acts *buddhilāghavāt* (from light-mindedness). There follow thirty-seven *ślokas* of recrimination and an exhortation for strong and virile kingship.[14]

yathaiva pūrṇād udadheḥ syandanty āpo diśo daśa
evaṃ rājakulād vittaṃ pṛthivīṃ pratitiṣṭhati

XII.8.32

Just as water from fullness in the ocean runs to the ten points,
So from the clan of the king wealth is established on earth.

Yudhiṣṭhira, as the audience has seen throughout the course of the poem, tends toward hopeless inactivity if faced with a crisis; his decency does not relish the

[13] This desire of Yudhiṣṭhira to embark upon a life of renunciation and to live in the forest finds a certain symmetry with Balarāma, the brother of Kṛṣṇa, who is similarly expressive of such a life, although his interest lies in pilgrimage among sacred sites. The relationship between these two princely figures is undefined, yet in this pacific respect they do mirror each other. This desire of Yudhiṣṭhira to live apart from the world is enigmatic for it lacks title; Buddhism, Jainism, and asceticism in general bear such a curious, indefinite, and undeclared role in the poem.

[14] Arjuna always speaks in this tough and quasi-militant manner; it is as if he is the senior martial figure in the Pāṇḍava camp, the 'general'. Certainly, he is the only one to own the superhuman cosmic weaponry. See McGrath 2012.

likelihood of violence. On these occasions, it is his brothers and often his wife who recharge his mental alacrity, as Arjuna does now. It is this occasional vacillation of the king and his steady dependence upon his brothers and wife that allow the poets to dramatise and give voice to what *should* amount to good kingship, and this kind of equivocation on the part of the king acts as a dramatic trope enabling such declamation.

Once again, it is the rhetoric of the situation that makes for effective pronouncement: for the real audience is *outside* of the poem and not within the words themselves. That is where the enactment of the poetry is directed, through metaphors that are interpreted and electrified by the poets via their performance. Meaning lies in the drama writ large and not simply in the particular statements: a rhetorical duality of message for an audience is implicit in the nature of the poem. In other words, there exists a meaning behind—or actually *beyond*—the words (and not simply *within* the language). The message of the poem lies along a trajectory between the poets and the audience; that is, the medium and the epic are simply and only the grounds for that communication. It is this axis that we, as critical analysts, need to fathom and comprehend if we are truly to understand this great Bhārata Song.

Arjuna now encourages his brother to perform the horse sacrifice:

> taṃ cen na yajase rājan prāptas tvaṃ devakilbiṣam
>
> XII.8.34
>
> O king, if you do not sacrifice it, you obtain the offence of the deities!

In return, the king makes a statement the audience has often heard from him before:

> araṇye phalamūlāśī cariṣyāmi mṛgaiḥ saha
>
> XII.9.4
>
> I shall go in the forest, eating roots and fruit with the beasts.

Yudhiṣṭhira exhibits an intense attraction towards the renunciant way of life, despite all the grand rituals and the magnitude of war and policy; it is a curious dichotomy in his persona. On the one hand, there is his frugal and inflexible passion towards kingship, and yet simultaneously he craves the quiescence of forest life. It might be the case that the poets are just staging the contrasts of possible *kinds* of life: that is the message. Even though Kṛṣṇa pronounced the Gītā to his companion, Arjuna, the brother who is actually closest to the life of divine association is in fact Yudhiṣṭhira, at least in aspiration and expression. Arjuna is the potently dangerous and strict hero of superhuman ability who loves his supernatural weapons; he is also the most sexually active of the Pāṇḍavas. Or, is it that the belief system of the Gītā is completely different from that of Yudhiṣṭhira's expressed spiritual ambition, and the hero and the king possess two intangibly different visions of the world?[15] It is difficult to fathom what it is exactly that Yudhiṣṭhira believes, at least in terms of his cosmic understanding. All that the audience repeatedly hears is this firm desire for a withdrawn, silent, and mystical life; yet the mystical initiations in the poem all go to Arjuna.[16]

Now the king describes the world as:

> evaṃ saṃsāracakre'smin vyāviddhe rathacakravat
>
> XII.9.32
>
> Thus on this various wheel of saṃsāra, like a chariot wheel ...

These are metaphors that one usually associates with Buddhist teaching; in fact all these pacific cravings are arguably Buddhist or Jaina in form and do not simply derive from the *āśrama* system of a gradual life—and certainly not from the common *kṣatriya* code of vitality.

Next, brother Bhīma enters the conversation, similarly trying to dissuade the king from retirement and urging him to rule more vigorously. He tells him, *tān hatvā bhuṅkṣva dharmeṇa ... mahīm imām* (having killed them by right [the Kauravas], enjoy this earth!) (XII.10.8). Bhīma is shocked that so much death will have no consequence for the Pāṇḍavas and that all their killing will be mere fecklessness if Yudhiṣṭhira withdraws from the kingship. Then suddenly the narrative slips into another edifying discourse and the poetry assumes a completely different tone. As we have observed before, this is very much the centrifugal fashion of epic *Mahābhārata*: specifically *kṣatriya* literature changing with brahminical exhortation, often given in the medium of animal allegories. Here, it is a bird who is speaking to some *ṛṣis* (XII.11.7).

Nakula and Sahadeva add their words to this long remonstrance, and their elder brother becomes quiet, but then Draupadī speaks. The poets say that she is *abhimānavatī nityaṃ* 'always arrogant', especially towards Yudhiṣṭhira. She reminds him of his powerful words spoken during their forest exile and of how he promised them not only victory but good consequences of victory (XII.14.6ff.). She too uses the word *klība* (an emasculated man) in her peroration, and, as

[15] Nīlakaṇṭha, in a note to I.105.39, states: *paraṃ dharmaṃ nivṛttirūpam / aparaṃ dharmaṃ pravṛttirūpam* (the highest *dharma* is withdrawal, the lesser *dharma* is exertion). The former is what attracts Yudhiṣṭhira, whereas Arjuna is the one—as described by the Gītā—to accomplish the latter kind of activity.

[16] See McGrath 2014.

usual, Draupadī's words exhibit icy sarcasm and acerbity; her speech progresses, her feelings become wound up like a steel spring, and her voice is always propounding the intransigent principles of *kṣatriya* culture.[17] Draupadī is always careful to flatter and speak with compliments that cajole the listener—and then she quickly breaks tempo and suddenly delivers a ferocious insult like a dart.

> tavonmādena rājendra sonmādāḥ sarvapāṇḍavāḥ
>
> XII.14.32
>
> O Indra of kings, by your madness all the Pāṇḍavas are mad!

Draupadī is rarely gentle or generous towards the *dharmarāja*, at least not in her speech.

Her furious discourse is continued by Arjuna who talks of the importance of *daṇḍa* 'the punitive', and he says that *daṇḍaḥ śāsti prajāḥ* (the punitive rules the people); that is, the king's capacity to punish is what maintains a polity. He adds that *nāghnātaḥ kīrtir astīha* (there is no fame without killing), *eva devā hantāras* (even the deities kill) (XII.15.15–16). All this is moving a long way from Yudhiṣṭhira's express predilection for a peaceful life in the woods as once again his family compel him to follow in their strictly *kṣatriya* view of the world. It is as if Yudhiṣṭhira is the profile of the Pāṇḍavas—for it is they who determine policy, while he is the one designated to enact its force in the kingdom. It is a strange compact of kingship where the king receives his real impetus from his close kin while remaining without overt aggression himself: this is rule by association. In a sense, these views on what should constitute *justice*, for the Pāṇḍava Bhāratas are always modelled in reaction to what they have experienced as *injustice* at the hands of the Dhārtarāṣṭra Bhāratas. What Bhīṣma propounds in his long discourses are models for the sustenance of justice that are active rather than simply responsive.

***

Essentially the arguments that condone what happened at Kurukṣetra turn upon the belligerence of Duryodhana, and how he—along with his gang—treated Draupadī; that is, the crime and its punishment generate the axis of narrative. Arjuna argues forcibly for the necessity of the 'punitive', again and again repeating the words *yadi daṇḍo na pālayet* (if the punitive would not protect), and listing all that would therefore fail in the polity. According to his view of the universe, the *daṇḍa* is both *natural* and *cosmic*. It is a profoundly necessary force in how *all* of life functions—and without its action there would not even be any

[17] For further considerations of Draupadī as the voice of *kṣatriya* culture, see McGrath 2009, chap. IV–V.

sacrifices, which maintain the inherent stability of life, or the four *varṇas*, the 'classes', which inhabit the middle *triloka* (the three worlds) (XII.15.35). The three duties of a king, says Arjuna, as he ends his powerful speech of fifty-seven *ślokas*, are:

> yaja dehi prajā rakṣa dharmaṃ samanupālaya
>
> XII.15.53
>
> *sacrifice*, give, protect the populace, maintain dharma!

These are the ritual, the martial, and the judicial components of sovereign life. Now that the war is over and the kingdom secure, it is the last that counts most; and, soon, with the conduct of the horse sacrifice, the first of these activities will be implemented on an imperial and magnificent scale. This speech of Arjuna is reminiscent of the Gītā, insofar as he is urging his king towards *action* and the absolute necessity of practicing the *dharma* of a king. Reformulating the words of the charioteer Kṛṣṇa, Arjuna terminates his discourse by mystically saying:[18]

> avadhyaḥ sarvabhūtānām antarātmā na saṃśayaḥ
>
> XII.15.56
>
> Doubtless, the inner soul of all beings is indestructible!

Despite all this enforcement by the *daṇḍa*, soul cannot be destroyed, and thus there is a natural validity for a king's punitive action. It is through such activity that life moves from body to body, says Arjuna:

> evaṃ jīvaḥ śarīrāṇi tāni tāni prapadyate
>
> XII.15.57
>
> Thus life enters body after body.

It is as if the interlocutors of the king here—and I discount the words of the twins Nakula and Sahadeva as being in a minor tone and more on the level of an echo or resonance concerning sacrifice and death—enjoin Yudhiṣṭhira towards being a strong *rāja*; this is the point of Arjuna's speech.[19] Draupadī and Bhīma, who are always close in the poem, for he is her chosen protector, propose a *dharma* that

[18] Vyāsa also 'becomes' present at this family gathering that attempts to raise Yudhiṣṭhira's weak spirits and to soothe his grief. His words also echo the Gītā at one point: *hantīti manyate kaścin na hantīty api cāpare* (one thinks, *he kills*, and others think, *so—he does not kill*) (XII.26.15–16, which recalls VI.24.19).

[19] There is something slightly epicene and undeveloped about these two younger heroes, and it is as if they for some reason have not been amplified as characters.

responds to crisis; while what the king himself is expounding as well as desiring is a policy that would allow him personal *mokṣa* 'release' from earthly and mortal confinement. As the audience will soon perceive, this ordering supplies the structure of the Śānti *parvan* writ large: Arjuna's principles of practical kingship, Draupadī's principles for *āpad* or 'crisis', and Yudhiṣṭhira's own principles of spiritual freedom, in as much as these are the similar triform expression of the sage and pedagogic Bhīṣma to his young and royal scion.

Says Arjuna:

jitvārīn kṣattradharmeṇa prāpya rājyam akaṇṭakam
vijitātmā manuṣendra yajñadānaparo bhava

XII.22.10

Having conquered enemies by kṣatriya dharma, having acquired a thornless kingdom,
O Indra of humans: having conquered the self, be devoted to gifts and to sacrifices!

To be victorious, to rule, and to sacrifice, these are the activities of a *rāja*; or, to hold the *daṇḍa*, to deal with crisis, and to maintain a priestly office.

***

The poets periodically activate the personae of both Vyāsa and Kṛṣṇa in these early *adhyāyas* of the book. They are not party to the narrative, but simply appear and disappear spontaneously as they join the company of the Pāṇḍavas and Draupadī in offering speeches that contribute to the drama of trying to raise the despondent humour of Yudhiṣṭhira, who remains guilty and grievous for his deceased kin. Kṛṣṇa, in the voice of Nārada, tells a story of sixteen mythical and famed kings from the ancient past, beginning with Marutta, and including Bharat and Rāma, and closing with Pṛthu: all of these kings were celebrated sacrificers, and they all performed many *aśvamedhas* (XII.29.16–136).[20] Then Vyāsa speaks at length about ritual atonement, something that is of great interest to Yudhiṣṭhira because his sorrow still remains unmitigated. He reminds the king that Indra, having destroyed the demonic Daityas, performed an hundred *kratus* 'horse sacrifices':

ekaikaṃ kratum āhṛtya śatakṛtvaḥ śatakratuḥ

XII.34.27

Having offered a sacrifice a hundred times, one by one, [he was] Śatakratu.

[20] Belvalkar, in the Critical Notes to Volume 13 of the 1961 Pune text, gives a Table of this Ṣodaśarājakīyam comparing a similar, but not identical, listing given in the Bombay text of the Droṇa *parvan* VII.55.37–70.25.

Certainly, the mood of recompense or *śānti* that epic *Mahābhārata* is supposed to generate in an audience is sustained by these early *adhyāyas* of Book Twelve; yet, once Bhīṣma commences his oration, that aesthetic soon vanishes from the narrative, and the poem becomes thoroughly didactic.

***

Now let us shift towards another paradigm, as the poem itself does in Book Twelve; for as we have observed throughout the poem, kingship in Yudhiṣṭhira's case—or in the case of epic *Mahābhārata*—is not a singular office but concerns a small group of people (including Dhṛtarāṣṭra—and even Draupadī and Gāndhārī are involved at times). As a *sacrificer*, Yudhiṣṭhira certainly conducts his kingship in an individual manner, but that station is restricted to the sovereign sponsor of a supreme ritual. We have also noted in the first chapter how influential the immediate populace is to the extent of constituting a coherent part of what was known as a *saṅgha*. I would now argue that the familiarity of kingship, its immediacy of clan-orientation, and its reliance on the informal institution of a *saṅgha*, are phenomena specific to premonetary and pre-urban society.[21] These are the elements of kingship that signal how Yudhiṣṭhira and his brothers come to dominate *bhāratavarṣa* and how the family of Pāṇḍu, or the nominal family of Śaṃtanu, come to possess complete hegemony over Northern India.[22] Although, as we know, ultimately the Yādavas are to supplant this standing, their aim constituting a delicate subtext throughout the course of the poem and their story supplying hypostasis for the epic.

Once secondary urbanisation begins to establish itself in the upper subcontinent, the economy, political system, and religious culture change. With the advent of the Mauryas, there is a renewed impetus towards non-rural life, which in itself is dependent upon a surplus of commercial goods that could sustain such an urban society, goods that are to be exchanged—or 'converted'—for money in an activity mediated by a rapidly burgeoning merchant class.[23] With the development of a monetary system (of coinage), human relationships became open

21 I would argue that Hāstinapura is conceived of as a fortified town and *not* a city, the criterion for such being quantitative, economic, or commercial. Such a situation existed prior to Northern India's secondary urbanisation.

22 Kauṭilya, commenting on the idea of a *saṅgha*, observes that *kāmbojasurāṣṭrakṣatriyaśreṇyādayo vārttāśastropajīvinaḥ / licchivikavṛjikamallakamadrakakukurakurupāñcālādayo rājaśabdopajīvinaḥ* (the Kāmbojas, the Surāṣṭras, *kṣatriyas*, *śreṇis*, and so on, maintain a livelihood of weaponry and trade; the Licchivikas, Vṛjikas, Mallakas, Madrakas, Kukuras, the *Kurus* [my emphasis], the Pāñcālas, are living by the name of king) (XI.1.4-5). Kangle (1972, part 2:454) comments: "The Licchivis, the Vṛjis and the Mallas are well-known from Buddhist and other sources. Kukuras are a member of the Andhaka-Vṛṣṇi league according to the *Mahābhārata* ... Most of the *saṅghas* mentioned belong to the north and north-west of India."

23 By money I mean *coin*, as a medium of exchange and as a store of wealth.

to trade as a market developed, for human connection was no longer simply founded upon patronage, immediate kinship, and mutual obligation.[24] With the increase in production that occurred during this period due to commerce—both internal and external—there was a specialisation and a surplus of goods generated; these created a different range of material values and social life.[25] Standards of value found a new location in the abstract and unattached phenomenon of *money*; to paraphrase Seaford, money is impersonal, unlimited, and universal, and hence its utility is such that all the old premonetary systems of affiliation—which were personal, limited, and particular—became rapidly defunct.[26] Money enables a new system of value in which there is one simple standard because currency is no longer fundamentally diverse.[27] Seaford, writing about this similar eco-political transition in the Hellenic world comments: "This brave new world of money is a very recent development in the experience of the human species, and the first poetic genre to be created in it was tragedy, which centres around an unprecedented individual known also from historiography and philosophy: the *tyrant*, isolated from the gods and even from his own kin, obsessed with money, a transgressor against the ancient moral codes of reciprocity, the sacred, and kinship. Because money embodies impersonal power, and lends itself to individual possession, it promotes an unprecedented degree of individual autonomy, and so seems to loosen its possessor from the old moral codes, even from dependence on kin and gods."[28] To quote from Dodd: "money heralds the triumph of quantity over quality, a world in which some[thing] must be *measurable* against something else in order to be deemed of value." He similarly notes: "monetary

[24] See Stark (in Stark et al. 2012, 109), commenting on this kind of social community, who states: "Membership ... was based on personal bonds between each member and the 'leader'. These bonds resulted in mutual obligations between the leader and his followers: in principle, loyal services were compensated by material gifts and, consequently, social prestige." As we have already observed, the redistribution of moveable wealth that occurred at festivals and ritual ceremonies played a key function in this early pattern of economy.

[25] See Brown 1922; Wiser 1936; Spellman 1964; Kosambi 1965; Sastri 1967; Earle and Ericsson 1977; Shell 1982; le Goff 2010; Graeber 2011.

[26] Seaford 2004, 147–172. Sahlins (1972, 279) remarks: "Exchange too is a moral conduct and is so regulated." Premonetary exchange is founded upon a mutual recognition of loyalties or dependency, whereas a monetary system operates according to supply and demand, which find equilibrium in terms of an abstract and impersonal 'price.' Loyalty possesses a moral agency, whereas price does not; price concerns contract, not fidelity.

[27] To paraphrase Graeber (2011, 22): obligation is social and moral, whereas *debt* is quantifiable and requires money, and can also be exchanged as a commodity itself. Wiser (1936) offers a practical portrait of such a premonetary economy. Heitzman (1984) portrays Buddhist mercantile patronage during the period of early secondary urbanisation.

[28] Seaford 2006, 148–149.

exchange and gift giving tend to be mutually exclusive. Gifts are emotionally charged, morally loaded, and reciprocal. Monetary exchange, by contrast, seems to lack emotional significance, morality, and reciprocity."[29]

***

In sum, the nature of kingship, which we have been examining during the archaic preliterate period—before the Mauryas—as something fungible and mobile among a small oligarchic social group, became displaced by a new form of kingship that was monarchic and discrete; this latter type is what Bhīṣma describes at such meticulous length beginning with the Śānti *parvan*.[30] I would aver that this shift was a matching corollary to the shift from premonetary economics of service to a market economy where currency is exchanged for goods.[31] The point being that, with the use of money, the *source* of value, rather than being dispersed and multiple, became unitary and standardised, as *fungibility* became singular rather than various or several. This is also a period when what we know as early Hinduism found its sources as brahminical culture both advanced and then retreated; it is also a period, of course, of terrific Buddhist and Jain hegemony, and many of the patrons of early Buddhism and Jainism were merchants, and not *kṣatriyas* or *brāhmaṇas*. In this new political model, there is no place for any *fraternal* kingship, and certainly the *saṅgha* is viewed as old-fashioned, useless, and conducive of political disaster; monarchy becomes autarchic.[32]

[29] Dodd 2013, 30.

[30] In the words of a modern North Indian intellectual, "The Shanti Parva of the Mahabharata emphasizes that it is the duty of the king to extend all assistance to the trader and the businessman." (Varma 2004, 67.)

[31] One could well ask, therefore, why is there no mention of money or coinage in the Śānti *parvan*? I would simply respond that the poets are ostensibly describing an heroic age, an age that was mythical and long prior to the beginning of the first millennium of the Common Era. There is thus a blurring of historic and poetic reality.

[32] Concerning the development of secondary urbanism, Shimada (2013, 199) has noted: "As indicated by the disappearance of large social/kinship groups in late period inscriptions at Amarāvatī, the increasing heterogeneity and complexity of society may have fragmented traditional social structures based on spatial and kinship ties, and developed new social systems composed of individuals or individual families as independent socio-economic units." He also writes (189–190): "In this sense, exchange in a market place was radically different from the traditional idea of exchange ... The activity of selling and buying neither depended upon, nor established, any personal link between sellers and buyers. Goods in a market are thus in the 'neutral' position situated between sellers and buyers ... Money is not linked to any particular goods but can be converted into any goods and services. It can also circulate among many people, but hardly leaves any trace of its handling. The exchange system based on money effectively breaks any link between goods and their original producers and owners."

ii. Installation

The moment ultimately arrives when the poets visualise for the audience the formal entry of the new king into Hāstinapura, from which Yudhiṣṭhira and family have presumably been absent for about fourteen years. The poets draw upon the usual metaphor that is ascribed to him—almost as *his* sign or emblem—that of *rājā nakṣatrair iva candramāḥ* (the king, like a moon with stars) (XII.38.30). This image of the moon is repeated three more times as his personal simile.

The old king Dhṛtarāṣṭra leads the procession *narayānena* (with a carriage drawn by men); Yudhiṣṭhira is praised by the deities and *brāhmaṇas* as he enters *svapuraṃ* 'his town'.

> tato rathaṃ navaṃ śubhraṃ kambalājinasaṃvṛtam
> yuktaṃ ṣoḍaśabhir gobhiḥ pāṇḍuraiḥ śubhalakṣaṇaiḥ
> mantrair abhyarcitaḥ puṇyaiḥ stūyamāno maharṣibhiḥ
>
> XII.38.32
>
> Then the new bright chariot covered with deerskin and woollen cloth,
> Yoked with sixteen white, finely decorated oxen,
> Hymned with auspicious mantras, praised by the great ṛṣis ...

Bhīma is the charioteer, and Arjuna bears the imperial white umbrella; the twins carry the ceremonial yak-tails. The poets say that the brothers are *pañca ... bhūtānīva* (like the five elements) (XII.38.37). Yuyutsu is in the next chariot, which is followed by the vehicle of Kṛṣṇa, both chariots being drawn in the typical manner by equines. Foot soldiers, elephants, and horses all follow, all being praised by various kinds of poets: *vaitālikaiḥ sūtair māgadhaiś ca subhāṣitaiḥ stūyamāno yayau rājā* (the king went, being praised by well-wishing eulogists, by poets, and by panegyrists) (XII.38.43). It is said that the people are all very happy and that the *rājamārga* 'royal route' and the town are decorated with white garlands, banners, pedestals, incense, and scented powders, and that girls are present, and full pots of water are placed at gates. Yudhiṣṭhira makes his entry *suhṛdvṛttaḥ* (surrounded by good friends).

Thousands of people greet him, and once again the simile is that of a moon. The houses are crammed with women, who are praising the Pāṇḍavas as they pass along the *rājamārga*, and the buildings *prākampanteva bhāreṇa strīṇāṃ pūrṇāni* (tremble, crammed as it were with the weight of women) (XII.39.3). His people, the *brāhmaṇas*, all meet the king and welcome him as he enters the *bhavanaṃ ... devarājagṛhopamam* (palace like the house of the king of the deities [that is, Indra]). The first task of Yudhiṣṭhira is to honour the deities within the building, and this is done in a unique manner that previsions what we now think of as the practice of *pūjā*, for such devotion to figurative objects is in no way part of the pre-Hindu or Vedic tradition.[33]

> praviśyābhyantaraṃ śrīmān daivatāny abhigamya ca
> pūjayāmāsa ratnaiś ca gandhair mālyaiś ca sarvaśaḥ
>
> XII.39.14
>
> Having entered the interior the fortunate one approached the statues,
> And he thoroughly worshipped with sweet garlands and precious objects.

Then again, the audience hears this simile of the moon, and one wonders what such an emblem connoted at the time of performance; was this also the standard of the patron who commissioned the poem?[34] Great jubilation and festival rejoicing ensues with drumming and the sound of conches being blown. This is a rare interlude in the course of Books Twelve and Thirteen, and it depicts in vivid and vivacious detail a scene the poets appear to have actually witnessed, for there is an air of realism about the poetry illustrating these moments, insofar as the words are neither formulaic nor in any way clichés.[35]

A curious little scene now occurs in which a mendicant *brāhmaṇa*, said to be a *rākṣasa* ('a fiend' or 'daemon') appears and insults the king and curses him for causing the death of his kinsmen and elders. He is described as *śikhī tridaṇḍī* (wearing a hair-tuft, carrying a three-branched stave), like a *parivrājaka* (a wandering renouncer) (XII.39.23). He is also said to be *duryodhanasakhā* (a friend of Duryodhana). He cries out to Yudhiṣṭhira:

> dhig bhavantaṃ kunṛpatiṃ jñātighātinam astu
>
> XII.39.26
>
> Damn you, wicked king, destroyer of kin!

[33] It is Kṛṣṇa who first raises the model of *pūjā* as a medium of worship at VI.31.26. There is virtually no indication of this classical manner of devotion in the epic, however. There is Ekalavya, at I.123.12ff.; there are also the statues we have already mentioned, at VI.108.11; and there is the golden cow, at III.121.11; none of these are really full instances of *puja*, however. There is also mention of a boy (in the Sāvitrī episode) who *karoty aśvāṃś ca mṛnmayān / citre'pi ca likhaty açvāṃś* (makes earthen horses and scratches horses in a picture) (III.278.13), which does indicate the practice and recognition of figural depiction.

[34] Let us repeat that the son of Samudragupta, Candragupta Āditya, flourished between 380 and 413 CE. His name means 'protected by the moon'.

[35] In my own experience of participating in the public rituals of Mahārao Pragmulji III in the Kacch of Western Gujarat, such scenes as the poets describe here in the early Śānti *parvan* are strongly akin to what I have witnessed in and about Bhūj on ceremonially festive occasions, particular in terms of the *sounds* of the event—the drumming and the singing—and the massed bodies of admiring people and the particular manners of womenfolk.

He adds, *mṛtaṃ śreyo na jīvitam* (death is better than living), meaning living with Yudhiṣṭhira as ruler. The king replies in his usual extremely formal, dignified, and mild fashion.

> prasīdantu bhavanto me praṇatasyābhiyācataḥ
> pratyāpannaṃ vyasaninaṃ na māṃ dhik kartum arhatha
>
> XII.39.30
>
> May the submissive request of mine to you succeed:
> You should not make such damnation of me who is rendered unfortunate!

Then the assembled *brāhmaṇas* take over and begin to shout and scorn the man, and, with their mantric powers, cause the figure (whose name is Cārvāka) to instantly die.[36]

This is an odd scene and uncanny in its uniqueness; it is as if an earlier rite—where a recently nominated or installed king is formally denounced and ritually insulted as an apotropaic element to the occasion—had been curiously added to the narrative, but with adjustments. It is as if the poets, or the tradition itself, have forgotten the prior and inceptive meaning, and all that remains is this uncanny instance. It is as if the poets are aware of the practice and the procedure that is involved, but the significance and meaning of the rite have been lost from their conscious performance.[37] The scene ends, *rājā ca harṣam āpede* (and the king acquired joy) (XII.39.37). Finally, his sorrow and grief are dissipated.

The installation continues, Yudhiṣṭhira now being referred to by the poets as *kuntiputro rājā* (the king, son of Kuntī). The authenticity of the scene is sustained as he takes a seat *param āsane* (on a superb chair) of gold and faces in an easterly direction (XII.40.1). Kṛṣṇa and Sātyaki, his Pāñcāla allies, sit on stools covered with precious quilts and face the king; Bhīma and Arjuna also sit on stools behind the king. All the family are there: Kuntī, Sahadeva, Nakula, Vidura, Dhaumya (the house-priest), and Dhṛtarāṣṭra with Gāndhārī, and Yuyutsu and Saṃjaya. This is what the poets describe as *jñātisaṃbandhimaṇḍala* (a circle of kin), and it is such a circle he should always keep about him (XII.81.41). As we know, Yudhiṣṭhira never fails to do that, and, in fact, his authority and decisiveness is

[36] Perhaps this enigmatic little scene is a folk memory taken from what was once a ritual verbal contest between either king and outsider, or *brāhmaṇa* and outsider? To quote from Keith (1925, 347): "The human sacrifice as prescribed in two of the ritual texts is based closely on the horse sacrifice." Perhaps this instant in the epic is a dramatic vestige of such a memory? A *cārvāka* is a 'materialist', which is in nice counterpoint to the steady phenomenology of Yudhiṣṭhira.

[37] This is a movement that is common for *all* rituals, however; where it is really only the longevity or temporal metonymy of a tradition that remains as the one element to carry it on in time or to charge a ritual with its force.

thoroughly founded upon this 'circle of kin' and their company; such is the basic ground and formation of Yudhiṣṭhira's corporate and archaic kingship.

Objects are brought in for the king to touch: white flowers, earth, gold, silver, and pearls (XII.40.7). Then the populace appears, led by a house-priest, and they offer symbolic and auspicious objects as they gaze at the king.[38] Gold, earthen, and jewelled objects are brought for the *abhiṣeka* (the king's anointment); vessels filled with liquids and foods, milk and sacred grass, kindling for the fire, ghee, and all the ritual implements are assembled, and Dhaumya designs the fire-precinct. Draupadī, who has not yet been mentioned, now enters the ceremony, for the sacrificer *must* have a wife.[39] King and queen are seated together, and Dhaumya pours an offering into the fire, and then, *dāśārheṇābhyanujñātas* (authorised by Dāśārha [or Kṛṣṇa]), *abhyaṣiñcat patiṃ pṛthvyāḥ kuntīputraṃ* (he anointed the son of Kuntī as king of the earth).[40] This line is followed by the text *dhṛtarāṣṭraś ca rājarṣiḥ sarvāḥ prakṛtayas tathā* (and also all the people, the *rājarṣi*, and Dhṛtarāṣṭra)—appearing to indicate that the coronation was also performed by these individuals, which is remarkable. Such only enforces our understanding of what constitutes the Kaurava *saṅgha*.

Once again the audience observes how it is that Kṛṣṇa is overseeing all procedure concerning Yudhiṣṭhira, as he has done throughout much of the poem. It is also noteworthy, here at this most sacred and vital moment, that the new king's title or epithet is a metronym, *kuntiputro*, referring to his matriline; for metronyms in a matrilineal culture possess higher status than patronyms, in terms of how someone is being addressed (XII.40.15).[41] After so many years of ordeal and struggle, Yudhiṣṭhira has achieved his aim, or, more particularly, the aim of his family. It is remarkable that this is the *second* royal anointing Yudhiṣṭhira has received, for he underwent the *abhiṣeka* as part of the *rājasūya* ceremony; that is, this rite occurred at Indraprastha *and* at Hāstinapura. Such is rare and is certainly unique in terms of kingship in the epic.[42]

38 That is, they receive *darśan*, or the 'benediction of his glance'. See Eck 1981.

39 See Jamison 1996.

40 This echoes the *rājasūya* ceremony in the Sabhā *parvan* in which *tenābhiṣiktaḥ kṛṣṇena tatra ... abhavat* (there, he [Yudhiṣṭhira] was anointed by that Kṛṣṇa) (II.49.15). As we have noted continually, Kṛṣṇa has a unique position of both power and authority vis-à-vis the Kuru *rāja*.

41 We should recall that Kuntī is a member of the clan of the Yādavas, that is, Kṛṣṇa's people. The Bhārata Song is arguably therefore a *yādavakathā*, a Yādava Epic. It is a Yādava, Vāsudeva Kṛṣṇa, who is soon to bring into the world the baby Parikṣit (at XIV.68.23), the child who becomes the future *rāja*.

42 Keith (1914, vol. XVIII:cxi–cxiii) notes: "In the ritual texts the Rājasūya is an offer of great complication ... the centre being the Abhiṣecanīya day, when the actual anointing of the king took place ... The important feature of the whole [rite] is that the king is sharply distinguished from the priests."

All the many drums are sounded, and the king makes the usual gesture of presenting gifts to the *brāhmaṇas*, who the poets say are *haṃsā iva ca nardantaḥ* (sounding like geese).

> pratipede mahad rājyaṃ suhṛdbhiḥ saha bhārata
>
> XII.40.22
>
> O Bhārata, he received the great kingdom together with friends.

Then, in his first speech, Yudhiṣṭhira begins by referring to all of his brothers, not simply to himself, saying: *dhanyāḥ pāṇḍusutā* (the fortunate sons of Pāṇḍu); again the audience hears the statement that kingship is not simply sole in status (XII.41.2). He immediately speaks of Dhṛtarāṣṭra as *mahārājaḥ pitā no daivataṃ param* (the great king, our father, supreme divinity); and he adds that *asya śuśrūṣaṇaṃ kāryaṃ mayā* (I am obedient to him). This is the kingship of Yudhiṣṭhira as he and as the poets and editors of the Bhārata Song understand it: it is a rule of immediate clan and there is *no* sense of individual control. The poets then speak of how the king allots these family members to the various offices about him, beginning with Bhīma who is next to him in age:

> yauvarājyena kauravyo bhīmasenam ayojayat
>
> XII.41.8
>
> The Kaurava appointed Bhīmasena as crown prince.

Vidura is his counsellor; Saṃjaya is to oversee wealth; Nakula is to control the forces of the kingdom, while Arjuna is their commander; Dhaumya is their family priest; and Sahadeva is to be Yudhiṣṭhira's personal guard. Thus, the new king is surrounded by those who share the conduct and office of rule. There is no mention of the *mantrins* 'ministers' who surround a solitary monarch as officiates of state. As we shall soon see, these *mantrin* counsellors and political intimates are crucial elements in the polity and system of kingship, which Bhīṣma is soon to describe.

***

One can observe here in a definite light a political system that is neither absolutist nor singularly patriarchal, but one that is founded upon lateral and familiar relations; it is also one where the voices of both Draupadī and Kuntī are given much credence.[43] There is no solitary and unimpeachable king who stands at the apex of a strict hierarchy. That is the reason why success could have

[43] Mahārāṇī and Rājmātā in contemporary terminology. The works of Jhala (2008 and 2011) show how these figures were active in an early twentieth-century princely setting.

been so disputed and become a locus for such ferocious contention. I would again propose that a system like this was founded upon the conditions of premonetary economy and preliterate culture, and it was only with the developments of secondary urbanisation and the accumulation of wealth *as money*, and as a new and absolutely impersonal 'symbol', that absolutist autocracies (that is, the Mauryas and then the Guptas) evolved. Then, once writing becomes an established medium of rule and of social domination—and here I include the writing inscribed upon coins—a culture becomes immediately organised in a different fashion: whoever controls the writing possesses the power to organise what is being written. Paid service replaces dependable kinship in the offices of rule, as a late archaic culture becomes what we now know of as early 'classical'. It was also during this inchoate classical period that Sanskrit received its renewed force as a language of political culture.[44] The first written texts of the *Mahābhārata*, or written *parts* of the *Mahābhārata*, probably, as Bronkhorst has asserted, possessed a distinctly ideological force in the courtly and political culture of the early first millennium CE in Northern India.

To recapitulate what we already noted above, human relations become simply more negotiable, or commodified, and loyalties acquire quantifiable and exchangeable value when there is trade and metallic currency on an advanced and extensive scale; where capital is made up of money rather than moveable wealth, payment replaces genetic loyalty or fidelity. In such a situation, kinship and personal duty become displaced as a market develops where purchase is possible, and all exchange is homogenised in accord with a single system of valence; this causes a new pattern of wealth and a redistribution of how moveable wealth was formerly localised.[45] In sum, with the development of a money economy and a money-based culture, familial and kinship relations become—by varying degrees—replaced by paid or commercially funded faithfulness: human worth becomes a product that is universally convertible, and not socially entailed, since labour can be rented and not simply exchanged or served. Urbanisation also affects the nature of a king's entourage in that land-based wealth and such patterns of inheritance or service are no longer the fount from which a king's advisors and servants are drawn.[46]

44 See Pollock 2006 and 2010.

45 See Goody 1977. There will still continue to be what le Goff (2010, 233) refers to as "thésaurisation," that is, the accumulation of highly valuable moveable wealth, perhaps in the form of *niṣkas* ('gold ornaments' or 'ingots'), or what contemporary Anglo-Gujarati refers to as 'gold biscuits'.

46 Literacy also allows the organisation of a bureaucracy that is founded upon standards of uniform written competence and numeration. The Moghuls perfected such a form of state bureaucracy.

It is epic *Mahābhārata*'s creation of an ideally heroic past set in an imaginary Bronze Age that projects such a system of kingship, one that was completely clan-orientated as a social organism; what ensued—in terms of Bhīṣma's discourse—was materially and vertically more hierarchical in organisation. The temporal axis of epic poetry is thus strangely abstract, and yet it must have been highly pertinent to whoever held or dominated its patron régime. For us today, however, to decode that message is complex, particularly as the term *rāja* is employed so extensively and without particular singularity or exact distinction. What we can say is that the former system was an aspect of preliteracy, while the latter model of kingship reflects a culture where literacy existed as a medium of record and transaction.

***

The king then has the *śrāddhāni* 'further obsequies' performed for those unnamed kin who fell during battle; these rites consist of food and moveable wealth offered as gifts (XII.42.1-6). As we have seen earlier, the task of king as sacrificer on such occasions is not simply to conduct the rites, but, more importantly, to deliver largesse, given to the brāhmaṇas and their company who perform the ceremonies. The idea of reciprocity is fundamental, if not actually necessary, to the successful action of any rite, and here the poets say:

> dhanaiś ca vastrai ratnaiś ca gobhiś ca samatarpayat
>
> XII.42.5
>
> He satisfied them with cattle, jewels, garments, and wealth.

Yudhiṣṭhira has halls, cisterns, and ponds established in honour of the deceased, and for those women who had lost warrior sons he makes dispensations.

> ānṛśaṃsyaparo rājā cakārānugrahaṃ prabhuḥ
>
> XII.42.11
>
> The splendid king, devoted to kindness, organised benevolence.

At last the inconsolable despair of Yudhiṣṭhira—through all these rituals and tasks as he re-orders the kingdom—is dissipated, and the poets say of him that he is *sukhī* 'happy', an extremely rare word in his personal life. To Kṛṣṇa he says, *prāptam idaṃ rājyaṃ pitṛpaitāmahaṃ mayā* (this ancestral kingdom has been obtained by me!). The ancestors here are in the nominal patriline, although technically Yudhiṣṭhira's genetic paternity is actually outside of that lineage.[47] The

[47] As we have already noted, in terms of the matriline it is the Yādava clan who come out with the ultimate *jaya* 'victory' in the succession. See Trautmann (1974 and 1981) on the nature of Dravidian kinship, that is, where the matrilineal system of kinship predominates.

king makes *namaste* to Kṛṣṇa, thanking him for the vital alliance and allegiance that made this possible (XII.43.3–4). He then sings a praise-song of eleven *ślokas* for his companion with whom he had virtually shared sovereignty for so long, and in this he pronounces an uncommon array of Kṛṣṇa's sacred names. The poets say, *evaṃ stuto dharmarājena kṛṣṇaḥ sabhāmadhye prītimān* (thus praised by the *dharmarāja* in the middle of the *sabhā*, Kṛṣṇa was pleased), and so he verbally gratifies the king responsively. Yudhiṣṭhira is returned to his dignified and capable self now and is enjoying the graciousness of being *mahārāja*; his guilt and grief are passed.

The king, after this long day of ceremony and the concomitant expressions of gratitude to all present at the *sabhā*, at last permits his brethren to return to what are their new domiciles, that is, the rich habitations of their former enemy-cousins. Bhīma, of course, receives the *bhavanaṃ* 'palace' of Duryodhana, well supplied with jewels and servants; this is *dhṛtarāṣṭrābhyanujñātaṃ* (authorised by Dhṛtarāṣṭra) (XII.44.7). It is as if the family are now ruling at Hāstinapura, with old Dhṛtarāṣṭra—to use a modern analogy—as president and Yudhiṣṭhira as prime minister, and the various senior males in the clan appointed to key central offices of power. This is no solitary and absolute kingship, but a diffusion of political and martial strength among a near-kin-group, one whose links are cognate, affiliate, and in the case of Saṃjaya, of fealty.[48] Arjuna receives the household of Duḥśāsana; Nakula that of another of Duryodhana's brothers, Durmarśaṇa; Sahadeva is given the dwelling of Durmukha—and all these establishments come with great appointment of wealth and property. Kṛṣṇa, of course, is said to reside with Arjuna *vyāghro giriguhām iva* (like a tiger in a mountain cave) (XII.44.15).[49] So ends the first day of the *kururāja*'s residence at Hāstinapura after many years of exclusion, exile, and struggle. Apart from his juvenile time, he had not dwelled there for almost all of his life, and so this day marks a true 'homecoming.'

One of his first actions as king, say the poets, is to arrange the order of the *varṇas*, sustaining and enforcing those divisions of society and culture.

cāturvarṇyaṃ yathāyogam sve sve dharme nyaveśayat

XII.45.4

He caused the four varṇas to settle, each in their own dharma, as is fit.

[48] Only the moiety of Dhṛtarāṣṭra are agnates.

[49] Kṛpa, who is of the generation of Śaṃtanu, the nominal great-grandfather of Yudhiṣṭhira, and who participated in the horrific destruction of the Pāṇḍava heirs in the Sauptika *parvan*, is in no way punished, which seems odd, and it is as if the poets are unaware of that event or that *parvan*. Perhaps the Sauptika *parvan*, being so Śaiva in nature, was a 'newer' phase to the epic. They say, *kṛpāya ca mahārāja guruvṛttim avartata* (and to Kṛpa, the great king conducted a *guru* relationship) (XII.45.8). Kṛpa had been their archery instructor when the five brothers were boys.

It is then, on Kṛṣṇa's advice, that Yudhiṣṭhira, presumably on the second day of his kingship—although the temporal transitions in the Śānti *parvan* are vague and almost imperceptible—visits the dying Bhīṣma. Thus, the narrative that began with the brothers' exclusion from Hāstinapura is closed, and the poem enters a new *kind* of speech. We are now entering upon what earlier in this book we distinguished as the transition between what we referred to as 'nature' and what was to be termed as 'culture.'

iii. Classical Ideals

The king, as he makes his way towards Bhīṣma, is as usual accompanied by his siblings, and also by Kṛpa and Kṛṣṇa; they drive by chariot back towards Kurukṣetra to pay homage to the wounded arch-hero. Bones and skulls still litter the earth, weapons and cremation pyres are everywhere upon the ground, fiendish ghosts and *rākṣakas* are in the vicinity, and the situation is ghastly.[50]

The plural and diverse teachings of Bhīṣma in the Śānti *parvan* have already been prefigured in the long soliloquy of Vidura when he was requested to speak about Yudhiṣṭhira and certain moral points by the sleepless old king (V.33.16ff.), a thoroughly didactic section of the poem often referred to as Vidura-*nīti* 'Vidura's precepts'. This and the edifying discourse of the dying Bhīṣma eventually culminate in the much later and carefully explicit formulations of statecraft that came to be gathered together and known as the Arthaśāstra of Kauṭilya, traditionally a minister to Candragupta Maurya.[51]

The Śānti *parvan* projects an image and narration of kingship that is very different—in general—from the other books in the epic. In Book Twelve, the ideal of kingship is not so deeply coloured nor imbued with Indo-Āryan forms and qualities, but offers a courtly, philosophical, and often urbane picture of a more classical king and entourage.[52]

[50] Belvalkar, in his Introduction to the Śānti *parvan*, Volume 16 in the 1966 Pune Edition, on p. clxxxvi notes: "the distance between Hastināpura situated on the Ganges, and the Kurukṣetra near the rivers Dṛṣadvatī and Sarasvatī where Bhīṣma was lying on the Śaraśayya, must have been about one hundred miles. The audience used to go and return every day."

[51] He is said to come from Takṣaśilā in the fourth century BCE.

[52] Thapar (2013, 309) remarks: "The recording of dynasties after the Kurukṣetra war indicates a perception of difference in the nature of power in the kingdoms. The war is a watershed in the Puranic periodization of the past. Whereas earlier all were included under the umbrella terms of *rājā* or *kṣatriya*, now the social status of individual dynasties is given." She also discusses the lineage system at work within the earlier Candravaṃśa genealogies of the *Mahābhārata* (ibid., 228–294.)

The Śānti *parvan* essentially expresses various kinds of traditional teachings that supply the ethos of kingly governance and understanding; plus, in the later sections of this long *parvan*, there are extensive teachings on theology, myth, and spiritual or 'liberation' philosophy—and these chapters of the book are at times given in voices other than that of Bhīṣma. It is a substantially huge document of more than fifteen thousand verses, and its manner of teaching is dramatised in several ways by the poets as maxim, allegory, discourse, injunction, and myth. Essentially, the first section of this vast book is instructive of royal ethic and of the necessary diligence—both violent and cunning—of successful kings; it is not what I conceive of as epic poetry *qua* warrior culture and song, and my comments and observations here are more of a passing overview than a careful analysis; they are given as brief counterpoint to what has been argued so far in this book. Other scholars, like Bowles, Fitzgerald, and Hiltebeitel—as we observed earlier in chapter 1—have already made considerable, lengthy, and important studies of this *parvan*.[53]

There is little metonymy between the earlier books of the poem and the Śānti *parvan* that would facilitate any continuity of narrative once Bhīṣma formally commences his discourse at XII.56.10, and it is as if the epic *Mahābhārata* has been 'attached' to this part of the poem, such is the lack of joints or seams in the great speech that would fuse the two kinds of verbal action.[54] If one removed the names of the two speakers, Bhīṣma and Yudhiṣṭhira, from the Śānti *parvan*, *nothing* would be in any way affected in the dialogue: the words have no emotional, intellectual, or even dramatic effect on either persona. Epic *Mahābhārata* takes up the heroic narration again in the Āśvamedhika *parvan* at XIV.70.[55]

[53] In part, the Śānti and Anuśāsana *parvans* often read like Machiavelli, or even von Clausewitz at times, and they are much in the style of a handbook on government, like the Arthaśāstra; they catalogue and document the knowledge that would possess utility for a governor or ruler. See Varma (2004, 29) for a contemporary view of this text: "The Shantiparva, a section of the Mahabharata devoted to the elaboration of statecraft, can have few rivals in the history of political theory for its hard-bitten pragmatism." Added to these teachings are certain spiritual values in terms of their practice and certain injunctions concerning the four *varṇas*. There is even a section on *strīsvabhāva* (the disposition of women) at XIII.38–39. Much of these two documents are explicitly in the genre of pedagogy.

[54] The Anuśāsana *parvan* makes this cursory comment at its end: *so' bhiṣikto mahāprājñaḥ prāpya rājyaṃ yudhiṣṭhiraḥ* (Yudhiṣṭhira, the very wise, having obtained the kingdom was anointed) (XIII.153.3). It is as if the poets or editors, at the close of this massive document, are suddenly reinstating the narrative they had essentially ignored for many thousands of lines.

[55] The micro-narrative of XII.146.2ff., about Janamejaya, son of Parikṣit, exemplifies this lack of metonymy between the narrative of epic *Mahābhārata* and the leading discourse of the Śānti *parvan*; for at the time of this speech by Bhīṣma, Parikṣit had not been born. That event occurs later, in the Āśvamedhika *parvan*.

Both the Śānti and Anuśāsana *parvans* participate in no temporal narrative or occasion apart from their own discourse or pronouncement; apart from the transition from the first to the second day, they are timeless in the sense of being without day or night, or having any mediate relation with the epic as given in the previous eleven *parvans*.[56] The sole structure of these two books is organised by whatever particular speaker is active at any one moment. These two books—which compose about a third of the *Mahābhārata* as we have it today in the Pune transcription—do not connect with the chronological sequence in the rest of the poem, except in the scene we have just examined where the *rāja* finally claims his capital; only a self-contained and self-defined dialogue exists and almost in capsule form. As we know, when editors or poets 'attach' a narration or document to another text, they make the affix either at the beginning or at the end of the material being appended. This practice is evident many times throughout the poem, where praise-song for Kṛṣṇa or Śiva, for instance, is attached to a *parvan*, or when some deviation—what we have referred to as *bricolage*—occurs in the narrative text.

The many characters, all of whom are now sung by the poet Vaiśaṃpāyana, also control their own voices, as when someone gives an account that is spoken by a third figure; it is such *levels* of speech that provide format to these essentially hortatory *parvans*. The form of much of this poetry is like a catalogue at times, and there are small steady oscillations of sentiment that revive the language and metaphors of the Gītā. These two books explicitly moralise the conditions and nature of kingship—much in the manner of Vidura speaking to the old Dhṛtarāṣṭra in the Udyoga *parvan* one night, as we noted above, when the old man is also suffering from great anguish (V.33.1ff.). Vidura then also spoke in a timeless manner, offering a discourse—the Vidura-*nīti*—that had no dramatic connection with the preceding or ensuing narrative.

It is difficult for us to imagine what the performative and dramatic situation of such verses must have been—how it was to listen to the poets sing these long and thematically various passages. At times the words appear to quote from more vigorous *kṣatriya* literature, and they sometimes seem to emulate a directly *śāstric* tradition, but this is certainly not the genre in general, insofar as the form

[56] In some manuscripts, the Anuśāsana *parvan* was incorporated into the text of Book Twelve and was not a separate *parvan*. Dandekar, in his Introduction to the 1966 Pune Edition of this chapter comments (on p. lxxiv): "One thing which strikes the reader of the *Anuśāsanaparvan* rather prominently is the complete lack of any logical order in the arrangement of its subject matter ... The commentator Nīlakaṇṭha has tried to discover some kind of logical unity in the successive adhyāyas, but his attempt must be said to have failed miserably." This is, in other words, what we have been referring to as a technique of *bricolage*.

of the discourse is that the young king asks a question upon which the elder hero extemporises at length.

Presumably these two magnificent and compendious *parvans* were pedagogic in how they were performed, and one can imagine young princes listening to the verses and being tested by their *ācāryas* as they were being schooled in the recitation of such formulaic allegories of rule.[57] In the latter part of the Śānti *parvan*, when the poets supply a commentary on the nature of *mokṣa* or 'spiritual freedom', it is even more difficult to imagine who the audience might once have been for the words are frequently esoteric.

***

When Yudhiṣṭhira first meets with Bhīṣma, fifty-six days remain—or two complete lunations—before the winter solstice, which is when the ancient hero expires, and hence the discourse must extend throughout this period; thus, the actual performance possibly lasted for such a duration (XII.51.14). The exposition of Bhīṣma begins with his stating, eight times: *sa māṃ pṛcchatu pāṇḍavaḥ* (let the Pāṇḍava ask me), and the question is to concern *dharmān* ('the laws' or 'the orders'; 'right') (XII.55.3ff.). His initial words are: *dharmo ... kṣatriyāṇāṃ ... samare dehapātinam* (the *dharma* of *kṣatriyas* causes bodies to fall in battle, or, more lucidly, the *dharma* of *kṣatriyas* is violence). Bhīṣma is thus initially dealing with Yudhiṣṭhira's dubiety about his bloody policy at Kurukṣetra. He adds, further absolving the king from his exceeding sense of culpability, that Yudhiṣṭhira was only performing his duty or *dharma*:

> āhūtena raṇe nityaṃ yoddhavyaṃ kṣattrabandhunā
>
> XII.55.17
>
> A kṣatriya who is challenged in battle musts always fight.

Yudhiṣṭhira touches the elder's feet, and the old hero sniffs the head of the king, and so the long moral discourse commences. During this performance Bhīṣma, who is moribund, imitates—just as the poets are imitating or enacting the voice of Bhīṣma—the many tens of speakers who compose this long verbal display of edifying principles, stories, and recollections; despite the morbidity of the old warrior, this is a dramatic performance with dozens of voices and many emotions being played. In this sense, the discourse is unlike what is presented

[57] In Suhravardī's Sufi romance, Mirigāvatī, which dates from ca. 1503 at the Moslem court of Jaunpur, stanzas 144–146 illustrate a young prince, the hero of the poem, being tested to see if he is truly royal; among the many mandatory accomplishments he must demonstrate—gambling, polo, classical Indian languages, *śāstra*, augury—is a knowledge of *Mahābhārata*. The poem is in fact replete with references to the epic, and Yudhiṣṭhira is typically cited for his 'sense of duty'.

in the Arthaśāstra, where the form is simply an edifying monologue without any action. Despite the lack of narrative, the constant change in the voicing of characters must have given the performance of this part of the poem terrific drama and energy, and it is not by any means a monologue, not internally.

***

Let us first make a quick overview of the ancient hero's point of view specifically as it relates to *rājadharma* (the lore of kingship), and then let us examine some of the more theoretical foundations of his thought.

Bhīṣma's first discourse begins with a sudden and radically marked shift in the narrative, away from the epic poem, as the audience has known it so far, towards another abstract and almost wholly intellectual and atemporal world. What the old hero begins to portray in these gargantuan and encyclopaedic speeches is a different kind of kingship from what has so far been demonstrated in the epic. Now the *saṅgha* has no place; in fact such an operation of power is condemned for its potential weakness. There is certainly no fraternal kingship in Bhīṣma's *Il Principe*, but a single and central solitary figure, who never hesitates to use open or discreet force in order to sustain his *puissance*; even a *guru* is to be removed if he becomes disaffected, says Bhīṣma (XII.57.7). As I proposed earlier, this new model of monarchy is a corollary of the new system of monetary economy; it reflects not only a different polity but a completely different social system and politics.[58]

For instance, the king—and Bhīṣma uses the word *rāja* here, as he almost always does—should make extensive use of *cāras* 'spies' in order to learn about the kingdom (XII.57.39); this is a new practice. Similarly, he should be regarded as *devavat* (like a deity), a quality that was never ascribed to Yudhiṣṭhira (XII.59.130), as in the following:

> mahatī devatā hy eṣā nararūpeṇa tiṣṭhati
>
> XII.68.40
>
> For he stands a great divine figure with the form of a human.

This is a common refrain of Bhīṣma's concept of kingship; yet nowhere before in the Kuru narrative has such a claim of inviolable sanctity or divinity been announced.[59] Even the incorrigible Duryodhana, in his greatest verbal flights,

[58] We should recall that the political culture of Cyrus II, Kuruš the Great, who flourished between ca. 600 and 530 BCE, and who established the vast and potent Achaemenid Empire, might have had great influence on political forms and thinking in the subcontinent during this time.

[59] This divine status of the king, however, does fit well with what happens in the seventeenth *parvan*, where, as we shall see, Yudhiṣṭhira does not actually die, but is simply absorbed or assumed into heaven.

never made such a pronouncement. Conversely, Bhīṣma counsels Yudhiṣṭhira against all trust and amity, and he says with emphasis:

> jñātibhyaś caiva bibhyethā mṛtyor iva yataḥ sadā
>
> XII.81. 32
>
> Always controlled, you should fear kinsmen, like death!

This of course goes completely against the grain of all that the audience has heard about Yudhiṣṭhira's form of familial kingship during the course of the poem so far, where his brothers have acted as if they were his conscious equals in all but title.

Bhīṣma then advises his young protégé at length concerning the qualities of his *mantrins* 'ministers' (XII.81–86). Again, during the course of the Kuru narrative, such counsellors were essentially absent, for there was only family or clan in the vicinity of the Pāṇḍava ruler. One presumes that these *mantrins* were paid officers in the new government; they were not loyal members of the family or clan of Yudhiṣṭhira.

Soon Yudhiṣṭhira asks his mentor about the *gaṇa*, a term that denotes an institution akin to the *saṅgha*, implying that this is either a political entity of the past or one that is found elsewhere than at Hāstinapura. He says, *gaṇānāṃ vṛttim icchāmi śrotum* (I want to hear the manner of *associations*) (XII.108.6). Bhīṣma describes how unstable and potentially hostile such communities are, and, again, it is implicit that what exists in the Kuru world in his eyes is not a *gaṇa* or anything like a *saṅgha*. He is completely cynical about how troublesome and unstable such bodies are, and states that:

> bhedād gaṇā vinaśyanti bhinnāḥ sūpajapāḥ paraiḥ
>
> XII.108.14
>
> Gaṇas are destroyed due to schism, split, inspired to rebel by enemies.

One of the signal and dynamic terms of epic *Mahābhārata* is this word *bheda* ('partition' or 'schism'). In fact, this is the one word Janamejaya asks about when he poses the question that inspires the *whole* and complete telling of the original epic (I.58.19). It is notable that Bhīṣma now condemns such oligarchic activity in his vision of this new and monarchic politics.

All this I would propose represents a more classical view of kingship than the older and archaic version that the audience has heard about in the course of the poem up to Book Twelve. The political modelling accomplished by the old hero in these prolonged and protracted discourses has no relation to the political system that we have observed during the rest of the poem, in the same way that the two narrative forms are unconnected. Bhīṣma closes this short commentary on such 'primitive' kinds of polity by saying:

> tasmāt saṅghātam evāhur gaṇānām śaraṇaṃ mahat
>
> XII.108.31
>
> Therefore people say that the close union of gaṇas is a great protection.

This neatly portrays what occurred between the Pāṇḍavas, the Pāñcālas, the Yādavas, and the Vairāṭas.[60] Note the conjoining of the terms *saṅghāta* and *gaṇa* here.

***

Let us now turn to the more theoretical aspects of this dramatic monologue and its formal interlocutor. Yudhiṣṭhira commences the exchange by requesting Bhīṣma to *rājadharmān viśeṣeṇa kathayasva* (tell especially the lore of a king) (XII.56.3). Bhīṣma responds:

> na hi satyād ṛte kiṃcid rājñāṃ vai siddhikāraṇam
>
> XII.56.17
>
> For the cause of perfection of kings is not anything but truth.

As a consequence of this *satyam* 'truthfulness', Bhīṣma later makes the important observation:

> prīyate hi haran pāpaḥ paravittam arājake
> yadāsya uddharanty anye tadā rājānam icchati
>
> XII.67.13
>
> For the wicked person is pleased taking the wealth of another in a kingless place;
> As others take of him, so he desires a king.

Thus it is that the intellect of a king is formed to apprehend veracity in the universe, and simultaneously it is the earthly presence of the king that oversees and works to preserve the possession of property and wealth. This contact with, or consciousness of, *satyam* 'truth' is what facilitates the blamelessness of the king as a punisher, and equally it is the potential of such punishment that sustains the security of wealth in a kingdom. There is thus an implicit and profound bivalence about kingly life and practice: there is the necessary relationship with

[60] These allies, with the exception of the Pāñcālas, are connected to the Pāṇḍavas by blood ties and marriage; the Pāñcālas are joined only by marriage.

natural, or cosmic and universal, *truth*, and also an active material and coercive relationship with physical property.

According to this view, the position of the king is founded upon a secure holding of object possessions, which is a view that certainly does not indicate a system of economy where all wealth is symbolically possessed by the king and where those below his standing receive a proportion of annual production generated by such wealth, like cattle or fields, livestock and land. Ideally, it is from his superior ethical position that a king possess the right to employ *daṇḍa* 'violence', either judicially or martially, thus implicitly sustaining a situation of praxis as it concerns land and all that is attached to land, and its firm or protected tenancy.

It is for this reason, because of the *pāpa* 'the criminal' that people once—long ago in an hypothetical past—entered into agreement and made covenants with, says Bhīṣma:

> tāḥ sametya tataś cakruḥ samayān iti naḥ śrutam
>
> XII.67.18
>
> Those ones then having assembled made compacts: thus it is heard.

Again, as with the formation and conduct of the *saṅgha*, which we discussed earlier, there is this notion of an 'ancient' social contract that existed between those who possessed property and those—the kings—who were bound to sustain such asset possession. It is the *samaya* 'the agreement', which in a preliterate world is highly formalised by reciprocity and ritual exchanges, that once institutionalised this relationship underlying kingship and its customary existence. An active community with the authoritative *brāhmaṇas* was central to this system.[61] The situation, then, according to Bhīṣma's antique view of society, is that a king is ethically superlative and therefore morally justified in acting punitively when property is not respected and treated. Underlying this view of the past is the pragmatic condition of an 'accord' between those who are ruled and the ruler, and central to this view is the social group that encompasses the king and behaves in the manner of a constantly and ceaselessly referential *saṅgha*, that group who are party to the *samaya*.[62] That is the *old world* of kingship, according to Bhīṣma.

He continues with his discourse, telling of how the *prajā*, the 'people', then formalised the contract, and made it substantial and feasible. This was in

61 See Heesterman 1985.

62 In his commentary to Arthaśāstra XI.1.1–5, Kangle (1972, part II:456) notes: "*Saṅgha* is a form of rule evolved from clan rule. Fairly big states were formed with councils of elders to rule over them ... a *saṅgha* had more than one chief or *mukhya*. In some *saṅghas*, the chiefs styled themselves *rājan* or king. *Saṅgha* is best rendered by 'oligarchy'."

antiquity, the olden days when Manu lived, and such a time occurred *before* the present—that is, the epic here and now where the old hero relates his great counsel to the young king.

> paśūnām adhipañcāśadd hiraṇyasya tathaiva ca
> dhānyasya daśamaṃ bhāgaṃ dāsyāmaḥ kośavardhanam
>
> XII.67.23
>
> We shall give a treasury-increasing allotment: a tenth
> Of the grain, a fiftieth of cattle, and of gold also.

These 'people' say that *saṃsthaṃ no bhaviṣyati* (it will become our standard); hence the army, hence the power of judicial retribution, and hence the wealth necessary for the sacrifices—although this last component appears to require further and more particular prestations. In the case of the *rājasūya*, this final category was constituted by the spectacular conquests made in four compass directions, and for the *aśvamedha* there was the expedition towards the Himālayas in order to secure the wealth hidden there. Oddly enough—because this is simply our modern presumption—there is no explicit mention of land tenure or any direction given as to the management and tenancy of landholdings. Whether *all* the land is owned by the king, who takes a percentage of production, or, if the land is actually owned by other individuals or by clans, guilds, or other associations, who offer the king a percentage of their produce, is not succinctly stated and remains a curious and inexplicable elision. Even when Bhīṣma restates the suzerain's percentage, the nature of land tenure remains unclear:

> baliṣaṣṭhena śulkena daṇḍenāthāparādhinām
> śāstranītena lipsethā vetanena dhanāgamam
>
> XII.72.10
>
> You should desire to obtain wealth by stipends for teaching and conduct,
> By the punishment of criminals, by customs-tax, by the sixth-tax.

This is the king's *price* for the 'contract', and it is this access to wealth that is the 'root' of a sovereign's power and existence.[63] Bhīṣma later says, in an oblique manner concerning ownership of wealth:

> abrāhmaṇānāṃ vittasya svāmī rājeti vaidikam
>
> XII.78.2
>
> The Veda states, 'the king is the master of the property of non-brāhmaṇas.'

[63] This 'sixth' is mentioned in the Manusmṛti at VII.130.

This would seem to indicate that monarchy controls all property that is *not* held by *brāhmaṇas*; yet whether this continues from the Vedic period into the 'real-time' present of the Śānti *parvan*, Bhīṣma does not state. As we have observed above, as a direct consequence of the *brāhmaṇas* performing sacrifices for a king, they receive material grants as their just due.

Bhīṣma concludes this first part of his long teaching about how politics were organised in the old and remembered *past* by reemphasising the importance of physical wealth for a king *now*. He consistently stresses the importance of riches if a king is to maintain order in a flourishing polity. He says:

> kośād dharmaś ca kāmaś ca paro lokas tathāpyayam
>
> XII.128.49
>
> From a treasury are order and desire and the next world, as is this one.

The final message then—drawing upon the historical reminiscence of *the past*—is that *wealth*, cattle, jewels, servants, armies, and all the matériel of kingship, lie at the basis of sound princely governance—what was soon to become known as 'money.' This 'past,' I would propose, is constituted by the preceding eleven books of the poem. Morality and intelligence are secondary to such an appraisal of the 'new' kingly system, and this is Bhīṣma's principal injunction, disregarding emotion and transcendental desire and certainly the human loyalty of kinship and affinal association. One must remember that the only significant mention of land tenure and the king occurred in the poem when the Pāṇḍavas, during the exchanges made during the Udyoga *parvan*, requested the secession of control of five villages.[64]

***

It is curious that during these long perorations of the Śānti *parvan* no mention is made of the Bhārata war, or of any of the campaigns that preceded the *rājasūya*, or of the relevant geopolitical situation of *bhāratavarṣa*.[65] All this would be in recent memory, one would think, and it is as if such exclusion of a present situation makes the exposition appear to be taken from another tradition of poetry because there is such a complete disjunction or occlusion of memory. The references that Bhīṣma employs in his speeches are all taken from historical myth, or are allegories of animals, or the teaching is simply abstract, programmatic, or epigrammatic.

[64] *Yudhiṣṭhiraḥ puraṃ hitvā pañca grāmān sa yācati* (Yudhiṣṭhira having lost the town asks for five villages) (V.54.29). Perhaps implicit here is the notion that Dhṛtarāṣṭra controls *all* the villages in the kingdom?

[65] There is a cursory mention of the battle at XII.151.32–33.

We should recall that during the *kali yuga*, when there exists little natural order in the world, a king's policy concerns expedience and opportunism, with a constant state of perpetual responsiveness; human relations during this age lack steadiness and parity. If there are no prescriptive or abstract principles by which moral action is to be guided or judged, the question is: What is the nature of this kind of preponderant *adharma*? This is almost a paradoxical or irrational state in which survival is the only justification for action, *post hoc*. In a sense, this is the appropriate kind of *dharma* for the *kali yuga*—for this is arguably a cosmic season of *āpad* or 'misfortune'; and if an action is despicable or reprehensible, as long as it allows the agent to survive, it is morally passable. If the doer is aware of the error and does not only act unconsciously or compulsively, then the act is permissible: right is performative, rather than constitutional or moral, and thus *dharma* during such a *yuga* exists to be performed in a thoroughly teleological manner.

> evaṃ vidvān adīnātmā vyasanastho jijīviṣuḥ
> sarvopāyair upāyajño dīnam ātmānam uddharet
>
> XII.139.92
>
> Thus the wise one, distressed, standing in disaster, desiring to live,
> Understanding expedience, by all expedience he should rescue his distressed self.

This is practically how the Pāṇḍavas and their Vṛṣṇi ally Kṛṣṇa conducted themselves during the eighteen days of fighting at Kurukṣetra; the Kauravas were *not* so reprehensible. Thus, in a sense, the Pāṇḍava side of the family inhabit the *kali yuga* much more than their fellow moiety, except for Duryodhana's treatment of Draupadī.[66] Yet, as we know, due to the tenuous nature of *dharma* during the early *kali yuga*, it is almost impossible for any moral situation or any moral agent to be completely 'right,' because the poem is really concerned more with the complex nature and portrayal of a preponderant *adharma*.

***

Bhīṣma, in the third of his three discourses, directs his words to the abstractions that support life and to the intellectual foundations of kingship. He says, *prajñā pratiṣṭhā bhūtānāṃ* (judgement [or 'intelligence'] is the stability of beings) (XII.173.2). This mental situation—as opposed to the practical or the expedient—is the focus of Bhīṣma's final teaching: it is the *intellect* that frees and

66 This unique treatment of Draupadī when she was in what was a *taboo* state, might sit well with our view of Duryodhana as a *shaman*, or one adept in sympathetic magic, insofar as this scene represents his successful manipulation of 'dangerous' natural forces. Purity and danger are thus practically, or even ritually, opposed in such a view; tampering with the nature of blood is bad for a community.

liberates human existence from its earthly and material imperatives. Bhīṣma, speaking in the voice of Bhṛgu, the great *ṛṣi*, says:

> satyaṃ brahma tapaḥ satyaṃ satyaṃ sṛjati ca prajāḥ
>
> XII.183.1
>
> Truth is Brahma; spiritual austerity is truth, and truth creates a populace.

This is the *truth* that ideally supplies Yudhiṣṭhira with his vision and the basis of his political action.[67] Most of this long explanation by Bhīṣma is spiritual ontology in its expression; its description of human activity exceeds the narrative domain of Yudhiṣṭhira that we have examined so far in this study, and it is more in the form of an *upaniṣad* than in the pattern of *kṣatriya* poetry as we have been pursuing it up to this point (and as the poets have recounted in the preceding eleven *parvans*).

***

It is remarkable that in all this telling of the ideals of *nītiśāstra* or 'good kingship', Bhīṣma draws upon a traditional system of lore that is animal, fabulous, and truly allegorical; he informs Yudhiṣṭhira in so many instances, not programmatically or historically, but with stories about wise, magical, or cunning animals. This is a kind of exposition that culminated in the Hitopadeśa tales that were put into written form in about the twelfth century and that recalled a much earlier Pañcatantra tradition of fables. One wonders why so much of the teachings of the Śānti *parvan* is expressed in this form: Does this in some way indicate for us the nature of a possibly youthful audience?

During the ensuing Anuśāsana *parvan*, the form of the poetry is that Yudhiṣṭhira asks Bhīṣma a question, and then the old warrior responds in dramatic or mimetic fashion. The topics do not really have much to connect them to the epic narrative, and one can understand these *adhyāyas* as being pedagogical in utility, possibly a central component in the education of young elite or cadet *kṣatriyas*.

At the end of this vast section of the poem, the old hero expires and receives his funerary service. There is little in the Bhārata Song that now concerns itself with kingship or the conduct of Yudhiṣṭhira, and the epic turns toward concluding the narrative strands: firstly with the *aśvamedha*; and then in the brief four books that terminate the poem and deal with the deaths of Kṛṣṇa

[67] It was this idea of *truth* that lay behind the political activity of the Mahātmā Gandhi, described in his Autobiography. Here, truth concerns the nature of consciousness itself, rather than any single reasonable and demonstrable proof.

and his Kuru allies. The poem in no way concerns itself with their successors, except right at the beginning of the epic in the Ādi *parvan*, where the audience hears something about Janamejaya, the great-grandson of Arjuna.[68] The only kingly function that the audience perceives adhering to Janamejaya is that of an occasional sacrificer and also the fact that he is the royal patron of a great epic performance.[69]

***

In sum, then, the ideals of *Mahābhārata* kingship (before the Śānti *parvan* and Bhīṣma's teaching), which the poets have pictured for an audience, are multifarious and multi-fold. There is no solitary autocratic ruler, and what exists in this poetry is the rule of a clan where a fraternity—and a powerful wife and her mother-in-law—dominate, with the eldest of the brothers as its leading figure, the one who bears the title. This fraternal company, as we noted earlier, is itself intrinsically founded upon the consensus and approbation of popular society: a presence that is voiced in and out of the poetry as a constant steady refrain, but only and *always* in reference to the kingly office. The combination of these two political components, inner clan and peripheral populace, amount to what twentieth-century Indian historians viewed as a *saṅgha*, whose verbal accord was necessary for a ruler's succession and viable government.[70] It is the combination of these three voices—king, clan, and vocal populace—that expresses the nature of how kingship functions in sovereign Hāstinapura polity as depicted by the poem *up to* Book Twelve (a form of kingship based upon cooperation). With

[68] Janamejaya is said to have as his principal wife Kāśyā, a Vārāṇasī woman. She gave him two sons, and of the eldest, Candrāpīḍa, a hundred sons were born, the eldest of whom, Satyakarṇa, was king after Janamejaya. Satyakarṇa had a son called Śvetakarṇa, who himself had a son called Ajapārśva with his wife Yādavī. (Harivaṃśa, 114.2ff.). Note the continuing practice of taking a Yādava wife here. Law (1941, 94) notes: "After the death of Janamejaya, the Kuru kingdom was split up into several parts ... The junior branch probably resided at Indraprastha or Indapatta ... which probably continued to be the seat of kings claiming to belong to the Yudhiṭṭhilagotta (Yudhiṣṭhira-gotra), long after the destruction of Hastināpura and the removal of the elder line of Kuru kings to Kausāmbi." Commenting on the Majjhima Nikāya II, p. 65ff., Law (96) adds: "but in the Buddha's time the Kuru country was being ruled by a titular chieftain called Koravya, and evidently had little political importance of its own."

[69] In terms of the sacrifice, I wonder if one could construe the *nāgas* 'snakes' that are cast into the fire in lieu of an oblation as metaphors of Buddhism or Jainism? They would be members of a clan of such religious devotion. It is telling that on Duryodhana's banner a snake was depicted (IV.50.12).

[70] Allow me also to reiterate strongly the fundamental duality of kingly sovereignty itself, which underlies this kind of organisation of associate power, a topic that we addressed in chapter 1 and revisited in chapter 2. On such a not, Mallory (1989, 141) remarks on the "dual political leadership among the early Indo-Europeans. Citing Homer's account of the Achaian forces in the *Iliad* ... how frequently the tribes listed are led by two rulers."

literacy and the invention of monetary currency, all this changes, as Mauryan, and then later, Gupta, politics supercede.

I would strongly aver that it is this latter society and polity that Bhīṣma portrays, and not what the poets depict in epic *Mahābhārata* prior to Books Twelve and Thirteen. Bhīṣma's modelling of kingship is monarchic in its domination and not corporate. The epitome of kingship implied in this later part of the poem concerns a 'cultural' conception of rule as opposed to one that is conceived of as 'natural,' in that the earlier type of governance is one that is viewed as being thoroughly founded upon a universal order generated by the natural world. Kingship in Bhīṣma's present explication concerns a world that is mediated by money and by purchase, or by cultural forms that do not subscribe to such 'natural' universality, but to a far more human practicality.[71]

What Bhīṣma describes during his great four-part speech does *not* describe kingship in such terms of the *saṅgha*; in fact he decries such a model of polity. What we have noted from a close reading of epic *Mahābhārata* is different from what the arch-hero describes in his discourse, and the two situations of kingship do not often connect or appear similar, even on a simple temporal or narrative level. As we observed, the Śānti and Anuśāsana *parvans* do not actually mention any of the events or moods of the poetry that precede their telling: there is a curious mutual exclusion between these two kinds of singing, the two forms of poetry and the two patterns of suzerain power. These are two traditions or two performances that have been arbitrarily—although successfully—joined by literary editors. I would propose that the detailing of kingship that the poets accomplish during the earlier course of the poem concerns more archaic *kinds* of princely rule, whereas what Bhīṣma describes in his timeless oratory relates more to classical forms of kingship.[72] The first situation is actually oligarchic and collective, whereas the second constitution is definitely autocratic and individual,

71 In the ten History Chronicles of Shakespeare—and let us not forget that kingship also supplies the theme to many of his other dramas, like *Julius Caesar*, *King Lear*, and *Anthony and Cleopatra*, to name a few—the two kinds of kingship are similarly stylised and expressed. There is the 'natural' (or anointed) and sacred king, and there is the new pattern of kingship that is more directed by machination and calculation, or what came to be termed the Machiavellian. *Richard III* is a fine indication of this latter kind, and *Richard II* or *Henry V* is a good example of the former. Historically, the argument is that the old and good, or the more 'natural' type of crown, the late mediaeval, was being ousted by the early modern and more bureaucratic and commercial or rational model of rule; the Tudor dynasty recapitulated that earlier form of kingship as a mode of legitimacy. *Killing of the king* is also an important theme for Shakespeare, followed by royal rejuvenation.

72 Flannery and Marcus (2012) have analysed this transition from systems of chiefdom to hierarchical monarchy from a more global perspective.

and these represent two distinctly separate ideals of kingship *and* two different kinds of economy.

One also must remember a necessary and essential fourth dimension: epic *Mahābhārata* is poetry and not a record. It is a song that represents an idealised old world that is *not* a portrait of an historical reality, but a pictured heroic time when deities and humans lived, occasionally loved, and sometimes died together in situations that were often extraordinarily beautiful, thanks to the play of their enactment and the narration of their metaphors and myths. The only true criterion of validity and integrity lies—or lay—in the satisfaction of the intended audience and the pleasure experienced from listening to this poetry; and sometimes in the pacification of a warrior's grief.

4

The End

The question as to how Yudhiṣṭhira's model of kingship has come to be represented, portrayed, and delineated in the course of this epic is without any one precise picture: for as we have seen there is no single plane, no one just figure, but an amalgamation of many dimensions of possible forms and models of kingship concurrently extant in the poem. He is *rāja*, but sovereignty is discreetly shared with Kṛṣṇa; he is *rāja*, but only in the company of his brothers and with the steady presence of his *prajā*, the 'populace'; and he is a king who is also a magnificent ritualist. During epic *Mahābhārata*, however, Yudhiṣṭhira is *not* king as Bhīṣma describes that office during his four great discourses.

Yudhiṣṭhira in the earlier epic is a model of receptivity, of extraordinary assurance, a man of strong vision concerning kingship, yet he is someone who constantly shares his decisions with those who advise him, principally Kṛṣṇa, and to some extent also Nārada and Vyāsa. His half-brothers and his principal wife do tend to dominate him, which he judiciously accepts: such is the tacit dialectic of the family association and direction. In his dealings with his primary wife, he accepts her embittered, cynical, and often outrageous language—and sometimes this is almost abusive—with calmness and decency, and he constantly worries about how she and his mother, Kuntī, will react when hardship or death come close.

Yudhiṣṭhira enters the world of the *rājasūya* almost naively and yet manages to glide through the process. His tremendous remorse at the loss of *all* the next generation of Pāṇḍava menfolk, those of the next age who should inherit his kingdom, vitiates all possible jubilation that he might experience after the costly victory of Kurukṣetra. The *aśvamedha* sacrifice seems to affect him only moderately, although it does appear to cleanse him of being psychically possessed by mourning. There is little emotion in the portrait that we see of Yudhiṣṭhira, apart from this steady reiteration of sorrow and the two quick or flamboyant occasions of anger that he demonstrates towards Arjuna and towards Kuntī. The poets do tell of how he becomes martially enraged after the death of Śalya, but this, like most of Yudhiṣṭhira's behaviour during the war, is essentially formulaic. There is no hint of the transcendent about Yudhiṣṭhira. He is not a mystical figure nor does he experience spiritual illumination at any point in the poem; *dharma* for him concerns praxis, and it is in no way a medium of enlightenment. He is a moralist, not a mystic. He *never* abjures responsibility by claiming that *daiva* has caused his actions, and he is a reserved and almost silent king; yet he is a character of firmness and quiet resilience, always flexible and responsive towards the words of those nearest to him. It is this paradox of superb power and yet perpetual receptivity that makes for a complex and enigmatic *rāja*; he is a figure of potence and of gentleness, and, some would say, of great and unmixed beauty. Also, he never appears to grow old in any way, remaining curiously youthful.

Within the poem are merged the myths and the kingly rituals: there are the warrior or *kṣatriya* paradigms of Bronze Age kings, and there are the ideals of hypothetical rule, as well as a *mirror* of kingship in terms of its *realpolitik*.[1] What we think of as 'heroic religion' is in fact really only an expression of a projected kingship where varieties of supernal deities who exist in a more elevated *status* are activated in a purely verbal ritual as they interact with heroes.[2] This is a ritual of epic song or epic performance in which heroes work to support different models of royal chiefdom. Thus, right kingship, as evinced by epic performance, is *like* the poetic activity of the aerial and mundane deities who ideally supply blessings to a community. These forms of benefit, or what we might consider more pragmatically as distributions derived from ritual sacrifices, are *like* the activation of emotion that occurs when the poetry that describes such super-mundane behaviour is being sung or performed. The performance of epic song is causative and efficacious of intellectual, affective, and pleasurable *change* in an audience: as we have observed, the poem reiterates this again and again. In sum, singing of heroes—who are half-divine—and about their actions with deities is socially and naturally *good*.

The most distinguishing feature of Yudhiṣṭhira's paramountcy is his role as a sacrificer, for it is in this manner that the narrative of the poem appears to

[1] Bronze Age warrior kings who lived in the palatial strongholds in what we now call Greece can be dated back to the seventeenth century BCE. They used chariots and their materially rich culture had collapsed by the twelfth century. It is that society the Iliadic poets did their best to recapitulate; just as the epic *Mahābhārata* poets and the later editors attempted to reconstruct a poetry that represented an early second millennium world of Northwest India.

[2] To quote from the masterful recent work of Flannery and Marcus (2012, 548): "Most likely our ancestors also believed that the first humans had abilities beyond ours. Those 'old ones' had taken on the role of betas in society's dominance hierarchy and, when treated properly, would intercede on their descendents' behalf with the alphas of the spirit world."

establish its basic sequence; the overall structure of epic *Mahābhārata* is founded upon this activity of the king. It is a nominal title, though, insofar as the king really only commissions or sponsors the rites, and his role is more specifically to reallocate masses of moveable property once the rites have been performed, and, of course, to acquire that wealth before the rite actually commences.

As the sanguine Vidura—speaking of the nature of princely life—says to his old king:

> lekhāśmanīva bhāḥ sūrye mahormir iva sāgare
> dharmas tvayi mahān rājann iti vyavasitāḥ prajāḥ
>
> V.85.3
>
> Like a scratch on stone, radiance in the sun, like great waves in the sea,
> O king, the *people* are convinced great dharma is in you!

This is the mysterious nature of kingship, where, if the king is true, his *dharma* is intrinsic to, and ingrained within, his nature, and so emanates among the polity and community; but note that the referent or the adjudication comes from the *prajā*, the 'people'. Kingship in this view concerns *natural* law and derives its effects from such a condition: the king both represents and enacts the *truth* of the cosmos, and it is this ethical dignity that exonerates him from the blame of having to punish in a corporeal manner any infringements that he perceives of this truth. Use of the *daṇḍa* is polluting, yet the intellectual and spiritual dignity of the king exculpates him, just as his sacrifices similarly acquit him if they are accomplished correctly. The many dimensions and qualities of kingship portrayed in this epic, however, radiate with such a multiplicity of princely models that at times they appear to contradict or to cancel each other.

***

The recurrent lamentations of the old king Dhṛtarāṣṭra, for his own folly and sorrow at the slow and steady destruction of his side of the clan, must certainly have been an explicit message to any kingly audience of the poem. Dhṛtarāṣṭra is a figure of indulgence, and his blindness is more than simply real. Duryodhana, the one son to whom Dhṛtarāṣṭra was overly partial and to whom he was excessively indulgent in tacitly supporting his son's lust for sole power, Duryodhana is the most intricate and opaque of all the heroes in both character and message. It is as if, at times, the words of this valiant, young, and fully mortal king have been drawn from another poetic tradition—even a Buddhist or Jain tradition—and his truculence and minatory belligerence are dramatic qualities that have been laid upon another kind of *earlier* character. This is speculative, however, for there is no significant evidence that will allow us to construct any firm inference about this hero; he simply remains wholly paradoxical, especially in his death. We can say though that Duryodhana is strangely solitary, unlike Yudhiṣṭhira.

Yudhiṣṭhira is quietly central within the epic, distinguished, imposing, and nearly always scrupulous in his words and noble manner. Concerning a reputed literary relationship between the Yudhiṣṭhira of epic poetry and the historical Aśoka, there is little salient or direct connection, and it is difficult to discern any possible equation. Certainly, Yudhiṣṭhira demonstrates no understanding of literacy or of writing, although the public use of script was a powerful medium for the Buddhist emperor.[3] There is no reference to any of the prestigious Aśokan Edicts in the epic text, and certainly there is little historical record of the *cakravartin* or emperor Aśoka as a *sacrificer*.

***

Let us now—in closing—turn to the final four books of the poem: the Āśramavāsika, the Mausala, the Mahāprasthānika, and the Svargārohaṇa *parvāṇi*, which are more like appendages to the main work of the epic. It is even as if they are drawn from another style of poetry. These, especially the final part of Book Fifteen, the Putradarśana *parvan*, are generally concerned with the manifestation of death and its corollary mourning; all the allied heroes and kings are deceased, and the poem now coalesces around the closed and idealised family of Vyāsa.

One of the first problems that the narrative or the new king must address is what to do with the displaced chief of the clan, Dhṛtarāṣṭra? The poets say that for fifteen years:

> pāṇḍavāḥ sarvakāryāṇi saṃpṛcchanti sma taṃ nṛpam
>
> XV.1.6
>
> The sons of Pāṇḍu consulted that king for all tasks.

Thus, the seniority of rank continues to possess a more than nominal authority, and it is said that even Kuntī offered obeisance to Gāndhārī, Dhṛtarāṣṭra's principal wife. Concerning Vyāsa and his son Dhṛtarāṣṭra, the poets comment:

> vyāsaś ca bhagavān nityaṃ vāsaṃ cakre nṛpeṇa ha
> kathāḥ kurvan purāṇarṣir devarṣinṛparakṣasām
>
> XV.1.12

[3] Seven rock edicts, eleven pillar edicts, and nineteen minor rock edits are all that presently remain. None of the speeches of Yudhiṣṭhira are in any way like the prose form or sentiments of these edicts; there are no resonances or echoes in the language of Yudhiṣṭhira that might possibly point to any of these inscriptions. See Talim 2010.

For the lord Vyāsa always made a home with the king,
Making epic—of rakṣasas, kings, divine mystics, wizards of old.

In accord with the standards of the *āśrama* system, the old king eventually wishes to retire to the forest and live an asocial life, withdrawing from political existence and the world of Hāstinapura.[4] However, in order to do this, he requires the permission and acceptance of Yudhiṣṭhira, the new king. Yudhiṣṭhira, of course, wishes to join his uncle and to pass on kingship to his nominal cousin Yuyutsu, the one remaining son of Dhṛtarāṣṭra. To this end, Yudhiṣṭhira says: *astu rājā* (let him be king), *yaṃ cānyaṃ manyate* (and anyone else who is considered) (XV.6.7). Thus, within the inner workings of the Hāstinapura *sabhā*, kingship—just as we have noted before—is a fluid condition able to be passed among the central few who live together in a situation of princely and oligarchic reciprocity. This is the location of what I would identify as a *saṅgha*, an 'association': the social and political currency of those in the immediate vicinity of the king.

Vyāsa again intervenes and directs Yudhiṣṭhira to accept the old king's desire. Yudhiṣṭhira responds by saying that the *ṛṣi* is *pitā rājā guruś ca* (father, king, and *guru*) and so cannot be refused anything (XV.8.8). Throughout the poem, Vyāsa has frequently intervened to direct his young nominal grandson, but never before was Yudhiṣṭhira in such a position of power as during these later stages of the epic; yet Vyāsa still manages the throne, just as he is said to manage the poem. How an audience would conceive of such an authority is difficult to reconstruct, for *ṛṣis* are not human beings but divine creatures of great and atemporal magic.[5] Yet Yudhiṣṭhira considers Vyāsa to be 'king', which, as he is ostensibly the master narrator of the Bhārata poem, as well as the reputed progenitor of the clan, is a correct entitlement.[6]

Before he actually departs, Dhṛtarāṣṭra recounts the lineage to those of his subjects who attend on him at the palace; they are the *paurajānapadā janāḥ* (the town and country people), who have consistently appeared throughout the poem and taken an active part in the functioning of kingship at Hāstinapura; they are a vital part of the *saṅgha* model of politics. Now, it is as if the old king is reaffirming or proclaiming the succession as he prepares to secede. He begins with Śaṃtanu, then Vicitravīrya, Pāṇḍu, himself, and then he includes Duryodhana, with Yudhiṣṭhira in the sixth place of succession (XV.14.1–10). This is the simple

4 See Olivelle (1993) on the four customary and temporal stations of male life.

5 Certainly, *devarṣis* like Nārada are fully divine, while *brahmarṣis* and *rājarṣis* possess supernatural powers. In McGrath 2016, chap. 6, I describe and analyse the life cycle of Nārada.

6 On the level of myth, Lincoln (1991) would associate Vyāsa with the supra-deity Brahmā.

public pronouncement of how the kingdom has passed from one ruler to another and how kingship is sometimes shared between two generations.[7] There is no mention of further succession after Yudhiṣṭhira for presumably it is up to him to proclaim that Parikṣit will become king.[8]

Then, the poets reveal to the audience, once again, how active the populace is in the polity of Hāstinapura, for the old king specifically requests of the people that they formally dismiss him and Gāndhārī from the office of kingship, saying:

> gāndhāryā sahitaṃ tan māṃ samanujñātum arhatha
>
> XV.15.5
>
> Please dismiss me together with Gāndhārī.

In response to this, the people all begin to weep with grief, and one of them, a *brāhmaṇa*, speaks on their behalf, admonishing the aged couple not to retire and depart towards the forest. Once again we see how deeply founded this Kuru kingship is upon its populace, and the *brāhmaṇa* even claims how well Duryodhana ruled for them, saying that they were *duryodhenāpi rājñā suparipālitāḥ* (so very well protected by king Duryodhana) (XV.15.20). He also claims that the war and destruction were not the fault of Duryodhana but of *daiva* ('fate' or 'destiny'), and so the clan is absolved of any guilt. As we know, this is an aspect of kingship that the poem has consistently projected, a model of rule that is deeply founded upon the constant affirmation by a group of subjects who are near to the king—really a popular *chief.* The *brāhmaṇa* also assents to the rule of Yudhiṣṭhira *and* his brothers, and, as we have repeatedly observed, it is notable that Yudhiṣṭhira's conduct as king in the public conception is rarely distinct from, or separated from, the immediate presence of the half-siblings. The *brāhmaṇa* says of this group:

> adharmiṣṭhān api sataḥ kuntīputrā mahārathāḥ
> mānavān pālayiṣyanti bhūtvā dharmaparāyaṇāḥ
>
> XV.16.22
>
> So the great charioteers, the good sons of Kuntī, having become
> Devoted to dharma, will protect even the adharmic humans.

7 Neither Dhṛtarāṣṭra, Pāṇḍu, nor Yudhiṣṭhira was actually conceived in this patriline. In fact, there is no patriline here. Similarly, Śaṃtanu has no real issue, for both his sons die, and it is Vyāsa, the son of Parāśara, who actually generates the line, but not including Yudhiṣṭhira. Vasiṣṭha was the grandfather of Parāśara.

8 Parikṣit's mother is Uttarā, who comes from the clan of the Mātsyas. The first story in the song of Vaiśaṃpāyana, given at I.57.1ff., tells of the origins of the Mātsyas: this is how he begins the *Mahābhārata*. The twin sister of the eponymous king Matsya is Satyavatī, the mother of Vyāsa. The grandfather of these twins is Uparicara, who ruled the Cedis; the children were begotten within a fish and not a human.

The message of epic *Mahābhārata* as it concerns the idea of kingship is thus both complex and various, and partakes of no simple or unitary model—certainly not in the sense of a *single* person.

The poets thus portray three pictures of rule: Dhṛtarāṣṭra, Duryodhana, and Yudhiṣṭhira, and we observe three distinct patterns with presumably the last taking priority in terms of the poem's message, while the other two models offer counterpoint or shadow. How far the modelling generated by the poetry and by the poets—and possibly the later editors—actually reflects an historical condition is not possible to ascertain. Even to propose that the image of kingship generated by the performance of the poem is communicative of moral judgement—that this *should* be the practical ideal of kingship—is to make claims that cannot really be supported by dependable evidence, neither within the text or (most certainly) beyond it. This even applies to the words of Bhīṣma. Nevertheless, there must have been some moral consensus among patron and poets, or audience and poets, at some point, for such was the necessary and creative social tissue of all epic poetry.

***

Some time after the elder king has retired to the forest, Yudhiṣṭhira and his immediate family determine to visit Dhṛtarāṣṭra, who was by then dwelling as a renunciant upon the shores of the Yamunā. There, Yudhiṣṭhira inquires after Vidura and is directed towards the woods where he sees a naked, filthy, emaciated, and quite distracted Vidura, whom he approaches, calling out his name. Vidura retreats, but eventually pauses beside a tree, and, in a yogic trance, simply gazes at the king. The poets then describe a preternatural occurrence:

> viveśa viduro dhīmān gātrair gātrāṇi caiva ha
> prāṇān prāṇeṣu ca dadhad indriyāṇīndriyeṣu ca
> sa yogabalam āsthāya viveśa nṛpates tanum
>
> XV.33.25
>
> Vidura entered the wise one, limb by limb,
> And breath into breath, he gave his senses into the senses;
> He, having taken the power of yoga, entered the body of the king.

The physical body of Vidura remains beside the tree, thoroughly dead. Yudhiṣṭhira wishes to cremate the remains of his nominal half-uncle, but a bodiless voice announces that *na dagdhavyam etad* (this is not to be burned) (XV.33.31). Thus, Yudhiṣṭhira received into his own being that *élan* of the previous generation, of the half-brother of his own nominal father. Of those three offspring of Vyāsa, Vidura was always the sage, the prudent and learned one, and master of *nītiśāstra* (the teaching of kingly conduct), so this transmigration of *psyche* is appropriate.[9] This is the only male embodiment that Yudhiṣṭhira ever receives from that generation.[10]

***

As the poem closes, it is said that Yudhiṣṭhira, now the *kauravo rājā*, passes on the kingdom to Yuyutsu, his nominal cousin and the one son of Dhṛtarāṣṭra who survived, for he had chosen to fight on the Pāṇḍava side having crossed the battle lines in Book Six. The kingdom is also passed to Parikṣit, Yudhiṣṭhira's nephew.[11]

> rājyaṃ paridadau sarvaṃ vaiśyaputre yudhiṣṭhiraḥ
> abhiṣicya svarājye tu taṃ rājānaṃ parikṣitam
>
> XVII,1,6
>
> Yudhiṣṭhira bestowed all the kingdom on the son [of] the vaiṣya woman,[12]
> Having anointed Parikṣit king in his own sovereignty.

It is Yudhiṣṭhira who performs the royal anointment here, and he says specifically to Subhadrā, *te putraḥ kururājo bhaviṣyati* (your [grand]son will become king of the Kurus). Once again, this would appear to be a dual kingship, for Parikṣit at this point would be almost twenty years of age, and so sovereignty thus draws in both moieties of the Kuru clan.[13] It is also said that Vajra, a son of Kṛṣṇa, and so Yudhiṣṭhira's

9 Allen (2012, 41–42) neatly summaries the life of Vidura from the point of view of Dumézil.

10 It is a moot question—or a modern and twenty-first century question—as to whether the 'sons' of Pāṇḍu were actually aware of their true progenitors. Certainly Yudhiṣṭhira has been so informed by his male progenitor, the divinised Dharma, at III.298.6. At III.44.20ff., Arjuna is received by his progenitor Indra with great paternal intimacy, although the father never announces his paternity to the son; only the poets say this to the audience.

11 Parikṣit is married to Mādravatī, from Madra on the Jhelum (in a region that is now known as the Punjab), who bears him the son Janamejaya (I.90.93). Again, the primary brides of these high status Kauravas are taken from Āryāvarta, the old and 'sacred' homeland; whether this refers back to ancient Vedic clan connections or to later migrations from that region is disputable. Falk (2006, 145) writes: "The third phase [of south-westward migration] is dominated by intruding Westerners, be they of Iranian, Scythian, or Kushana stock. Around 50 BCE they start to advance from Gandhara into the Indian mainland; many move further down to east, south and central India. The Kṣatrapas start to govern most of the Indus plains and western India. They are followed by the Kushanas ..."

12 Yuyutsu was not the son of Gāndhārī, but had been born to a co-wife, a *vaiṣya* and not a *kṣatriya* woman (I.107.35–36). Likewise, Vidura, in the previous generation had been born of a *vaiṣya* mother.

13 Events in the later life of Parikṣit receive cursory description at I.36.8–40.5, where he is killed by a snake, and at I.45.6–15. He is said to be a *nṛpati* (I.38.14). Janamejaya's life is briefly encapsulated at I.40.5–11. Parpola (2015, 146) comments that "The 'proto-epic' Vedic verse preserved in the Brāhmaṇas (AB 8.21.3 and ŚB 13,5,4,2) glorifies the horse sacrifice of King Janamejaya, a descendent of the Kuru king Parikṣit known from the Atharvaveda."

cousin-once-removed, is appointed to rule at Indraprastha.[14] Yudhiṣṭhira informs Subhadrā, the wife of Arjuna and grandmother of Parikṣit, that:

> parikṣidd hāstinapure śakraprasthe tu yādavāḥ
> vajro rājā tvayā rakṣyo mā cādharme manaḥ kṛthāḥ
>
> XVII.1.9
>
> Parikṣit in Hāstinapura, the Yādava in Śakraprastha.[15]
> King Vajra is to be protected by you, and do not set your mind on adharma!

The injunction is that Subhadrā is *not* to scheme and plot, and should not supplant Vajra in favour of her own grandson—the implication being that women in the court can devise means for usurping a king's express will and design. Kṛpa is appointed as the *guru* of adolescent Parikṣit, he being of a similar generation to Bhīṣma, and so becomes the *ancient* of the clan and family and court, the office of princely *guru* being a formal position, just as Droṇa had once held the office of *guru* for the Pāṇḍavas (XVII.1.13).

As this scene closes, there is the curious additional statement describing the court:

> kṛpaprabhṛtayaś caiva yuyutsuṃ paryavārayan
>
> XVII.1.25
>
> Then led by Kṛpa they surrounded Yuyutsu.

Yet of the other joint-sovereign, the poets say:

> śiṣṭāḥ parikṣitaṃ tvanyā mātaraḥ paryavārayan
>
> XVII.1.26
>
> The remaining other mothers surrounded Parikṣit.

It is as if the poets, in closure, are nicely and exactly delineating the political dynamics of this new *sabhā*. There is a careful reality about this observation concerning where the handles and reins of power are actually situated, a precision in such non-formulaic and particular pictures in the poetry that would imply that this is something that has been witnessed, and not heard, by our poets. It is

14 Law (1941, 93–94) writes: "The Kurus are described by Buddhaghosa as a people who had migrated in large numbers from Uttarakuru to Jambudvīpa and founded a kingdom ... which was 300 leagues in extent, comprised several districts, towns and villages, and its capital Indapatta (Sk. Indraprastha near the modern Delhi) was seven leagues in circuit. Hastināpura (Pali Hatthipura), known in earlier times as Āsandīvat, appears to have been the earlier capital."

15 Śakraprastha is Indraprastha, and the Yādava is Vajra.

uncommon in this epic, as we have seen, for such detailed and unconventional specificity to be supplied by the poets, and it makes one wonder as to how it was that these poets were sometimes actually connecting in a highly familiar or intimate level with their audience (a kind of historicity that is now lost for us).

***

As the first ritual officer of the kingdom, Yudhiṣṭhira establishes the final obsequies for members of his family and for Kṛṣṇa. This is his concluding ritual act in the poem because Yudhiṣṭhira is soon to move towards another level of existence, one that is beyond the sublunary and mortal. In a sense, then, this rite is a token of his departure from the world, and it closes his kingly presence in the *sabhā* at Hāstinapura. Following this moment, Yudhiṣṭhira, accompanied as always by his brothers, begins to turn away from the kingdom, this time not towards the forest but towards another life altogether. These concluding four books of the epic are of an increasingly otherworldly nature and take the narrative of the poem away from the political and material earth.

ity uktvā dharmarājaḥ sa vāsudevasya dhīmataḥ
mātulasya ca vṛddhasya rāmādīnāṃ tathaiva ca
bhrātṛbhiḥ saha dharmātmā kṛtvodakam atandritaḥ
śrāddhāny uddiśya sarveṣāṃ cakāra vidhivat tadā

XVII.1.10

The alert Dharmarāja, the dharma-souled one, having spoken,
Together with his brothers, having made the obsequies
For the wise Vāsudeva and the elder maternal uncle and also of
Rāma and others,
Having stipulated the last rites he then made them appropriately for all.

As the terminal ceremony to these obsequies, he distributes, as a royal sacrificer should, jewels, clothing, villages, horses, chariots, and cattle to the principle *brāhmaṇas*.[16]

Then Yudhiṣṭhira, now described by the poets as *rājarṣi* (the royal seer) (XVII.1.14), calls upon the *paurajānapadā janāḥ* (town and country folk) and informs them of these arrangements and of his plans to finally retire from kingship. They become displeased and disapproving, rebuking the king:

naivaṃ kartavyam iti te tadocus te narādhipam

XVII.1.16

"This is not to be done by you," they then said to the king.

[16] Note the presence of land that is now part of this distribution of wealth.

Again, we observe how significant the popular voice is in the practice of kingship and its determination: this is the *saṅgha* still, no matter how paramount and great the king has become. Yudhiṣṭhira ignores them, *na ca rājā tathākārṣīt* (and the king did not do thus), and so of course succeeds in this final design. Accompanied by his brothers and by Draupadī, they undress and remove their jewelry and put on *valkalāni* (garments made of bark), the customary dress of ascetics (XVII.1.19). Their appearance is as it was when they—more than thirty years before—had set off towards the forest after the dicing-match, and again they are followed by the populace for a short while.[17]

Now, as they commence this *mahāprasthāna* (the great going out), they are also accompanied by a dog, *śvā caiva saptamaḥ* (the dog as a seventh member) (XVII.1.23). The group sets off in an easterly direction, then turns southward, and then towards the west and up towards Dvārakā, having circumambulated the kingdom in their peregrination, when they finally turn northward towards the mountains. This pilgrimage is given simply in a few *ślokas*, a pedestrian journey that would have taken—in geographical or temporal reality—far more than a single year: this is the condensed epic-time of the poem.

One by one the members of the family collapse and die, leaving only the king and the dog who continue to proceed alone together. There is no indication of any death ritual for the fallen, and it is as if—at this point in the poem—there occurs a transition from the political world of kingship into a mythical *other*-world where such practices are unnecessary as being only mundane. The narrative in this otherworld continues to be related by Vaiśampāyana, as once more the poem moves onto a supernal plane and the king becomes visibly immortal: this is a unique moment for Yudhiṣṭhira. There occurs another instance of ring composition here, for at the outset of the Ādi *parvan* a dog had also appeared, the son of the bitch Śaramā.[18] The animal had fouled a ritual and been struck, and so Śaramā had cursed Janamejaya, the king and great-grandson of Arjuna and patron of the narrative that encircles and encompasses the Bhārata Song.[19]

[17] When they had set off that first time, a son of Dhṛtarāṣṭra had been in control at Hāstinapura, Duryodhana; now it is another son of the blind old king who is regnant there, Yuyutsu. Again, we see an instance of ring composition *qua* symmetry in the narrative. The poets or editors are perhaps demonstrating an irony here, in that so much totally destructive warfare seems in fact to have borne little of consequence: at least for the Pāṇḍavas, but *not* for the Yādavas.

[18] A dog also appears at XII.116–119, but this dog soon transforms into other creatures. Another instance of ring composition at this point in the poem is supplied by the appearance of the deity Agni, who enjoins Arjuna to cast his bow and double quiver back into the sea, Varuṇa, from where it originated in Book One (XVII.1.33–39).

[19] The dog is arguably a metaphor of the uncleanliness of mortality, or the contamination of the temporal world, that ritual attempts to exceed or remove; therefore it cannot possibly enter heaven

Now, the divine Indra appears and requests that Yudhiṣṭhira mount the chariot. To this, the king refuses for he cannot leave his kin, saying:

na vinā bhrātṛbhiḥ svargam icche gantuṃ sureśvara

XVII.3.3

I do not desire to go towards heaven, Sureśvara, without brothers.

He includes Draupadī in this expression. Indra responds that the brothers and their wife are already there and that Yudhiṣṭhira will see them, *nikṣipya mānuṣaṃ dehaṃ*, for they 'have cast off human form'. Indra makes the comment however, that Yudhiṣṭhira:

anena tvaṃ śarīreṇa svargaṃ gantā na saṃśayaḥ

XVII.3.6

You, doubtlessly, will go to heaven with this body.

This is an unusual statement, avoiding death and compounding the mortal and immortal worlds. Certainly, when Arjuna in Book Three visits Indra in his particular cosmic realm, he does—so it would appear—in human and embodied form. The epic blurs this physical relationship between mortal and immortal, both in terms of person and in terms of place, and the convergence between the two conditions often happens, usually of person and rarely of place. Genetically, and also in a locative sense, heroes and deities do not observe terrestrial bounds, an aspect that gives the poem greater ritual force *qua* its own performance insofar as the deities themselves participate and act in the poem: the situation of the epic is *not* the natural world.

Yudhiṣṭhira now requests that the dog accompany him in this progress, and Indra advises him to abandon the animal, which the king refuses to do on principle because the animal is *bhakto māṃ nityam* (always my devotee), and the king must reciprocate that bond, just as he was obliged to reciprocate the loyalty and affiliation of the *saṅgha*.[20] This is a famous little story in contemporary Indian

---

or be part of anything that seeks to contact the atemporal. This dog had appeared at a *sattra* (a great soma sacrifice), which was being held at Kurukṣetra and which king Janamejaya happened to attend. More generally, the poem is constructed in near-perfect ring composition, beginning in the Ādi *parvan* with Janamejaya's *sarpayajña* 'snake sacrifice', and then ending on that same note, at that same event. Janamejaya, of course, is not yet actually born at the end of poem when Yudhiṣṭhira is assumed into heaven, for Parikṣit, his father, is then a youth. Thus, it is not the case that there is more or further *implicit* narrative concerning the Kurus, because in terms of the narrative itself the poem begins at the end and ends at the beginning, as it were: it is a complete cycle, representative of the fine artistry of these poets. Such forms of chiasmus are a kind of *telling* that are typical of preliteracy.

20 As we have seen, Bhīṣma's model of kingship in his four discourses is one that is patterned more after an autarchic authority where reciprocity between king and people—even those of the immediate clan or family—is not obligatory; in fact, the case is quite the opposite.

folklore as the hound happens to be Yudhiṣṭhira's divine father in disguise, and so Dharma admires the *anukrośa* 'compassion' of his son (XVII.3.16–17).[21] The father tells the son:

abhijāto'si rājendra pitur vṛttena medhayā

XVII.3.17

O Indra of kings, you are learned, with the practical intellect of your father!

This is only the second time in his earthly life that Yudhiṣṭhira has encountered his father; the previous occasion had been during the forest exile (III.298). The father informs him that *prāpto'si ... divyām gatim anuttamām* (you achieve the highest divine end) (XVII.3.21). Thus king Yudhiṣṭhira becomes a divine being, just like Yayāti (I.82).[22]

Yudhiṣṭhira is then mounted on a chariot by the deities, Dharma and Indra and the Maruts and the Aśvins—the fathers of the Pāṇḍavas—and:

ūrdhvam ācakrame śīghraṃ tejasāvṛtya rodasī

XVII.3.24

Quickly he ascended, having covered with energy the sky and earth.

He does not actually perish or die, but is simply assumed upwards by these divinities, and there is no overt disembodiment. The poets say that:

lokān āvṛtya yaśasā tejasā vṛttasaṃpadā
svaśarīreṇa saṃprāptaṃ nānyaṃ śuśruma pāṇḍavāt

XVII.3.27

Having covered the worlds with glorious energy, by excellent action—
Achieved with his own body: we have heard of none other [doing this] than the Pāṇḍava.

Neither Yudhiṣṭhira nor his brothers expire in a good *kṣatriya* manner, fighting like warriors, and these deaths are transcendental, painless, unlamented, and profoundly unheroic, which is a strange and unfitting conclusion for such a strongly *kṣatriya* epic. After all the many tens of thousands of lines about the importance of *kṣatriya* ideals and the encoded mores of a warrior, these five heroic brothers simply decease without effort and even without recognition of extinction; is it because—as *the* most exemplary of heroes—they are ultimately

[21] See Lincoln (1991, 96–106) on the Indo-European motif of the hound of the underworld, the 'hellhound.' This is the dog that attends the passage of those who transit from life to death.

[22] Let us recall that it was the two sons of Yayāti, Yadu and Pūru, who established the dynasties of the Yādavas and the Kauravas.

exempt from both time and death? It is a paradoxical ending, though, especially for Arjuna and Bhīma who have been such vigorous warriors, and it is as if a suddenly different view of cosmos is being invoked or presented. One can explain this by referring to the fact that the Pāṇḍavas are only semi-human, unlike Kṛṣṇa or the sons of Dhṛtarāṣṭra who are completely mortal and who can thus experience a natural death.

Greeted by Indra, who is surrounded by other deities, Yudhiṣṭhira simply refuses to accept his new situation unless the brothers and Draupadī can also be present; he outrightly refuses to be without them. Even in the supernatural world, the king cannot be without his wife and brothers, his identity is so completely engaged with these kin.

> gantum icchāmi tatrāhaṃ yatra me bhrātaro gatāḥ
>
> XVII.3.35
>
> I want to go there where my brothers have gone.

He fondly includes Draupadī in this demand. Kingship for Yudhiṣṭhira, even when mortally deceased, cannot be separated from his immediate kin; the pattern does not change even in death.

***

Soon the king and hero attains to *svarga*, which is usually translated as 'heaven', it being a shining and light place that is spatially upward and skyward rather than an underworld (XVIII.1.3). There he observes Duryodhana, and, at the sight of his nominal cousin enveloped in such splendour, Yudhiṣṭhira becomes *amarṣitaḥ* 'angrily indignant'. Nārada, who happens to be present, tells him:

> eṣa duryodhano rājā pūjyate tridaśaiḥ saha ...
> sa eṣa kṣattradharmeṇa sthānam etad avāptavān
>
> XVIII.1.13
>
> There is king Duryodhana worshipped with the Thirty Deities ...
> He, by kṣatriya dharma, obtained this place.

Certainly, Duryodhana did end his life in fine warrior and heroic fashion, unlike the Pāṇḍavas or Kṛṣṇa.[23] Even in this heavenly place, however, Yudhiṣṭhira wants to be with Karṇa and his other half-brothers, and Draupadī and asks to be with them. To this end, he is escorted by a *devadūta* 'divine herald' to a revolting and punitive realm of hellish and malodorous torment where he is shown the

[23] This is all reported to Janamejaya by the poet Vaiśaṃpāyana who is said to have learned his song from Vyāsa. It is the cosmic vision of the *ṛṣi* that allows him access to such supernatural and otherworldly events.

suffering dead. There, the infernal souls all acclaim his beatific presence and beg for him to remain with them; on inquiry, these are the miserable spirits of his brothers and wife (XVIII.2.40–41). Contemplating this disturbing sight, Yudhiṣṭhira becomes possessed by *krodham tīvraṃ* 'bitter rage'.

The *dharmarāja* immediately expresses his wish to remain in their company in the foul and torturous *naraka* (world of fatal misery) that they inhabit: it is his preference. Once he has proclaimed this allegiance to kinship rather than to material or spiritual comfort, all the torments vanish, and all the old Vedic deities arrive to honour and praise him: Indra, the Vasus, the Rudras, the Ādityas, the *siddhas* and *ṛṣis*. It is Indra, as *king* of the deities who welcomes him, saying that it was due to his *vyāja* 'deceit' of Droṇa that this visual punishment was inflicted upon him (XVIII.3.14).

The eschatology implicit in these scenes is strangely blurred, for earthly *karma* engages with a universal system of causality that has moral force, and yet the idea of rebirth is not fully absent. Moral consequence is twofold: that of infernal anguish or heavenly bliss and that of worldly reincarnation. There exists in this hybrid view both penance and reward, as well as rebirth. This vague distinction is something that Janamejaya is curious about, and he inquires of his poet:

> āho svic chāśvataṃ sthānaṃ teṣāṃ tatra dvijottama
> ante vā karmaṇaḥ kāṃ te gatiṃ prāptā nararṣabhāḥ
>
> XVIII.5.5
>
> O best of the twice-born, what was the perpetual station of
> those there?
> Or, what end did those bull-men obtain of their action finally?

He is implying that they might have remained *svarge* 'in heaven' eternally, or that they might have returned to the sublunar world and a further life of *karma* 'worldly effect'. This idea of a 'perpetual station' for those after they have expired from earthly life, contrasted with a causal cycle of constant reincarnation, is new in the poem, unless, of course, the situation of the *indraloka*, the 'place', where deceased heroes go after falling in battle is also conceived of as an eternal condition.[24] The definite counterpoint of *svarga* and *naraka* is also new expression in the poem. The poets—or editors—are not explicit in this depiction or conception, and in fact many forms of afterlife are compounded within the poem, just as the many religious cultures and periods are fused into one ideal Pan-Indic society.

[24] These are pertinent questions: Where does the *nadī* of bloody battle go? Does it convey the immaterial being, the spiritual envelopes of the deceased warriors, to that place? Is there some real connection between the house of Yama and the *indraloka*?

Yudhiṣṭhira is urged to bathe in *gaṅgāṃ devanadīṃ puṇyāṃ* (the sacred celestial Gaṅgā), and to discharge his mortal envelope:

avagāhya tu tāṃ rājā tanuṃ tatyāja mānuṣīm

XVIII.3.39

The king having submerged abandoned his human body.

Then, *divyavapur*, as a 'divine body', he is *vṛto devaiḥ kururājā yudhiṣṭhiraḥ* (the king of the Kurus Yudhiṣṭhira, surrounded by deities) (XVIII.3.41).[25] There, he witnesses his kin and companions:

dadarśa tatra govindaṃ brāhmeṇa vapuṣānvitam

XVIII.4.2

He saw there Govinda embodied with Brahmā.[26]

All the Kuru clan are present in this theologically diverse tableau in divine and cosmic form as the figures of the Bhārata Song are now represented in their universal or *mythical* state: Soma is said to have been Abhimanyu, Sūrya is Karṇa, Draupadī is Śrī, Bhīṣma is among the Vasus, Bṛhaspati is Droṇa, Nakula and Sahadeva are the Aśvins, as all the old-time Vedic pantheon is represented.

***

In conclusion, during the final passage of the poem, the poets return to the earlier verses of the Ādi *parvan*, for the epic is said to have been first sung at Takṣaśilā, a city in the Northwest—the Tehsil of modern Punjab—that flourished in the latter half of the first millennium BCE. In the Ādi *parvan* itself, however, Takṣaśilā is not mentioned as the location of the snake sacrifice.[27] It was once a famed centre of learning, and scholars travelled from far to study there; it was also a particularly Buddhist *locale* of knowledge. The reputed composer of the Arthaśāstra, Cāṇakya or Kauṭilya, supposedly the teacher of Candragupta Maurya, is said to have assembled the classic text on the practice of good kingship while residing at Takṣaśilā. During the time of Aśoka, the town became an even more famous nucleus of Buddhist teaching.

As the *Mahābhārata* now reaches closure, the poets once more gravitate to the three voices who exist on the outer rim of the poem: the *sūta* Ugraśravas,

[25] Genetically he is not a Kuru, let us recall, but a Yādava.

[26] Govinda is one of the youthful names of Kṛṣṇa; it is an old name referring to his cow-herding adolescence.

[27] It is thus perhaps highly pertinent that our oldest manuscripts of parts of the poem are Kashmiri or Śārada in form. Law (1941, 87) notes: "In the Jātakas and the Great Epic, Gandharā is described as the kingdom with Takkasilā (Sk. Takṣaśilā) as its capital." This is where Duryodhana's mother came from and his uncle Śakuni.

the poet Vaiśaṃpāyana, and king Janamejaya. The *sūta* performs the voices of the other two, and Ugraśravas is, of course, spoken by another nameless master-poet, whoever it is that actually performs the work, whenever and wherever that was.[28] He says of Janamejaya that, having performed his sacrifice:

tatas takṣaśilāyāḥ sa punar āyād gajāhvayam

XVIII.5.29

Then he went from Takṣaśilā again to Hāstinapura.

The entire poem, the poet declares, was performed *yajñakarmāntareṣu* (during the pauses in the actions of the ritual). In other words, the king had sponsored both the sacrifice and the performance of the poem, and the two were coterminous: Vaiśaṃpāyana has been declaiming—throughout the course of most of the poem—what he heard the *ṛṣi* Vyāsa sing during that ritual immolation of snakes.

jayo nāmetihāso'yaṃ śrotavyo bhūtim icchatā

XVIII.5.39

Jaya is the name of this story, to be heard by one desiring power!

This is an injunction that indicates the epic is to be heard *by* kings, those who desire power: according to the poem itself, this is its purpose or utility in the world.

For us nowadays (in the twenty-first century) to say *who* those kings were is not yet feasible. What we are able to claim, however, is a tentative reconstruction of the models of kingship that the epic represents for us, and to conceive of how those models pointed at earlier historical *experience* and also at later poetic *ideals* of good kingship. Thus, we can examine the narrative as a myth in which kinship patterns organise how the poetry and its acoustic metaphors were developed via enactment or performance. This has been my aim during the course of the present study.

The claim of Bronkhorst that the *Mahābhārata* was a medium of cultural movement eastwards towards Magadha thus seems to be an interesting idea, but it does lack the textual support that could substantiate such an inference. What were the metaphors that engaged such an axis of transference, for instance? One could similarly hold the opinion that the Mānava Dharmaśāstra was also part of an ideological movement eastwards as *brāhmaṇa* culture extended from central Northern India towards the coast, crossing regions that had once been the founding terrain for early Buddhism and Jainism; but there is no evidence for this claim either.

[28] *Na gāthā gāthinaṃ śāsti bahu ced api gāyati* (the song does not proclaim the singer, even if he sings a lot) (II.38.17).

***

The immediate future of *Mahābhārata* Studies in the West lies in the methods pursued by Mahadevan and Hiltebeitel in an analysis of the poem's textual transmission through time: in terms of the object movement and material conveyance of the work *qua* manuscript. Certainly, the study of how Nīlakaṇṭha proceeded to collect textual variants and the principles of critical inquiry he invoked deserves much more attention; Minkowski has already opened up this field remarkably. My own exegeses in the tradition of the Parry-Lord-Nagy school of analysing oral poetics have, I would like to think, developed a new conceptual understanding of what it means to *closely read* this poetry as a preliterate phenomenon in its originality. I only hope that sincere humanistic endeavour is not inhibited by narrow methodological and *nay*-saying contention in the years to come and that these various and different methods of analysis proceed in a generous manner.

What we can aver, in sum, is that the epic *Mahābhārata* represents a human impulse to acquire and integrate all the then known evidence of social life in a single anthology.[29] One can perceive this impulse in the Homeric epics, which—in late sixth-century Athens at the Festival of the Panathenaia—drew into one voice much of an intellectually conceived past and so *re*-made part of the old Bronze Age epic poetry as Pan-Hellenic.[30] Similarly, the history plays of Shakespeare—just like the *Mahābhārata*—integrated an envisioned historical tradition in order to give legitimacy and weight, if not political credence, to the new régime of the house of Tudor. If we could somehow find textual evidence that would link the Bhārgava clan with, say, Samudragupta or a ruler like him, then we would be able to advance our understanding of the Sanskrit epic markedly.[31] Macdonell

[29] We can observe this impulse today with the expressed ambition of collections like Getty Images who seek to acquire all known images in the world; or with the explicit motivation that has generated the ongoing world documentation by an organisation like the Wikipedia digital *bibliothèque*. There is nothing new in such human endeavour.

[30] This movement or production was the movement "from Homer the pre-classic to Homer the classic," where the *polis* of Athens supplied the political and imperial impetus. See Nagy 2010, 376. I would also draw the reader's attention to Douglas Frame's excellent revision of the *Homeric Question* in which he proposes models for clan, kingship, *polis*, and also festival in terms of how these aspects of epic performance and patronage might have once functioned for the Homeric epics. See Frame 2012.

[31] Magnone (2012, 110–111) comments on a similar point: "This dominance of brahmanical axiology is hardly surprising, considering the hand brahmans had in shaping the epics in their extant form. Admittedly, in edifying their literary monuments, brahmans have often employed pre-existing narrative materials through a process of adaptation to make them subservient to aims and developments originally alien. Besides these purposeful elaborations, the ancient stories have often incurred alterations of a more haphazard nature over the course of transmission: they have been expanded or condensed, curtailed or supplemented, deliberately or accidentally modified through misunderstandings, errors or memory defects."

and Keith, in their Vedic Index for the lemma Bhṛgu, note: "in the battle of the ten kings the Bhṛgus appear with the Druhyus, possibly as their priests." For the lemma Druhyu, they state that "the Druhyus were a north-western people and the later tradition of the epic connects Gāndhāra and the Druhyu."[32] Let us recall that the Northwest is where Janamejaya conducts his snake sacrifice, whereas the East is where the Naimiṣa Forest is located—in Uttar Pradesh—and where Ugraśravas performs the complete poem.

As we have frequently observed, the poem projects an ideal and heroic past, and in that poetic situation manages to involve and to draw in elements of many different cultural, political, literary, and religious traditions, unifying and binding them into a single narrative. I would go so far as to propose that what existed at that period constituted, in part, what we would today describe as an *heroic religion*, where heroes were worshipped and were the recipients of ritual attention.[33] Certainly, in twenty-first century India, heroes continue to receive great devotion and spiritual attention.[34] There is in the poem a consistently conscious stratagem that is almost antiquarian in manner, which emulates and imitates an hypothetical archaic past; yet, though the words succeed, the lack of experience or of any witness makes for a cursory text, and it is as if the poets have heard of something, but they have never actually *seen* such events. Certainly the four Kurukṣetra Books and parts of the Virāṭa *parvan*, in that they describe an ancient and Bronze Age warrior tradition, are chronologically older—at least in terms of style—than those parts of the poem represented in the Śānti *parvan*, for instance.[35] There has been a successful fusion of two *types* of poetry here, of two forms of art, that of the heroic and the didactic, making for the epic as we have it now.

[32] See Macdonnell and Keith 1912. They cite RV VIII.3.9; 6.18; 102.4; and VII.18.6.

[33] There are verses in both the Ādi *parvan* and in the Svargārohaṇa *parvan* that announce the spiritual and ritual efficacy of performing the epic (I.2.235ff., and XVIII.5.35ff.). Epic *Mahābhārata*, in its activation during performance, makes heroes come to life, and just like any rite causes change in the human microcosm, ideally change that is beneficial for the mortal beings who sponsor the ritual.

[34] One has only to look to the violent struggles that occurred at the birthplace of the hero Rāma in 1992, at Ayodhyā. In Western Gujarat today there are many *kīrtistambhas* 'hero stones' that are frequently the object of much devotion. See Sax (2002) for how *Mahābhārata* heroes receive worship in the Garwhal; also see Hiltebeitel 1988. See McGrath 2004, chap. VI on hero-worship in the epic. Cult worship is of course an essential aspect of *cultivation* or agriculture in preliterate and premodern societies.

[35] Raghu Vira, in the Introduction to his 1936 edition of the Pune Virāṭa *parvan*, p. xvii, notes: "It was natural that such a piece [the Virāṭa *parvan*] should enjoy a greater popularity than any other parvan of the *Mahābhārata*. It even, in a way, supplanted the Ādi. The Mbh. reciters commenced their sessions with the Virāṭa and not with the Ādi. The Virāṭa came to be the *maṅgala* [auspicious opening song] of the *Mahābhārata* recitation."

Much of the poem, however, attempts to cast itself back into an older world of warrior life, a world where Indra, Mitra-Varuṇa, Brahmā, and such Indo-Āryan deities received worship, a time when Rudra-Śiva the Mahādeva still walked among the indigenous pre-Āryan folk. For reasons of intellectual and cultural hegemony, all these components of a known and unknown cultural past became simultaneously involved in a single great poem, the Bhārata Song, and as with any human tradition, much of it was simply invented rather than actually received, or, shall we say, it was *re*-conceived. Conversely, along with such a conceptual trajectory went a strange—to us today—sensibility that managed to elide all signification of Buddhist and Jaina experience, including the greatness of someone like Aśoka, as well as to forget the majestic and imperial cultural achievements of the Indus Civilisation peoples whose traces must have certainly existed in common memory during the later part of the first millennium.

***

The final words of Yudhiṣṭhira concern his beloved half-brothers with whom he had consistently shared *all* power. Having witnessed them suffering in a place that is hellish, he refuses to leave them, saying:

na hy ahaṃ tatra yāsyāmi sthito'smīti nivedyatām
matsaṃśrayād ime dūta sukhino bhrātaro hi me

XVIII.2.52

Messenger, let it be said: I am here, for I shall not go there.
For these, my brothers, are happy because of my protection.

Thus, his last statement in the epic concerns those whom he loves most, these half-brothers with whom he shared the kingdom, war, and rule, who in many ways, along with their joint wife, directed him. Yudhiṣṭhira was their elder and leader, but he was also the whole-hearted recipient of their advice and injunctions: this was no monistic office that he maintained. Many words remain to be spoken *to* Yudhiṣṭhira, said by various divine figures, but he himself remains silent hereafter. The poet Vaiśaṃpāyana, in his address to the patron of the poem, Janamejaya, soon refers to Yudhiṣṭhira as *tava pūrvapitāmahaḥ* 'your ancestor'; in fact he is the nominal great-grand-uncle at this moment in the poem (XVIII.38).[36]

We can finish with a small and almost private scene taken from one night towards the end of the Bhīṣma *parvan*, where the armies have withdrawn from the field and the *śūrās* 'the heroes' have returned to their camps.

[36] Let us recall that in terms of simple chronological time, Janamejaya is not yet born; it is the super-subtle artistry of the poets and editors than manages his inclusion here.

kṛtasvastyayanāḥ sarve saṃstūyantaś ca bandibhiḥ
gītavāditraśabdena vyakrīḍanta yaśasvinaḥ
murhūrtam iva tat sarvam abhavat svargasaṃnibham
na hi yuddhakathāṃ kāṃcit tatra cakrur mahārathāḥ

VI.82.54

Congratulations done, the glorious ones disported;
All were praised by poets with instruments and song.
Momentarily all that was *just like heaven*,
Not one great warrior there made any poetry of war.

In heaven, there is no destruction nor any ferocity, and, if one can relate place to time, heaven is therefore *like* the *kṛta yuga*. It was the dissension between elements of kinship, where rivals—nominal cousins in fact—were contending for a throne, which led to such mutually violent disorder, to *bheda* (the 'partition'). Good kingship and its rightful efficacy maintain themselves without war, an activity that epic *Mahābhārata* both extols and disdains: such is the dualism of its message.

It is this dualism of expression that we can observe in the moods and emotions of *rāja* Yudhiṣṭhira as he struggled with the moral, political, as well as the spiritual, claims that kingship brought to him and his family, a family for whom he felt both terrific ambition and yet great responsibility; a family to whom he was genetically connected only by his mother.[37] The poetry of the Bhārata Song, with its innumerable metaphors of death and ordeal, and its repeated expressions of dreadful grief, makes beautiful the classical view of how one kind of kingship was retrospectively conceived, how it struggled to achieve its station, and how it should endure. This narrative ideal of kingship strangely blends the memory of a *saṅgha* with the picture of a fraternal ruler who always attends to the popular voice. The epic poem actually *develops* its picture of kingship during the course of the narrative, for kingship during epic *Mahābhārata* undergoes a maturation in itself, as if it too were a character in the story. It is as if the poem were providing an aetiology of kingship in Northern India for early classical times. In this historical picturing, Bhīṣma has the final voice.

37 As a coda to all the above, we might append a brief passage from Anthony (2007, 134), where he offers an aetiology of the poetics of early Bronze Age kingship: "At the beginning of time there were two brothers, twins, one named Man (**Manu*, in Proto-Indo-European) and the other Twin (**Yemo*) ... Man became the first priest, the creator of the ritual of sacrifice that was the root of world order ... After the world was made, the sky-gods gave cattle to 'Third man' (**Trito*). But the cattle were treacherously stolen by a three-headed, six-eyed serpent (**Ngwhi*, the Proto-Indo-European root for *negation*). Third man entreated the storm god to help get the cattle back. Together they went to the cave (or mountain) of the monster, killed it ... and freed the cattle. **Trito* became the first warrior." In this reading, Yudhiṣṭhira would arguably figure as *Manu."

Let us say then in conclusion that epic *Mahābhārata* summarises all the historical possibilities, if not temporal developments, of kingship in Northwestern India during the latter half of the first millennium BCE and during the early centuries of the Common Era. The experience of listening to the performance of such intricate, but vastly faultless, beauty must have been—ultimately—an ideally transformative event for a *kṣatriya* audience, both emotionally cleansing and intellectually acculturating.[38]

[38] To reiterate an earlier note, William Shakespeare, during the late sixteenth century and early seventeenth century, composed a sequence of ten dramas about the kings of England; these were not written in temporal sequence. Plus, many of his other plays—*King Lear*, *Hamlet*, *Julius Caesar*, to name only a few—similarly dramatised the nature and crises of kingship, and the vicissitudes of monarchic rule. Apart from the first of the English dramas, *King John*, the (subsequent) plays concerned the contention between the two cognate houses, the House of Lancaster and the House of York, both descended from Edward III (1327–1377). The reign of Elizabeth thus received what can be called a demonstration of its historical legitimacy, manifest on both the private and royal stage of court and in the public theatre. Shakespeare made much of the sanctity or 'anointment' of kingship as a force or element of nature, where the mettle of a king was genetic and sacred, and he moralised upon this kind of natural political agency in these dramatic and memorial enactments. Providence and power, violence, cruelty and egotism—what he refers to as *commodity* (KJ II.i.561)—all are given active causality in the plays, where hereditary aspects of rulership and the accidence of 'fortune' work together in political time. Shakespeare of course drew upon previous literary and prose works, that of Hall and of Holinshead, as well as from Plutarch, in order to supply himself with characters and plots, as well as historical or evidential material. To quote from Tony Tanner (1994, xiii), in his introductory essay to the history plays, "The Elizabethans, of course, had writings, but they also still had 'tellings'—myths, apocrypha, legends, and a very active oral tradition," which playwrights quarried for their productions. I say all this simply to give a moment's counterpoint to our present study of kingship as it appears in the Great Indian Epic.

Appendix on Epic Time

Time in epic *Mahābhārata* is represented in many forms and manifestations, and Yudhiṣṭhira is arguably the central figure about whose presence *kāla* 'time' circulates; in fact, from the moment that the *rājasūya* is first mooted after the great hall has been fabricated, it is about the kingly office of Yudhiṣṭhira that the poem revolves. *Kāla* is also a well fitting metaphor of kingship itself because of its invisible and immanent dominance of the world: as Nārada says, *kālo hi parameśvaraḥ* (for time is the supreme lord) (V.110.20). At the outset of the poem, Saṃjaya summarises the potency of time for the benefit of the old king Dhṛtarāṣṭra, beginning:

> kālamūlam idaṃ sarvaṃ bhāvābhāvau sukhāsukhe
>
> I.1.187
>
> All this is the root of time, being and not being, happy or not.

This little discourse on *kāla* continues for four *ślokas*, commenting on how all-generative and all-destructive and dominant is time, for *kālaḥ sarveṣu bhūteṣu carati* (time wanders among all beings).

One of the possible non-temporal meanings of *kāla* is 'death', which sits well with this idea of time as the ultimate ruler, death in this case being linked to the king's use of the *daṇḍa* 'punitive violence'. In this way, there occurs the phrase *kāla ivāntakaḥ* (time—like death), or, *kāla coditāḥ* (impelled by time), said when someone either approaches death or dies (XII.117.11 and VII.1.9). This is the sense of time as an autonomous cosmic force that is engaged when Kṛṣṇa uses the word *kāla* in the Gītā, when he claims, *kālo'smi lokakṣayakṛt* (I am time, destroying the world) (VI.33.32). As we have repeatedly seen, the purpose of Bhīṣma's long oration upon the implicit nature of the universe was given in order to assuage Yudhiṣṭhira's enormous grief—caused by his belief that Pāṇḍava ambition had destroyed the known world, thus linking *kāla* and king in this usage of Kṛṣṇa.[1]

Arguably, when Kṛṣṇa makes the claim *kālo'smi*, and we translate this word *kāla* as 'time' rather than 'death', this moment supplies the epic with its navel, as it were, or the most *inward* instance of time in the poem. For it is from this point that Kṛṣṇa looks upon the inexpressible and ineffable *brahma* and begins to describe the cosmos where he identifies himself as 'time', and it is at this epiphanic moment that the source or precursor of the whole universe is posited as it is unveiled in the language of Kṛṣṇa's Chariot Song of the Gītā. Such a moment does not occur elsewhere in the poem, and thus one could argue that it is during these lines that *time*—quite literally—takes it origin in the epic. If we think of the poem as Kṛṣṇa's Epic, or what could be called the *kārṣṇaṃ vedam* (the Veda of Kṛṣṇa)—and Kṛṣṇa in this usage would be Kṛṣṇa Vāsudeva Yādava and not Kṛṣṇa Dvaipāyana Vyāsa—then this moment where Kṛṣna makes his claim about time *qua* his own person would really and truly function as the central temporal focus in the epic: narrative is in a sense *time*, and it is at this second of theophany that the narrative itself states that time finds its cause.

From an *outward* point of view, regarding the production of the poem itself and the transit—which is chronological—that this represents, we can again apply a twofold comprehension of phase between what was the Bhārata and what became the *Mahābhārata*.[2] The poem, as we have been arguing throughout the course of this book is stylistically 'double,' therefore, being composed of the 'classical' poetry that has incorporated an archaic and preliterate background, where the latter is in fact the primary document; this is one of the fundamental hypotheses of the present book. This view of the epic would reflect a later and literal arrangement of the text where the divine Kṛṣṇa and the paired

[1] Vassilkov (1999, 26) comments on the phrase *coditāḥ kāladharmaṇā* (impelled by the order of time), a formula that is deployed by the poets to gloss the moment of death: "it ought to have been *kāladharmeṇa*, but the formula retains the archaic Indo-Aryan ('Vedic') form which enables us to suggest that the *kālavāda* ideas in the MBh were present fairly early. The distribution of the formula led Georg von Simson to remark . . . that the term was absent from the battle books." By *kālavāda*, Vassilkov understands "the Doctrine of Cyclical Time."

[2] To repeat a point that we made in chapter 1, Ugraśravas claims that Vyāsa initially composed the *bhāratasaṃhitām* (the Bhārata collection) in twenty-four thousand verses (I.1.61). In the *parvasaṃgraha* (the digest of books), from the installation of Bhīṣma as *senāpati* 'commander' to the Sauptika *parvan*, with the eighteen sub-*parvans* the number of verses amounts to 23,795. I argued for this conception of the core *Jaya* epic in McGrath 2011. These figures are supplied at I.2.154–190, and I would argue for a pertinent correspondence between these two figures. Sukthankar (1944, 423) comments on the unit of measurement: "They are not 'ślokas' or stanzas as we ordinarily understand them; but are, properly speaking, what are technically known as, 'granthas,' a grantha being a unit of measurement of written matter equal to 32 akṣaras."

naranārāyaṇau have become fully active—by insertion—within an earlier and simply heroic narrative. As Sukthankar observed concerning the Bhagavadgītā, it serves as "the keystone of the whole new superstructure of the remodelled Bhārata and which has passed into world literature."[3] The word "new" is the key term in this sentence.[4] As I argued in the previous chapter, in this sense then there occur two *outward* forms of time in the poem: those materials drawn from the archaic period and those materials that were founded during classical times. To quote from Sukthankar again: "In our version of the *Mahābhārata* there is a conscious—nay deliberate—weaving together or rather stitching together of the Bhārata legends with the Bhārgava myths."[5] In this view, the legends supplied the archaic material, and the myths were from a more classical period.[6]

***

Time is constituted by transition, or rather by serial connectivity supplied by metonym. Where there occurs a shift in the narrative—something that often happens in the *Mahābhārata*—there exists a disjunctive moment in the narrative metonymy that makes for temporal conjunction: suddenly another story is being performed and the metonyms shift to another register of signification. Time is also one of the most complex and divergent metaphors in epic *Mahābhārata*, for time in the poem is simultaneously multifold, polytropic, and never uniform, which for us as modern readers (who think in terms of the reasonable and the literary) might appear illogical; chronology in our Western linear or vernacular sense possesses or manifests only a minor key in the epic.[7]

3 Sukthankar 1944, 307. One could point to a single sentence of this wonderful scholar which summarises this view as well as his view of the clan of Bhṛgu: "The infiltration of masses of Bhārgava material in the shape of Bhārgava myths and legends, the manner of its treatment, and even that strange admixture of the epic with the Dharma and Nīti elements, which latter especially had so long puzzled many inquirers into the genesis of the *Mahābhārata*, thus appear to find a simple and straightforward explanation in the assumption of an *important unitary diaskeuasis of the epic under very strong and direct Bhārgava influence*."

4 In McGrath 2012, I argued that the phenomenon of the *naranārāyaṇau* was a classical condition of the poem. This article developed ideas that I had also posed in McGrath 2013. In brief, during archaic times Arjuna was the divine element in this twinning, being part of the *dvau kṛṣṇau* 'two Kṛṣṇas', whereas in classical times Kṛṣṇa had taken on that supernatural aspect and Arjuna was considered mortal, within the *naranārāyaṇau*.

5 Sukthankar 1944, 332.

6 The idea concerning the distinction between archaic and classical, and between literate and preliterate, is a central tenet of this book; I develop this idea more specifically in the following chapter, the "Appendix On Epic Preliteracy." I would thus reverse the terms of Sukthankar's statement insofar as *mūthos* concerns 'authoritative speech' while *legend* concerns that 'which is to be read'.

7 Curiously, this word has no reliable etymology. *Kāla* is only mentioned once in the Ṛg Veda and that is in the late Tenth Maṇḍala, at X.42.9. Time in the Vedas centres upon ritual and orthoprax

It is this large and cosmic system of time, so lightly underlying the surface appearance of the narrative, that supplies the poem with its wonderful majesty and grand artistic success. The illusion of temporal affinity unites all the elements of what we have been referring to as *bricolage* into a single *myth* that is energised and made active in the nuanced voice and gestures of the poets. In that sense, the *idea* of time is the invisible master signifier that joins all the hundreds of varying kinds of narrative speech into what seems to be a homogenous and mono-rhythmic story.[8] Time wears many masks in the epic and in doing so brings into apparent uniformity a vast array of diverse narrative elements. Grief itself—what we have been describing as the signal emotion of epic poetry—is thoroughly conditioned by a sense of loss or irrefutable departure: the transience of those with whom one shared sentimental affiliation as they move out of time into that which possesses no duration, that is, the kingdom of death.

In this brief chapter, I would like to simply summarise all these various conceptual features of time (the participatory 'overlord') as they have been displayed by the poets in the course of the great Bhārata Song; these are given in eight particular *topoi*. This would also be an occasion to revisit and to clarify how it is that we have viewed these inlaid dimensions during the course of the present book, strands that often run simultaneously and that in their combination represent what is in effect *poetic time*. Poetic time is the time engaged by the medium itself, by performance, regardless of the logic or the elision and expansion that occurs within the syntax of narrative.

***

Firstly, in terms of the larger structure of poetics, there exists an explicit temporal frame that in a practical sense occurs externally to the main body of the poem

precision, and the Vedic poets do not refer to an abstraction of time; there is *ṛtu*, but this signifies foundational 'order' rather than any chronometric situation, and this is fundamentally linked to the movement of heavenly bodies. These poets use the words *pūrva* and *paurvam* to indicate the past, and for the future the subjunctive is employed; there is little use of the future tense in Veda. See Pingree (1981, II:8): "Many Vedic sacrifices are to be performed at specific times determined by the position of the Sun relative to its northern (*uttarāyana*) or southern (*dakṣiṇāyana*) path, the synodic month and the night within it, or the position of the Moon with respect to the *nakṣatras* . . ." Time in the Vedas relates to natural phenomena rather than to the philosophical or conceptual; references are merely to night and dawn (I.13.7), the lunar months (I.25.8), and to such physically obvious signs of temporal passage. In I.155, time appears to be associated with Indra and Viṣṇu, and the metaphor of a wheel and spokes recurs in many of the hymns. I am grateful to Susan Moore and to Amarananda Bhairavan for sharing their learning with me on this subject.

8 In the Mānava Dharmaśāstra, time is created by *svayaṃbhur bhagavān* (the self-made lord) (I.6). In the order of creation, *karmātmanāṃ ca devānāṃ so'sṛjat prāṇināṃ prabhuḥ* (the potent one discharged the divine breaths and the form of rituals) (I.22); then the creator made fire and wind and the Vedas, followed by *kālaṃ kālavibhaktīś ca'* (time and its partitions) (I.24). After this come the heavenly bodies. Time in this conception is very much a material component of the universe and acts—like the deities or the rituals—as a dominant force.

in that it brings shape to the master narrative. Specifically, Ugraśravas opens the poem and immediately recounts how he *heard* the song being declaimed by Vaiśaṃpāyana in the recent past. Vaiśaṃpāyana, in his singing, tells of how he had *heard* Vyāsa perform the hypothetical and original Bhārata Song at the snake sacrifice of Janamejaya. Somewhere between these two situations, the visionary song of Saṃjaya is heard as he declaims, before his patron and king Dhṛtarāṣṭra, all that he sensibly observed during the warfare on the fields of Kurukṣetra: these are the four Kurukṣetra Books.[9] In terms of human life, Saṃjaya lived four generations before Vaiśaṃpāyana, and so within the course or form of the overall narrative there exists this implied sequence of years apart from the other and various orders of natural or mythical time in the poem's received performance. There is the song given in the presence of old Dhṛtarāṣṭra, the song that is supposed to be performed before Janamejaya, and there exists the later song that takes place in the Naimiṣa forest.

This irrational and complex form supplies an outer envelope for all the internal temporal series that take place within the poem itself and add to the irreducibly beautiful system of the interior text.[10] It is as if the poets, and/or the editors, of our *Mahābhārata* had consciously worked to create such a sophisticated and intricate poem that in its way reveals another and non-Euclidean fourth dimension of time, one that is more than earthly in its non-logical representation, a world where deities and heroes live together.[11] I would submit that this dimension derives from an arrangement made by the editors of the text rather than being composed by the poets themselves; it was a formation that occurred when the epic was first consigned to a written document. This is a guess, however, for there are no grounds that could enforce such an inference.

Let us note, however, adding further complexity and sophistication to this narrative form, that Saṃjaya, although he usually sings of what he mentally and visually perceives in present time, sometimes actually retrojects his account into an accomplished past. This occurs through the formulaic model whereby his interlocutor, Dhṛtarāṣṭra—on being told by the poet that such a hero had been felled—then inquires *katham* 'how' this occurred. It is then that Saṃjaya begins to perform the *parvan*, commencing in an initially retrospective and thereafter

9 I have analysed this seamlessly beautiful structure in McGrath 2011.

10 It is irrational for two reasons: because of the great temporal disjunction between Saṃjaya and Vaiśaṃpāyana; and because the series of three frames is not absolute due to Saṃjaya not keeping to his frame but appearing in the epic prior to the opening of *his* own song—the four Kurukṣetra Books.

11 In this sense the poem is a matrix for many different planes of narrative that occur simultaneously, in the same way that a Cubist painting projects many dimensions or aspects of a view within one image or upon a single canvas; there is no one continuum. See Hinton's (1904) study for a discussion of the concept of the tesseract or hypercube as a phenomenon of the fourth dimension.

proleptic manner, in which both past and present are compounded within the immediacy of performance. Such cases occur at VI.15 and VII.8, at the opening of the first two of the Kurukṣetra Books.

***

Secondly, there is the cosmogonic time of revolving *yugas*, these four reiterative and giant immutable envelopes that enclose all earthly existence within a hierarchy.[12] The narrative itself, according to Kṛṣṇa, sets the poem at the outset of the *kali yuga*, the last of these cyclic periods.[13] Occasional references to the Rāmāyaṇa tradition point towards another epic worldview that is situated in the *tretā yuga*, the second of the universal cycles and one that was long prior to the events of the Bhārata Song; Rāma as a hero—in terms of the poetry—greatly antedates the lives and conflicts of the Kurus.[14] At I.85.1, the poets indicate that Yayāti, who is the progenitor of the peoples described in this poem, was of the *kṛta yuga*, for he is referred to as *kārtayugapradhāna* (chief of the *kṛta* yugic time).[15]

The *kṛta yuga*, where *dharma* is actually completely fulfilled on earth, represents an era that is essentially unchanging, for all was then harmonious and in balance and no social nor macro-microcosmic disequilibrium existed, and, in that golden or perfect condition, there occurred no conflict or competition, and, of course, no work and ideally no death.[16] The poem's usage of this kind of *supra*-chronology, however, is more concerned with the metaphor of dharmic integrity and its diminution than with any distinct memory of a more morally substantial and less imperfect past: the *yugas* are a metaphorical system. The knowledge of this 'past' is of course only accessible to the poets with their skills of intellectual vision, for such actual recollection of gigantic time or *aeon* is not possibly human. The *kṛta yuga* is a moral ideal and not a record; it is a myth and not a fact, and thus—like any myth—requires interpretation. In terms of human ontology, this myth possesses great utility, and its reference is never really astronomical nor chronological but simply heuristic. In a sense, it is a manner for

[12] González-Reimann (2002) offers the best summary of this system as it occurs in the epic. At III.148.10, there is a summary of this myth of ages given by Hanūmān; and at III.186.17, Mārkaṇḍeya offers his overview of the sequence.

[13] Stated at V.140.6–15.

[14] The *Rāmopakhyāna* commences at III.257. Saṃjaya mentions in passing the fight between Rāma and Rāvaṇa at VII.71.28, and the *Mahābhārata* poets or editors obviously know of this other epic tradition.

[15] This connection with the *kṛta yuga* that Yayāti holds is despite the fact that in genealogical time he is only about seven removes from the generation of Śaṃtanu.

[16] During the reign of king Duḥṣanta, the father of Bharata, such natural harmony was mythically extant (I.62.3–14).

telling of human potential in a fully moral situation and of delineating a model of that decline.

***

Thirdly, there are the *devas* and the *pitṛs* (the 'deities' and 'ancestral dead') beings who principally inhabit the *other*-world, a place that is not affected by ephemeral time for they are indefinite. These divine beings sometimes enter into the mortal, or sublunar, world to participate in human activity, especially at the rituals. At one point in the poem, when the deities enter upon the living terrain, they are said to be *hṛṣitasragrajohīnān* (possessing garlands that are fresh and dustless), whereas of the human Nala it is said that he is *mlānasragrajaḥ* (possessing a dusty garland that is wilting) (III.54.23–24). Mortality is thus finitely signalled by the unavoidable decay of time's passage or presence, for nothing can endure in time except for such beings of divine origin. The divine beings, of course, do not experience pain or grief, for these are qualities of the temporal world.

We have seen how Agni, Śiva, Indra, Sūrya, and Dharma have appeared 'on earth' in the poem, and, conversely, how Arjuna had entered into the world of Indra; similarly the deceased kin of the Kurus appear in XV.41 arising out of the Gaṅgā, and, at the very close of the poem, the Pāṇḍava brothers enter into a timeless and undecaying *svarga*. There is thus at times a merging of the temporal and atemporal, the natural and supernatural, both vividly and visually within the poem. There is also a strongly marked presence of the timeless earthly beings, the *cirajīvin* 'long lived', as with Vyāsa, Nārada, and Hanūmān, to name but a few imposing figures who are not deities, but who possess an undying or an unspecified quality of the immortal. They enter into the song and disappear from the narration without any sign of mortal transition or physical gravity.

***

Fourthly, there is the sidereal, or annual, time of the cyclical year, and its repetitive calendar. Karṇa, towards the end of his unique dialogue with Kṛṣṇa as they drive together on a chariot, states the planetary conditions of the passing occasion. He begins:

> prājāpatyaṃ hi nakṣatraṃ grahas tīkṣṇo mahādyutiḥ
> śanaiścaraḥ pīḍayati pīḍayan prāṇino'dhikam
> kṛtvā cāṅgārako vaktraṃ jyeṣṭhāyāṃ madhusūdana
> anurādhāṃ prārthayate maitraṃ saṃśamayann iva
>
> V.141.7

> The super-brilliant harsh planet Saturn oppresses the heavenly body Rohini,
> Oppressing living beings exceedingly; and Mars,
> Having placed his face in the lunar mansion Jyeṣṭha,

Sets out toward Anurādhā, the lunar mansion presided
Over by Mitra, as if to extinguish [it], Madhusūdana.

Thus the poem situates itself exactly in terms of universal time, a point of reference that has allowed Indian astronomers to locate the precise instant of the great battle at Kurukṣetra to a year in the fourth millennium BCE.[17] Similarly, Kṛṣṇa describes the actual calendar day when battle is about to begin: it is a time of *amāvāsyā* 'new moon' during the month after the rains, when there is grass and also when the harvests have been taken (V.140.16–18); this is about the autumnal equinox.[18] This is the only occasion in the poem when an exact and empirical time is offered by the poets.[19] It is a moot point, why the poets or editors paid such careful attention to supplying the moment of battle with clear astral and seasonal definition, unlike any other event in the poem; what is the relevance of this particular date and to whom was it once germane?

There are also mentions of the very 'real' durations of eighteen days or twelve years or one year, for instance, or lucid indications of the diurnal and nocturnal aspects of the poem that situate the reader in a quite certain narrative 'reality' where sunlight and darkness alternate.[20] In the Āraṇyaka *parvan*, the poets make an uncommon statement about specific weather, for instance:

nidāghāntakaraḥ kālaḥ sarvabhūtasukhāvahaḥ
tatraiva vasatāṃ teṣāṃ prāvṛṭ samabhipadyata

III.179.1

While they were dwelling there monsoon commenced;
A time—bearing happiness to all beings, the end of the hot season.

17 Chandra (1978) offers an example of this kind of thinking. He dates the battle to 3137 BCE.

18 At the outset of the Kurukṣetra Books, Vyāsa describes in fine detail the astronomical situation that marks the opening of battle (VI.3.11–17).

19 As we have already noted above in chapter 3, there is the statement that Bhīṣma expires after the winter solstice, but this is not as precise as the date given for the eighteen days of battle. The poets say that Yudhiṣṭhira was born *aindre candrasamāyukte muhūrte' bhijite' ṣṭame* (on the eighth hour of the second half of the month Mārgaśīrṣa on the day of Indra) (I.114.4). Bhīma and Jarāsaṃdha fight their duel *kārttikasya tu māsasya . . . prathame' hani* (on the first day of the month Kārttika) (II.21.17). Kṛṣṇa also informs Yudhiṣṭhira that his horse sacrifice will begin, *caitryāṃ hi paurṇamāsyāṃ ca tava dīkṣā bhaviṣyati* (for your initiation will be on the full moon in the month Caitra) (XIV.71.4). None of these dates is supplied with full astrological definition, however.

20 The transit of days (and sometimes of nights) is described in the Kurukṣetra Books. Most of these four books are composed of finely modulated formulaic expression, and the narrative is often static for this reason, being given over to long passages of simile and metaphor in a manner that occasionally borders on the ekphrastic. It is with the advent of literacy that narrative, which privileges the medium of metonymy more than metaphor, takes precedence over pattern.

This kind of time is not of great narrative importance in the poem, however, and such observations are without much force in terms of what the poets are doing with their words.

***

Fifthly, there is also the 'reality' of ritual time, the temporal movement of particularly formulated events founded upon solemn ceremonies, which are themselves ideally mimetic of cosmic sequence.[21] These rituals almost *enact* time, insofar as they are markers of natural or social sequence; the *aśvamedha* is a particular example of this, for there is the projection of the apparently historical, a chronological time made explicit in the sequence of events in the poem. These movements, as we have demonstrated, can be formally grouped according to a series of rites that organise the narrative: the *svayaṃvara*, the *rājasūya*, the *dyūta*, the *śastryajña*, and the *aśvamedha*. Ritual actually gives tempo to the process of the poem, and, in that sense, these ceremonies are quite literally rites of passage in the life cycle of a king.

The poem commences with the statement that the opening scene occurs *dvādadaśavārṣike sattre* (during the twelve-year *sattra* rite) of Śaunaka, thus indicating the external, or outer temporal frame, of the whole epic, which is said to be sung by Ugraśravas (I.1.1).[22] Merely in terms of the poem itself, those twelve years mark its absolute containment or extent, thus signalling a temporal periphery. In ultimate counterpoint, infinity or eternity exists only *within* the poem's internal expressions, as with the two theophanic demonstrations of Kṛṣṇa, or depictions of heavenly situation as in the final *parvan*.

However, when there are moments that depict such human or equine peregrinations of *bhāratavarṣa*, or depictions of pilgrimage among *tīrthas* (the 'holy sites'), the actuality of pedestrian time is irrelevant, and time is simply a vehicle that possesses no solar reality, being compressed into a matter of one or two lines: for the *passing* of time is irrelevant to what in fact constitutes poetic time. Time on these occasions merely expands or is compressed according to the words of the poets and the constraints of performance; it is often the case that spatial movement or landscape is similarly condensed in such a progress.[23]

21 See Nagy (1979, sec. 30): "What is recurrent in ritual is timeless in epic tradition."

22 At I.189.1, the poets mention that *purā vai naimiṣāraṇye devāḥ sattram upāsate* (in the beginning the deities attend a *sattra* in the Naimiṣa forest). There is a pertinent recapitulation here.

23 This is something that cinema cannot accomplish except in terms of specific metaphor such as speeded up footage of passing clouds; cinema only has access to real time, the flashback or the reverie, and to montage, which implies the passage of time. I would urge the reader to view Christian Marclay's film *The Clock* to see how the experience of an exacting metonymy creates the illusion of temporal duration.

The temporal conditions of the Gītā, for instance, are virtually negligible for the same reason, and it is as if the envelope of the narrative parts momentarily: such theophanic 'periods' occur in what is in fact a timeless fashion.[24]

***

Sixthly, there is the genealogical presence of fugitive human time as represented by birth, life, and the contingencies of death; in this there are seven sequential human generations of physiological economy between Śaṃtanu and Janameja, inclusively.[25] The poem takes place during the reign of the latter king and retrojects the events of the song, what in cinema studies is referred to as a 'flashback'. The retrojection is not simply an act of recollection, but a visualisation by the poets, causing the audience to *see* the story, and, in this sense, the poets themselves are the genesis of this kind of phenomenal time.

Conversely, there is also a threefold projection of time that occurs in the Ādi *parvan*, firstly where the old king Dhṛtarāṣṭra sings a proleptic monody summarising much of the epic, beginning at I.1.102, and running for fifty-six verses. Then there occurs the *anukramaṇī*, or 'digest', of one hundred micro-narratives of the poem; followed by the *parvasaṃgraha* (digest of the books) (I.2.34ff. and I.2.72ff.). Each of the Kurukṣetra Books also opens with Saṃjaya telling his patron how it was that a particular hero perished, and then, on being asked by Dhṛtarāṣṭra, he recapitulates the narrative that precedes that instant of death.

In particular, there is the temporal cycle that Draupadī dramatises in terms of her menstrual period, which, through the public abjection of that condition, becomes destabilised. It is that instant of instability, that 'untiming' of her natural rhythm, which drives the wrath of the king's brothers to seek vindication, and, strangely, that act of almost magical subversion of feminine reproductive capability, is what leads to the long-term sterility of the Pāṇḍava lineage. For as we have seen, none of Draupadī's progeny survive the battle to become heirs to the kingdom, and it is the Yādava allies who ultimately triumph and who assume rule.[26] Likewise the poets are constantly making passing reference to the obligation that men have to honour and to satisfy their women-folk during

24 I argue, in McGrath 2016, chap. 3, that all ritual conditions are generated by the atemporal experience of theophany.

25 We have already noted above in chapter 2 how there is no memorial tradition in epic society, no monumental record is ever mentioned that would remember the dead and so reduce their removal from the temporal world of human sentiment; the past is in no way—in this poetry—materially sustained or integrated into the present and future. In a sense, epic itself is the only 'record' of these lives that were once 'situated' in the past.

26 As an act of magic, Duryodhana succeeds in this denigration of the Pāṇḍava queen insofar as he commences a movement that ultimately destroys her heirs.

their monthly cycle, and of the vital importance of engaging in timely sexual intercourse or fruitful insemination during the season of ovulation. Time in this very corporeal or biological sense possesses an ethical necessity and must not in any way be treated as erratic or volatile. In terms of the generation of the poem's main narrative, it is the disordering of this one tempered course that creates the movement of the song: for only if this cycle is harmonious and effective is the kingdom a balanced polity.

***

Seventhly, there is also, as we have already stated, the performative time that is presented by the poets as they cast their voices *backward* in years in order to recapitulate past events, telling of former kings, heroes, and deities who lived and acted in past days of old kingship; their knowledge is thus so informed or inspired. As we observed in the previous chapter, due to the express ring composition of the work, the epic possesses *no future* beyond itself. The poem at its conclusion reverts back towards events of the Ādi *parvan*: that is, the overall narrative as a temporal form is circular and not linear; it is a *closed* system. The only future presented by the moment of closure is the time that is represented by the moral efficacy caused by the performance of the epic, of the benefits that *will* accrue to those who learn or commission or recite the song. The benefits of ritual occur *after* participation in this event. The poem also begins at a point in time that is actually long after the events in the poem have occurred.

The poem itself is of course imperishable and unbounded, and it cannot decay or disintegrate: *nārado'śrāvayed devān ... vedasamitam* (Nārada caused the deities to hear the equal-to-the Vedas), that is, the *Mahābhārata* (XVIII.5.42–43).[27] As a work of divine art, it is beyond time, and we as an audience—through the eyes and via the words of the poets—look into this stationary and conceptual world of the kings, heroes, and deities, almost as if we are observing—in our mind's eye—motion upon a single screen.

The untimely quality of many of the micro-narratives of the Āraṇyaka *parvan* seems to hover in the general impetus of the narrative, although these micro-narratives are reputedly *historical* in substance.[28] There are also interjections into the narrative, as at the beginning of the Bhīṣma *parvan* or during lengthy genealogical accounts in the Ādi *parvan*, for instance—like the Pauṣya and Āstika episodes—that also step out of the overall narrative into another age,

27 The Bombay Edition of the poem in closing mentions the great moral and cosmic efficacy of *bhāratakathāṃ* (the Bhārata epic) (XVIII.5.68).

28 Mārkaṇḍeya appears in the narrative at III.180–283 and commences to tell edifying stories about the mythical and ancient 'past,' about figures like Manu, Angiras, Rāma, and Sāvitrī.

one that is almost prelapsarian; thus, Nārada tells the mournful Yudhiṣṭhira an account of sixteen long-dead kings at XII.29.16–136.[29] So narrative time, historical time, and mythical time can be compounded in one unitary sequence of words or poetic *montage*.

The four long non-diachronic discourses of Bhīṣma shift the tempo of the song onto another register that does not take part in the apparently annual or diurnal properties of the master narrative. As we have remarked, most of the Śānti *parvan*, insofar as it pays no respect to the passage of time, thus supplies its catalogue of injunction with a timeless imperative, so enforcing the moral import and prescription of its poetry, implying that these formal maxims or allegories are somehow *eternal* in their veracity: the absence of time implying great ethical distinction or truthfulness.

Specifically, in terms of poetic voice, there is the verbal time engaged by the definite and prospective time of an heroic speech act, as when Arjuna tells his charioteer Kṛṣṇa, *paśyāmi dravatīṃ senāṃ ... paśyāmi karṇaṃ samare vicarantam* (I see the army running, I see Karṇa attacking), when he informs his driver as to what he is about to do (VIII.52.5); these perceptions are in only Arjuna's mind's eye, and he is simply forecasting them. Boasting or vaunting, because it is ideally effective—and the alternative to this efficacy for the speaker is of course death—by definition is to *make* a futuristic statement, or to actually conduce or cause an event to occur in the future. In this particular instance, Arjuna not only makes a speech act, but he empowers it with a compelling visualisation of what is *going to happen*. Prophetic speech and curses are likewise futuristic in their effects.[30]

***

Eighthly, and finally, time in the epic takes on a myriad of aspects and measurements all of which are perfectly compounded during performance, where the poet or poets move between the various chronological planes while simultaneously activating one verbal or visualised stage, where figures from different temporal levels in the cosmos behave. This is not simply a manner of retrojection, or 'flashback,' that is mixed with a hypothetical or dramatic present (that also sometimes projects its own future); there is also a spontaneous shifting of narrative types: as when Bhīṣma tells Yudhiṣṭhira fabulous moral tales about magical or allegorical animals or micro-narratives about heroes in heavenly non-worldly settings. When Kṛṣṇa offers a theophany to Arjuna or to the members of the *sabhā*, living time is disengaged for the revelation that by definition must be timeless.

[29] In Book One, there is also the Śakuntalā episode, which is part of the genealogical background.

[30] As at VII.158.60.

The repeated and frequent use of *upamā*, or 'simile', likewise disengages the narrative—or the audience—from related or present time, as the poetry become unfixed in an untimed state or other mental situation. We noted earlier how a great deal of the Kurukṣetra Books are given in the form of simile, the *nadī* being the most typical and recurrent of these complex images.[31] These similes are static and 'fictional,' being drawn into, or mortised within, the ongoing narrative, and yet their existence is elsewhere and without chronological record.

The framing of a poet's voice within another poet's voice is a particular technique of moving among temporal registers, as when the poem opens with Ugraśravas singing his poem, which contains the major voice of Vaiśaṃpāyana who himself reputedly envelops the minor voice of Saṃjaya—each voice in fact occurring in a different *locale* and in another time.[32] Each of these voices also, on many occasions, imitate or enact other voices of further internal drama, heroic characters who sometimes—as we have noted—continue to perform the words of even another voice. Time thus slips and shifts with great theatrical facility in the work of these master poet-actors or speakers, time in this case being profoundly architectonic rather than temporal; for changes in voice *qua* time are indicated by changes in the emotion a poet is at any moment representing.

***

At its very basis the poem incorporates a grounding narrative of about fifty years, the duration of time between the boyhood of Kuntī's sons and the youth of her great-grandson Parikṣit; this is the essential story of the *Mahābhārata*. Into this account are introduced tales from the past that supply the epic with its vertical extension or warp, as well as the entries and exits into the song of those divine and non-natural beings like the deities, who bring a certain lateral extent or weft to the work. This is the overall *textus*, the 'fabric' of the epic, weaved of these various kinds of thread.

In sum, it is this play and conflation of the many expressions of temporal universality that make for the grandeur and magnificence of the epic, allowing

31 Tsagalis (2012, 344–345) comments on such poetic usage in the *Iliad*: "Similes are much more frequent in battle scenes, not only because they allow the narrator to present his audience with something familiar in their own experience (since their subject matter is drawn from daily life), which stands in contrast to the unfamiliar (and hard to map) battle scenes, but also because similes are organized on the basis of solid spatial constraints that allow the storyteller to 'find his way' amid the spatial vagueness created by continuous fighting . . . The pictorial output of simile is much greater than that of a simple scene or episode . . . In this way, the oral tradition's spatial nature becomes plainly evident: similes are the spatial hooks on which visual imagery is hung, making memory recall 'on the run' a reality of the performance." This practice of recalling formulaic simile also, of course, engages the poet with a previous time—the moment when he first heard or performed such similes.

32 I described and analysed this poetic system at length in McGrath 2011.

the poem to incorporate *at once* all the cosmos in its limitless manifestation, the living, the dead, and the supernatural; there is no single or unitary semantic field of time. In this overall and all embracing *poetic time*, there is a complete suspension of disbelief on the part of an audience. For us today, a moment in time only exists in terms of the sequence in which it is a part, and, in order to recall that moment, one can only trace or retrace the succession of moments to arrive at that instant or particular event; time in this sense is purely metonymical. Poetic time in the *Mahābhārata*, however, is profoundly and nearly always elliptical, and omits much or almost all of these sequences. To express this differently, the individual moments of time can be said to represent microcosmic instants, whereas the totality of all the sequencing represents the macrocosm. For an audience, the poem oscillates between these two formations, hence in part its great literary beauty and success.

Time in epic *Mahābhārata* is an economy of these many diverse kinds of measurement and metaphors of duration, all united as one in the poetry and its mimetic telling. This unique illusion of unity and of uniform progress is fully and completely accomplished by the poets as they move among the hundreds of differing voices in the poem; for if there is any one particular calibre that can be said to signify the many specifics of time, it is simply the expression of any one *voice* at any one moment.

The correlative of all this is, of course, the notion of space, the cartography of both permanent and impermanent as they amalgamate in the poetry. There is the *triloka* (the three worlds) of the aerial, the earthly or temporal, and the underworld, and at times, as we have seen, these converge in the narrative: as when a divinity appears on earth or a mortal enters one of the timeless locations like *svarga*. Location and the timely function in close concordance. The presence of time in the poem, as I have shown, concerns the aesthetics of the work rather than representing any formally chronological pattern of situations. This is a poetic time that gives the epic its shining and marvellous effect: it is a perfectly and magnificently created illusion and that is inceptive genius. One must also recall that heroes are not always mortal human beings and that this is especially the case with the half-human Pāṇḍavas and the charismatic or paranormal Duryodhana; hence the changes between time and place are not always so unnatural.[33]

***

I hope that this brief overview has shown how time in epic *Mahābhārata* is essentially conceptual and poetic, and only rarely does it exhibit an empirical

[33] Draupadī is not human at all, being born from a ritual fire: she is *ayonijā* (not born of a womb).

significance. Time in the poem is simply another aspect of a larger system of metaphor and vehicle of the many and various instances of narrative worth. It is this perpetually shifting tempo of story that is superficially founded upon a reality of solar, or world, time in the poem, moving backward and forward, out of and into, the atemporal *super*-natural, as well as engaging with moral or yugic time while being marked by ritual tempo. As we know, this *reality* of earthly time is most vividly and powerfully expressed in reference to menstruation, how it is that the feminine body inflexibly and unconditionally marks time and human reproduction and so structures the generative emotion of anger in the poem.

It is not simply that epic *Mahābhārata* encompasses, involves, or implies all of Indian *history* dating from the unrecorded, but obviously recalled, time of the Indus Civilisation peoples. It also recalls the Indo-Āryan world of Indra and other Vedic deities, and those concomitant ritual practices and habits, along with an archaic heroic world that is given some temporal status by virtue of its language and its technology—chariots, premonetary economy, the *saṅgha*—along with the classical world of what I have proposed is early Gupta kingship. Moreover, this vast drama continues to inform contemporary Indian culture in so many ways today.

To be a *classic* is in a sense to be *timeless* and intransitive, it is to represent the values that are more than germane to the continuity and sustenance of a culture or society; by encasing these values within a structure that engages with many possible dimensions of time, the poetry thus imbues the work of art with an 'invariable' quality.[34] The syntax of the poem is made up of all these integrated temporal components, and the grammar, as it were, informs this syntactical regularity with its well-tempered locative seams: how it is that the multitude of varying elements are inflected into a single harmonious and radiant whole by the *deictic* speech of the poets.

Time in the *Mahābhārata* is an illusion generated by the marvellous skills of the poets, and, I would strongly aver, by their ancient editors. It is this compounding of so many moments in time within one single linguistic theatre of poetry, in a manner that is perfectly fitted and ultimately discrete in its artistry, that makes for what we understand as *the myth* of modern India. Hence the durability of this epic results from a multiplicity of expositions that are apart from the simply poetic or textual.

[34] We have already noted how the 'classical' impulse also attempts to incorporate and represent a spatial totality in terms of all known or named topographic references. We see evidence of this, for instance, in the passages of the poem relating to pilgrimage, where numerable places are listed or catalogued within a collapsed or fused manner of time. Similarly, human journeys of great duration are usually collapsed into a few lines.

As I have shown, epic *Mahābhārata* frequently draws upon social systems and rituals that are at least two and a half thousand years in age. It is not simply the case that these various and multiform cultural elements are merely conflated into one poetic system, but that the metonyms involved are faultlessly united and merged so that the overall effect of the poem is that of a unified and radiant whole.

As a rider to all of the above it might be worth adding a brief note on the corresponding idea of *spatiality* in the epic: how it is that space and the sensibility for spatial understanding and perception are rendered by the poets.

Half of the poem as we know it today, that is, Books Twelve and Thirteen, the Śānti and Anuśāsana *parvans*, offer no indication at all of their environment, and there occurs virtually no spatial representation; these areas of the poem are simply verbal declamation without any attempt at pictorial verisimilitude. There also exists little architecture in the poem, and, where such is mentioned—as with the *sabhā* fashioned by Maya in Book Two (II.3.19)—it is in a somewhat mannered style.

When scenes are described that take place within interiors, there is similarly little to indicate the architectonic arrangement or decoration of such rooms. Exterior scenes such as landscapes are also given cursory depiction: there are trees and the geniality of rustic and idyllic settings perhaps, at times, but these too are general and lack particular qualities. Landscape in the epic is more a matter of nomenclature rather than of detailed topography, and the terrain of pilgrimage and journey also receives slight definition beyond simple idiom.

The poetry of the epic is concerned with voice and emotion; even individual character is only supplied in terms of speech, and there exists little description of physiognomy or dress. Similarly, space in epic *Mahābhārata* is supplied by the nuanced words of the poets, by the expression of the heroes and heroines and the affect generated through their speech; in a sense, this is a world of *drama*, but one given by monologue acted out by the poets as they imitate the characters. That is the foundational nature of *epic space*: it is purely emotional or theatrical.

Even the vivid battle scenes of the four Kurukṣetra Books and the small battles elsewhere—as in the Virāṭa *parvan*—receive no particular description of *setting*, and the forest of Book Three is almost fully conceptual. This is not a poetry of realism nor of naturalism, but one of verbally affective drama where the spatial does not extend much further than an arm's length from the human body; and when it does, this is portrayed in formulaic terms, in language which is drawn from the old-time poetic tradition. Epic *Mahābhārata* is a song that is primarily concerned with emotion, and secondarily, with genealogical and moral learning. Given such a definition and manner of art, the skills and theatrical brilliance of these poets must have been truly remarkable. There is no ceiling, or wall, or horizon to this space where heroes and deities pass before the eyes of an audience, for there exists simply a hierarchy of affective causality.

***

Let us now close this appendix with a brief quote from Viṣṇu Sukthankar where he comments upon the "philosophy of the *Mahābhārata* ... which has given this venerable old monument of Indian antiquity its rank as Smṛti and its abiding value and interest to the Hindus, nay to all true children of Mother India."[35] This idea of *antiquity* is—as I have indicated—polymorphous and intrinsic to the essential aesthetic system of this great poem.

[35] Sukthankar 1944, 335.

Appendix on Epic Preliteracy

Preliteracy was the cultural medium for the creation of epic *Mahābhārata*, and elements of the poem arose from a social matrix that existed long before writing became a phenomenon of record and of literary artistry in Northwest India.[1] Like much cognate Indo-European epic song, the poem is founded upon a preliterate ground of great antiquity that long preceded any written record of its many forms.[2] However, what we have now in the Pune Critical Edition of the work is without doubt originally drawn from a sophisticated and well-edited composition that was profoundly literary in organisation.[3] Even though the Pune text demonstrates an integrity of form and composition, the various *parvans* frequently evince great stylistic difference, which would indicate an aggregation of several poetic traditions into one final and well-produced poem. Additions to these *parvans*, what are commonly referred to as 'later' accretions, usually occur

1 In support of this, allow me to quote from Phillips-Rodriguez' finely tuned essay (2012, 216-217): "The reality is that at the beginning of the analysis the textual critic very rarely knows what the original text was like. He may have a fair idea of certain matters of style, language, metrics, etc. but only in a few cases would he be able to tell in the first instance an archetypal reading from a non-archetypal one ... Firstly, as an oral document it [the *Mahābhārata*] can be traced back to several centuries BC. Secondly, it kept growing and shaping itself freely in every recitation for several centuries till the time it was committed to writing and began a different phase of transmission in the first centuries AD. All this means that the text has gone through several centuries of undocumented oral transmission followed by at least ten more centuries of lost written evidence, and it has kept continually changing ever since."

2 I have already suggested that the poem was first transcribed into a written text during the reign of Samudragupta. See Mahadevan (2008 and 2011), and also Hiltebeitel (2011a), for their succinct views on when this first record of the poem might have occurred. The use of writing is first dateable during the Mauryan period. Shimada (2013, 139) makes the observation: "In the Dharma *sūtra*-s, the earliest group of Indian classical texts, there is no statement on the procedure of making legal written documents. This is also true of *Manusmṛti*, dated roughly around 100 BCE–200 BCE or even later, although the presence of such documents is mentioned." He is referring to where Manu, at VIII.168, states—concerning evidence or record—that *balād dattaṃ balād bhuktaṃ yac cāpi lekhitam* (whatever is derived by force, enjoyed by force, or also written due to coercion ...).

3 In the manner of what Nagy (2010, 313) describes as "an oral tradition that evolves through a streamlining of variations."

at the beginning and end of the books, for from a scribal point of view this is simply 'easier.'

To argue that the composition of the *Mahābhārata* was accomplished in writing at one particular moment in time—even if by a *committee*—is to ignore the nature of human literary and poetic culture; archetypes in this sense exist only as an *ideal*. Such poetry is never simply written *ab ovo*, but it draws upon tradition and precedence and example. That is the nature of human culture; its production is always metonymical and recipient rather than uniquely creative or original. The Homeric and Hesiodic poetry, the poetry of Shakespeare, of John Milton, the operatic music of Wagner, to name but a few such artistic endeavours, all received much from the success of previous traditions. Doubtless, the great Bhārata must have been arranged in a literary fashion at some point in time, but this was accomplished by poets—and later by editors—who knew perfectly well the variety and longevity of poetic materials they were including in their work.

Synchronically speaking, the tradition of heroic song or narrative existed—and continues to exist—in three fundamental forms. Firstly, there is the amorphous and popular, the common stories and songs about heroes that exist in the minds and telling of people, the 'audience'—such as folklore or mural illustration or lyric song itself and local drama. Secondly, there is the more professional and restricted form that was relayed by the preliterate poets, who knew the formulae and themes and motifs of their song, which were infinitely variable, depending upon their audience's needs. Lastly, there exists the epic as a 'commodity,' a material object in a written and bound, or simply accumulated, state; this last form of the poem possesses a value that can be bought and sold and exchanged like any material object, and thus owned, stored, or transported. These three 'stations' of the poem can be considered as immanent, performative, and material.

Let us now review seven summary points that allow us to comprehend more effectively and lucidly this system of poetry and its beautiful synthesis of song culture and writing. These points have all appeared in the course of this book and are fundamental to the conception and organisation of this present study.

***

Firstly, the Parry-Lord-Nagy system of analysing oral poetics provides us with a basic conceptual apparatus for understanding the techniques of preliterate song composition.[4] With their commentary written about field work in Bosnia in the early half of the twentieth century, Milman Parry and Albert Lord have

4 Parry 1932; Lord 1960; Nagy 2010 and 2013. Bynum (1974) supplies the historical and intellectual background for these theoretical positions.

enabled us to understand epic in terms of its production as an event that was achieved *during* performance. This was by virtue of the poet's skill in drawing upon themes and motif of song and upon a mental store of formulaic expressions that were possessed by the poet as an intellectual hoard, as something that had been learned and internalised as a potential *repertoire*. The poetry of the four Kurukṣetra Books of the *Mahābhārata* is almost wholly composed of such systematic and carefully arranged formulae, and for much of the time there is actually no narrative at all in this part of the poem. The beauty of this kind of poetry is that the formulaic metaphors are constantly being minutely varied so that there exists no reduplication or simple repetition of phrase; it is a poetry of great mastery and infinite artistry.

A poetic formula need not necessarily be an exact duplication of a previous phrase or expression, but it can be lexically varied; it can also be ultimately ideal or conceptual rather than simply morphological. Likewise, the ability of an epic poet either to expand or contract such a performance at will, according to the needs or wishes of an audience, patron, or the physical conditions of the performance, was an essential functional dimension of this kind of poetic production.

Gregory Nagy has developed this apparatus further by demonstrating how differently the poets worked in first millennium BCE Greece, illustrating the distinction between an *aoidós* and a *rhapsōidós*. These were the two kinds of poets who practiced within a manner of inspiration that drew upon, in the former case, conceived visual stimuli or the images that came to mind during performative composition; and, in the latter case, the poetry that came from the recital of memorised verse, or the poetry that had been heard and learned verbatim and then re-performed precisely upon occasion like an unwritten script.[5] I have shown how the *aoidós*, as typified by the poet Saṃjaya, is essentially 'earlier,' at least in style, if not in time, than the 'later' *rhapsōidós*, as typified by Vaiśaṃpāyana.[6]

The use of ring composition is another component or method in this scheme of poetics, whereby a certain particular signifier or indication will open and close a frame or sequence within the poem. This can be a word, image, or a descriptive activity. We noted earlier, for instance, how the poem commences with the final

5 See Nagy 1996b.

6 See McGrath 2011. Homeric epic poetry was inspired acoustically by the Muses, whereas the inspiration for Saṃjaya is visual. For Vaiśaṃpāyana, inspiration is not a critical moment in the production of the poem because he merely repeats what he has previously heard. Visual inspiration entails a critical act on the part of the poet who must make judgements as to what he is going to relate or say; verbal inspiration requires no critical act on the part of the poet for there occurs only a repetition of what has been received.

scene and then finally ends where the poem began. In such a manner of ring composition, time is curtailed, and the poem possesses no future beyond its own performance; the only effect is moral.

***

Secondly, this kind of epic poetry is polysemic, that is, it possesses no one single or uniform order of communication, for meaning varies and shifts throughout the course of the poem, as we have seen above with the concept of kingship. Due to the multitextual and inclusive nature of this kind of poetry where composition is necessarily centripetal in form, there are many kinds of expression joined into one work of art; whereas a directly written text or 'script' is fixed and fundamentally exclusive in form for it is 'established.'[7] What we have in the now written and 'finalised' epic is a flawless combination of these two forms, the preliterate and literate, where a system of polysemic signification developed: hence the word 'king' bears different interpretations at different points in the poem, for instance.[8]

Conversely, yet similarly, in epic *Mahābhārata* there exists a terrific range of nominal synonymity due to this kind of composition, where many customs—geographic, cultural, ritual, linguistic, and nominal—as strands of poetry have been simultaneously bound into what is now ostensibly a single and 'recorded' performance. Here, a *system* of composition that extends and ranges through potentially vast amounts of time and areas of place, certainly centuries and possibly millennia throughout the whole subcontinent, is represented as one temporal and uniform event.[9] Within this one integral poem, many conventions

7 One should recall that preliteracy and literacy are *not* mutually exclusive conditions or situations; illiterate poets can exist and flourish in times of great literacy. In fact, this is often the case today in parts of rural and non-metropolitan India.

8 Franklin Edgerton, in his Introduction to the 1944 edition of the Sabhā *parvan*, on p. xxxv–xxxvi, comments: "It appears then that probably all, certainly most, MSS. of every recension contain some readings which are neither inheritances from the original nor independent changes, but due to the contaminative influence of forms of the text which stood outside of the recension in question. This, I have suggested, may be due to peculiar features of Indian literary tradition. This on the one hand is characterized by the extensive development of regional versions of the same literary work, but on the other hand by extensive inter-relations and later-influences between such versions. Doubtless much of this confusion is attributable, particularly in the case of such a work as the Mbh., to the great popularity of oral recitation in India, and to the characteristically Indian institution of pilgrimage on a large scale (possibly also of the wandering monkhood)." Thus, rhapsodic poets, or poets who recite a song, will often 'adjust' their work, not simply to accord with time constraints, but they will also introduce figures or metaphors into the text so that the poem is metonymically more connected with its audience and place: on the one hand, there is *repertoire*, and, on the other hand, there is an attunement of 'reception.'

9 Burgess (2001) has demonstrated how this kind of inclusiveness might have occurred for the Homeric *Iliad* as it drew upon the much larger tradition of the Epic Cycle, particularly as it concerned the Aethiopis.

of meaning and word usage have been drawn, and during the long duration of what was, in effect, a centralising activity, they lost and often forsook certain qualities of their peculiar originality. We have noted the many words indicating kingship, for example: ideas as to the nature of kingship come from many geographical regions of a landscape, as well as being taken from many historical varieties of polity and traditions of poetic performance that have then been formed into a single amalgam of one sole Bhārata Song, supposedly produced as a discrete incident.

Likewise, in this epic, we see different periods and manners of theological expression fused into a single religious culture. This includes not simply the attentions offered towards the Indo-Āryan and early Hindu supernal deities and towards terrestrial and aerial semi-divine figures, such as *gandharvas, apsarās*, and the daemonic *dānavas*, but also to what must have been a strongly practiced heroic religion where the ritual singing of epic poetry activated the cosmos ideally in favour of humanity.[10] As we have seen, the epic repeatedly comments on the microcosmic efficacy of its own performance as a ritual event; to attend a recitation of the poem or the ritual dramatisation of some of its events, as well as to sponsor either kind of performance is 'good.' Epic *Mahābhārata* continues to display these sacerdotal qualities even today in the subcontinent, for when the poem is sung in temples this is accomplished by *paṇḍitas* or *pūjāris* (the 'temple priests').[11] Unfortunately, this range of diverse unity is changing due to the poem becoming monopolised by sectarian forces in the polity: "The arrival of *Mahabharat* on Doordarshan [the national television station] only reemphasized ... the representation of the Pandavas with the story of *bharat*. The BJP [the Hindu nationalist party] was able to use these articulations in its political struggle, in challenging the dominance of the Congress-led political center in New Delhi."[12]

10 See McGrath 2012.

11 I speak here about fieldwork done in Western Gujarat during the early years of the twenty-first century. Taking this idea of *medium* even further, Mitra (1993, 132) comments on the late twentieth-century televised epic: "*Mahabharat* and *Ramayan* on Doordarshan have also been reproducing a Hindu hegemony by circulating two epics that are typically connected with Hindu ideology and Hindu practices." Ironically, the scriptwriter for the *Mahābhārata* series was Moslem and some of the characters—Arjuna, for instance—were played by non-Hindus, Sikhs and Moslems. To quote further from Mitra (138): "In some episodes Krishna offers a blessing, and the camera closes up on him, keeping the receiver of the blessing out of the frame, collapsing the textual receiver of the blessing with the viewer at home ... Here it is no longer Arjun or Yudhistir who is the recipient of the blessing, but the people watching Krishna." Nowadays, to discuss the *Mahābhārata* with people in the non-metropolitan and rural parts of the country means to refer not to the various kinds of written text but to the televised version; this has now become the source of popular knowledge about the epic.

12 Mitra 1993, 150–151.

***

Thirdly, in this poetry that was founded upon the use of formulaic expression there existed no particularly overt individuality of character. This is a poetry of kinship and of defined figures; it is not an art form where characters possess distinctly *visual* and personal traits or apparel. Almost never does an audience hear about *how* a single person in the poem appears, for what exists is more a form of typology, and we do not hear what the heroes are *like* except in terms of simile: trees, ritual fire, and rivers, for instance. Certainly, there is characterisation of manner and especially of speech, but in terms of outward distinction—apart from certain innate qualities as with Karṇa's inborn earrings and cuirass—there are no unique specifications that distinguish these heroes, deities, and kingly or queenly figures. The poetry functions in terms of *types* or models of manner and kinship and not in terms of explicitly perceptible appearance, for the poem almost always draws upon the experience of the tradition and not upon the particular and individual experience of a poet.[13] The sensibility is towards the linguistic convention of this kind of poetry and its formulated custom, rather than primarily towards a poet's worldly apprehension; this lends to the ultimately Pan-Indic success of the work.

As a rider to the above, as we have remarked earlier, it is remarkable that there occurs virtually no mention of sculpture or painting in the epic for nearly all depiction of the plastic and visual arts is for some reason occluded.[14] This certainly indicates a strong practice of aniconism as one aspect of preliterate poetics. Was it the case in this culture that deities and other divine and semi-divine creatures only existed—in terms of iconography—as objects of poetic song and hymns of praise? Or, perhaps this phenomenon is due to the fact—as we have already noted—that the first stone statuary in the subcontinent was Buddhist in manufacture and representation, and all indication of Buddhism, as we know, has been thoroughly excluded from the poem.

***

Fourthly, the epic poets were skilled in the art of visualising their narrative for their audience-spectators, and what the audience received as an acoustic communication was in fact a narrative that was composed of visual arrangements and imagery: the audience was mentally *caused* to see a poetic development. This is a

13 We have already remarked on how the *levée* scene of Yudhiṣṭhira in the Droṇa *parvan*, and the entry of the king into Hāstinapura in the Āśvamedhika *parvan*, are unique instants in the poem. It would appear that the poets on such occasions are actually describing perceived events rather than simply drawing upon what they have heard about such moments.

14 Śikhaṇḍinī is said to be adept in *lekhya*, which can mean either 'painting' or 'writing'; this is a unique instance of such a talent in the poem (V.190.1).

vital dimension in the art of this genre of preliterate poetry, and it is a technique in which the Homeric poets excelled superlatively. For an audience, their experience of the poem is auditory, yet their memory or reminiscence of the epic is paradoxically visual.

The *truth* of this kind of poetry lies in its use of metaphor and simile. What we as twenty-first century readers understand as logically demonstrable truth does not always apply to such an archaic and poetic structure of narrative; the truth of written prose is founded upon the activity of reasoned metonymy that underlies the narrative, so informing it with plausible coherence. In this, the literate and preliterate are to be profoundly distinguished, for these are two thoroughly different systems of organising how meaning is to be expressed. Hence in preliterate song there are 'inconsistencies' of many different kinds: repetitions, contradictions, reiterations, narrations repeated from varying perspectives and/or voices that make for not identical dimensions. Rational truth in preliterate poetry is not a primary criterion of production: the aesthetic virtue of such a work of art lies not in its logical reasoning, but in its beautiful use of metaphor (for example, in such poetry even death and violence are made lovely).

Similarly, the narrative movement in preliterate poetry is more akin to what we might observe in bas-relief or chromatic depiction of events, as demonstrated at the late first millennium BCE *stūpas* of Bharhut, Sāñcī, and Amarāvatī, by the mural frescoes of Ajanta, or by the more contemporary painted cloths or painted and glazed paper screens that itinerant poets have used in the nineteenth and twentieth centuries in Western India.[15] To clarify, the movement of the narrative is not necessarily diachronic or based upon a system of visually immediate metonymy; this is what we have referred to in this book as *bricolage*, or narrative that is not organised according to temporal sequence, such as we—as readers—would expect today; meaning is organised more structurally.

***

Fifthly, metaphor as a trope is always and only to be interpreted, for there is no immediate communication of meaning or of truth when one draws upon the usages of metaphor: there are many possible interpretations or *nuances* of expression that are available to an audience—concerning the polyvalent referent of metaphor—but no one separate and unique statement. Such communication is therefore never absolutely direct, since all reception of meaning must necessarily be mediated by an act of critical interpretation.

In that sense, in preliterate poetry there exists a twofold situation: there is the narration itself, and in preliterate and premonetary culture this is *always*

[15] See J. D. Smith 1991; Knox 1992; Spink 2005–2009.

founded upon the workings of kinship; and then there exists the actual *performance* of the narrative, something that is necessarily to be dramatic and theatrical if the poem is to achieve creative success. As we have seen during the course of this present book, these are the two inseparable dimensions or conditions of epic *Mahābhārata*: what we have referred to as the *myth* and the *enactment*, the object narrative and the subjective performance.

During performance the poets must *interpret* the language and the expressiveness of the words they are singing: that interpretation is, I would propose, by definition a judgement and pronouncement of a metaphorical nature. How is it, for instance, that a poet declaims the sorrow of, say, Arjuna, or the virulence of Draupadī, or the volatile bombast of Duryodhana or grandeur of Karṇa? The poet supplies qualities of affect to his words—the sound—and then an exacting delineation to the visual images that he verbalises. Such performance by necessity requires an interpretive act on the part of the poet, if the emotion of the moment is to be thoroughly and convincingly conveyed. For instance, if a word or phrase is to be spoken ironically or cynically, this depends on the poet's interpretation: it is the poet who charges the expression with its particular feeling, for there exists no indication within the poetry itself as to *how* the words are to be verbally, or even gesturally, demonstrated and made *explicit* in terms of emotion. The language of emotion is always subject to such performative, and necessarily delicate, considerations; it is an act of conversion, and, as such, that manner of language is by definition metaphorical. It is the performance that is the vehicle of the emotion concerned and not the language merely in itself.[16]

Concerning the mechanics of this kind of work, in preliterate poetry there are usually only two *voices* at the most: for presentation cannot accommodate the drama of more than two persons being simultaneously played by a single poet. Ideally, preliterate song only expresses one speaker, and sometimes two, and for a poet to extend this *theatre* to several voices is practically excessive. Such dramatic *virtuosity* rarely occurs in the poem, since the shifts of interpretation—where the voices and emotions are played by just one poet—would be too great to accomplish viably. This is a realistic constraint upon the mechanics, or *praxis*, of epic declamation. A solitary poet is constrained in the affective expression, or meaning, to be achieved during performance by virtue of the fact that one poet must enact different voices; if this is a passionately tense scene, it is almost impossible for a poet, no matter how gifted, to imitate more than two voices simultaneously in dialogue. The dialectic of epic performance is framed by this

[16] The language of emotion vis-à-vis the poet concerns sound: how it is that the poet supplies a word with affect. The language of emotion vis-à-vis the audience concerns vision: how it is that the audience experiences grief or sorrow by a transference of affect between image and the recollection.

practical requirement, where, say, the discussion of policy in a *sabhā* is in fact a series of dialogues, or, moreover, a litany of monologues.[17]

Thus, to repeat, what occurs in the substance of the narration in epic poetry concerns kinship, that is, the narrative form that is so unlike the modern novel or cinematic plot where kinship is more often than not an absent condition. We can thus say that, on the one hand, there exists a narrative, and, on the other hand, there exists the interpretation of this narration by the poet; this latter condition in a sense means that the performance itself is utterly metaphorical insofar as the poet *interprets* the words or the mood of the voice and the emotion of the character, so demonstrating and making vivacious that judgement in the action. It is this drama or generation of emotion by the poet that therefore limits the number of voices or characters that can be played at any one moment during performance.

Nowadays, we—as readers of a text—only have access to the words themselves and not to the emotions that were formerly active during performance. It is as if we were reading a musical score of an orchestral symphony without being able to actually listen to the various instruments playing and to the qualities of such performance: we are limited by the mere signs of the score.

***

Sixthly, in this kind of poetry, whose sources are possibly late Neolithic or early Bronze Age in production, we have observed in epic *Mahābhārata* a constant manifestation of duality: as a pattern of characterisation and as a process of creativity.[18] I would go further than simply repeating that what we perceive in epic *Mahābhārata* is merely a representation of the Indo-European form of twins and twinning. In fact, I would strongly aver that our perception of a dynamic and active *dualism* in the text—as both condition *and* procedure—is in fact a profoundly inherent system of duality *qua* the very nature of cognitive process for such preliterate poets.[19] This manifest duality is how they worked, how it was that they composed this poetry, and how the poem *came to mind* in terms of a

17 On a similar note, the poets rarely describe what a character in the poem is privately *thinking*; there are descriptions of things and of individual figures and of their speech, but only occasionally is the thought of a character expressed, and this is usually in direct speech. The thought process of Śuka, for instance, the son of Vyāsa, who, *saṃcintya manasā* (having thought with his mind), is rendered by the poets (XII.318.46ff.), and likewise, the thoughts of Yudhiṣṭhira are verbally expressed at VII.102.9ff. and VII.103.32ff.

18 I would like to connect this praxis of duality in the creative processes of the poets with a condition of matrilinearity in the culture of that 'time'; but at present I can find no firm grounds to support such an inference. This remains therefore a general *sensibility* that I perceive in my readings of the poem.

19 See above, p. 5, for more textual reference on this point. In McGrath 2016, I have examined the hero Arjuna from the point of view of how this *dualism* is manifest in his life cycle.

creative method: an activity of composition-in-performance that was syllogistic in form or developed through twofold modulation.[20]

We have seen in this present study how king Yudhiṣṭhira operates in a near-dyarchic fashion in the company of his close ally and advisor, Kṛṣṇa;[21] and how kingship in the epic is often a matter of dispute or contention between two brothers, or, on another level, between two cousins, or even further, between two moieties of a clan. Likewise, there are often two males, a husband and another male figure—a progenitor—and it is the latter who successfully inseminates the woman, usually a queen. As we have often seen, the great heroes always have their appointed *bhāga* (a binary 'opponent'), and the unique relation that exists between charioteer and hero is another fashion of this kind of duality. Also, combat and battle are typically described in terms of duels between two heroes, which is the *nature* of the dialectic in this poetry. In terms of the procedure for poetic declamation, the relationship between poet and patron, between *sūta* and king, supplies the practice of how this class of *kṣatriya* poetry was pronounced.[22] Ring composition is similarly a form of duality that organises a narrative structure by virtue of an extended symmetry.

The most important quality of this nature of *duality* as it exists—almost as an hypostatic form in the epic—is that this is the nature of mental process for that time and culture, how it is that the poets *thought* as they performed their work. The progression of narrative in such a kind of verse is founded upon a practical or active dualism: this is how the poem moves and how the poets constructed and mentally formulated their work. In fact, I would go so far as to describe this as a fundamentally necessary duality in the nature of the poem's generation; thus, in the poem, all the major scenes in the plot are based upon a feud between two individuals or the two moieties of the clan. I would also strongly argue that this fashion of composition is not simply a condition of preliteracy, but is also a function of premonetary culture where there existed no unitary or universal epitome of currency in a society. The *Iliad* is similarly informed in its procession of narrative.[23]

20 In speaking about duality, I am here referring to a finite diachronic process and not to a synchronically organised binary structure.

21 I have developed this argument more fully in McGrath 2013, chap. III.

22 See McGrath 2011 for a depiction of the king-poet model; and McGrath 2013 for a portrayal of the powerful condition of amity and dependence that exists between a charioteer and his hero.

23 For instance, there is Achilles and Patroklos and Diomedes, and Achilles and Apollo and Agamemnon and Hektor: the first group being in a relationship of likeness and the second in a relationship of difference. With Apollo, Achilles is in an *agonistic* relationship, with Patroklos, the relationship is one of substitution, and with Diomedes, Achilles has what is a *doublet* relationship (where both heroic

To repeat, the monologue never really exceeds the dialogue form, and, if it does—and this is very rare—it is in the fashion of a series of speeches that simulate dialogue; there is no *stichomythia*, or what we would now call conversation. Thus, duality is intrinsic and innate—almost as a force of simple opposition—to how the epic was composed and organised as a narrative and as a system of characters. This is not simply counterpoint in narrative, but occurs similarly in terms of double agency in the story, making for a kind of creativity that can be said to be almost *fugal* in its progress. In sum, this duality is a cognitive process that informs poetic matter.

***

Seventhly, and finally, we speak about preliteracy and its culture, but what we are actually discussing is not simply preliteracy, but also its corollary, the concomitant premonetary economic situation.[24] I would argue that these two forms of social order are inseparable in the late Bronze Age period that we have been examining as it is manifest in the epic: they were obverse and reverse to the one same social situation. Poetry, in a natural economy or a preliterate and premonetary society, circulates just as money flows in a monetary economy, and both sustain and maintain values that pertain to human livelihood and judgement.

Certainly, this poetry is artificial insofar as the poets and editors are representing in their work a kind of culture that did not actually ever exist, for such poetic syncretism of religious periods—the archaic Indo-Āryan joined with an indigenous pre-Hindu, and with early classical Hindu culture and even suppressed aspects of Buddhist or Jaina life—represents a society that never really occurred and that is only hypothetical or an artistic pretence. Similarly, the retrojection of an idealised *heroic* world is also a matter of artifice: where a world of *semi*-divine beings, who are not naturally or mortally human, and who, conversely, are not yet fully timeless and divine, is *remembered* and described by the poets as if these beings had once lived and walked the earth. It is as if that world—the *myth*—became actually present in terms of an heroic religion: a quality of life that was enacted and so activated by the performance of the epic or parts of the epic as a work of ritual devotion.[25] The performance of the poem thus creates and transmits, or sustains, *value* for a community as it exists within a

---

narratives are sometimes expressed in the same fashion). These various kinds of *polarity* are amplified and developed throughout the progress of the poem.

24 In chapter 3 of the current book, I have supplied more details of this 'natural' premonetary form of economy and its development into a monetary system.

25 Let us recall that it is *work*, and I use the word in an ontological sense here, that creates value for a society or culture. See Graeber 2001. The *Mahābhārata* as a poem *and* as a ritual is thus very much a *work* of art in which an economy of metaphors is active.

larger macrocosm, and the ritual mediates and stabilises the various dimensions of the microcosm as it exists within a conceived cosmos or *triloka*.

In the late Bronze Age society referred to by the epic, not only was there no writing, but there was no medium of exchange; the economy then was not a monetary one but one founded upon a system of services and loyalties that were exchanged, for money did not exist.[26] The intellectual consequences of this kind of social organisation cannot be stressed too much, for there existed *no* single standard of value in such a community; value was dispersed and various, and there was *no* one form of economic currency. Value, then, was thus wholly dependent—in its genealogy—upon a system of kinship based loyalties or services, themselves defined and maintained by rites. The establishment of a unitary symbol of primary worth only occurs where such a discrete sign is produced: this arrives with the introduction of coinage and the standards of weight therein established.[27] As we know, one of the first recorded demonstrations of writing occurred with the impress and fabrication of coinage.[28]

***

Value is, of course, not a natural phenomenon; it is a thoroughly conceptual and socially fungible token that only arises in acts of exchange, and I include here the exchange of words. Without the norm or measure supplied by a royal coinage—in fact the first such coinage in India was actually minted by the *śreṇi*, the 'guilds', in the later centuries before the Common Era—there existed *no* single paradigm of value. What existed was an order of exchanges of fidelity founded upon kinship relations and allegiance. Now, for us today as distant readers of the poem, the only occasions where moveable wealth is perceptible in the epic are twofold: either at the great sacrifices or at prestigious weddings, the marriage of princesses and heroes or princes. On both occasions moveable wealth is distributed and circulated, these being in the form of jewels, weapons, livestock, servants, but not land. Wealth is also exchanged in gambling, but this is a unique occasion in the poem.

26 As we have earlier observed, in this kind of society there was no market, and hence no domestic barter; although in terms of long distance trade, barter certainly existed. See Wiser 1936; Earle 2002; Seaford 2004.

27 Rapson (1897, 2) writes: "The most ancient coinage of India, which seems to have developed independently of any foreign influence, follows the native system of weights as given in Manu VIII.132ff. The basis of this system is the *rati* (*raktikā*), or *guñja*-berry, the weight of which is estimated at 1.83 grains = .118 grammes. Of the gold standard coin, the *suvarṇa* of 80 *ratis* = 146.4 grs. or 9.48 grms., no specimens are known; but of the silver *purāṇa* or *dharana* of 32 *ratis* = 58.56 grs. or 3.79 grms., and of the copper *kārṣāpana* of 80 *ratis* (same weight as the *suvarṇa*), and of various multiples and subdivisions of these, numerous examples have been discovered in almost every part of India."

28 Certainly, in the Hellenic world letters were also employed as signs of numeration.

It is not simply the case that preliteracy and premonetary society are simply prior in form to what occurred in classical times, but that consciousness itself and the relationship between consciousness and objects are very different during the archaic time. As we have seen, kinship is different in a premonetary culture from what obtains in a monetised system, and kinship is the matrix that generates consciousness. Objects, once money appears, move in very different courses among a community, not being obliged to remain in channels that are conditioned only by kinship structures and those types of affiliation. It then becomes possible for power to become much more unique and detached because its sources and its energy no more derive from the tissue and attachments of blood relations and such social empathy; power, or what we have been discussing as 'kingship,' then becomes potentially autarchic, depending only on the possession and use of quantities of currency or the richness of the treasury.

Full or absolute preliteracy occurred during an historical period when such a 'natural' economic system became established, and I would argue that these two registers of meaning existed inseparably; it is not by chance that some of the first human script occurred on coins. It is this system of how meaning is encoded that is one of the forces creating so much polysemy and multitextuality in the poem, for there existed then no single and authoritative *standard* of significance. Although, one could argue that kingship, insofar as it commissioned the ceremonial singing of the epic, was in a sense generating that spectrum of value as represented by the poem and its performance.

***

In sum, epic *Mahābhārata* was born from such a vast and inconceivable range of formation as I have attempted to delineate in the above lines; its aetiology is unlimited simply because we lack sufficient record or data to apprehend such ancient human experience. The nature of kingship manifests just one aspect of this kind of poetry, as does the nature of those more-than-natural beings, the heroes: superhumans who became supernatural in the terms and frames of ritual. Both kingship and heroic action were essential components in the practice of epic as a ritual form of devotion directed towards the many contending elements of an envisaged macrocosm: the deities, daemons, and natural spirits.

In closing, let us not make the not so uncommon error of presuming that the preliterate is always 'older' than the literate. Stylistically this may be the case, but even then this is not necessarily always true. On the one hand, as we have already noted, illiterate and itinerant poets exist today in Western India in situations of great social literacy.[29] On the other hand, simply because something

[29] See Randhawa 1996; J. D. Smith 1991.

in a poem would indicate that it is a phenomenon of a *written* text does not necessarily indicate that it is a 'later' instance in the formation of poetry.[30] What is overtly an indication of 'writing' could in fact be drawing upon extremely ancient ideas and words that had never before been engaged by epic poetry; the *text* as we have it today is not in any way absolute nor all-comprehensive in its inclusion of human experience. The literary artists—either as poets or editors—could simply be drawing upon a tradition that was profoundly ancient and that was at one point in time a condition of preliterate culture; but as an expression of cultural, ritual, or poetic practice, it had not been *included* in the text until much later. Hence, the seamless and imperceptible compounding of the archaic and classical. This manner of confusing the older and the later with the preliterate and the literate is a fallacy, for we must presume that the epic text is not an unqualified totality, even though it does make this claim about itself, as any ritual text would.[31]

The nature of human culture, and specifically of literary culture, is not possibly innovative or creative, but simply draws upon what has existed or does exist in recollection, presentation, or combination. Culture survives, or takes place in time, by virtue of metonymy: there is no unique or discrete instance or phenomenon; for the literate and preliterate—and *even* the illiterate—all engage upon one continuous surface of known human experience, and when change does occur creatively it is only by virtue of *re*-arrangement or *re*-combination of elements. We can observe this phenomenon in the overtly and explicitly hybrid constitution of epic *Mahābhārata* with its variform religious customs, practices, and beliefs, and its combination of archaic and classical political conditions all which are flawlessly founded within one great poem.[32]

30 See McGrath 2012, where I contrast the potentially 'early' form of the expression *dvau kṛṣṇau* with the potentially 'later' or 'newer' term *naranārāyaṇau*, and where both phrases refer to the same two heroes. My argument here, in the first case, was based upon the semi-divinity of Arjuna: his father was Indra, in contrast to the full humanity of Kṛṣṇa who had only mortal parents. Whereas in the second instance of a *dvaṃdva* compound, it is *nara* who represents the mortal Arjuna and *nārāyaṇa* who stands for the divine and cosmic Kṛṣṇa. I argued that *dvau kṛṣṇau* was a preliterate expression and that *naranārāyaṇa* was a literate phenomenon with the rider that such inference was *not* firm in any way and such argument was at best only a strong possibility. Certainly, linguistically the former indicates an earlier cultural model while the latter indicates a later cultural situation: but that is all that we can say, simply because the text is *not* absolute. From a more objective point of view, we can say with certainty that these two figures were receiving worship by the second half of the fifth century CE, as evidenced by their fine bas-relief representation in a Gupta period Viṣṇu *mandir* in Deogarh, Uttar Pradesh; see Lubotsky 1986.

31 *Yad ihāsti tad anyatra yan nehāsti na tat kvacit* (whatever is here—that is elsewhere; what is not here—that is nowhere) (XVIII.5.38).

32 For instance, in McGrath 2013, I showed how the classical deity Kṛṣṇa grew out of much earlier and archaic historical and literary forms.

It is only within the material substrate of culture that original or unique shifts happen, as with the invention of money or alphabetical systems, or the discovery of iron or steel production. Through the techniques of sequence, aggregation, or dispersal, the poets and the editors struggled in their work and effort to recreate or reformulate that *one myth* of human presence and awareness, which, in terms of kingship, became the ideology of the great Bhārata poem; where, as I have shown, the king was the primary ritual officer in the community, surrounded by family, clan, and the company of principal allies who all went to compose his *saṅgha*.[33] Just as on the Shield of Achilles, where a totality of the earthly *kosmos* was represented, it is the *basileùs*, the 'king', who is at the very centre or focus of the community, surrounded by reapers harvesting in a field and heralds who prepare a sacrifice.[34] In the Bhārata poetry, the reapers become the fighting heroes and the ritual agents the *brāhmaṇas*.

***

Unlike the various epic poems of the Western tradition, the genius of epic *Mahābhārata* continues to flourish today in the subcontinent as a dynamic and profoundly intrinsic component of not simply Hindu culture, but of Indian culture in general, including its diaspora throughout the world; for the *immanence* of the poem within Indian society remains energetic and vibrant. This is not only in literary terms, but also in the visual arts, sculpture, cinema, and moral, political, and religious culture, as the old epic heroes remain constant figures of great ritual and practical devotion.[35] Mitra, in his study of the *Mahābhārata* and television in India, asserts that "in India the viewing of a program like *Mahabharat* on television does not only constitute a reading practice, but is also a religious practice of worship, where the reader of television is participating in a religious activity by turning on the television set on a Sunday morning and involving the entire family."[36] In contemporary India, there are presently *many Mahābhāratas* that have proceeded from those ancient preliterate origins and

[33] For this idea or theory of the hypostatic *one* myth or one narrative form, see Propp 1928; Witzel 2012. The *Mahābhārata* itself, as we have observed, expresses this notion concerning its own perfectly complete and autonomous existence.

[34] This occurs in Scroll XVIII of *Iliad*, lines 550–560. In this depiction the king is completely silent yet pleased.

[35] See Hiltebeitel 1988; Tharoor 1989; Mankekar 1999; Sax 2002; Varma 2004; and Das 2009—to name but a few authors in this field. As we noted earlier, the hero Rāma has become in the last decades a point of political, if not geopolitical, contest in which many people have died in the ensuing communal riots.

[36] Mitra 1993, 64.

completely unknown sources.[37] Yet nowadays, the several Sanskrit versions of the poem are merely one small plane of that vital and constantly self-renewing current of Indic sacred song in which moral beauty as a constantly edifying form is once more expressed.[38]

Let us now close this appendix with two thoroughly empirical examples of how it was that the oral tradition or preliterate culture once operated in late bronze age Indian antiquity. These two factual or textual specimens will illustrate just how it was that those early poets worked and then later, once literacy had become an aspect of society, how it was that the editors sometimes dealt with this poetry.

Firstly, looking back to the early part of this book where we examined the role of Magadha in the epic conflict, it soon becomes obvious that this allegiance of Magadha is murky, and that is also changes as the poem progresses: it is as if the poets and editors differed in their understanding of the coalition at different moments in the narrative. Or, was it that they were drawing upon very differing narratives and combining them with an occasional lack of conscious precision?

At VII.91.24, a duel begins between Sātyaki and Jalasaṃdha (who is portrayed as king of the Māgadhas) in which the latter is felled. At VIII.4.85, a champion of the Māgadhas is mentioned as being felled by Bhīṣma. At VIII.5.22, the poets say that the *māgadho rājā* was allied to Karṇa; however, it is said that *arautsīt pārthivaṃ kṣattram ṛte kauravayādavān* (he obstructed the *kṣatriya* princes except the Kauravas and Yādavas). At VIII.8.19, the Māgadhas are once again advancing with the Pāṇḍava force, but then, at 13.3ff., Arjuna and Kṛṣṇa advance against the *pravara* 'champion' of the Māgadhas. At VIII.17.2, the Māgadhas are on the side of the Kauravas, and at VIII.51.23, the poets say that Jayatsena, the *adhipati* of the Māgadhas, had been killed by Abhimanyu. In the Strī *parvan*, Gāndhārī observes the body of Jayatsena upon the battlefield, but does not say

[37] The modelling of Yudhiṣṭhira's kingship that we have been examining and analysing during the course of this book has become—in twenty-first century India—a patterning and paradigm of wisdom and bare human fortitude, but apart from the image of ruler as sacrificer and ritual officer. The *rājanīti* of modern politics is such, though, that, in years to come, this outline of a ruler who is religiously proper and also ritually active might possibly return quite forcefully. In those circumstances, one might expect to see a resurgence of hero cult, where archaic heroes once again receive formal adoration and ceremonial respect, and national leaders are treated as almost divine beings.

[38] In closing, let us add that epic *Mahābhārata* quotes from, summarises, and refers to the poetic tradition of the Rāmāyaṇa on many occasions during the course of its narrative. Apart from the *Rāmopakhyāna*, it is in exchanges between the old king Dhṛtarāṣṭra and his *sūta* Saṃjaya that these references are generally to be found. Sathaye 2007 has written a brilliant essay on how both *Mahābhārata* and Rāmāyaṇa retell the Viṣvāmitra episode, where he focuses upon how each epic generates its own particular epithets for this common narrative.

who killed him (XI.25.7). In the Āśvamedhika *parvan*, Arjuna attacks the king of Magadha and vanquishes him (XIV.83), and Kṛṣṇa is said to have subdued the Māgadhas at XVI.6.10.

Whether these variances indicate a slip on the part of the poets or editors or if this is simply an indication of *bricolage* whereby elements of various preliterate traditions have been synthesised, is a moot point. Our rational twenty-first century attitude to narrative systems always anticipates logical coherence, whereas in preliterate antiquity, due to a performative tradition that often privileged emotion over reason and where transmission was verbal rather than literal, this was not always the case. It is remarkable that Sörensen, for the lemma Jayatsena, places a few question marks among his notations, emphasising this ambiguity concerning the Māgadhas.

Secondly, in the Bombay version of the poem when the *parvans* are listed along with the particular foods to be distributed during each book's performance, the Sauptika *parvan* is not mentioned. What is mentioned in its place, however, is the *gadāparvaṇi* (the books of the club) (XVIII.18.66). This refers to the minor *parvan* presently referred to as the *gadāyuddha parvan*, which is what closes the Śalya *parvan*; in the Pune CE text this constitutes IX.54–64. It is telling that the profound Śaivite Sauptika text is omitted in this listing.

According to this same summary, after the Āraṇyaka *parvan* there occurs the Āraṇeya *parvan* (III.295–299 PCE). Then between the Strī and the Śānti *parvans* occurs the Aiṣika *parvan*, which describes the contest of missiles between Aśvatthāman and Arjuna (presently at IX.10–18 in the PCE). In this same ordering, there is *no* Anuśāsana *parvan*, although this might simply indicate its inclusion within the Śānti *parvan* as an *ensemble*.

Nīlakaṇṭha makes no comment on this system of serial form and this ordering begins with the Āstīka *parvan* (I.13–53) and concludes with the Harivaṃśa *parvan*, a sum of twenty books. One wonders as to what tradition of the poem is being referred to here? We must also remember that the Bombay text of the poem was *not* the text of the epic that Nīlakaṇṭha carefully assembled; his commentary was simply appended to that first 1836 printing.[39]

Sukthankar, in his Introduction to the Pune Edition of the Āraṇyaka *parvan*, Part 1, xxxiii, writes, "The Bombay Edition, like the Calcutta, is based on the Nīlakaṇṭha version but (like yet other editions of the *Mahābhārata* prepared in the same fashion, e.g., the Chitrashala Edition) does not represent the Nīlakaṇṭha tradition very faithfully. In the footnotes to the text, and the critical notes at the end, I have frequently drawn attention to unwarranted

39 See Minkowski, 2004 and 2010.

departure from Nīlakaṇṭha's original text ... They prove very clearly that *without any conscious effort at alteration or emendation—and perhaps, notwithstanding the half-hearted efforts to preserve intact the received text—discrepancies do arise in the course of time, and the text does drift away from the norm, imperceptibly, within a relatively short period of time*."

Bibliography

Primary Texts

Aitareya Brāhmaṇa of the Ṛg-veda. 1895-1906. With the commentary of Sāyana Áchārya. Edited by Satyavrata Sāmaśramī. Calcutta: M.N. Sarkār, Satya Press.

Ānandavardhanāchārya. 1965. *Dhvanyāloka with the Lochana of Abhivinagupta*. Varanasi: Chowkhamba Vidyabhawan.

Bāṇa. 1883. *Harṣacarita*. Edited by Iśvarachandra Vidyasagara. Calcutta: Sanskrit Press.

Dīgha Nikāya. 1890. Edited by T. W. Rhys Davids and J. Estlin Carpenter. Oxford: Pali Text Society.

Kauṭilīya Arthaśāstra. 1972. 3 vols. Edited by K. P. Kangle. Delhi: Motilal Banarsidass.

Mahābhārata. 1933–1966. Pune Critical Edition. 19 vols. Edited by V. S. Sukthankar, S. K. Belvalkar, and P. L. Vaidya. Pune: Bhandarkar Oriental Research Institute.

Mahābhāratam. 1979. With the commentary of Nīlakaṇṭha. 6 vols. Edited by Pandit Kinjawadekar. New Delhi: Oriental Books Reprint Corporation.

Manusmṛti. 1983. With Sanskrit commentary by Manvartha-Muktāvalī of Kullūka Bhaṭṭa. Delhi: Motilal Banarsidass.

Nītiprakāśika. 1953. With *Tattvavivṛti* of Sītārāma. Edited by T. Chandrasekharan. Madras: Government Oriental Manuscript Series, Government Press.

Proclus. 1983. "Fragments of the Epic Cycle." In Hesiod, *The Homeric Hymns and Homerica*, Loeb Classical Library 57, translated by H. G. Evelyn White, 480–539. Cambridge, MA: Harvard University Press.

Suhravardī. 2012. *The Magic Doe: Qutban Suhravardī's Mirigavati*. Translated by Aditya Behl, edited by Wendy Doniger. New York: Oxford University Press.

Secondary Sources

Agrawal, Ashvini. 1989. *Rise and Fall of the Imperial Guptas*. Delhi: Motilal Banarsidass.

Agrawala, P. K. 1965. "The Depiction of Punch-Marked Coins in Early Indian Art." *Journal of the Numismatic Society of India* 27: 170–176.

Agrawala, Vasudeva S. 1952. *India as Known to Pāṇini*. Varanasi: Prithvi Kumar.

Allen, N. J. 1996. "The Hero's Five Relations: A Proto Indo-European Story." In *Myth and Mythmaking*, edited by J. Leslie, 5–20. Richmond, Surrey: Curzon.

———. 1999. "Arjuna and the Second Function: a Dumézilian Crux." *JRAS* (third series) 10: 403–418.

———. 2002. "Mahābhārata and *Iliad*: A Common Origin?" *ABORI* 83: 165–177.

———. 2012. "Bhārata Genealogy: The Close Parental-Generation Males." In Brockington 2012, 39–50.

Anthony, David W. 2007. *The Horse, the Wheel, and Language*. Princeton: Princeton University Press.

Austin, Christopher. 2011. "Evaluating the Critical Edition of the Mahābhārata." *Journal of Vaiṣṇava Studies* 19: 71–86.

Austin, J. L. 1962. *How To Do Things With Words*. Cambridge, MA: Harvard University Press.

Bachhofer, Ludwig. 1939. *Early Indian Sculpture*. London: Pegasus Press.

Bakker, Egbert J. 1997. *Poetry in Speech*. Ithaca: Cornell University Press.

———. 2005. *Pointing at the Past*. Hellenic Studies Series 12. Washington, DC: Center for Hellenic Studies.

Balzani, Marzia. 2003. *Modern Indian Kingship*. Oxford: James Currey.

Barber, E. J. W. 1991. *Prehistoric Textiles*. Princeton: Princeton University Press.

Beissinger, Margaret H. 1999. *Epic Traditions in the Contemporary World*. Berkeley: University of California Press.

Bellavia, David. 2007. *House to House: An Epic Memoir of War*. New York: Free Press.

Benveniste, Emile. 1969. *Le Vocabulaire des Institutions Indo-européennes*. 2 vols. Paris: Les Editions de Minuit.

Bhattacharji, S. 1992–1993. "Social Pressures Behind the Bhārgava Interpolation of The Mahābhārata." *ABORI* 72–73: 469–482.

Bhattacharya, Pradip. 2012. *Narrative Art in the Mahabharata: the Ādi Parva*. New Delhi: Dev Publishers.

Bigger, Andreas. 1998. *Balarāma im Mahābhārata*. Beiträge zur Indologie 30. Wiesbaden: Harrassowitz.

Bird, Graeme D. 2010. *Multitextuality in the Homeric Iliad*. Hellenic Studies Series 43. Washington, DC: Center for Hellenic Studies.

Blackburn, Stuart H., ed. 1989. *Oral Epics in India*. Berkeley: University of California Press.

Bod, Rens. 2013. *A New History of the Humanities*. Oxford: Oxford University Press.

Bowles, Adam. 2007. *Dharma, Disorder, and the Political in Ancient India*. Leiden: Brill.

Bray, Sir Denys. 1913. *The Life-History of a Brāhūī*. London: Royal Asiatic Society.

Brockington, J. L. 1984. *Righteous Rāma: The Evolution of an Epic*. Delhi: Oxford University Press.

———. 2010. "The Spitzer Manuscript and the Mahābhārata." In Franco and Zin 2010, 1:75–87.

———, ed. 2012. *Battle, Bards and Brāhmins*. Delhi: Motilal Barnarsidass.

Brockington, J. L., and Mary Brockington, trans. 2006. *Rāma the Steadfast: An Early Form of the Rāmāyaṇa*. London: Penguin Books.

Brockington, Mary, and Peter Schreiner, eds. 1999. *Composing a Tradition: Concepts, Techniques and Relationships*. Zagreb: Croatian Academy of Sciences and Arts.

Bronkhorst, Johannes. 1993. *The Two Sources of Indian Asceticism*. Bern: P. Lang.

———. 2007. *Greater Magadha*. Leiden: Brill.

———. 2011a. *Buddhism in the Shadow of Brahmanism*. Leiden: Brill.

———. 2011b. *Karma*. Honolulu: University of Hawaii Press.

———. 2011c. *Language and Reality*. Leiden: Brill.

Bronkhorst, Johannes, and Madhav M. Despande. 1999. *Aryan and Non-Aryan in South Asia*. Harvard Oriental Series, Opera Minora 3. Cambridge, MA: Harvard University Press.

Brown, Cecil Jermyn. 1922. *The Coins of India*. Calcutta: Association Press.

Brown, W. Norman. 1972. "Duty as Truth in Ancient India." *Proceedings of The American Philosophical Society* 116: 252–268.

Bühler, G., and J. Kirste. 1892. "Indian Studies, no. II, Contributions to the History of the Mahābhārata." *Sitzungsberichte der Philosophisch-Historischen Classe der Kaiserlichen Akademie der Wissenschaften* 127:1–58.

Burgess, Jonathan S. 2001. *The Tradition of the Trojan War in Homer and the Epic Cycle*. Baltimore: Johns Hopkins University Press.

Bynum, David E. 1974. *Four Generations of Oral Literary Studies at Harvard University*. Cambridge, MA: Center for the Study of Oral Literature, Harvard University.

Byrne, Francis J. (1973) 2001. *Irish Kings and High-Kings*. Dublin: Four Courts Press.

Chandra, Asit Nath. 1978. *The Date of the Kurukshetra War*. Calcutta: Ratna Prakashan, Oxford Book & Stationary Co.

Chakrabarti, D. K. 1992. *The Archaeology of Ancient Indian Cities*. Delhi: Oxford University Press.

Candraśekharvijay Gaṇi, Paṅnyās. 1985. *Jain Mahābhārat*. 2 vols. Ahmedabad: Kamal Prakāśan Trust.

Christensen, Arthur. 1936. *Les Gestes des Rois dans les Traditions de l'Iran Antique*. Paris: Librairie Orientaliste Paul Guethner.

Claessen, Henri J. M., and Jarich G. Oosten. 1996. *Ideology and the Formation of Early States*. Leiden: Brill.

Coomaraswamy, Ananda K. 1992. *Essays in Early Indian Architecture*. Edited by Michael W. Meister. New Delhi: Indira Gandhi National Centre for the Arts: Oxford University Press.

Das, Gurcharan. 2009. *The Difficulty Of Being Good*. Delhi: Allen Lane.

Davidson, O. M. 1998. "The Text of Ferdowsī's *Shāhnāma* and the Burden of the Past." *JAOS* 118: 63–68.

———. 2013. *Poet and Hero in the Persian Book of Kings*. Third Edition. Cambridge, MA: Ilex Foundation, Harvard University Press.

Davis, Donald R., Jr. 2010. *The Spirit of Hindu Law*. Cambridge: Cambridge University Press.

Davis-Kimball, Jeannine. 1997. "Warrior Women of the Eurasian Steppes." *Archaeology* 50: 44–49.

DeMarrais, Elizabeth, Chris Gosden, and Colin Renfrew. 2004. *Rethinking Materiality*. Cambridge: MacDonald Institute for Archaeological Research.

Dharma, P. C. 1989. *The Rāmāyaṇa Polity*. Second Edition. Bombay: Bharatiya Vidya Bhavan.

Drews, Robert. 2004. *Early Riders*. London: Routledge.

Dodd, Nigel. 2014. *The Social Life of Money*. Princeton: Princeton University Press.

Dué, Casey, and Mary Ebbott. 2010. *Iliad 10 and the Poetics of Ambush*. Hellenic Studies Series 39. Washington, DC: Center for Hellenic Studies.

Dumézil, Georges. (1940) 1948. *Mitra-Varuna*. Leroux: Presses Universitaires de France. Reprint, Paris: Editions Gallimard.

———. 1968. *Mythe et épopée*. Vol. 1, *L'idéologie des trois fonctions dans les épopées des peuples indo-européens*. Paris: Gallimard.

———. 1977. *Les Dieux Souverains des Indo-Européens*. Paris: Gallimard.

Dumont, Louis. 1966. *Homo Hierarchicus*. Paris: Editions Gallimard.

Eck, Diana L. 1981. *Darśan: Seeing the Divine in India.* Chambersburg: Anima Books.

———. 2012. *India, a Sacred Geography*. New York: Harmony Books.

Earle, Timothy K. 1997. *How Chiefs Came to Power*. Palo Alto: Stanford University Press.

———. 2002. *Bronze Age Economics*. Boulder: Westview Press.

Earle, T. K., and J. E. Ericsson. 1977. *Exchange Systems in Prehistory*. New York: Academic Press.

Edgerton, Franklin. 1924. *The Panchatantra Reconstructed.* Vol. 1, *Text and Critical Apparatus*. American Oriental Series 2. New Haven: American Oriental Society.

Elmer, David. 2013. *The Poetics of Consent*. Baltimore: Johns Hopkins Press.

Emeneau, M. B. 1953. "The Composite Bow in India." *Proceedings of the American Philosophical Society* 97: 77–87.

Evans, Kirsti. 1997. *Epic Narratives in the Hoysaḷa Temples*. Leiden: Brill.

Falk, Harry. 2006. "The Tidal Waves of Indian History." In Olivelle 2006, 145–166.

Faust, Drew Gilpin. 2008. *This Republic of Suffering: Death and the American Civil War*. New York: Alfred Knopf.

Feller, Danielle. 2004. *The Sanskrit Epics' Representation of Vedic Myths*. Delhi: Motilal Banarsidass.

———. 2012. "Epic Heroes Have No Childhood." *Indologica Taurinensia* 38: 65–85.

Fenik, B. 1968. *Typical Battle Scenes in the Iliad*. Wiesbaden: F. Steiner.

Figiel, Leo S. 1991. *On Damascus Steel*. Atlantis, FL: Atlantis Arts Press.

Fitzgerald, James. 2001. "Making Yudhiṣṭhira the King: the Dialectics and Politics of Violence in the *Mahābhārata*." *Rocznik Orientalistczny* 54: 63–92.

———. 2006. "Negotiating the Shape of Scripture." In Olivelle 2006, 257–286.

———. 2010. "No Contest Between Memory and Invention." In Konstan and Raaflaub 2010, 103-121.

Flannery, Kent, and Joyce Marcus. 2012. *The Creation of Inequality*. Cambridge, MA: Harvard University Press.

Fleet, J. F. 1888. *Inscriptions of the Early Gupta Kings and their Successors*. Corpus Inscriptionum Indicarum 3. Calcutta: Government of India, Central Publication Branch.

Fortson, Benjamin W. 2004. *Indo-European Language and Culture*. Oxford: Blackwell.

Forrest, W. G. G. 1968. *A History of Sparta*. London: Hutchinson.

Frame, Douglas. 2009. *Hippota Nestor*. Hellenic Studies 37. Washington, DC: Center for Hellenic Studies.

Frame, Douglas. 2012. "New Light on the Homeric Question: The Phaeacians Unmasked." In *Donum Natalicium Digitaliter Confectum Gregorio Nagy Septuagenario a Discipulis Collegis Familiaribus Oblatum*, edited by Victor Bers et al., chs.harvard.edu/CHS/article/display/4453. Washington, DC: Center for Hellenic Studies.

Franco, Eli, and Monika Zin, eds. 2010. *From Turfan to Ajanta: Festschrift for Dieter Schlingloff*. 2 vols. Bhairahawa: Lumbini International Research Institute.

Friedrich, P. 1966. "Proto-Indo-European Kinship." *Ethnology* 5: 1–36.

———. 1989. "Language, Ideology, and Political Economy." *American Anthropologist* 91: 295–312.

Gandhi, M. K. 1927. *Autobiogaphy: My Experiments with Truth*. Ahmedebad: Navajivan Publishing House.

Garcia, Lorenzo. F., Jr. 2013. *Homeric Durability*. Hellenic Studies 57. Washington, DC: Center for Hellenic Studies.

Gitomer, David L. 1992. "King Duryodhana. The Mahābhārata Discourse of King and Virtue in Epic and Drama." *JAOS* 112: 222–232.

Gode, P. K. 1942. "Nīlakaṇṭha Caturdhara, the Commentator of the Mahābhārata." *ABORI* 23: 146–161.

le Goff, Jacques. 2010. *Le Moyen Age et l'Argent*. Paris: Perrin.

Goldman, Robert P. 1995. "Gods in Hiding: The Mahābhārata's Virāṭa Parvan and the Divinity of the Indian Epic Hero." In *Modern Evaluation of the Mahābhārata*, edited by Satya P. Narang, 73–100. Delhi: Nag Publishers.

———. 2015. "Poet as Seer, Poetry as Seen: Reflections on Visualization as a Critical Element in the Conceptualization of Kāvya." In *Beyond Rules: Essays Honoring the Life and Work of Frits Staal*, edited by George Thompson, pp. 1–26. Honolulu: International Journal of Buddhist Studies, in collaboration with the University of Hawaii Press.

Gonda, J. 1966. *Ancient Kingship from the Religious Point of View*. Leiden: Brill.

González-Reimann, Luis. 2002. *The Mahābhārata and the Yugas*. New York: Peter Lang.

Goody, Jack. 1977. *The Domestication of the Savage Mind*. Cambridge: Cambridge University Press.

———. 2010. *Myth, Ritual, and the Oral*. Cambridge: Cambridge University Press.

Graeber, David. 2001. *Towards an Anthropological Theory of Value*. New York: Palgrave.

———. 2011. *Debt: The First 5000 Years*. New York: Melville House Printing.

Granet, Marcel. 1929. *La Civilisation Chinoise*. Paris: Editions Albin Michel.

Hallisey, Charles. 1995. "Roads Taken and Not Taken in the Study of Theravāda Buddhism." In *Curators of the Buddha*, edited by Donald S. Lopez, Jr., 31–61. Chicago: University of Chicago Press.

Hamblin, William James. 2006. *Warfare in the Ancient Near East to 1600 BC*. London: Taylor & Francis.

Handlin, Lilian. 2012. "The King and his Bhagavā." In *How Theravāda Is Theravāda?*, edited by Peter Skilling et al., 165–236. Chiang Mai: Silkworm Books.

Heesterman, J. C. 1985. *The Inner Conflict of Tradition: Essays in Indian Ritual, Kingship, and Society*. Chicago: University of Chicago Press.

Hegarty, James. 2012. *Religion, Narrative and Public Imagination in South Asia: Past and Place in the Sanskrit Mahābhārata*. New York: Routledge.

Heine, N. 1986. "Epic Sarvabhūtahite Rataḥ: A Byword of Non-Bhārgava Editors." *Annals of the Bhandarkar Oriental Research Institute* 67: 17–34.

Heitzman, James. 1984. "Early Buddhism, Trade and Empire." In *Studies in the Archaeology and Palaeoanthropology of South Asia*, edited by K. A. R. Kennedy and G.L. Possehl, 121–137. New Delhi: Oxford.

Helms, M. 1993. *The Broken World of Sacrifice*. Chicago: University of Chicago Press.

———. 1998. *Access to Origins: Affines, Ancestors, and Aristocrats*. Austin: University of Texas Press.

Hiltebeitel, A. 1976. *The Ritual of Battle*. Chicago: University of Chicago Press.

———. 1979. "Kṛṣṇa and the Mahābhārata." *ABORI* 60: 65–107.

———. 1988. *The Cult of Draupadī*. 2 vols. Chicago: University of Chicago Press.

———. 2001. *Rethinking the Mahābhārata*. Chicago: Chicago University Press.

———. 2005a. "Buddhism and the Mahābhārata." In Squarcini 2005, 107-131.

———. 2005b. "Not Without Subtales: Telling Laws and Truths in the Sanskrit Epics." *Journal of Indian Philosophy* 33: 455–511.

———. 2006. "Aśvaghoṣa's Buddhacarita." *Journal of Indian Philosophy* 34: 229–286.

———. 2010. *Dharma*. Honolulu: University of Hawaii Press.

———. 2011a. "On Sukthankar's 'S' and Some Shortsighted Assessments and Uses of the Pune Critical Edition." *Journal of Vaiṣṇava Studies* 19: 87–126.

———. 2011b. *Reading the Fifth Veda*. Leiden: Brill.

———. 2011c. *Dharma: Its Early History in Law, Religion, and Narrative*. New York: Oxford University Press.

Hinton, Charles Howard. 1904. *The Fourth Dimension*. London: Sonnenschein & Co.

Holtzmann, A. 1892. *Zur Geschichte und Kritik des Mahābhārata*. Kiel: C. F. Haeseler.

Hopkins, E. Washburn. 1888. "The Social and Military Position of the Ruling Caste in Ancient India." *JAOS* 13: 57–372.

———. 1894. "Henotheism in the Rig-Veda." In *Classical Studies in Honour of Henry Drisler*, 75–83. New York: Macmillan and Co.

———. (1901) 1993. *The Great Epic of India*. New York: Scribner and Sons. Reprint, Delhi: Motilal Banarsidass. [Citations refer to the Motilal Banarsidass edition.]

———. 1907. "The Sniff-Kiss in Ancient India." *JAOS* 28: 120–134.

———. 1915. *Epic Mythology*. Strasburg: Trübner.

———. 1926. "The Original Rāmāyaṇa." *JAOS* 46: 202–219.

———. 1931. "The Divinity of Kings." *JAOS* 51: 309–316.

Hudson, Emily T. 2013. *Disorienting Dharma*. New York: Oxford University Press.

Humphrey, Caroline, and Stephen Hugh-Jones, eds. 1994. *Barter, Exchange, and Value*. Cambridge: Cambridge University Press.

Hurford, James R. 2007. *The Origins of Meaning*. Oxford: Oxford University Press.

Jakobson, Roman. 1981. *Essais de Linguistique Générale*. Paris: Les Editions de Minuit.

———. 1987. *Language in Literature*. Edited by Krystyna Pomorska and Stephen Rudy. Cambridge, MA: Harvard University Press.

Jamison, Stephanie. 1994. "Draupadī on The Walls of Troy: *Iliad* 3 From an Indic Perspective." *Classical Antiquity* 13: 5–16.

———. 1996. *Sacrificed Wife/Sacrificer's Wife*. Oxford: Oxford University Press.

———. 1997. "A Gāndharva Marriage in the *Odyssey*: Nausicaa and Her Imaginary Husband." In *Studies in Honour of Jaan Puhvel*, Part 2, *Mythology and Religion*, edited by J. Greppin and E. C. Polomé, 151–160. *JIES* Monographs 21. Washington, DC: Institute for the Study of Man.

———. 2007. *The Rig Veda Between Two Worlds*. Collège de France, Publications de l'Institut de Civilisation Indienne, Série in 8, Fascicule 74. Paris: Editions Diffusion de Broccard.

Jhala, Angma Dey. 2008. *Courtly Indian Women in Late Imperial India*. London: Pickering and Chatto.

———. 2011. *Royal Patronage, Power and Aesthetics in Princely India*. London: Pickering and Chatto.

Jhala, Jayasinhji. 1991. *Marriage, Hierarchy, and Identity in Ideology and Practice: An Anthropological Study of Jhālā Rājpūt Society in Western India, against a Historical Background, 1090-1990 A.D.* PhD dissertation, Harvard University.

Karashima, Noburu, ed. 1999. *Kingship in Indian History*. New Delhi: Manohar.

Keith, Arthur Berriedale. 1914. *The Veda of the Black Yajus School, Entitled Taittirya Sanhita*. 2 vols. Harvard Oriental Series 18–19. Cambridge, MA: Harvard University Press.

———. 1920. *Rigveda Brahmanas: The Aitareya and Kauṣītaki Brāhmaṇas of the Rigveda*. Harvard Oriental Series 25. Cambridge, MA: Harvard University Press.

———. 1925. *The Religion and Philosophy of the Veda and Upanishads*. 2 vols. Harvard Oriental Series 31–32. Cambridge, MA: Harvard University Press.

Keny, L. B. 1942. "The Origin of Nārāyaṇa." *ABORI* 23: 250–256.

Klostermaier, Klaus K. 1984. *Mythologies and Philosophies of Salvation in the Theistic Traditions of India*. Ontario: Canadian Corporation for Studies in Religion.

Knox, Robert. 1992. *Amaravati*. London: Trustees of the British Museum.

Kohl, Philip L. 2007. *The Making of Bronze Age Eurasia*. Cambridge: Cambridge University Press.

Kölver, Bernhard. 1997. *Recht, Staat und Verwaltung im Klassischen Indien*. Munich: R. Oldenbourg.

Konstan, David, and Kurt A. Raaflaub, eds. 2010. *Epic and History*. Chichester, West Sussex: Wiley-Blackwell.

Kosambi, D. D. 1965. *The Culture and Civilisation of Ancient India*. London: Routledge and Kegan Paul.

Kristiansen, Kristian, and Thomas B. Larsson. 2005. *The Rise of Bronze Age Society*. Cambridge: Cambridge University Press.

Kulke, H. 1992. "The Rājasūya. A Paradigm of Early State Formation." In *Ritual, State and History in South Asia: Essays in Honour of J.C. Heesterman*, edited by A. W. van den Hoek, D. H. A. Kolff, and M. S. Oort, 188–198. Leiden: Brill.

Lal, B. B. 1973. "Archaeology and the Two Indian Epics." *Annals of the Bhandarkar Oriental Research Institute* 54: 1–8.

Law, Bimala Charan. 1924. *Some Kṣatriya Tribes of Ancient India*. Calcutta: University of Calcutta Press.

———. 1941. *India as Described in Early Texts of Buddhism and Jainism*. Delhi: Bharatiya Publishing House.

Law, N. N. 1921. *Aspects of Ancient Indian Polity*. Oxford: Oxford University Press.

Lévi-Strauss, Claude. 1991. *Histoire de Lynx*. Paris: Plon.

Lienhardt, Godfrey. 1961. *Divinity and Experience*. Oxford: Oxford University Press.

Lincoln, Bruce. 1991. *Death, War, and Sacrifice*. Chicago: University of Chicago Press.

Lord, A. B. 1960. *The Singer of Tales*. Cambridge, MA: Harvard University Press.

Lubotsky, Alexander. 1996. "The Iconography of the Vishnu Temple at Deogarh." *Ars Orientalis* 26: 65–80.

MacDonell, A. A., and A. B. Keith. 1912. *Vedic Index of Names and Subjects*. London: John Murray.

Magnone, Paolo. 2012. "Uttaṅka's Quest." In Brockington 2012, 101-128.

Mahadevan, J. P. 2008. "On the Southern Recension of the Mahābhārata, Brahman Migrations, and the Brāhmī Paleography." *Electronic Journal of Vedic Studies* 15: 43–147.

———. 2011. "Three Rails of the Mahābhārata Text Tradition." *Journal of Vaiṣṇava Studies* 19: 23–69.

Mair, V. 2006. *Contact and Exchange in the Ancient World*. Honolulu: University of Hawaii Press.

Malik, Aditya. 2005. *Nectar Gaze and Poison Breath*. New York: Oxford University Press.

Malinar, Angelika. 1996. *Rājavidyā: Das königliche Wissen um Herrschaft und Verzicht*. Wiesbaden: Harrassowitz.

———. 2012. "Duryodhana's Truths: Kingship and Divinity in *Mahābhārata* 5.60." In Brockington 2012, 51–78.

Mallory, J. P. 1989. *In Search of the Indo-Europeans*. London: Thames and Hudson.

Mallory, J. P., and Douglas Q. Adams. 1997. *Encyclopedia of Indo-European Culture*. London: Fitzroy Dearborn.

Mankekar, Purnima. 1999. *Screening Culture*. Durham: Duke University Press.

Mangels, Annette. 1994. *Zur Erzähltechnik im Mahābhārata*. Hamburg: Verlag Dr. Kovac.

Mani, Vettam. (1964) 1975. *A Purāṇic Encyclopaedia: A Comprehensive Dictionary with Special Reference to the Epic and Purāṇic Literature*. Reprint, Delhi: Motilal Banarsidass. [Citations refer to the 1975 edition.]

Martin, R. P. 2004. "Home is the Hero: Deixis and Semantics in Pindar's Pythian 8." *Arethusa* 37: 343–363.

Matilal, Bimal Krishna, ed. 1989. *Moral Dilemmas in the Mahābhārata*. Delhi: Motilal Banarsidass.

Matsubara, Mitsunori. 1990. *Monotheistic Theory of The Early Vaisnavas: Vyuha Theory in the Early Pancaratra*. Delhi: Motilal Banarsidass.

Mauss, Marcel, with Henri Hubert. 1902–1903. "Esquisse d'une Théorie Générale de la Magie." *Année Sociologique* 7: 1–146.

———. 1925. *Essai sur le Don*. Paris: Alcan.

Mayrhofer, Manfred. 1956. *Kurzgefaßtes etymologisches Wörterbuch des Altindischen*. Three vols. Heidelberg: Carl Winter.

McGrath, Kevin. 2000. Review of *Splitting the Difference: Gender and Myth in Ancient Greece and India*, by Wendy Doniger, *American Anthropologist* 102: 417.

———. 2004. *The Sanskrit Hero: Karṇa in Epic Mahābhārata*. Leiden: Brill.

———. 2009. *Strī: Women in Epic Mahābhārata*. Cambridge, MA: Ilex Foundation, Harvard University Press.

———. 2011. *Jaya: Performance in Epic Mahābhārata*. Cambridge, MA: Ilex Foundation, Harvard University Press.

———. 2012. "A Short Note on Arjuna as a Semi-Divine Being." *Journal of Vaiṣṇava Studies* 21: 199–210.

———. 2013. *Heroic Kṛṣṇa: Friendship in Epic Mahābhārata*. Cambridge, MA: Ilex Foundation, Harvard University Press.

———. 2015a. "Acts and Conditions of The Gītā." In Tsoukalas and Surya 2014, 43–92.

———. 2015b. *In The Kacch*. Jefferson, NC: McFarland and Company.

———. 2016. *Arjuna Pāṇḍava: The Double Hero in Epic Mahābhārata*. New Delhi: Orient Black Swan.

———. Forthcoming. "Kingship, Landscape, and the Hero." Chapter 4 in *Genealogy, Archive, Image* , edited by Jayasinhji Jhala. Warsaw: De Gruyter Open.

McHugh, James Andrew. 2012. *Sandalwood and Carrion: Smell in Indian Religion and Culture*. Oxford: Oxford University Press.

Mehendale, M. A. 1995. *Reflections on the Mahābhārata War*. Shimla: Indian Institute of Advanced Study.

Meillet, Antoine. 1908. *Les Dialectes Indo-Européens*. Paris: Champion.

Michaels, Axel, ed. 2001. *The Pandit: Traditional Scholarship in India*. Delhi: Manohar.

Mierlo, Wim Van, ed. 2007. *Textual Scholarship and the Material Book*. Variants 6. Amsterdam: Rodopi.

Minkowski, Christopher Z. 1991. *Priesthood in Ancient India*. Publications of the de Nobili Research Library 18. Vienna: Institut für Indologie der Universität Wien.

———. 2004. "Nīlakaṇṭha's Instruments of War: Modern, Vernacular, Barbarous." *Indian Economic and Social History Review* 41: 365–385.

———. 2005. "What Makes a Work Traditional? On the Success of Nīlakaṇṭha's Mahābhārata Commentary." In Squarcini 2005, 225–252.

———. 2010. "Nīlakaṇṭha's Mahābhārata." Seminar [Web Edition] 608 (April 2010): http://www.india-seminar.com/2010/608/608_c_minkowski.htm.

Mitra, Ananda. 1993. *Television and Popular Culture in India: A Study of the Mahabharat*. New Delhi: Sage Publications.

Morley, Iain, and Colin Renfrew, eds. 2010. *The Archaeology of Measurement*. Cambridge: Cambridge University Press.

Muellner, Leonard. 1996. *The Anger of Achilles: Mēnis in Greek Epic*. Ithaca: Cornell University Press.

———. 2012. "Discovery Procedures and Principles for Homeric Research." *Classics@* 3: http://chs.harvard.edu/CHS/article/display/1321.

Nagy, Gregory. 1974. *Comparative Studies in Greek and Indic Meter*. Harvard Studies in Comparative Literature 33. Cambridge, MA: Harvard University Press.

———. 1979. *The Best of the Achaeans*. Baltimore: Johns Hopkins University Press.

———. 1996a. *Poetry as Performance*. Cambridge: Cambridge University Press.

———. 1996b. *Homeric Questions*. Austin: University of Texas Press.

———. 2003. *Homeric Responses*. Austin: University of Texas Press.

———. 2004. "Poetics of Repetition in Homer." In *Greek Ritual Poetics*, edited by D. Yatromanolakis and P. Roilos, 139–148. Hellenic Studies 3. Washington, DC: Center for Hellenic Studies.

———. 2009. *Homer the Classic*. Hellenic Studies Series 36. Washington, DC: Center for Hellenic Studies.

———. 2010. *Homer the Preclassic*. Berkeley: University of California Press.

———. 2013. *The Ancient Greek Hero in 24 Hours*. Cambridge, MA: Harvard University Press.

Neelakantan, Anand. 2013. *Ajaya: Epic of the Kaurava Clan*. Mumbai: Platinum Press.

Oberlies, Thomas. 2003. *A Grammar of Epic Sanskrit*. Berlin: De Gruyter.

Oguibénine, Boris. 1998. *Essays on Vedic and Indo-European Culture*. New Delhi: Motilal Banarsidass.

O'Hanlon, Rosalind, and David Washbrook, eds. 2011. *Religious Cultures in Early Modern India*. London: Routledge.

Okpewho, Isidore. 2014. *Blood on the Tides: The Ozidi Saga and Oral Epic Narratology*. Rochester, NY: University of Rochester Press.

Oldenberg, Hermann. (1894) 1988. *Die Religion des Veda*. Berlin: W. Herz. Translated by Shridhar B. Shrotri. Translated edition, Delhi: Motilal Banarsidass.

Olivelle, Patrick. 1993. *The Āśrama System: The History and Hermeneutics of a Religious Institution*. New York: Oxford University Press.

———, ed. 2004b. "Dharma: Studies in its Semantic, Cultural, and Religious History." Special issue, *Journal of Indian Philosophy* 32 nos. 5–6.

———, ed. 2006. *Between The Empires: Society in India 300 BCE to 400 CE*. New York: Oxford University Press.

———. 2009. *Aśoka*. Delhi: Motilal Banarsidass.

———, ed. 2009. *Dharma: Studies in its Semantic, Cultural, and Religious History*. Delhi: Motilal Banarsidass.

———. 2011. *Ascetics and Brahmins*. New York: Anthem Press.

Pal, Pratapaditya. 1986. *Indian Sculpture*. Vol. I, *Circa 500 B.C.–A.D. 700*. Los Angeles : Los Angeles County Museum of Art.

Pargiter, F. E. 1908. "The Nations of India at the Battle between the Pāṇḍavas and the Kauravas." *JRAS* (1908, part 1): 309–336.

———. 1922. *The Ancient Indian Historical Tradition*. London: Oxford University Press.

———. 1913. *The Purana Text of the Dynasties of the Kali Age*. London: Humphrey Milford.

Parkman, Francis. 1849. *The California and Oregon Trail*. New York: G. P. Putnam.

Parpola, A. 1994. *Deciphering the Indus Script*. Cambridge: Cambridge University Press.

———. 2002. "Pandaiē and Sītā: On the Historical Background of the Sanskrit Epics." *JAOS* 122: 361–373.

———. 2004–2005. "The Nāsatyas, the Chariot, and Proto-Aryan Religion." *Journal of Indological Studies* 16, 17: 1–63.

———. 2015. *The Origins of Hinduism*. New York: Oxford University Press.

Parry, M. 1932. "Studies in the Epic Technique of Oral Versemaking. II, The Homeric Language as the Language of Oral Poetry." *Harvard Studies in Classical Philology* 43:1–50.

Peabody, Norbert. 2002. *Hindu Kingship and Polity in Pre-Colonial India*. Cambridge: Cambridge University Press.

Phillips-Rodriguez, Wendy J. 2007. "A Discussion About Textual Eugenics." In Van Mierlo 2007, 163–176.

———. 2012. "Unrooted Trees." In Brockington 2012, 217–229.

Pingree, David Edwin. 1981. *Jyotiḥśāstra: Astral and Mathematical Literature*. Wiesbaden: Harrassowitz.

Pollock, Sheldon. 2001. "New Intellectuals in Seventeenth Century India." *Indian Economic and Social History Review* 38: 3–31.

———. 2006. *The Language of the Gods in the World of Men*. Berkeley: University of California Press.

———, ed. 2010. *Epic and Argument in Sanskrit Literary History*. Delhi: Manohar.

Printz, Wilhelm. 1910. "Bhāsawörter in Nīlakaṇṭha's Bhāratabhāvadīpa und in andere Sanskritkommentaren." *Zeitschrift fur vergleichende Sprachforschung* 44: 69–109.

Proferes, T. 2007. *Vedic Ideals of Sovereignty and the Poetics of Power*. American Oriental Society Series 90. New Haven: American Oriental Society.

Propp, Vladimir. (1928) 1968. *Morphology of the Folktale*. Translated by Laurence Scott, with an Introduction by Svatava Pirkova-Jakobson. Reprint, Austin: University of Texas Press.

Puett, Michael J. 2002. *To Become a God: Cosmology, Sacrifice, and Self-Divinization in Early China*. Cambridge, MA: Harvard University Press.

Purves, Alex C. 2010. *Space and Time in Ancient Greek Narrative*. Cambridge: Cambridge University Press.

Randhawa, T. S. 1996. *The Last Wanderers*. Ahmedebad: Mapin Publishers.

Rao, Venkat D. 2014. *Cultures of Memory in South Asia*. Heidelberg: Spriger.

Rapson, E. J. 1897. *Indian Coins*. Strassburg: K. J. Trübner.

Reichl, K., ed. 2000. *The Oral Epic: Performance and Music*. Berlin: VWB, Verlag fur Wissenschaft und Bildung.

Rosenfield, John M. 1967. *The Dynastic Arts of the Kushanas*. Berkeley: University of California Press.

Runciman, W. G., ed. 2001. *The Origin of Social Institutions*. Oxford: Oxford University Press.

Sahlins, Marshall D. 1961. "The Segmentary Lineage: An Organisation of Predatory Expansion." *American Anthropologist* 63: 332–345.

———. 1982. *Stone Age Economics*. Chicago: Aldine Atherton.

———. 1985. *Islands of History*. Chicago: University of Chicago Press.

Salomon, Richard. 1995. "On Drawing Socio-Linguistic Distinctions in Old Indo-Aryan: The Question of Kṣatriya Sanskrit and Related Problems." In *The Indo Aryans of Ancient South Asia*, edited by Georg Erdosy, 293–306. Berlin: De Gruyter.

———. 1998. *Indian Epigraphy*. Oxford: Oxford University Press.

Samuel, Geoffrey. 2008. *The Origins of Yoga and Tantra*. Cambridge: Cambridge University Press.

Sastri, K.A Nilakanta, ed. 1967. *Age of the Nandas and Mauryas*. Delhi: Motilal Banarsidass.

Sathaye, Adheesh. 2007. "How to Become a Brahman: The Construction of *Varṇa* as Social Place in the *Mahābhārata*'s Legends of Viśvāmitra." *Acta Orientalia Vilnensia* 8: 46–67.

———. 2010. “The Other Kind of Brahman: Rāma Jāmadagnya and the Psychosocial Construction of Brahman Power in the Mahābhārata.” In *Epic and Argument in Sanskrit Literary Theory Essays in Honor of Robert P. Goldman*, edited by Sheldon Pollock, 185–207. Delhi: Manohar.

Sax, William. 2002. *Dancing the Self: Personhood and Performance in the Pāṇḍav Līlā of Garhwal*. Oxford: Oxford University Press.

Scharfe, Hartmut. 1989. *The State in Indian Tradition*. Leiden: Brill.

———. 1992. “Sacred Kingship, Warlords, and Nobility.” In *Ritual, State and History in South Asia: Essays in Honour of J.C. Heesterman*, edited by A. W. van den Hoek, D. H. A. Kolff, and M. S. Oort, 309–322. Leiden: Brill.

von Schelling, F. W. J. 1857. *Philosophie der Mythologie*. Stuttgart.

Scheuer, Jacques. 1982. *Śiva Dans le Mahābhārata*. Paris: Presses Universitaires de France.

Schlingloff, Dieter. 1969. “The Oldest Extant Parvan List of the Mahābhārata.” *JAOS* 89: 334–338.

Seaford, Richard. 2004. *Money and the Early Greek Mind*. Cambridge: Cambridge University Press.

———. 2006. *Dionysos*. Oxford and New York: Routledge.

Searle, J. R. 1969. *Speech Acts*. Cambridge: Cambridge University Press.

Selvanayagam, Israel. 1992. “Aśoka and Arjuna as Counterfigures Standing on the Field of Dharma.” *History of Religions* 32, no. 1: 59–75.

Sen, Amartya. 2005. *The Argumentative Indian: Writings on Indian History, Culture and Identity*. London: Penguin Books.

———. 2009. *The Idea Of Justice*. London: Allen Lane.

Sharma, J. P. 1968. *Republics in Ancient India*. Leiden: Brill.

Sharma, Tej Ram. 1989. *A Political History of the Imperial Guptas*. New Delhi: Concept Publishing.

Sharma, Ram Karan. 1966. “Elements of Oral Poetry in the Mahābhārata.” In *Proceedings and Transactions of the All-India Oriental Conference. Twenty-first Session, Sringar, Kashmir, October, 1961,* Vol. 2, Pt. 1, 43–49. Poona: Bhandarkar Oriental Research Institute.

Shay, Jonathan. 2002. *Combat Trauma and the Trials of Homecoming*. New York: Scribner.

Shayegan, M. Rahim. 2012. *Aspects of History and Epic in Ancient Iran*. Hellenic Studies Series 52. Washington, DC: Center for Hellenic Studies.

Shell, M. 1982. *Money, Language, and Thought: Literary and Philosophical Economies from the Medieval to the Modern Era*. Baltimore: Johns Hopkins University Press.

Shimada, Akira. 2013. *Early Buddhist Architecture in Context*. Leiden: Brill.

Simmel, G. 1900. *Die Philosophie des Geldes*. Leipzig: Duncker & Humblot.

von Simson, Georg, ed. 2011. *Mahābhārata. Die Große Erzählung von den Bhāratas*. Berlin: Verlag der Weltreligionen.

Singh, Bhrgupati. 2011. "Agonistic Intimacy and Moral Aspiration." *American Ethnologist* 38: 430–450.

Sircar, D. C., ed. 1922. *Early Indian Political and Administrative Systems*. Calcutta: University of Calcutta.

Skjærvø, Prods Oktor. 1994. "Hymnic Composition in the Avesta." *Die Sprache* 36: 199–243.

———. 1998. "Eastern Iranian Epic Traditions I: Siyāvaš and Kunāla." In *Mír Curad, Studies in Honour of Calvert Watkins*, edited by Jay Jasanoff, H. Craig Melchert, and Lisi Olivier, 645–658. Innsbruck: Sonderdruck.

———. 2000. "Eastern Iranian Epic Traditions III: Zarathustra and Diomedes. An Indo-European Epic Warrior Type." *Bulletin of the Asia Institute* 11: 175–182.

———. 2011. *The Spirit of Zoroastrianism*. New Haven: Yale University Press.

Smith, J. D. 1987. "Formulaic Language in the Epics of India." In *The Heroic Process: Form, Function, and Fantasy in Folk Epic*, edited by B. Almqvist et al., 591–611. Dublin: Glendale Press.

———. 1991. *The Epic of Pābūjī*. Cambridge: Cambridge University Press.

Smith, M. C. 1975. "The Mahābhārata's Core." *JAOS* 95: 479–482.

———. 1992. *The Warrior Code of India's Sacred Song*. New York: Garland Publishing.

Snodgrass, Jeffrey G. 2006. *Casting Kings: Bards and Indian Modernity*. Oxford: Oxford University Press.

Smith, Vincent A. 1909. *The Edicts of King Aśoka*. Broad Campden: Essex House Press.

Sneath, D. 2007. *The Headless State. Aristocratic Orders, Kinship Society, and Misrepresentations of Nomadic Inner Asia*. New York: Columbia University Press.

Spellman, John W. 1964. *Political Theory of Ancient India*. Oxford: Oxford University Press.

Sörensen, S. (1904) 1978. *An Index to the Names in the Mahābhārata*. Copenhagen. Reprint, Delhi: Motilal Banarsidass.

Spink, Walter M. 2005–2009. *Ajanta: History and Development*. 5 Vols. Leiden: Brill.

Squarcini, Federico, ed. 2005. *Boundaries, Dynamics, and Construction of Traditions in South Asia*. Florence: Firenze University Press.

Stark, Sören, Karen S. Rubinson, with Zainolla S. Samachev and Jennifer Y. Chi. 2012. *Nomads and Networks: The Ancient Art and Culture of Kazakhstan.* Princeton: Princeton University Press.

Strauss Clay, Jenny. 2011. *Homer's Trojan Theater*. Cambridge: Cambridge University Press.

Sukthankar, Vishnu S. 1944. *Critical Studies in the Mahābhārata*. Bombay: Karnatak Publishing House.

———. 1957. *On The Meaning of the Mahābhārata*. Bombay: Asiatic Society of Bombay.

Sullivan, Bruce. 1990. *Kṛṣṇa Dvaipāyana Vyāsa and the Mahābhārata*. Leiden: Brill.

Talim. M. V. 2010. *Edicts of King Aśoka*. New Delhi: Aryan Books.

Tanner, Tony. 1994. Introduction to *Histories*, Vol. 1, by William Shakespeare, ed. Sylvan Barnet. Everyman's Library. New York: Alfred Knopf.

Thapar, Romila. 2003. *Early India: From the Origins to AD 1300*. Berkeley: University of California Press. Originally published as *The Penguin History of Early India*, Delhi: Penguin Press (2002).

———. 2013. *The Past Before Us*. Delhi: Permanent Black, Orient Black Swan.

Tharoor, S. 1989. *The Great Indian Novel*. New Delhi: Penguin Books.

Thompson, G. 1997. "On Truth-Acts in Vedic." *Indo-Iranian Journal* 41: 125–153.

Thornton, C. P., and C. C. Lamberg-Karlovsky. 2004. "A New Look at the Prehistoric Metallurgy of South-Eastern Iran." *Iran* 42: 47–59.

Tieken, Herman. 2004 "The Mahābhārata After the Great Battle." *Wiener Zeitschrift für die Kinde Südasiens* 48: 5–46.

Tomlinson, Gary. 2015. *A Million Years of Music*. New York: Zone Books.

Trautmann, T. R. 1974. "Cross-Cousin Marriage in Ancient North India?" In *Kinship and History in South Asia*, edited by T. R. Trautmann, 61–103. Ann Arbor: University of Michigan.

———. 1981. *Dravidian Kinship*. Cambridge: Cambridge University Press.

———. 2000. "India and the Study of Kinship 'Terminologies.'" *L'Homme* 154–155: 559–572.

Tsagalis, Christos. 2012. *From Listeners to Viewers: Space in the Iliad*. Hellenic Studies Series 53. Washington, DC: Center for Hellenic Studies.

Tsoukalas, S., and Gerald Surya, eds. 2014. *Studies in the Bhagavad Gita*. Vol. 1, *Ontology*. Lewiston, NY: Edwin Mellen Press.

Tsuchida, Ryutaro. 2008. "Considerations on the Narrative Structure of the Mahābhārata." *Studies in Indian Philosophy and Buddhism* 15: 1–26.

———. 2009. "Some Reflections on the Chronological Problems of the Mahābhārata." *Studies in Indian Philosophy and Buddhism* 16: 1–24.

Tuck, A. 2006. "Singing the Rug: Patterned Textiles and the Origins of Indo-European Metrical Poetry." *American Journal of Archaeology* 110: 539–550.

Turner, James. 2014. *Philology: The Forgotten Origins of the Modern Humanities*. Princeton: Princeton University Press.

Varma, Pavan K. 2004. *Being Indian*. New Delhi: Penguin Books.

Vassilkov, Yaroslav. 1999. "*Kālavāda* (the Doctrine of Cyclical Time) in the *Mahābhārata* and the Concept of Heroic Didactics." In Brockington and Schreiner 1999, 17–33.

Verardi, Giovanni. 2011. *Hardships and Downfall of Buddhism in India*. Delhi: Manohar.

Verardi, G. V., and S. Vita, eds. 2003. "Images of Destruction: An Enquiry into Hindu Icons in their Relations to Buddhism." In *Buddhist Asia. Papers from the First Conference of Buddhist Studies, Naples, May 2001*, edited by Giovanni Verardi and Silvio Vita, Vol. 1, 1–36. Kyoto: Italian School of Eastern Asian Studies.

Vidal-Naquet, Pierre. 1981. *Le Chasseur Noir*. Paris: Maspero.

Walsh, Thomas R. 2005. *Fighting Words and Feuding Words*. Lanham, MD: Lexington Books.

Ward, Donald. 1968. *The Divine Twins: An Indo-European Myth in Germanic Tradition*. Berkeley: University of California Press.

Watkins, Calvert. 1985. *The American Heritage Dictionary of Indo-European Roots*. Boston: Houghton Mifflin Company.

———. 1995. *How To Kill a Dragon: Aspects of Indo-European Poetics*. Oxford: Oxford University Press.

van Wees, H. 1992. *Status Warriors: War, Violence, and Society in Homer and History*. Amsterdam: J. C. Gieben.

West, M. L. 2007. *Indo-European Poetry and Myth*. Oxford: Oxford University Press.

Wilce, James M. 2009. *Language and Emotion*. Cambridge: Cambridge University Press.

Wiltshire, M. 1990. *Ascetic Figures Before and In Early Buddhism*. Berlin: Mouton de Gruyter.

Wiser, William Henricks. 1936. *The Hindu Jajmani System*. Hussainganj: Lucknow Publishing House.

Witzel, E. J. Michael. 1997. "Early Sanskritization: Origins and Development of the Kuru State." In Kölver 1997, 27–52.

———. 2012. *The Origins of the World's Mythologies*. Oxford: Oxford University Press.

Index

Myth and Poetics

A series edited by

Gregory Nagy

After Antiquity: Greek Language, Myth, and Metaphor
by Margaret Alexiou

Helen of Troy and Her Shameless Phantom
by Norman Austin

Poetry in Speech: Orality and Homeric Discourse
by Egbert J. Bakker

The Craft of Poetic Speech in Ancient Greece
by Claude Calame, translated by Janice Orion

Masks of Authority: Fiction and Pragmatics in Ancient Greek Poetics
by Claude Calame, translated by Peter M. Burk

Masks of Dionysus
edited by Thomas H. Carpenter and Christopher A. Faraone

The "Odyssey" in Athens: Myths of Cultural Origins
by Erwin F. Cook

The Poetics of Supplication: Homer's "Iliad" and "Odyssey"
by Kevin Crotty

Poet and Hero in the Persian Book of Kings
by Olga M. Davidson

Gender and Genre in the Folklore of Middle India
by Joyce Burkhalter Flueckiger

Ariadne's Thread: A Guide to International Stories in Classical Literature
by William Hansen

The Ravenous Hyenas and the Wounded Sun: Myth and Ritual in Ancient India
BY STEPHANIE W. JAMISON

Poetry and Prophecy: The Beginnings of a Literary Tradition
EDITED BY JAMES L. KUGEL

The Traffic in Praise: Pindar and the Poetics of Social Economy
BY LESLIE KURKE

Topographies of Hellenism: Mapping the Homeland
BY ARTEMIS LEONTIS

Born of the Earth: Myth and Politics in Athens
BY NICOLE LORAUX, TRANSLATED BY SELINA STEWART

Mothers in Mourning
BY NICOLE LORAUX, TRANSLATED BY CORINNE PACHE

Epic Singers and Oral Tradition
BY ALBERT BATES LORD

The Singer Resumes the Tale
BY ALBERT BATES LORD, EDITED BY MARY LOUISE LORD

The Language of Heroes: Speech and Performance in the "Iliad"
BY RICHARD P. MARTIN

Heroic Sagas and Ballads
BY STEPHEN A. MITCHELL

The Anger of Achilles: Mênis in Greek Epic
BY LEONARD MUELLNER

Greek Mythology and Poetics
BY GREGORY NAGY

Myth and the Polis
EDITED BY DORA C. POZZI AND JOHN M. WICKERSHAM

Knowing Words: Wisdom and Cunning in the Classical Traditions of China and Greece
BY LISA RAPHALS

Singing the Past: Turkic and Medieval Heroic Poetry
BY KARL REICHL

Heroic Poets, Poetic Heroes: The Ethnography of Performance in an Arabic Oral Epic Tradition
BY DWIGHT FLETCHER REYNOLDS

Homer and the Sacred City
BY STEPHEN SCULLY

Singers, Heroes, and Gods in the "Odyssey"
BY CHARLES SEGAL

The Mute Immortals Speak: Pre-Islamic Poetry and the Poetics of Ritual
BY SUZANNE PINCKNEY STETKEVYCH

Phrasikleia: An Anthropology of Reading in Ancient Greece
BY JESPER SVENBRO, TRANSLATED BY JANET E. LLOYD

The Swineherd and the Bow: Representations of Class in the "Odyssey"
BY WILLIAM G. THALMANN

The Jewish Novel in the Ancient World
BY LAWRENCE M. WILLS

CPSIA information can be obtained
at www.ICGtesting.com
Printed in the USA
BVOW03*0310170417
480715BV00002B/4/P